HISTORY OF PSYCHOLOGY
A Cultural Perspective

HISTORY OF PSYCHOLOGY
A Cultural Perspective

Cherie Goodenow O'Boyle
California State University
San Marcos

LAWRENCE ERLBAUM ASSOCIATES, PUBLISHERS
2006   Mahwah, New Jersey   London

Senior Editor: Debra Riegert
Editorial Assistant: Rebecca Larsen
Cover Design: Tomai Maridou
Full Service Compositor: TechBooks
Text and Cover Printer: Hamilton Printing Company

This book was typeset in 10/12 pt. Times, Italic, Bold, and Bold Italic.
The heads were typeset in Americana, Americana Italic, and Americana Bold

Lawrence Erlbaum Associates, Inc., Publishers
10 Industrial Avenue
Mahwah, New Jersey 07430
www.erlbaum.com

Library of Congress Cataloging-in-Publication Data
O'Boyle, Cherie Goodenow, 1950–
    History of psychology : a cultural perspective / Cherie Goodenow O'Boyle.
        p.   cm.
    Includes bibliographical references and index.
    ISBN 0-8058-5609-9 (casebound : alk. paper) — ISBN 0-8058-5610-2 (pbk. :
alk. paper) — ISBN 0-8058-5786-9 (casebound : alk. paper)
    1. Psychology—History—Textbooks. I. Title.

BF81.O26   2006
150.9—dc22   2005035824

Books published by Lawrence Erlbaum Associates are printed on
acid-free paper, and their bindings are chosen for strength and
durability.

Printed in the United States of America
10 9 8 7 6 5 4 3 2 1

This book is dedicated to my faculty colleagues at California State University, San Marcos. They are the most committed, hard-working, and generous professionals with whom I have ever had the privilege of being associated. This book could never have been written without their help and support.

Contents

Foreword

This text is fascinating, original, creative, and fun to read. Its content is well presented and organized in a coherent way. It is unusually "reader-friendly" and pedagogically sound, with a lively writing style as well as a feminist orientation that is missing in most standard texts on the history of psychology. A welcome alternative to the typically stuffy, detail-laden, deeply serious, and dry scholarly treatise, it tells a gripping, often fast-paced story that should be of interest not only to students but to many other readers as well.

Professor O'Boyle's bold and clever work may even generate a new trend in the teaching of the history of psychology: concentration on the history of ideas in their sociocultural and political context rather than the currently widespread practice of emphasizing biographical details concerning the lives of major figures in the history of psychology. It is a breath of fresh air in a field in which there is typically little variation among standard run-of-the-mill texts that focus on names and dates. Her account uses imaginative new features, such as the closing "The Times" section of each chapter, which gives the reader a feel for what everyday life was like during the age discussed in the chapter. Each chapter also opens with a well-chosen question, which piques the reader's interest. The consistent use of the present tense throughout the whole book generates a vivid immediacy to the ideas and events being discussed. Another successful innovation is the "Stop and think" questions interspersed generously throughout the volume. Yet another appealing feature of this book is that it begins much earlier than most standard textbooks in the field and covers much more than only the history of experimental psychology. Most significant is that Professor O'Boyle clearly knows how students think and what will capture their imaginations.

Professor O'Boyle has produced an intriguing new approach to the teaching of the history of psychology. I enjoyed reading it.

Michael Wertheimer, PhD
Professor Emeritus
University of Colorado at Boulder

List of Photographs
and Illustrations

Preface

This book is written for those who are curious about the history of scientific and intellectual thought within a Western cultural context, and about the mysteries surrounding thoughts, feelings, and behaviors. It is for anyone who wonders about the history of the art and the science of modern psychology.

History of Psychology: A Cultural Perspective is different from other texts in a number of ways. First, this book is a history of ideas, concepts, and questions, not of dates, events, or great minds. While historians may be fascinated by the biographies of individuals, most people are more interested in philosophical issues, scientific explorations, and questions about their own and others' thoughts, feelings, and behaviors. Histories of great minds are about other people, whereas histories of ideas, concepts, and questions are about us and are therefore as relevant today as they were for the first humans.

Second, this book explores more than the history of experimental psychology. Traditional texts approach the topic from within paradigms of psychology that prevailed during the middle of the last century. Times and paradigms have changed, and the historical record changes along with them. Therefore this book also explores the histories of applied, social, developmental, clinical, and cognitive psychology. Beyond the discipline, the history of all of science is inextricably intertwined with events in the surrounding environment. Thus, this history includes information about the intellectual and cultural context in which the history of psychology unfolds.

Finally, this is a critical, perhaps iconoclastic history, in that it holds no ideas sacred and regards no individuals as heroes. At the same time, it is a friendly history, written by an experimental scientist and psychologist who understands deeply why science came to be and the role that science plays as "a candle in the dark."

A FEW NOTES ABOUT STYLE
LEARNING TOOLS

The exploration of psychology began the first time one human wondered what caused thoughts, feelings, and behaviors. This journey through the history of psychology thus begins with the appearance of modern-day humans. Readers are invited to participate on this journey if they are willing to engage in an active pursuit of the answers to psychology's questions.

This journey is told in a style called the **historical present**. That means that this story is told in the present tense. This is an invitation to put oneself intellectually into the place and time presented in each chapter and to adopt that worldview. When it is necessary to jump temporarily to the actual present, the text is *italicized*.

Because this history is based on present-day scholarship, the times before the year 1 in the Western calendar will be referred to as BCE—Before the Common Era, as opposed to using BC, Before Christ, to designate this era. Similarly, the times from the year 1 and after will be referred to as CE, of the Common Era, as opposed to AD, Anno Domini.

Finally, the study of thoughts, feelings, and behaviors is not a strictly scientific enterprise. Therefore, this journey takes place in the rich context of everyday life that includes cultural influences including contributions from literature, music, and art. A variety of aspects of Western intellectual history are included, rather than regarding advancements in psychology as the contributions of just a few great men. This way, the contributions of many to philosophy, theology, and science are acknowledged. Contributions that often remain unrecognized are seen and ways in which, for some people, the pathways to intellectual achievement have been systematically blocked, are revealed.

Each chapter includes a section titled "The Times" here the zeitgeist or "spirit of the times" is captured. Descriptions of what life was like for ordinary people at the time are included, as well as information about important issues influencing the lives of those living then. The chapters also include short sidebars containing interesting stories or legends that illustrate important points related to the history of psychology. Along the way, **stop and think** questions are encountered. These are provocative questions intended to invite readers to stretch and explore the limits of their own intellectual landscapes. They are places to stop and ponder the important question that is presented. These intellectually challenging questions will enhance interest, curiosity, retention, and critical thinking.

Terms that may be unfamiliar to some readers are printed in bold-face where they are first used and are also listed in a glossary at the back of the book.

CONTENT HIGHLIGHTS

Because the answers to some psychological mysteries are based on the ways in which humans think, this journey begins at the time when homo sapiens appear on the Earth some 120,000 years ago. We then continue through ancient philosophical ideas in Classical Greece, explore the influences of theological thought in the West during the Middle Ages, and conclude in the scientific world of the future with questions such as the role that psycho-active medications play in informing us about the origins of personality.

Thus, the history of psychology is a very broad topic. Chapters 1 through 3 focus on two ways of coming to believe, trust and reason, and how those allow for speculation about the mysteries of the universe and humans' place in it. During this era, the big questions about how and why we think, feel, and behave as we do are answered by applying logical argument, philosophical speculation, preexisting beliefs, and theological systems of thought. In chapter 4 a third way of coming to believe, science, is born. In chapters 5 and 6 the mysteries of psychology begin to be approached through publicly observable experience and the systematic gathering of evidence. In psychology during this time, the curious still sometimes wander down the blind alleys of vitalism, spiritualism, and the occult arts. Chapters 7 and 8 explore the emergence of modern methods of psychology as a science, follow the transition of psychology from Europe to North America, and illustrate the shift from basic research to practical applications in the New World. Chapter 9 through chapter 12 explore the developments that led to current questions and present-day theories in the many domains of modern psychology. The histories of both experimental and descriptive research are examined, for example, and the early days of social psychology are explored, partly to learn why ethics became and remains an important consideration in psychological research.

MY GOALS

In embarking on this journey, I wish to achieve four goals. First, I want readers to understand what science is, and what it is not. Science education in the United States is widely acknowledged to be woefully inadequate to meet the political and economic challenges of our time. Especially in the field of psychology, there remains confusion about the methods of science as they apply to the study of thoughts, feelings, and behaviors.

Second, I want readers to know where psychology comes from so that they will better understand why Western psychologists make particular assumptions about thoughts, feelings, and behaviors and how those assumptions shape the questions that are studied in psychology today. Third, I want readers to examine and come to know why they believe what they believe. I hope this text helps to facilitate movement out of the intellectual stage in which everyone's opinion is as good as anyone else's and beyond the post-modern assertion that truth is whatever anybody decides that it is. I want readers to understand why evidence is sought and evaluated before accepting a belief. Finally, I hope that readers will become as captivated by the wonders and the mysteries of psychology as I am. At the end of the journey, I would like readers to be as curious as I hope they are at the beginning. Science, like philosophy, begins in wonder, and I hope that wonder of discovery stays alive throughout our journey through history.

INSTRUCTOR'S RESOURCE CD

A separate Instructor's Resource CD includes suggestions for teaching a history of psychology course. Provided are ideas for class activities and demonstrations, suggestions for small group and whole class discussions, a short list of films and videos related to the material in each chapter, and a test bank. The test bank includes both objective and essay items.

ACKNOWLEDGMENTS

Without the help and support of many individuals, this book would never have come into existence. It is with wonder at their dedication and undying gratitude for their time, advice, and support that I thank my colleagues in psychology, Wesley Schultz and Patricia Worden, who read and edited each chapter over a period of more than 4 years and made many valuable suggestions for improvement. At least 11 anonymous reviewers provided thoughtful comments and motivating opinions. I am most grateful for the clarifications, corrections, and encouragement provided by the esteemed Dr. Michael Wertheimer during the final revisions, and I am humbled by the very supportive foreword that he has kindly written for the book. Thanks are also due to many colleagues in many departments at California State University, San Marcos, who gave generously of their expertise and advice. My appreciation goes also to friends and family who were kind enough to read and comment on various sections and chapters, and who provided encouragement throughout. Finally, I am most grateful for the clarifications, corrections, and encouragement provided by the final reviewers: Michael Wertheimer, University of Colorado at Boulder; Alfred H. Fuchs, Bowdoin College; and John C. Malone, University of Tennessee, Knoxville.

AND SO WE EMBARK

This journey began before history and will go on as long as humans continue to exist. Right now my dog Scout is outside in the sun looking at me through the window as I sit at my computer, and he seems to be wondering why I am inside on such a beautiful day. If that is really what he is thinking (Do dogs think?), perhaps this journey will continue on even after humans have left the scene. In the meantime, enjoy your ventures into the history of psychology.

Bon voyage!

HISTORY OF PSYCHOLOGY
A Cultural Perspective

1

Origins of Psychological Thought: Why Do Other People Have Such Bizarre Beliefs and Behave So Strangely?

The purpose of this chapter is to identify some of the questions that have been or are considered within the purview of psychology and to introduce the ways in which humans think about such questions. There are universal human characteristics that influence how psychology's questions are answered, there are cultural differences, and there are learned influences that shape individual beliefs. Therefore, three ways of coming to believe something to be true are presented: trust, reason, and experience. These three ways of coming to believe establish a major theme of the text. Finally, the definitions of psychology, both in the past and today, are explored at the end of this chapter.

The real origins of psychological thought are lost in prehistoric mystery. In the Western world, psychology is broadly the search for the causes of thoughts, feelings, and behaviors. At various times and in various places, different assumptions about those causes have led to different answers and even different ways of seeking the answers, but the questions have remained much the same. And, after more than 3,000 years of written history, in many ways, the questions are still unanswered. Psychology is often a mystery.

THE QUESTIONS OF PSYCHOLOGY

For early humans, the most important problems probably concerned immediate survival: getting enough food, finding shelter, nurturing the young, and avoiding being eaten by more successful predators. Because our ancestors often depended on other people to help solve these problems, questions about the behavior of others and relationships between and among people became significant. Just as today, common questions probably included:

Why do other people behave the way they do?
How can I get other people to do what I want them to do?
Why are other people so different?

As the problems of immediate survival become more consistently solved, people might have become concerned with the following issues:

Where do thoughts and feelings come from, and how do they influence the body and behavior?
Do other people think and feel the same way you do?
Do other animals have thoughts and feelings?

Given enough leisure time, people may have asked questions about the place of humans in the universe and how much control it is possible to have over thoughts, feelings, and behaviors. Questions like these may have been asked:

How much of what happens to you can you control?
Can you control your thoughts, feelings, and behaviors?

Still other questions might have had to do with:

What is the source of human happiness?
What is the best way to live?

All of these questions still concern people today, and in one way or another, they have all become part of the discipline of Western psychology.

UNIVERSAL PSYCHOLOGICAL CHARACTERISTICS

There are many ways that these questions about ourselves, our relationships with others, and our place in the universe are answered. Among the influences on these answers are the psychological characteristics that are universal to humans. These characteristics have been selected for during evolution. Thus, humans exhibit

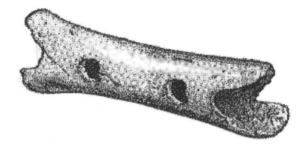

FIG. 1.1. Neanderthal bone flute *(On the Origins of Music,* by Robert Fink, 2003, Saskatoon, CA: Greenwich).

innate perceptual mechanisms that are the same across time and culture. We share with other animals many social responses that enhance survival when danger or threat is perceived and that allow us to get along with and work constructively with others. Reactions such as "fight or flight" in the face of immediate physical danger allow all animals to survive, to reproduce, and to adapt to a wide variety of environments. Various cognitive mechanisms enable all animals to discern meaningful information in a complex and sensory-rich environment. Even Neanderthals possessed the artistic and cognitive ability for abstract thinking, modeling, and manufacturing something other than tools (Marshack, 1972). For example, the flute shown in Fig. 1.1, found at a former Neanderthal hunting camp in Slovenia in 1996, indicates that Neanderthals possessed the ability to produce music and possibly to express the fears, longings, and joys in their lives. This enforces the idea that even Neanderthals had basic human behavior (Wilford, 1996). It is not possible to be certain which aspects of human thoughts, feelings, or behaviors can be traced to their common genetic inheritance, but because some characteristics appear across cultural and ethnic groups, it is safe to assume that at least some of them originate in the evolutionary past.

✓ **Stop and think.**
Do humans really all think the same way?

Perceptual and Cognitive Influences

It is true that the culture an individual belongs to can influence how questions about relationships with others or the sense of self are answered. There are also individual differences in how psychology's questions are answered. These sources of difference may lead us to think that the beliefs of others are bizarre or that their behavior is strange, but the perceptual and cognitive mechanisms that underlie these different beliefs and behaviors are quite similar. Understanding innate ways of perceiving and thinking may help illustrate why humans so often make the same mistakes in thinking, share similar incorrect assumptions, ignore important evidence if it does not support existing beliefs, and are thus likely to answer questions about psychological questions in similar ways. Researchers have begun to learn about some of these innate responses.

Simplicity

For example, humans prefer simple answers that can be readily understood, even for complex questions (Shermer, 1997). In an uncertain and confusing world, where sensory input is constant, intense, and at times overwhelming, humans quickly categorize new information and seek simple solutions and answers (Kagan, 1998). Humans need to quickly ascertain which incoming information has significance and which does not. In the evolutionary past, those individuals able to identify significant information and deduce simple and effective solutions fast were more likely to survive and go on to reproduce. Thus, the human brain today quickly categorizes incoming information and seeks out simple answers that have high **face validity**. An answer that has high face validity is one that looks, on the surface of it, as though it must be true.

> For every complex problem there is a simple answer, and it is wrong.
>
> H. L. Mencken

Pattern Recognition

Psychologists find that humans are predisposed to infer order, pattern, and meaning in what they experience, even when none is present (Kagan, 1998). The visual/perceptual system, for example, tends to "see" whole patterns from partial or even completely random evidence. We have all seen the shape of a Big Dipper among the stars at night, even though the only thing we have really seen are seven points of light:

> Humans, like other primates, are a gregarious lot. We enjoy one another's company. We're mammals, and parental care of the young is essential for the continuance of the hereditary lines. The parent smiles at the child, the child smiles back, and a bond is forged or strengthened. As soon as the infant can see, it recognizes faces, and we now know that this skill is hardwired in our brains. Those infants who a million years ago were unable to recognize a face smiled back less, and were less likely to win the hearts of their parents, and less likely to prosper. These days nearly every infant is quick to identify a human face, and to respond with a goony grin.
>
> As an inadvertent side effect, the pattern-recognition machinery in our brains is so efficient in extracting a face from a clutter of other detail that we sometimes see faces where there are none. We assemble disconnected patches of light and dark and unconsciously try to see a face. The Man in the Moon is one result. (Sagan, 1996, p. 45)

Humans infer patterns and meaning not only with visual perceptions, but with other information as well. Errors in logic are committed by drawing conclusions from a few facts, even when no such conclusion is warranted by the available evidence. Retailers know this when they announce low prices on a few very visible items, leading to the inference that overall prices are lower at that store (Pechmann, 1996).

People often treat single events as overly representative of whole patterns and small samples as overly representative of entire populations (Schwartz, 1998). If one person wins the lottery with a ticket purchased at the local mini-mart, that becomes the lucky location to purchase tickets. If one person hits it big in the stock market, the stock market begins to seem like the place to make a fortune.

Cause and Effect

These ways of thinking are part of why humans tend to think in terms of cause-and-effect relationships. In the search for simple answers, humans are prone to assume that events that occur together are causally related to one another (Gilovich, 1991).

If the assumption that two events that occur together must be causally related is a correct one (this fruit must be washed before it is safe to eat), it may aid in survival. If the assumption is incorrect (all fruit must be washed before it is safe to eat), it is a **superstitious** belief. A superstitious belief is defined as acquiring a response that is falsely believed to be associated with a reward. Using this definition, even nonhuman animals exhibit evidence of holding superstitious beliefs (Shermer, 1997). Some people have a superstitious belief that going outside in cold weather will cause them to "catch" a cold. Superstitious beliefs are very common and very easily formed (Vyse, 1997). Little evidence is required to develop a superstitious belief, especially if it is also a simple answer that has high face validity. People do catch colds more often during the winter months, and the idea that one can get sick from being uncomfortably damp and cold has high face validity. Of course, there are times when conclusions are drawn about causal relationships that turn out to be "accidentally" correct. Nearly all of the medicines in use today have their origins in folk medicines from earlier times and in other cultures, and the usefulness of these folk medications was almost certainly discovered through accidentally correct superstitious beliefs.

Biases in Processing Information

There are also biases that influence how incoming information is processed, such as a **motivational bias**, or the tendency to answer questions in a particular way because of a desire or wish to answer them in that way.

Filtering Evidence

Although there are many verifiable truths about nature, the universe, and the questions that concern psychologists, humans are not naturally predisposed to seek out and believe only the verifiable truth. Instead, we seek out and attend to evidence that supports what is expected and what is already believed to be true. Psychologists call this tendency to selectively attend to the available evidence **selective attention**.

Once a hypothesis has been formed or a conclusion drawn, humans are slow to change their minds, even in the face of disconfirming evidence. Psychologists call this a **confirmation bias**. Having already formed a hypothesis, we tend to pay attention only to evidence that supports the hypothesis and ignore evidence that refutes the hypothesis. In fact, the more educated people are, the more quickly they will form hypotheses and the more likely they will notice only evidence that confirms that hypothesis (Snelson, 1993). So when we think we already know what is true, we observe only evidence that will be most likely to support those preexisting beliefs.

There are also mechanisms of memory that filter evidence and allow for the maintenance of fondly held beliefs. Humans tend to remember only confirming evidence. That is, once a belief is accepted, the evidence that supports the belief is more likely to be remembered and the evidence that refutes the belief is forgotten. As a consequence of this, people come to believe that there is more supporting evidence than refuting evidence. Psychologists call this **selective recall**. Persons who call themselves psychics make predictions, only a few of which come to pass. But the client is more likely to remember the accurate predictions, or "hits," than the inaccurate predictions, or "misses," and is thus more likely to conclude that the psychic might really be able to foresee the future.

Desire for Social Consensus

The natural human desire and need to maintain bonds with significant others creates another motivational bias in thinking. Humans depend on one another for survival. Early **hominids** (erect, bipedal primate mammals, including ancestral forms of humans) were somewhat defenseless against predators because they did not have large claws or teeth to fight with and could not flee very fast or very far to escape. Like other prey animals, early hominids were dependent on others in their social group to provide sufficient warning to escape at the approach of danger and to join together when it was necessary to fight. Seeking the company of others is thus "hard-wired" into the human brain. Although there is individual variation in how much company is desired, humans tend to feel a sense of security in the presence of others, feel anxious when alone for long periods, and form emotional attachments to those with whom they spend time. This need for social acceptance is likely what explains why beliefs are often influenced by the presence of others and agreement within a group is sought.

The desire to maintain cohesion within social groups influences thinking, particularly in the ways that decisions are reached. For example, psychologists find that, in a group decision, everyone involved tends to center on the same focal points and that there is a tendency to overestimate the accuracy of consensus. We tend to think that if the group agrees with us that something is true, then it really must be true. We are even likely to change our opinion to match that of the group if the group's opinion differs from our own (Dawes & Mulford, 1996).

Personal Contact

Evidence is also filtered based on the degree of personal contact. Personal contact with an object or event results in more weight being given to that experience than other information (Clarke, 1995). For example, if you are acquainted with someone who actually knows the sister-in-law of a man who was purportedly cured of cancer by a psychic surgeon, you might be more likely to believe that particular myth than other people.

Optimistic Bias

Another motivational mechanism that influences how questions about ourselves and our relationships with others are answered is the human tendency toward unrealistic optimism (Weinstein, 1980). Most people under 60 years of age, especially males, tend to be overconfident about their ability to forecast the future, make correct decisions, and understand complex information (Schwartz, 1998). When asked, most people predict that they will be more successful than they turn out to be at answering questions and at comprehending difficult material (Fischhoff, Slovic, & Lichtenstein, 1977). What this means is that most people suffer from an unwarranted high level of optimism. Although this may mean that they are somewhat out of touch with reality, it is easy to imagine how being overly optimistic, that is, hopeful, might enhance survival and thus be a personality characteristic acquired through evolution.

All over the world, in all cultures and across time, humans use innate emotional reactions, perceptual and cognitive mechanisms, and motivational biases in formulating thoughts, feelings, and behaviors. During this journey through the history of Western psychology, we will find that the history of psychology is replete with answers that reflect these influences. As we examine answers to the questions of psychology, both past and present, we need to remain wary of both our own and others' tendencies to accept simple answers, form superstitious beliefs, assume cause and effect, filter evidence, and agree with others.

IMPORTANT DISTINCTIONS ACROSS TIME AND CULTURE

This book considers the answers to the questions of psychology as they are developed within the context of Western European and North American intellectual culture from the time of Classical Greece to the present. This is not the only perspective that can be taken on the answers to these questions. Although humans have common ways of thinking across time and culture, the answers that are developed to psychology's questions are often strikingly different based on varying assumptions made in different times and places. In what anthropologists and psychologists have called **worldview**, various times and cultures have taught their members to have perspectives that are divergent from those in other times and cultures. In particular, different perspectives are held on issues like the place of humans in the universe, understandings about relationships between the self and others, and the desire for power or degree of control that individuals have or should wish to have over events, the actions of others, and even their own actions.

The Place of Humans and Other Animals in the Universe

Cultures and times differ in the degree to which humans are seen to play a central role in the structure of the universe. In the Western view, humans are absolutely central. Humans are thought of as the "paragon of God's creations" and the reason that the Earth was created. In contrast, Classical Greek culture saw humans as incidental tools created and used by supernatural powers that had little or no concern for the lives or misfortunes of any single living being. Thus, the centrality of humans has changed dramatically across time.

Relationships Between the Self and Others

There are also differences in how the sense of self is experienced and how the self is viewed in relationship with others. In the West, people are taught to have a strong sense of themselves as separate individuals. Individuals learn to be independent and to rely most strongly on their own opinions and resources. According to Karl Marx and others, this individualistic focus is a necessary consequence of a culture divided by economic classes, especially one where a capitalistic ideology predominates (Wogaman, 1977). In other times, places, and worldviews, people have been taught that the self is only a small part of a large interdependent group. In these groups, people learn to work cooperatively and to consider the wishes and needs of others before making any decision. For example, among the Yoruba of West Africa, humans are believed to be created as beings-in-relationship to others. From birth to death each person is embraced within concentric circles of belonging from the family through the village and even across time and space by connections with ancestors and gods. Yoruba tribespeople go through life closely "attached" to others (Lowery-Palmer, 1980).

Desire for Power or Degree of Control That an Individual Can Have

In the West, individuals are usually thought to have absolute power over at least their own actions and some degree of control over many of the events that occur in their lives. Furthermore, this degree of control is thought of as desirable. It is believed that people are happier when they have, or believe they have, control over their actions and the events in their lives. In other cultures, the causes of behavior are thought of very differently. For example, before their contact with Europeans, the view of some aboriginal Native American peoples living in California was that everything both natural and supernatural was endowed with power. An individual could acquire more power by gaining knowledge about power and about the sources of power. But generally, only a moderate amount of power was considered desirable, as the possession of too much power could be potentially as dangerous as too little power (Kearney, 1984).

Also in these cultures, supernatural beings were believed to exert some control over one's fate, but most individual behavior was controlled by a strong set of social mores regarding cooperation and generosity. An individual gained power and influence in these cultures by sharing generously with others. Those who were generous and took care of others could be assured that others would take care of them when they were in need (Margolin, 1978).

In still other cultures, both past and present, an individual's actions may be thought of as determined by forces beyond the control of the individual. These might be supernatural forces or forces in nature. In either case, individuals have little control over their own actions and not much control over the events that occur in their lives. In these cultures, it is believed that people are happiest when they are able to give up the desire for control and accept whatever happens without complaint.

These are only a few of the contrasting worldviews that have shaped various times and cultures. Even though humans all begin with similar emotional responses, cognitive mechanisms, and social motivations, radically different answers to psychology's questions are developed depending, in part, on the culture or time period. It is important to remember that what may seem like significant questions to those of us imbedded in one time or culture may seem pointless or even nonsensical to people imbedded in another worldview. For example, the field of psychology itself is a product of a Western worldview, and the parameters of today's psychology appeared and evolved within the context of Western civilization.

WAYS OF COMING TO BELIEVE

✓ **Stop and think.**
What do you know to be true?

What do you know to be true? How do you know what is true? When do you decide for certain that something is not true? If emotions influence beliefs, if simple answers are sought and superstitious beliefs are easily formed, if evidence is selectively attended to and recalled based on what is already believed, if agreement with others is sought even at the cost of ignoring evidence, how do you know that any belief is true? What kind of evidence do you personally require before you believe something to be true? What kind of evidence do you need to overcome all of those ways in which your thinking can become confused? The study of knowledge and how knowledge is acquired is called **epistemology**. Epistemological questions originated in philosophy, but they have become central to the study of psychology as well.

Trust, reason, and experience are three ways of coming to believe that something is true. As this story moves through history, we will see that, in Western cultures, as in many others, trust in a variety of beliefs more often influences answers than reason or experience. But to a greater or lesser extent, all three ways of coming to believe have been used during nearly all time periods and in nearly all places.

Trust

For the purposes of this discussion, the word trust is defined as believing something to be true without either logical proof or publicly observable experience or evidence. It may sound paradoxical to say that psychological questions are sometimes answered by simply trusting in a given answer. Nevertheless, that is often exactly how those questions are answered. Your friend may say that the reason he has trouble with authority figures is because he had a difficult relationship with his father. When pressed for how he knows this to be true, he might respond by saying that he "just knows" that is the case or that explanation "just feels right." Trust that something is true comes from a variety of sources, including intuition, authorities, stories, and religions. In the case of modern Western cultures, his belief may come from the pervasive influence that Freud's theories have had in this culture.

✓ **Stop and think.**
Is it possible that he had a difficult relationship with his father because he has trouble with authority figures?

Intuition

One source of trust is intuition. Because we "just feel" something "must be true," we attribute truth to it. This reliance on intuition is very popular, probably because it is based in emotions, is simple, and usually has high face validity. **Intuition** might be defined as an awareness that seems to arise from within us so that we have direct and immediate knowledge. Although intuitions do seem to arrive in mind unbidden, in fact, intuitions probably arise from experiences that lie just outside conscious awareness. From that perspective, an argument could be made that intuition represents an experiential way of coming to belief, rather than a way of coming to believe through trust. However, the origin of intuitions usually lies outside conscious awareness. For example, imagine that you run into a friend whom you have not heard from in some time. Your friend seems happy to see you, but your intuition tells you she is not. She seems upset or angry with you. Did this belief just come to you intuitively? Or was there observable evidence of your friend's anger that you noticed but of which you were not consciously aware? Did you read your friend's "body language" to arrive at your intuition? Was there something in her tone of voice? Intuitions sometimes serve as powerful sources of belief, and they can be very convincing because they at least seem to arise solely from within, are a part of our immediate personal experience, and thus seem undeniably true.

✓ **Stop and think.**
Who do you believe?

Authorities

Authorities, defined as other people or institutions believed to have access to the truth, often serve as important sources of trust in beliefs. In the case of very complex questions, humans often seek out authorities for answers. Sometimes we prefer to be told what the truth is and not to have to figure it out for ourselves. There are also questions, especially complex ones, that each of us could never be expected to know the answers to and for which we must rely on the expertise of authorities. Whether we recognize it or not, and whether we even remember the source of our knowledge, much of what we believe to be true came to us originally through the voices of authorities:

> Even a casual scrutiny of history reveals that we humans have a sad tendency to make the same mistakes again and again. We're afraid of strangers or anybody who's a little different from us. When we get scared we start pushing people around. We have readily accessible buttons that release powerful emotions when pressed. We can be manipulated into utter senselessness by clever politicians. Give us the right kind of

leader and, like the most suggestible subjects of the hypno-therapists, we'll gladly do just about anything he wants—even things we know to be wrong. (Sagan, 1996, p. 424)

Stories and Narratives

Much of what humans believe to be true, both in the present and in the past, comes to us through stories. The Old Testament, for example, is a set of stories that gives one version of the origin of the Earth and of life on Earth. Greek mythology provided the Greeks with rules about how best to live, how to interact with others, and what personality characteristics to strive to achieve. Much of the handed-down wisdom in any culture comes in the form of stories.

Supernatural Powers

Humans do not seek knowledge purely out of curiosity. Many forms of adversity faced by humans seem inexplicable, and even trusted authorities cannot provide satisfying explanations. What explanation can there be for such seemingly inexplicable events? As human culture began to develop, as crops began to be cultivated and animals domesticated, understanding these bad events in nature became literally matters of life and death.

✓ **Stop and think.**
Why do bad things happen to good people?

These adversities in nature require explanation and solution. At some point in nearly all human cultures, what seems like the capricious and arbitrary forces of nature become attributed to supernatural forces (Vyse, 1997). The most important function of attributing events in nature to supernatural forces appears to be to provide simple and seemingly reasonable explanations for apparently unreasonable events and phenomena. Maybe bad things happen to good people because the supernatural forces have been angered. Maybe they have not been shown the proper respect or sufficient sacrifice has not been made. Even if the event seems inexplicable to us, it may make sense to the supernatural powers that caused it.

A belief in supernatural forces forms the foundation of all religions, both past and present. The belief that humans share the world with extraordinary, extracorporeal, and invisible beings is called **animism** and has been described as the most primitive form of religion (Tylor, 1924). Animism is nearly universal among human cultures. The evidence that we share the world with mostly invisible others is obvious to many and comes in many forms. Some of us wake up in the morning with vivid memories of seeing relatives or friends who have died. Memories of dreams are often as vivid as memories of what happened yesterday. Every time we walk out into the sunshine we see, moving along the ground beside us, an aspect of self, our shadow. When we look into a still pond, we see another aspect of self, our reflection. To some, these shadows and reflections constitute evidence of a spirit living inside. The physical body is only one aspect of the self. The body that is a part of nature dies, but the self that transcends nature lives on in a supernatural world.

If the supernatural forces are believed to be good or to have our best interests at heart, it can be comforting to believe in them. Bad things may still happen, but comfort can be taken from knowing that the supernatural forces have designed nature and cause it to function in a very purposeful way. Believing that there is an aspect of the self that transcends physical death and that can travel to and live on in a supernatural realm can be reassuring, too, if we believe that the supernatural realm is a happy one. Belief in the supernatural becomes the vehicle by which, symbolically, anxieties about misfortunes and even death can be calmed. Many explanations for belief in the supernatural have been offered by philosophers and theologians. Psychologists have suggested that these beliefs function to reduce anxiety about the capriciousness of nature, misfortune, and physical death.

Can Faith Heal?

Recently, a national magazine ran the above question as its headline for the month. Several popular television programs now have as their theme the notion that having faith can cause physical healing to occur. Many people believe that prayer can change the course of physical disease. Is this possible? Can faith really heal?

Psychologists would have to answer yes, absolutely! It is true that beliefs about what is true (the mental state) can actually alter the physical state. Does this mean that a supernatural being has intervened in our behalf and caused the physical illness to depart? If a supernatural being has not intervened, but faith can alter the physical state, then what is the mechanism that causes the cure to happen?

For psychologists, the mechanism that allows beliefs to alter the physical state is known as the **placebo effect**. A placebo is a neutral treatment, that is, one that objectively has no effect, like a sugar pill, but which the patient believes will have a beneficial effect. Placebos have repeatedly been found to be very effective treatments for a variety of conditions, as long as the patient has faith that they will be effective. In fact, a placebo condition is almost always included in any research protocol where the efficacy of various treatments is being tested because placebos alone are so often found to be helpful, even when no drug or treatment is provided. As one researcher reported, "The placebo component of drug administration can be as powerful or more powerful than the pharmacological component of drug effects" (Kirsch, 1985, p. 1192).

Reason

A second way of coming to believe that something is true is through the use of logical argument or reason. Reason is employed when a set of premises or observations can be associated together to form a coherent story. Sherlock Holmes used reason when he observed several pieces of evidence and then drew a conclusion about how the crime was committed.

Reason as Evidence

A coherent story put together through logical argument can provide strong evidence in support of a belief. For example, it seems reasonable that spanking children will cause them to behave, even though psychologists know that spanking results in several undesired outcomes (Deater-Dekard, Dodge, Bates, & Pettit, 1996).

Although logical arguments can be used to support beliefs based on trust, they are more often used to explain experiences and observations of the environment in useful ways. If you notice that when you take a hot bath, your sinus headache goes away, you may logically conclude that the hot bath has some curative power over the headache. You may then begin to speculate in logical ways about what aspect of the bath is influencing the headache. If it is simply the relaxation involved, then a nap should have the same effect. The speculation that a nap would also relieve the headache is a **hypothesis**. A hypothesis is a guess about a relationship between variables (the variables in this case being the headache and relaxation). Because humans seem predisposed to see patterns of cause-and-effect in any kind of correlation, they are constantly forming hypotheses. If you take a nap instead of a bath the next time you have a headache, you would be testing your hypothesis. Humans universally test hypotheses. This logical development and testing of hypotheses can be thought of as a rudimentary form of natural science, and it is something that humans do without being taught. Logical argument or reason is thus a way to tie together pieces of evidence that have been observed and to test the validity of the resulting conclusion.

The use of statistics is one of the most common instances of using reason as evidence. We will see that, in Western cultures, considerable trust is placed in evidence that is presented in terms of numbers.

Reasoning begins with **premises**, or assertions that are presumed to be true, and ends with conclusions logically supported by the premises. If all of the premises used to support a conclusion are true, then the logical conclusion must also be true. When the premises are all true, but the conclusion is not logical, some form of a rhetorical trick has probably been used to reach the conclusion.

Rhetoric

The skillful use of words to outline an argument is called **rhetoric**. Rhetoric is a useful tool to help people communicate ideas effectively to one another. Rhetoric can be used to outline both logical and illogical arguments. Most of us are vulnerable to a number of "tricks" in how words are used and can easily be convinced of the truth of a claim through the use of rhetorical tricks. Rhetorical tricks have even been used to support some answers to psychology's questions. A few such tricks are described in the following section.

For example, we can sometimes be convinced that if a claim cannot be disproved, then the claim must be true. If I tell you that I was visited in the night by an angel, can you prove that I was not? If not, then my claim stands. It is not even your word against mine, because you were not there to witness the visitation. Therefore, what I say must be true. Related to this trick are "black or white" arguments, in which either/or terms are used, and logical thinking is clouded. The "if you are not with us, then you are against us" argument is a common one.

Government Conspiracies

In 1948, something unusual fell from the sky near Roswell, New Mexico. Military officials from the nearby Army Air Force Base came out and collected the pieces of this strange object. They say that they examined the objects and then discarded them, reporting that the objects were part of an experiment launched a couple of weeks earlier by another government agency. Now, 50 years after the "incident," some people claim that this object was actually an extraterrestrial vehicle and that it was occupied by creatures from an extraterrestrial location. The Army Air Force Base in Roswell has been closed for 30 years, and other government agencies have no comment to make on these claims. Here come the rhetorical tricks:

What is the government hiding? Why won't they tell us what that object really was? Why won't they explain what happened to the remains of its occupants?

Wording questions in this way seems to make it obvious that something sinister is afoot. "The government" appears to be refusing to disprove these claims. What would the government say if nothing was being hidden? All agencies involved have already issued statements saying that the object was an experimental radio device sent up by the U.S. Air Force. What more could the government say if it really was just such a device? How could they explain what happened to its occupants if there were really no occupants?

Some rhetorical tricks involve claiming that the unexplained is inexplicable. In other words, objects or events for which no natural cause can currently be identified must therefore arise from some mysterious or supernatural cause. For example, no one is yet able to explain exactly how dreams happen, although there is considerable ongoing research into some of the neurological mechanisms involved. Does the fact that the origins of dreams cannot yet be fully explained mean that dreams must be the manifestations of spirits from beyond the physical world or messages from a supernatural realm? Is it necessarily true that a phenomenon that cannot be explained naturally must therefore have a supernatural explanation?

Arguments that use their own assertions as evidence of their validity are often used as rhetorical tricks to "prove" the logic of a position. These are referred to as **circular arguments**. Assuming that you are angry because you have been wronged, and the evidence that you have been wronged is that you are angry, is a circular argument. Here is another common example of a circular argument: Living things live because they are endowed with a "life-force," which is a form of energy that scientists have not yet discovered; even though scientists have found no evidence of this form of energy, it must exist because how could living things live without a life-force?

Similarly, arguments that reduce the issue to a level where it no longer makes any sense, called **reductio ad absurdum**, can also make something illogical seem logical. Zeno's paradox (see box, Zeno's Paradox) is a good example of a reductio ad absurdum argument. Psychologists are sometimes accused of using reductive arguments when they explain behavior on the basis of neurological functioning alone.

Zeno's Paradox

The Greek teacher Zeno submits this logical paradox for your puzzlement. Imagine that you are standing at the entrance to a great hall, and you wish to cross the room to the stage. Before you can cross all the way to the stage, you must first walk halfway across the room. That much is clearly logical. Having crossed half the distance, now you must cross half of the remaining distance. In fact, each time you wish to proceed you must first cross one half of the remaining distance. What this means logically is that you can never go all the way across because you must first cross one half of the remaining distance. The inevitable reductio ad absurdum conclusion: Logical argument has just proven that you can never get anywhere because first you have to get halfway there.

Logical argument requires the use of language to communicate that logic to others and is thus subject to rhetorical tricks. Despite the fact that it can be misused, logical argument or reason is an essential component of both what we believe to be true and how we seek knowledge.

Experience

A third way of coming to believe that something is true is through publicly observable experience. This usually means using sensory equipment (sight, sound, touch, taste, or smell) to observe the environment. All animals possess the ability to observe, but sensory abilities vary greatly. Dogs, for example, have senses of smell and hearing that are far superior to those of humans. Similarly, the visual equipment of most birds allows them to observe the environment in much more visual detail than can humans. The capabilities of the sensory equipment possessed by most humans seem to fall somewhere in the midrange to very modest range compared with that of other animals.

✓ **Stop and think.**
Can you trust your observations and experiences?

For most people in the Western world, experience forms the primary evidence that something is true. It can be hard to believe that someone close to us has died until we actually see the body of the deceased person. Because sensory experience forms the primary evidence for truth, it is important that we trust that our observations do reveal reality accurately. Fortunately, for most of us most of the time and for most practical purposes, observations do accurately reflect the real world. If you see a doorway in a wall, most of the time it really is a doorway that can actually be walked through.

Occasionally, however, observations turn out to be false. If a puddle appears in the middle of the road on a hot day far off in the distance, it may only be a mirage, meaning an accidental perception resulting from how the visual system functions. When running a very high fever, it is not unusual to "see" visions referred to as hallucinations. If you see a flying saucer glide across the sky while driving on a dark and stormy night, it might just be the reflection of light in a raindrop sliding across the windshield. From a practical standpoint, humans would not be able to function in the physical universe without trusting observations, but observations and experiences are not entirely foolproof.

✓ **Stop and think.**
What provides the best explanation for why we think, feel, and behave as we do, trust, reason, or experience?

FOLK PSYCHOLOGY

Given these various ways of coming to believe, how are questions about our own thoughts, feelings, and behaviors; our relationships with others; and our place in the universe answered? **Folk psychology**, sometimes called commonsense psychology, is a set of answers that are derived from superstitious beliefs, the desire to remain affiliated with others, trust, everyday reason, and unstructured observations. Folk psychology is made up of assumptions. **Assumptions** are beliefs that are not questioned or tested. They are like premises in a logical argument in that they serve as the foundation for a sequence of beliefs. If the assumptions are correct, the sequence of beliefs that follows should also be true. Unfortunately, a serious problem arises if the assumptions are not correct because not only may conclusions based on false assumptions be wrong, but also the assumptions themselves are not ever tested.

One example of an assumption of Western folk psychology is the belief that each person behaves in ways that they expect to find rewarding, although each person's definition of reward varies greatly. Other assumptions include that perceptions actually reflect what is real, that other people think and feel in similar ways, or that all people behave the way they do to achieve some purpose. The assumptions of folk psychology help us to understand ourselves and to interact successfully with other people. The problem with folk psychology in general is that the assumptions on which it rests often arise from collections of cognitive mistakes and motivational biases that turn out not to be supported by objective evidence. Remember, assumptions are not tested, and beliefs based on intuition, authorities, or cultural stories are similarly untested. It sometimes turns out that much of what seems like common sense to those in the present-day West has little or no evidence to support it and might not sound sensible at all to people from other cultures or from other times.

The assumptions of a particular folk psychology are specific to a particular time period or culture. For example, in the West, it is assumed that the way people behave as adults depends in large part on how their parents treated them when they were small children. Thinking of children as "lumps of clay" shaped by their environment is a nice, simple story. Casual observation might reveal that adults who behave badly grew up in "broken homes," so there seems to be a cause-and-effect relationship between early treatment and adult outcome. Authorities like Sigmund Freud, ancient writings, and cultural stories support this belief: As the twig is bent, so the tree will grow. So part of our answer to questions about the personalities of others will be something about how they were treated when they were young. This just sounds like common sense. It might surprise you to know that people in other cultures do not necessarily share this assumption.

Another part of Western folk psychology has to do with questions about motivation. Why do we behave as we do? If there is a single question that defines Western psychology today, this is probably it. Throughout history, a variety of answers to this question have been generated. Among these are that behavior is caused by an imbalance of fluids in the body, by supernatural powers, by what has been learned, by unconscious and repressed thoughts, or by the influences of genes. In the West, understanding the causes for human behavior has been an important issue. But in some cultures, the question itself sounds strange. Some cultures make the assumption that humans behave the way they do for the same reason that rocks behave the way they do. That is, humans behave the way they do because that is just how humans behave. Rocks have a rock way of behaving, birds have a bird way, and humans have a human way. Each aspect of nature plays its own respective role, and humans are part of nature. To ask why humans behave the way they do would be like asking why the rock just sits there year after year; that is what rocks do.

If folk psychology is just common sense, but the assumptions of folk psychology differ somewhat across culture and time, does that mean that some of the assumptions are wrong? How would you know which assumptions are true and which are not? Remember, folk psychology arises out of the ways that humans think and the untested assumptions that humans make. As long as the assumptions remain untested, no one will ever know which are true and which are not.

CONCLUSIONS ABOUT THE ANSWERS

Across cultures and times, humans rely on universal ways of thinking and cultural worldviews to answer questions about the nature of the universe, relationships between individuals, and the place of humans in the universe. We rely on intuition, we ask for and accept the word of authorities, we listen to cultural stories, and we practice religions to learn what to believe. In the face of uncertainty, and especially in situations of extreme importance, we resort to supernatural explanations.

Although thinking logically about a problem or collecting observational evidence in nature is something that most humans can do, it is likely to be done only in certain situations. Reason or experience are more likely to be used only when the evidence is clear, we have some sense of certainty about our answers, or the situation is of less immediate importance. The methods of logical explanation and collecting observational evidence take longer than simply believing, and the answers acquired through those means may be very different from those provided by authorities or believed by others. Given the desire for social consensus, accepting answers based on logic or evidence may be uncomfortable. No matter how valid you may trust your own answers to be, you may not wish to violate the social consensus of your group and risk becoming an outcast, or worse.

Questioning accepted wisdom is called **skepticism**. Skepticism has doubtless been present among all peoples, but the formal appearance of skepticism in Western thought occurs in about 800 BCE in the writings of Greek philosophers. These philosophers argued that, before something can be accepted as true, there should be some logical or observable evidence in support of the belief.

Skeptical questioning has been more acceptable in some cultures and in some times than others. At some times in Western culture, for example, skepticism has been severely punished. The astronomer Giordano Bruno was sentenced to death for teaching that the sun, not the Earth, is at the center of the universe. At the time, Christian Church doctrine, based not on the Bible but on Greek and Egyptian philosophy, asserted that the Earth was at the center of the universe. Thus, Church authorities found early astronomers' observations to be heretical and persecuted those who spoke publicly about them.

Skepticism was critical in the birth of science. On our journey through the history of Western psychology, we will examine the roles of trust, reason, experience, and skepticism in answering the questions posed by psychology.

✓ **Stop and think.**
What is psychology?

A SCIENCE OF PSYCHOLOGY

Psychology is studied as a science for the same reason that any aspect of nature is studied as a science. The previous sections illustrate that humans do not necessarily see the natural world as it is. Science, and psychology when it is practiced as a science, is a method for exploring and attempting to understand nature without being fooled by mistakes in thinking and perception. The science of psychology allows us to learn about how and why we think, feel, and behave as we do, without being misled by trust in preexisting beliefs, failures of logic, or misperceptions.

Before the journey to examine the history of psychological thought in the Western world can begin, the scope of the itinerary must first be clear. What exactly is psychology? What does the word psychology mean, both in the past and today?

The Greek Psyche

The word psychology derives from Greek and means the study of "psyche." But what is psyche? Therein lies the confusion, from ancient times until the present, about the scope of psychology. In the beginning, psyche was the name of a beautiful girl in a Greek story about love and immortality.

The Legend of Psyche and Eros

Once upon a time, a lovely mortal maiden, Psyche, was deeply but secretly loved by the young and immortal god Eros. Eros was the son of the god Chaos and the goddess of love, Aphrodite. Eros was a god of love and as such was considered one of the primeval forces of nature. Aphrodite was jealous of the attention that Eros paid to the beautiful Psyche so she commanded him to make Psyche fall in love with the ugliest and most despicable mortal man on Earth. But Eros was desperately in love with Psyche himself. So keeping his identity secret, he took her away to a remote hiding place, a palace with walls decorated with gold, where he could visit her in secrecy whenever he wished. He instructed Psyche to try to be content with the riches he provided in the palace. He forbade her ever to look at him in the light and visited her only in total darkness. But one night, Psyche was overcome with curiosity. She lit an oil lamp and saw the god of love sleeping beside her. A drop of oil from the lamp fell on Eros and awakened him. He angrily reproached Psyche for looking at him, then flew away, abandoning her to her fate. Psyche left the palace and wandered desolately in search of Eros. Eventually, she fell into the hands of Aphrodite, who forced her to perform a series of difficult tasks, including making a treacherous journey to the underworld. Finally, touched by Psyche's repentance and continuing love for him, Eros rescued her. He then persuaded Zeus to make Psyche immortal, and the story ends happily with Psyche's marriage to Eros (adapted from Grant, 1973; Grimal, 1965).

In this Greek myth, the story of Psyche and Eros serves as an allegory about the journey of a mortal, Psyche, as guided through life by love, Eros. When she becomes immortal, Psyche becomes a spirit. So the study of the psyche might be interpreted as the study of the part of the human (or other animal) that is not the body. What is meant by a "part of the human that is not the body" is not at all clear, however, and remains a subject of rancorous contention among psychologists even today.

The Greeks meant something very different by the word psyche than is meant today in the West when discussing an aspect of the human that is not physical. When used by Greek philosophers such as Plato, the word psyche refers to some aspect of a living thing that is not identifiable as part of the physical body. This is sometimes translated as, or understood to mean, the mind and its various functions, such as thought, perception, and memory. At other times, psyche is translated as spirit. But for these Greeks, psyche is not a spirit that goes on after the body dies. Instead, the word psyche refers in Greek writings to the biological processes that sustain life (Aristotle), or to breath (Homer).

Some Greek writings, especially later translations, refer to psyche as a life-force, a type of energy that differentiates living matter, like plants and people, from nonliving matter, like rocks or water. At first glance, living things do seem to be categorically different from nonliving things. Only living things are born, develop, sometimes move about, react to their environment, reproduce, and die. These characteristics are explained by attributing to living things a life-force that is not possessed by nonliving things. As long as the life-force is present, the thing lives, but when the life-force departs, the thing dies. This idea that living matter possesses a special type of energy, or life-force, is called **vitalism**. In many cultures, vitalism is, and has been, a popular belief. Today, scientists understand that there is no special life-force that causes things to live but that living things are subject to the same force, or forces, that govern all matter in the universe.

In English versions of the work of Greek philosophers, the word psyche is often translated as soul. In Western thought, the word soul usually means some aspect of the human that transcends the physical, that remains coherently identifiable as an individual after death, even in the absence of a body, and that is able to travel intact to metaphysical or other-worldly realms. It is important to remember that the Western understanding of the word soul is not what the Greeks meant by the word psyche. As an illustration of this, consider that Aristotle suggested that even plants have psyche or soul. By this, he meant only that plants have a life-force that leaves them when they die.

Modern Definitions

Modern definitions of psychology vary widely depending on who is being asked. This makes the scope of psychology very broad and the limits of psychology hard to define. The study of the history of this discipline will often wander far in any number of directions from where you might expect.

The questions that concern Western psychologists are questions about how and why animals (mostly human animals) think, feel, and behave as they do. Today, psychologists have organized themselves into two large professional organizations, each of which state a definition of psychology from the viewpoint of the individuals affiliated with that organization. For example, the largest of these organizations, the American Psychological Association (APA), founded in 1892, defines psychology as "the study of mind and behavior" and goes on to say that "the understanding of behavior is the enterprise of psychologists." Psychologists with many different perspectives belong to the APA, but clinical psychologists (practicing psychotherapists) are most strongly represented in this group. Another organization, the American Psychological Society (APS), was founded in 1988, and academic or research psychologists are most strongly represented in this group. This group offers a different definition of psychology, describing it as "the scientific study of thoughts, feelings and behavior."

✓ **Stop and think.**
What assumptions underlie these different definitions?

Throughout history, individual psychologists themselves have held varying opinions about the definition of psychology. These varying definitions are determined in part by the time period in which the psychologists are living and the assumptions that they make about the qualities of human nature.

Often, people who are not psychologists have very different opinions about what psychology is or should be. The most common definitions of psychology among nonpsychologists refer to the study of human behavior, or mind, and usually to clinical or therapeutic applications of that study.

At the advent of the 21st century, there are thousands of people throughout the world who call themselves psychologists, ranging from research scientists studying the neurochemical bases of brain functioning, to "parapsychologists" studying extrasensory perception, to therapists providing marriage and family counseling. One thing that unites all psychologists, however, is a passionate interest in the kinds of questions raised in this chapter.

⊕ The Times

What has life been like for most people? Seventy thousand years ago, anatomically modern humans were using controlled fire and practicing ritual burials. Ten thousand years ago, small settlements were being established. Five thousand years ago, larger settlements were appearing in various places on the globe, economies were changing from barter and trade to money, and writing was used, mostly to record transactions of goods and services. As trade increased, a merchant class arose, and leadership moved from spiritual powers or priests to secular powers. These stages of development toward civilization are universal across all cultures, although not simultaneous across time.

It is hard to know what daily life was like before written records were kept. Even when written records began to appear, much of early history recounts battles and wars. Histories are also more likely to be written about wealthy and influential individuals than about ordinary people. Throughout most of history, most people lived their lives in routines of meeting daily needs for food and shelter, sharing life with friends and family, and enjoying respites of occasional holidays and celebrations, much as is true today.

By the time historical records were made and preserved, human cultures were usually already well developed. Thus, it is difficult to know how early cultures were structured in terms of the roles of men and women. We do know that, in most groups, the status of women declined as the transition was made from a hunter–gatherer economy, where smaller populations are desirable, to an agrarian economy, where larger populations can provide more labor. Anthropologists and historians attribute this decline in the status of women, first, to the development of agriculture and the need for increased population, and, second, to the discovery of the fact that men also play a role in reproduction. The practice of agriculture provided an increased nutritional status for everyone, an increase in fertility for the women, and a decrease in infant mortality. Thus, women's roles in the community were more likely to be circumscribed by more frequent pregnancies and births, and their reproductive capacity began to be valued as a commodity. The discovery of paternity meant that men took control of women to own their reproductive capacity. Men also took control of agricultural surpluses to engage in trade with surrounding peoples. This gave men economic power, which they consolidated through the political and religious practice of patriarchy (Lerner, 1986). Although patriarchy is not universal, it is currently the predominant form of human social organization.

2

From Greek Philosophy to the Middle Ages: What and How Do We Believe?

The purpose of this chapter is to illustrate the transition from ancient supernatural explanations of natural phenomena to Classical Greek philosophy, where knowledge was sought through reason and in observations of nature. Many reasons this transition happened, and how this change influences the questions of psychology, are discussed. The chapter ends with the influence of Augustinian Christian doctrines on Western thought in the early Middle Ages.

WHAT WE BELIEVE AND HOW WE COME TO BELIEVE

We are about to visit the Classical Greek philosophers to see how they grappled with questions about what to believe and their reasons for believing. Before beginning the journey, we should review some important concepts that will be important for understanding the issues that concern these Greeks and the Western cultures that follow.

Ontology. **Ontology** is the study of what is real and the nature of reality. Is there anything that can be established as real beyond all doubt? For example, does reality include that which cannot be observed? This is a critical question for many psychologists.

Epistemology. As defined previously, epistemology is the study of knowledge and the methods by which we come to know. Trust, reason, and experience are three methods for coming to believe. Each of these epistemologies provides support for some, but not all, beliefs. Belief in the unobservable, for example, can only be achieved through trust or logic.

Psychology and the unobservable. Not only the origin of the universe but even questions about ourselves, our relationships with others, and our place in the universe can be and often have been explained as acts of the unobservable or supernatural. For example, through most of history in the West, "mental illness" has been attributed to the acts of supernatural forces. Even today, many people explain their actions or behaviors as resulting from supernatural powers, as in "the devil made me do it."

THE SIGNIFICANCE OF GREEK CULTURE

Our journey takes us to the islands and scattered settlements of Classical Greece. There are two reasons why this time and place serves as a good beginning for this exploration. First, the questions that were asked, the kind of knowledge that was sought, and especially the epistemological methods of Classical Greece are not seen before in human history. That is, as far as we know, no one before asked these questions or attempted to answer them in quite the same way as did the Classical Greek philosophers.

A second reason that this period is significant is because of the almost world-wide influence that Classical Greek philosophies had on human history. These philosophical ideas spread across the globe, carried by travelers like Alexander the Great and by the growth of the Roman Empire. Roman culture adopted many of the Greek ideas and much of Greek culture. Thus, Greek influences in art and philosophy are found as far away as India, Africa, England, the Middle East, and everywhere else that the Roman armies traveled. In no small way, the roots of Western culture lie buried in this intellectually fertile Classical Greek soil.

Greek Antiquity

The first **historical** Greek period, or time when written records are kept, is the Mycenaean age, roughly between 1600 and 1100 BCE. During this time, towns are established, along with stone fortresses and palaces, and a rich cultural and worldly life develops (Lommel, 1966). Literacy exists but is limited to members of the ruling classes. The collection of city/states that make up Greece is believed by its citizens to be the center of the world. So, for example, the settlement at Delphi, which is at the center of Greece, is referred to as "the navel of the world."

These Greeks trade with people living to the east as far as Persia and south along the coast of the African continent, and with a variety of smaller groups around the

Mediterranean. Thus, Greek culture is strongly influenced by the mythologies, supernatural beliefs, and values of the Mesopotamian, Babylonian, Sumerian, and Hebrew cultures to the east and the Egyptians to the south.

Written Greek mythology is born during this era, and beliefs in supernatural beings flourish among people of all economic classes. Literate upper-class Greek citizens are able to maintain their wealth by exploiting a large lower class of working people, including women, servants, and slaves. The religious beliefs that appeal to the people of the exploited classes are ones that promise some relief in a life after this one. These people think of the natural world as a living thing and believe that one is liable to encounter gods and goddesses everywhere in every form imaginable. When the deities appear, often as birds or small children, they give guidance or warnings but are also capable of deceiving or deluding humans into making bad decisions. Gods and spirits of the underworld make regular appearances. Faith healers, miracle-workers, and prophets wander the countryside in search of converts. Forms of magic like Babylonian **astrology**, or the foretelling of the future by the position of planets and stars, are widely accepted. Mystery cults flourish, in particular the **Dionysian** faith, practicing secret religious rites and promising benefits in an afterlife to believers. Ritual human sacrifice is still occasionally practiced, and animal and other types of sacrifice are routinely practiced, justified by religious beliefs (Bergmann, 1992).

As is true in most early human groups, women in both human and supernatural forms play decisive roles in the religious beliefs of this culture (Knox, 1993). The power of women to give birth is revered, and there are some indications that the status of women is substantially higher early in Greek history than during later periods (Demand, 1994).

The supernatural beings of literate and economically privileged Greeks are the gods and goddesses living on Mt. Olympus and described in the works of the poet Homer. Wealthy Greek citizens are more concerned with happiness in the present and less likely to believe in an afterlife. From early on, the Olympian deities seem to regard mortal humans as interesting distractions and playthings, but not of much import in the deities' own divine and immortal lives.

The Classical Greek World

Our exploration of Classical Greece begins in the area called Ionia and in particular in the seaport city of Miletus. Miletus is an important center of trade and commerce for the entire Mediterranean and becomes a center of learning and philosophy as well. The Classical Greek period begins at about the time of the appearance of the Pythagorean school in 530 BCE and lasts until about the death of Aristotle in 322 BCE.

Much of the evidence about Greek culture has been filtered, and only the history that others decided to preserve is available. The only evidence remaining about Greek civilization of any era is the artifacts and a few pieces of writing that were chosen by others to be saved. In particular, the Greek works that survive to influence Western thought were selected by the early Christians. These works were copied onto a more durable material, parchment, and thus made available to us. Those works that were not deemed important, or that conflicted with the tenets of early Christianity, either disappeared or were changed to fit Christian doctrines. For example, the Hippocratic Oath attributed to the Greek physician Hippocrates includes the phrase "I will not give to a woman an abortive remedy (the means to produce an abortion)" (Edelstein, 1967). Abortion was routinely practiced during the Classical Greek era, as it was in nearly all cultures of this era. So either this phrase was added by early Christians or the entire oath was written during the early Christian era and then misattributed to the Greeks as support for Christian doctrines (Gross, 1998; Edelstein, 1967).

Transitions in Ontology

If the primary epistemology in a culture is trust, as was true in the 6th century BCE in Greece, then questions about the origin of the universe are about who the supernatural powers are that made the universe and why they made it. When skepticism begins to cause doubt in cultural and religious stories, the origin questions change to ones about what the "stuff" of the universe is and the mechanics of how that "stuff" works in the universe.

Transitions in Epistemology

When the questions change, then the methods by which answers are sought also change. Greek philosophy comes into being just as epistemology based on trust shifts to other ways of coming to believe. The problem is how can beliefs based only on trust be supported? Are there other ways to establish the truth of a belief than to simply trust?

Reasons for the Transitions

Historians offer several explanations for why, at this place in human history, apparently for the first time, something other than intuition, religion, and folk wisdom is sought as the source for the truth about nature. These explanations include developments in literacy, medicine, trade, leisure, religion, and politics.

Literacy

In about 800 BCE, the Greek poet Homer writes an allegorical and historical account of wars between mainland Greece and Troy, basing his written history on a long oral tradition. The Olympian deities play starring roles in Homer's account, and his history of these wars is the first place that the personalities of the Greek deities are captured in writing. Homer's critics complain that he "ascribed to the gods all things that are a shame and a disgrace among mortals" (Bevan, 1913).

Once captured in writing, the deities lose some of their power and mystery and are brought down to a merely human level. This dethroning of the deities may contribute to Greek philosophers' willingness to give up their trust in stories and seek another way of answering questions about nature and the beginning of the universe.

Medicine

Prior to this era, Egyptian physicians made great progress in observing and describing physical illness, including serious brain injuries. This information became available to Greek doctors during the 7th century BCE. Earlier Greek cures for disease and injury relied on appeals to the gods, and illness was believed to be caused by supernatural forces. Cures involved sacrifices, incantations, prayers, and other rituals, *similar to those prescribed by faith healers today.*

By the 6th century BCE, Greek practitioners of medicine note many significant relationships between natural substances and health. Thus, these physicians are less likely to seek explanations for disease in supernatural factors and more likely to search in nature for both causes and cures.

Prosperity and Trade

The Greek upper classes of the 6th century BCE enjoy a high standard of living, due in no small part to the relative freedom from thievery allowed by conducting trade over the sea. The seaport city of Miletus becomes a center of trade for many surrounding cultures. Here, not only goods, but also ideas, are imported from Egypt, Persia, and many other settlements around the Mediterranean. Each of these cultures has its own religion and each its own story about the beginning of the universe, or **cosmogenic** story. Each culture's story regards its own citizens as the central and most favored group.

✓ **Stop and think.**
Which of these stories (if any) is the true story?

If you are a merchant in the city of Miletus, the first thing you might notice is that all of these cosmogenic stories are equally plausible. There is no evidence to support any of the stories; there are only people who believe them to be true. Each of these stories posits the existence of supernatural forces that cause the cosmos to come into being and place humans and other animals in it for some purpose.

Unfortunately, these stories are also mutually exclusive. That is, only one of them can be true. On what basis could you decide which one is the true one? Other people seem to believe just as strongly in their story as you do in yours. So who did create the universe, and why was it created? It becomes evident that stories, intuitions, and trust in authorities may not provide any evidence, even about something as basic as the origin of the universe.

The Babylonian Cosmogenic Myth

In the beginning were the waters, the sweet water, and Tiamat, the sea, containing within her the seeds of all life. She gives birth to all the gods and rules over the forces of Chaos in the cosmos. Her son, Marduk, emerges from the many, becomes the god of the sun, and threatens to take from Tiamat the power of renewal and of giving life. Marduk proposes to battle his mother, Tiamat, on the condition that he be given supreme power among the gods if he should win. Then Marduk, who is now called the Creator, mounts his storm-chariot armed with lightning and floods, slays Tiamat, slashes her into pieces, and then stands upon her body in triumph. He drives away the dragons and serpents of the army of Chaos and creates order in the cosmos. He builds a reed raft on the surface of the waters that becomes Earth. Then all of the gods sacrifice the god Kingu, and from his blood they create the creature Marduk names "man," whose purpose is to serve the gods that they might be "at ease" (Grimal, 1965).

Cosmogenic stories are not the only ideas being exchanged across cultures. By exposing themselves to different peoples and different ways of thinking, the Greeks of Miletus are creating for themselves a truly cosmopolitan social environment that almost certainly plays a role in opening their minds to alternative points of view. They are thus more likely to question the authorities of their own culture and to seek answers through some other means than accepting the word of others.

Leisure

Throughout Greece, the work of large numbers of slave laborers, nearly all women (Lerner, 1986), provide significant leisure time for upper-class males. Miletus is an especially privileged city economically because of its location as a center of trade. This advantage allows upper-class Ionians an unprecedented high standard of living and additional leisure time with which to consider important questions about reality and the nature of the cosmos.

Religion

The lack of concern with human affairs shown by the Olympian deities results in a religious environment that is less doctrinaire and dogmatic than is found in other cultures. It is uncommon in history for a single culture to support more than one religious system, but the Olympian religion of the upper class, and the Dionysian and other mystery religions of everyone else, coexist within the same culture in Greece. In addition, new peoples moving into the region are bringing their own belief systems with them. Eastern peoples bring the goddess Ishtar and her host of deities. The Egyptians worship Isis among many other deities. The Jews bring their unusual monotheistic belief in a single male god. Indeed, virtually every group that travels to the region believes in a different set of gods or goddesses than do the Greeks. It is likely that this plurality of religious beliefs is one factor that leads Greek culture to tolerate and foster the skepticism that eventually results in a radically different epistemology.

Politics

Instead of being a single geographically united state, the Greek world is really a collection of small cities scattered around the shorelines of the eastern Mediterranean. Each of these cities is ruled independently by its citizens (the free men). Each citizen is expected to pay attention to the political affairs of the city and to play an active role in decision making. Ideally, all opinions are to be voiced, each opinion is to be listened to with respect and tolerance, and differences of opinion are to be resolved through discussion. Thus, the Classical Greek political environment fosters tolerance for divergent perspectives and critical thinking. This type of political organization is also founded on an assumption that ordinary men are capable of discerning truth and right courses of action through reasonable discussion and without recourse to divinely informed rulers (Ehrenberg, 1968).

Choosing an Epistemology

So, here in Miletus in the 6th century BCE, there are changes in cosmogenic questions and in the way answers are sought. The importance of this period lies not in the truth of the answers that are found, but in this transition in epistemology. If there are three ways of coming to believe—trust, reason, and experience—and if skepticism arises about the beliefs reached through trust, then which way of coming to believe would be better?

> **✓ Stop and think.**
> Isn't it obvious that experience, including the direct observation of nature, would be a better way to know?

Observations and Folk Wisdom

Perhaps personal experience with the direct observation of nature would best reveal what is really real. Each individual can conduct personal observations using a variety of sensory modalities. From a practical point of view, the senses provide evidence about the physical world that is usually reliable. Ground that looks flat usually is flat. Food that smells bad probably should not be eaten. For most of us, most of the time, our own personal sensory experience is enough to establish that something is real.

Comparing Epistemologies: Observation and Trust

Although trust and observation are fundamentally different ways of answering questions about nature, they are in some ways similar. If you watch, you will notice that the sun changes its relationship to objects on the earth as the day passes. From the perspective here on Earth, it appears that the sun is moving across the sky. If someone asks you why the sun moves across the sky, you might make up a story about a god who attaches a beast to the sun and rides it across the sky each day. This kind of story is quite common in human cultures. But how would you answer the question about why the sun moves across the sky without reference to mythical or supernatural beings? In other words, what if you had decided to answer questions about nature using only explanations derived from nature and observable by humans?

✓ **Stop and think.**
Why does the sun move across the sky?

Any explanation you come up with will be essentially another story. For example, if you think of air as a substance, then you can think about the Earth and our sun both suspended in air. You may have also noticed that similar bodies seem to float past the Earth every night. So they are not just floating randomly, but are floating in a repeating pattern. From these observations, a story can be constructed about the sun and other objects in the sky suspended in air and floating around the Earth. You have no more evidence for this story than you have for the one about the god pulling the sun, but you have answered the question using only observations of nature.

You may have also noticed that objects floating on water seem to swirl together and maintain position relative to one another, so you can then add something to your story about some force in the air that pulls objects along together in the same way that water does. Now you have a fairly coherent answer to the question about the sun moving across the sky that uses only natural observation as evidence.

One difference between the natural explanation and the story about the god pulling the sun is that there is evidence in nature for the natural explanation, although it is important to note that not all of this explanation is supported by observable evidence. Neither the assertion that air is a substance in which bodies like the sun can be suspended, nor the suggestion that there is a force that pulls all of those bodies along together, is supported by observable evidence. These are assumptions and form the basis of a **theory** about why the sun moves. Theories are plausible but nevertheless hypothetical abstract ideas that are then tested through observation. That is, theories are predictions established through temporary trust until observational evidence is available. For example, you have observational evidence to support part of your theory about the sun and trust to support the assumptions. Those telling the story about the god pulling the sun have only trust that the god is there. There is no evidence in nature to support their story.

The other important difference between the explanation based on observable evidence and the story based on trust is that other people can make their own observations of nature, can follow the logical sequence of your explanation, and will probably come to a similar conclusion themselves. Observation is a fundamentally different epistemology than trust. Observation provides evidence. Furthermore, observations can be replicated by others who then will likely come to the same conclusion. Clearly, then, observation must be a better way to arrive at beliefs than trust. Or is it?

✓ **Stop and think.**

How many reasons can you think of for not relying on observation?

Man is the measure of all things.
                    Protagoras

Objections to Observation

The first problem with relying on observation as a way of knowing about reality is the selective perception of the person making the observation. Imagine that you and I are driving across the desert late on a dark and stormy night. Does my observation of a UFO flying across the sky establish the reality of that UFO? What if you look and observe only a raindrop sliding across the windshield (Sagan, 1996)? Does the UFO suddenly cease to exist and the raindrop suddenly come into being? If we measure reality one "man" at a time, if "man is the measure of all things," then things will come into being and disappear from being depending entirely on who is observing them. One Classical Greek philosopher, Socrates, rightly asks, why should man be the measure of all things? Why not make the dog-faced baboon the measure of all things? Then only that which the baboon observes will have reality.

A second reason that observations of nature may not be reliable in revealing what is real is that nature is always changing. In fact, this constantly changing nature is one of the perplexing facts about trying to establish what is real in nature. What color is the sky, really? The answer to this question should not depend on what time of day it is or what the weather is today. There should be some color that

the sky is really, shouldn't there? In spite of the fact that nature is always changing, some philosophers argue that there must be some part of the universe that is
real, certain, and unchanging no matter who is observing it or when they are
observing it.

✓ **Stop and think.**
Are objects that are not observable therefore not real?

A third objection to using observations to establish reality is that this limits
reality to things that can be observed. This might mean that only those things that
are accessible to sensory organs are real, an assertion we surely would not want to
make. Are there real objects in nature that are not, at least immediately, accessible
to our sensory organs? Like most people, you probably have to take the existence
of molecules, atoms, and subatomic particles on trust. But what about objects like
bacteria or viruses? If you cannot directly observe them, then you can at least
observe the consequences of their real existence as first one and then another of
your family comes down with a cold. And yet those viruses are inaccessible to
your unaided sensory equipment.

✓ **Stop and think.**
Can thoughts be observed? Can mind be observed?

Are thoughts real? Can the thoughts of others be observed? You are capable of
at least experiencing your own thoughts, but can you really observe your thoughts?
Do we really want to limit reality to only that which can be observed?

According to some philosophers of the Classical Greek era, neither trust nor
experience can establish the reality of anything. Trust provides no evidence, only
belief. And the evidence provided by experience and observation is unreliable,
varies as a function of a constantly changing nature, and does not reveal all of
nature anyway. Reason alone is left as a way of knowing some immutable reality.
Pure, abstract reason is the only road to sure truth about reality. This is the position
taken by the philosopher Pythagoras and later by Plato.

BELIEF SYSTEMS IN CLASSICAL GREECE

The True Reality of Numbers

Because he desires a reality that remains constant in spite of changes in nature and
has a distrust of both trust and observation, the Greek citizen Pythagoras develops
an ontology based on abstract reason alone. Abstract reason reveals the immutable

reality of numbers, and for this reason, mathematics becomes the foundation of reality for Pythagoras.

The bases of Pythagorean philosophy are the numbers 1, 2, 3, and 4. These numbers define reality because 1 defines a single point, 2 points define a line, 3 points define a plane, and 4 points are needed to define a solid. Pythagoras believes that mathematical formulas exist that define every relationship in nature. Even the relationships between the notes in a musical scale are defined by mathematical formulas.

The existence of supernatural gods or goddesses is not supported by any mathematical formula, so Pythagoras does not assume the existence of anything supernatural. Nature is the physical manifestation of the mathematical formulas; therefore, only nature and mathematics are real. Pythagoras does not worship deities, although later his followers develop a very mystical, almost religious, set of beliefs and come close to regarding Pythagoras himself as a god-like being.

Natural Philosophy

Pythagoras conducts the same observations of nature that humans have always conducted, but he combines these observations with a logical sequence of thought that both explains the observation and also predicts what may happen in the future. Using observation to describe nature and logic to explain and predict nature becomes the foundation of philosophy. **Philosophy** is (philo) the love of (sophia) knowledge or wisdom. Philosophy is the seeking out of knowledge through observation and logic.

Human Powers to Know

Asking questions like of what is the universe made or how nature works, suggests an underlying belief that humans have the capacity to understand the answers, even if they do not yet understand. Asking questions implies that the answers may someday be understood.

> All men, by nature, desire to know.
> Aristotle

Some of the conclusions the Greek philosophers reach cannot be true. The important point is not the conclusions they reach, but the ways in which they support and defend their beliefs. *It is necessary to keep in mind the intellectual distance between what you personally know now about science and philosophy and what Classical Greek natural philosophers knew. As you follow their arguments, try to step into their sandals and see the world through their eyes. Try to remember their context and what they knew or believed to be true.*

For example, Greek natural philosophy recognizes four elements in nature: earth, water, air, and fire. Everything in nature is composed of these elements combined in various ways. The sun, for example, is made of fire. These four elements form paired opposites. Water is the opposite of fire, and earth is the opposite of air. Much of nature in fact is arranged in these dichotomies. Hot is the opposite of cold, wet of dry, sweet of bitter.

The Greek Physis

Nature is constantly changing, transforming in state, color, position, temperature, sound, and appearance. Underlying this change, philosophers assume, must be some unchanging reality. What is that immutable reality? Everything that exists came from something before. Nothing can come from nothing. Thus begins the search for the one true, unchanging reality of which nature is made. Even before it is identified, the stuff of which everything else is made is called the physis, and those who are engaged in this search are called "physicists."

By using observations of nature tied to logical reason, the Greek physicist Thales decides that water is the one reality of which all of nature is composed. First, he observes that water is essential to life, all life forms need water to survive, and life begins in a watery environment. He further points out that all three of the other elements can be reduced to water.

✓ Stop and think.
Can you explain how all three of the other elements can be reduced to water?

The Soul

Thales also makes an observation about the unobservable psyche or soul. His definition is that soul is "that which is the cause of motion" in objects. Anything that is capable of independent movement, or that can cause motion, has soul. Soul is not a transcendent thing because on death, the ability to move is lost. Thus, Thales concludes, even a magnetic stone has soul because magnetic stones move toward metal (Bremmer, 1983).

Critical Thinking

Having suggested some answers to questions about nature, Thales next does something that is truly unusual in human history. He invites his students to examine the facts for themselves and see if they can come up with alternative explanations that fit the facts better. Perhaps Thales does this because of his background as a citizen of a Greek city. In any case, inviting critique is not something that is often done. Other later physicists come to different conclusions than Thales, but they use similar observations of nature tied to a logical sequence of thought to support their conclusions.

One student of Thales', Anaximander, suggests that choosing one of the four elements as the basis of the other three makes no logical sense, because each of them is the opposite of another. He decides that there must be something more basic than any of these four that serves as the physis and that can take on the properties of each of the four elements.

Atomic Theory

What Anaximander is suggesting is an atomic theory, and his ideas are similar to those of Democritus from the city Abdera near Macedonia. Democritus asserts that all objects are composed of atoms, or tiny pieces of matter. These atoms of matter are in constant motion, coming together and then breaking up, causing a constantly changing nature without the atoms themselves ever changing. Atoms are of many different shapes and come together through the laws of nature to form all objects in the physical universe, even humans. If Democritus had stopped here, physics may have made more progress in understanding the universe in the ensuing 2,000 years. But Democritus takes one more step and asserts that there is nothing in the universe except atoms, and the spaces in between the atoms called the void.

✓ Stop and think.
What about the gods? Are they made of matter also?

Suggesting that there is nothing in the universe except atoms and the void raises questions about the deities. If there is nothing except matter and the space between, then the gods must be made of matter also and are thus not supernatural at all. Using a rational argument, Democritus responds to these questions by saying that all belief in the supernatural, including belief in the gods, is motivated primarily by fear. The gods are not made of matter because they exist only as beliefs in the minds of frightened humans.

If the gods are only beliefs and if the universe is composed of atoms and the void, then of what are beliefs made, or thought, or will, or feelings, or what the Greeks call psyche? Democritus answers that psyche is breath, and breath is atoms of matter; therefore, there is no life-force, only atoms of matter interacting with other atoms. Thoughts are also made of atoms of matter and reason itself is made of atoms of matter interacting with other atoms. Even what is thought of as the will to act is simply atoms of matter acting on other atoms. These atoms are ruled by the laws of nature, and thus what is called free will is not free, but is determined by the laws of nature.

This assertion spells the end of Democritus' atomic theory for 2 millennia. The ideas that rational thought is made of matter, that all actions are caused by matter acting on matter, and that free will is only an illusion are profoundly disturbing. In fact, Plato is rumored to have wanted to burn all of Democritus' writings. Even centuries later, when Christian theologians examine Democritus' atomic theory, they repudiate it completely. An individual will that is assumed to be free forms the foundation of Christian morality. If the will is not free, but actions are instead determined by the laws of nature, individuals cannot be held responsible for their actions. Christian scholars suppress Democritus' ideas, and nothing resembling atomic theory is heard for another 2,000 years.

Platonic Philosophy

The work of the philosopher Plato has been interpreted in so many different ways that some argue that no one really knows what he may have meant in many of his writings. To confound the confusion, in many of his dialogs, Plato paraphrased the thoughts of his teacher, the philosopher Socrates. Although Plato lived and taught just a century after Thales, some critics suggest that it is hardly fair to describe Plato's work as a study of nature. In fact, some say, Plato's ideas offer an explanation of reality that relies on faith in the supernatural, in direct opposition to natural explanations (Gross, 1998). Other critics, however, provide convincing arguments that Plato's philosophy is grounded in the same naturalistic worldview that pervades the work of most Classical Greek philosophers (Kantor, 1963–1969).

Often, Platonic philosophy seems to paraphrase the beliefs of the Orphic mystery religion of his time. These beliefs include the idea that this earthly existence, and physical bodies, are only prisons in which human souls are trapped as punishment for past sins.

Rejection of Observation

Like Pythagoras, Plato is disturbed by a constantly changing nature and by unreliable human observations. Therefore, he seeks a way to find what is real that does not depend on observation by suggesting that the world of objects is really only a kind of reflection of reality. Reality itself does not exist on Earth, but exists instead on an ideal plane of existence in much the same way that mathematics does. In this view, reality consists of the ideal forms of objects, and each object that is encountered in the natural world is only an approximation of its ideal form. Thus, he argues, cats on Earth are only poor copies of the ideal form of cat, which exists, but does not exist in nature and is not observable with physical senses.

Observation relies on imperfect sensory systems and can only imperfectly reveal even the approximations of the ideal forms found on Earth. Thus, for Plato, observations are unreliable, although he does suggest that the senses of vision and hearing are more reliable than smell, taste, and touch. Fortunately, humans do not need to depend on observations to know reality, because humans already know the ideal forms. This knowledge derives from the time before each individual is incarcerated in a human body. The exercising of rational thought reveals knowledge of the ideal forms. Humans know because they have existed and will exist again on that ideal plane when this painful earthly life is over.

There is considerable controversy over what Plato means by these assertions. Early Christian writers interpret Plato's thoughts about this ideal plane of existence to mean that there is a perfect place, a heaven, where a transcendent part of the human, the soul, will live after physical death. However, given the naturalism of most Greek philosophy, notions about transcendent souls are probably quite foreign to Plato.

To get a better sense of the point Plato is making, consider a "right triangle." The perfect right triangle cannot ever be drawn by humans on Earth, but is determined by a mathematical formula and exists only as an idea, not as a real triangle. This is Plato's point. True, immutable, perfect reality exists only as ideas, never as real objects in nature. Thus, Platonic philosophy is similar to the Pythagorean idea that reality is realized only through abstract reason.

Plato transmits his ideas in written dialogs, like plays. These dialogs anticipate many of the questions considered by psychology in the ensuing centuries. For example, in *The Republic* (380/1993), Plato explores questions about what motivates human behavior.

✓ **Stop and think.**
What do you think motivates behavior?

Platonic Psychology

In *The Republic*, Plato has some of his characters taking the position that human behavior is motivated by desires of the moment, suggesting that humans behave in ways that they believe will bring them pleasure. Because people will inevitably come into conflict with one another if everyone behaves this way, there must be rulers to mediate conflict. Plato has other characters in the dialog argue that, although motivated by passionate desires, humans bring rational thought to bear on decisions about how to behave, so that behavior is also motivated by considerations of what is right and wrong. Thus, people most capable of rational thought, and by this Plato means the philosophers, should be the ones to rule. Plato's suggestion for how to get others to follow a leader is to either use brute strength and the threat of it, or to use persuasion and reason. His conclusion is that the most effective of these strategies is rational persuasion.

Plato is from an affluent family, and believes that only the best-educated citizens should rule. Of course, the best-educated citizens are also the wealthiest, and this accounts for Plato's reputation in history as a totalitarianist and an opponent of democracy. He advocates a classed society made up of three groups: common people, soldiers, and a group of wise rulers he calls the guardians. He suggests in *The Republic* that the best individuals within each class be brought together to breed better offspring. If any of these offspring prove to be defective in any way, they should be "exposed," that is, left outside to die.

The Platonic dialogs explore many of psychology's questions, but because the characters in the dialogs advocate a variety of answers, it is sometimes difficult to identify Plato's own beliefs on a given question. For example, he lives in a very patriarchal culture and Plato seems to agree with these patriarchal values. However, in *The Republic*, he describes an ideal city as one where girls and boys receive the same education and physical training and where women are as likely to be soldiers or guardians as are men, for "their original nature is the same" (as cited in Russell, 1945, p. 111). In spite of his general agreement with Classical Greek **androcentric** or male-centered values, Plato is probably the least **misogynistic** of all the Classical philosophers, that is, he exhibits the least hatred of women (Lerner, 1986).

The Aristotelian Milieu

Plato's student Aristotle is widely revered in Western culture, both past and present. Aristotle is unabashed in his denigration of women, asserting that the natural purpose of men is to engage in "politics, philosophy and rational discourse," and the natural purpose of women and slaves is to "minister to the needs of life" (Lerner, 1986, p. 209). Aristotle's androcentric philosophy ultimately has great influence over the development of theology in Europe, as do many of the books of the Old Testament, which are being compiled at about the same time that Aristotle is composing his works.

From Ethics to Anthropology

Instead of speculating about the nature of the universe or asking abstract questions about ethics and moral conduct, Aristotle is concerned with animal physiology and with the human experience. Psychological questions are addressed directly. How is the body built and how does it work? How does it influence immediate life experiences? What are thoughts and feelings? What role does friendship play in men's lives? Aristotle attempts to answer these questions using purely naturalistic explanations. That is, he conducts observations, writes descriptions, and attempts to tie these observations and descriptions to logical theories.

Illness and Nature

The son of a doctor, Aristotle is in every sense a biologist. For him, as well as for other educated Greeks, illness, including psychological illness, is attributed to bodily factors. By the 3rd century BCE, Greek physicians reject previous superstitious beliefs about illness and seek natural explanations for even mental illness through careful observation and case studies. Among the upper class in the Greek world, the practice of medicine is now separated from the practice of supernatural magic, although many people, even educated people, still seek the advice of both physicians and magicians when illness strikes.

The medical school in the city of Croton is renowned throughout the Greek world for its physiological approach to medicine. The study of physiology and anatomy by performing dissections of animals is first discussed in writings from this school. Alcmaeon, the school's most famous physician, examines the nerves of the visual system in these dissections and decides on the basis of his studies that the brain is the site of sensation and cognition. In another Greek medical school, Empedocles champions the heart as the central organ of intellect and blood as the medium of thought.

Greek physicians identify four fluids, or "humors," in the body: phlegm, black bile, blood, and yellow bile. Health, including mental health, is accomplished by maintaining a balance among these four humors. Thus, those with an excess of phlegm will develop a head cold, and the job of the physician is to help eliminate the phlegm and recover the proper balance of humors. Therapies consist of rest and quiet, soothing baths, and a simple but nutritious diet, all designed to help return the humors to balance. Treatments for mental illness are similar, because mental illnesses are also presumed to arise from an imbalance in the humors.

Certain personality traits or patterns of behavior are attributed to the humors of the body as well. For example, Aristotle asserts in *Problems* that children are physically moister and hotter than adults and are thus more hot-tempered, greedier, and tend to be angrier than adults. This physical difference also accounts for children's greater likelihood to express emotional passion; therefore, he regards childhood as the time when the appetite for pleasure is strongest (Barnes, 1984).

Descriptive Biology

The Lyceum is the school Aristotle founds in Athens for the purpose of facilitating the descriptive biological research that he organizes. Specimens and data are collected on every form of plant and animal life in the known world. One of Aristotle's former students, Alexander the Great, allows scholars from the Lyceum to travel with his armies, and some of his soldiers collect specimens to send back to Athens. Aristotle's goal is to make the natural world knowable to humans by describing nature and by using deductive logic.

The Causes

Aristotelian philosophy identifies four causes, or four bases on which everything can be explained. A thing can be explained on the basis of the material from which it is made, as in: An eye is made from various kinds of matter. A thing can be explained on the basis of the shape that it takes, as in: Matter put together in this way forms an eye. A thing can be explained on the basis of the force that causes it to take that shape, as in: Eyes are shaped by the laws of nature. Finally, a thing can be explained on the basis of the purpose that it serves, as in: The eye helps us to see and get around. This final cause, the purpose that something serves, is interpreted by later theological scholars to mean that there must be a designer who designed eyes with the intention of providing sight, but that is not Aristotle's intent (Kantor, 1963–1969).

The Problem of First Cause

Aristotle also discusses a puzzling logical problem. He notes that all living things move, and they move as a consequence of causes. That is, movement is caused by some previous cause. This line of causes could be followed back in time, but at some point, there has to be a first cause. Theorizing that everything is caused creates a logical dilemma by requiring a first cause that is not itself caused.

✓ **Stop and think.**
How would you resolve this dilemma?

Aristotle resolves the dilemma by naming this first cause the "unmoved mover," which is the first cause of everything in nature. By its very definition, nothing moves the unmoved mover. Later interpreters of Aristotle resolve this dilemma by assuming a supernatural first cause. In the Middle Ages, Christian scholars turn Aristotle's logical dilemma into evidence in support of the existence of a deity, but this conclusion is not supported in Aristotle's writings.

Aristotle's Psychology

In his role as a scholar of living things, Aristotle carefully describes human animals along with other animals, and so studies the psyche. Aristotle defines psyche as "that principle as a result of which any living thing comes to have life" and "the first principle of living things" (Robinson, 1989). For Aristotle, everything that lives has psyche.

Aristotle's Psyches

Aristotle differentiates three types of psyche:

1. Vegetative psyche allows a living organism to obtain nourishment and to reproduce its own kind. All living things, including plants, have vegetative psyche.
2. Sensitive psyche allows the organism to receive sensory information and perceive its meaning. Thus, pleasure and pain may be experienced, memories may be formed, and learning may occur. Both practical and specific knowledge may be acquired that is useful in facilitating survival. Aristotle refers to this kind of knowledge as passive reason. All animals, but not plants, have sensitive psyche.

3. Rational psyche yields what Aristotle describes as active reason. Active reason allows for knowledge about universal principles, rather than just specific pieces of information. For example, it is Aristotle's rational psyche that allows him to seek out the universal principles that govern the functioning of nature. Only men possess rational psyche, and it is man's nature to use this rational psyche to exercise active reason. Engaging in active reason is what gives men their greatest pleasure (Bremmer, 1983).

Aristotle clearly asserts that women do not possess rational psyches. In fact, after careful biological study, Aristotle concludes that, even in reproduction, women contribute only the material cause of life, the matter that makes up the new body. Men plant the psyche and the seed that contains the life, and thus men impart the shape that life takes, supply the force that causes it to take shape, and provide the purpose that it will serve (Lerner, 1986).

For those searching for one, there is a hierarchy implied in Aristotle's arrangement of the psyches, one that puts the male rational psyche in a position above those of all other living things. This apparent hierarchy comes to have far more significance in Western cultures than Aristotle gives it. For Aristotle, men have a rational purpose that makes them different from other animals, but men are still animals. Perceiving and understanding are not identical "for the former is universal in the animal world, the latter is found in only a small division of it" (Aristotle, 330/1961 BCE).

The Sensory Systems

According to Aristotle, information coming from one sensory system can interfere with conflicting information from another system, so that when attentively watching something, we sometimes cannot hear someone calling us. Our sensory system has a limited capacity and can be overloaded by excessive sensory input. At the same time, two (or more) sensory systems can yield confirmatory information. This confirmatory function of the senses Aristotle calls "common sense," such as having a common sense that a thing that looks soft also feels soft.

Like many before him, Aristotle believes that sensory information takes on the shape of the stimulus, the way that a piece of wax may take on the shape of something pressed into it. That shape can sometimes remain even after the stimulus has been removed. This accounts for the ability to remember stimuli that are no longer present. Thus, imagination is a case of the sensory system continuing to register a previously presented stimulus or combining several previous sensory inputs. Similarly, dreaming is caused by the form, or shape, of a previously experienced stimulus remaining in the senses.

Aristotle's speculations about dreams illustrate how different his naturalistic explanations are from superstitious and supernatural explanations. Supernatural explanations for dreams include that they are messages sent by deities or demons and that they foretell the future or warn of flaws in character. In contrast, the naturalistic view is that dreams are a consequence of the way that sensory systems function. Thus, any organism with a sensory system may dream.

The Emotional System

For Aristotle, emotions play a primarily motivational role, although they can also distract and distort perception and can amplify biologically based dispositions. All animals experience similar emotions, but there are different dispositions among species and even among individuals within a species, so that different individuals may be more or less likely to experience different emotions, depending on their individual dispositions. According to Aristotle, all animals seek those conditions that lead to pleasure. Thus, emotions motivate actions or behaviors designed to secure pleasure. All animals seek pleasures afforded by the physical senses because they are motivated to do so by their sensitive psyches. But for men, who possess a rational psyche, the greatest pleasure comes from acting in accordance with their rational nature, not from sensory pleasures. Men who seek only sensory pleasures are no different from women or animals. In Aristotle's view, fulfilling one's natural function, flourishing as a man, means using active reason to come to understand the universal principles underlying one's perceptions.

The Mind

In spite of having access to advanced medical knowledge, Aristotle denies the central role of the brain in sensation and movement, saying instead that it is the heart that receives sensory information and generates physical movement. He cites observational evidence of this, as well as logical deductions, illustrating that even very careful description coupled with logic can sometimes be wrong.

Like other philosophers of the time, Aristotle is unconcerned with a conscious mind that is independent of the body. For him, thinking is the act of compiling sensory information and generating physical movement. This process is the same for all animals, including humans. There is little sense in the Greek world of consciousness or mind as something distinct from the body. The rational psyche is a part of the physical body, and the pleasure of exercising the rational psyche ends when life ends. For Aristotle, what gives meaning to men's lives is the flourishing of the rational psyche in the present, and what gives meaning to women's lives is ministering to the needs of others.

Meaningful Social Relationships

Classical Greek culture takes a very different perspective on what constitutes meaningful relationships with others than do present-day Western cultures. Today, heterosexual romantic love and the maintaining of close biological family ties are usually cited as the most meaningful relationships with others. For Greek citizens, and for Aristotle, friendship serves the role that romantic love is said to play in the present. He identifies three types of friendships. The first is based on considerations of sensual pleasure, and this friendship survives only as long as the sensual pleasure does. The second is based on considerations of utility and lasts only as long as the two are useful to one another or until someone else comes along who would be more useful. Both of these types of friendship are self-focused, that is, your concern in maintaining these friendships is with meeting your own wants and needs. The third type of friendship Aristotle calls the perfected friendship, which is characterized by equality and mutual concern for the other. This friendship is based on the desire to promote the best interests of the other. Thus, one's concern in a perfected friendship is in helping the friend to achieve the friend's goals, and each reveres and celebrates the other for the other's sake, not for any reward. Curiously, the topics of love and friendship are not ones about which psychologists have had much to say in the centuries since, but Aristotle provides something to start with in his thoughts on these subjects.

End of an Era

Virtually every question that is of importance to present-day psychologists is addressed by one or more of the philosophers of the Classical Greek period, as they seek naturalistic explanations for human experience. But the Classical period lasts roughly 300 years, after which progress in Greek philosophy ends. Initially, Greek philosophy is interrupted by civil wars, resulting in an increasing focus on personal and immediate gratification. Then it is seriously disrupted by the takeover of Greece by Rome. Eventually, Greek philosophical thought is subsumed under Christian and Islamic religious doctrines by theologians seeking support for their beliefs.

TRANSITION OF POWER TO ROME

As so often happens in human history, war halts, or at least dramatically alters, social, cultural, economic, political, and philosophical progress. During the 3rd century BCE, philosophical speculation about the nature of reality and the place of humans in nature declines in favor of concerns about how to live a good life, and the focus is on attaining personal happiness. As Rome's power and influence grows in the middle years of the Roman Empire, the standard of living goes up in the outlying provinces. A class of tradesworkers and craftsmen come into being, and Roman stone architecture, based on that of the Egyptians, appears. Political organization in most Roman provinces is **oligarchic**, meaning that only a few select and wealthy individuals hold power. In the view of the Romans, the wealthy and powerful should rule, and getting others to do as the powerful want is a simple matter of having the advantage in physical strength, economic resources, and political cunning.

Roman culture is characterized by a focus on tradition, and Romans have little interest in skepticism or tolerance for change. Like the Egyptians before them, the Romans respect established authority, value civic order, and maintain long-standing cultural traditions. The individual, and individual opinion, is subordinated to the state. Roman society and politics are strictly patriarchal, and women, slaves, and nonlandowners have no power or place in public life. There is widespread respect for the achievements of Greek scholars and philosophers, but little advancement in original intellectual thought among the Romans.

One sign of intellectual progress during the Roman era comes in medicine, exemplified by the work of Galen. He gathers extensive clinical experience during his tenure at a gladiatorial school in Pergamon, where he is able to conduct animal dissections. Most of the information that he gathers about anatomy, and especially about brain functioning, survives to influence the study of these issues later in Byzantium and much later in Europe. For example, he distinguishes two different nerve pathways, one for sensory nerves and one for motor nerves, and establishes that it is the brain, not the heart, that is the center of nerve impulses.

Galen elaborates on the Greek idea of the elements by tying them to four bodily humors (phlegm, blood, yellow bile, and black bile) and applying the influences of the bodily humors to psychology and personality. According to Galen, personality characteristics are associated with these four humors, such that some people are born with a biological predisposition to be more phlegmatic, and thus more melancholic (depressed) than others, for example. However, most people are primarily cheerful because humans have a lot of blood, and blood is the humor associated with a happy disposition (Diogenes, 500/1972).

PHILOSOPHIES OF PERSONAL HAPPINESS

Toward the end of the Roman Empire in the 4th century of the Common Era, there is a further decay of respect for independent thought and more emphasis on practical concerns. People are interested in how to be happy and how to maximize personal gains in a time of rapidly changing fortunes. A series of emperors take over political power, usually by brutal means. Beliefs in supernatural forces grow stronger, and the conviction is widespread that whatever happens must be happening toward some purpose. People determine that whoever takes power, and by whatever means, the gods must have decided that it should be so.

The philosophies that prosper during this period help people to cope with an uncertain environment. Skepticism and Cynicism are philosophical systems that have been around since Greek times, but they are not very comforting systems of thought. Both Skepticism and Cynicism suggest that one should not trust others, either in word or deed, and Cynicism even recommends removing oneself from the company of other people. The systems of thought that people find most comforting during this time are Stoicism, Epicureanism, and various mystery religions.

Stoicism

Stoicism is a set of beliefs founded on the simple cause-and-effect idea that there is an underlying rational principle or cosmic order in nature that is responsible for all that exists and all that happens. This rational principle should serve as a guide for how to live. This principle leads to a set of laws that govern everything in nature and that supercede civil laws. Furthermore, civil laws only promote justice to the extent that they mirror natural laws. Happiness for humans lies in living in accordance with natural laws. This rational principle, or cosmic order, is like the ideal right triangle: It exists outside the bounds of temporal lives and temporal circumstances. But, and of this the Stoics are certain, it is not a god.

Because there is a rational principle that underlies everything that happens, people are encouraged to accept whatever happens to them. No matter what the misfortune, it must ultimately make rational sense, if not in the moment then at least in the context of the cosmic order. In this way, Stoicism, like many other philosophies and theologies, is teleological.

Teleology is the idea that there is some design or purpose in nature, an assumption that is shared by nearly all folk psychologies and religions. Countless examples of organisms perfectly suited to their environments can be seen in nature. Natural processes that seem to work perfectly are apparent, such as the adult salmon slowly disintegrating into fish food just as its spawn emerge and need to eat. Clearly, there is a simple, logical, cause-and-effect explanation for such perfect systems that is supported by unstructured observation of the natural world. That explanation is the telos, the design and purpose in nature, the ultimate cosmic order behind it all.

Stoicism helps people who live in an uncertain world feel better by pointing out that the individual who lives by natural law has a kind of freedom and independence from within that no despotic ruler can take away. Individuals can take comfort in the sure knowledge that there is a cosmic order and that everything is unfolding as it should.

Some of the influence of Stoicism extends to the present day in systems of religious thought that derive from late Roman times. Other aspects of Stoicism are lost, or deliberately suppressed, and must be re-articulated centuries later. For example, the Stoic philosopher and Roman slave, Epictetus (138/1948) suggests how emotional equilibrium might be maintained: "Remember that it is not he who gives abuse or blows, who affronts, but the view we take of these things as insulting. When, therefore, anyone provokes you, be assured that it is your own opinion which provokes you" (p. 23), and "Never say about anything, 'I have lost it,' but only, 'I have given it back' " (p. 23).

It is the duty of a Stoic to participate in public life and in the forming of civil laws to oversee their adherence to natural law. If, however, one wishes instead to withdraw from public life, then one should undertake the study of another philosophy.

Epicureanism

Epicureanism originates in part from the religious practices at the oracle at Delphi. Here, the priests focus on the idea of human limitations and encourage a wisdom of the middle line, of "never too much." The inscription on the temple at Delphi, often mistakenly attributed to Socrates, says "Know Thyself" (Freeman, 1956). This is not an exhortation to introspection but a prescription for maintaining that comfortable middle ground. Know what it is that excites you too much, and avoid it. Know what leaves you feeling empty, and avoid it as well. For Epicureans happiness lies in seeking tranquility through moderation, such as is found in friendships, and by avoiding intense passions, especially erotic love.

Epicureanism is a naturalistic philosophy. It is not teleological, nor does it posit supernatural worlds or promise an afterlife. In fact, Epicureans argue that, for most people, the idea of an afterlife is frightening. Most people are living a hand-to-mouth existence with far too little pleasure and far too much pain. To tell them that this life is not the end, that there will be no rest, and that they will go on living in another life is simply too upsetting. Epicureans believe there is nothing beyond nature and that we are each composed of a chance combination of matter that exists here and now and will not come together in this way again. Therefore, we should try to take advantage of this existence by enjoying moderate pleasures and minimizing pain.

Mystery Religions

Religions are another pathway to comfort during late Roman or any uncertain times. Mystery religions, so called because they are organized around a mystery of some sort, are an important part of the early human landscape. They persist even through the Classical Greek period among the lower classes. A number of these mystery religions, usually of Eastern origin, experience a resurgence in popularity in Rome as the Empire begins to disintegrate during the first few centuries of the Common Era. Among the most popular of the older mystery religions is one organized around the Persian god Mithras, whose birthday is celebrated on December 25. Another ancient and popular mystery religion is the worship of Isis, the Egyptian mother goddess, who is often depicted tenderly holding her divine infant. And throughout the Greek and Roman eras, Dionysian religious rituals persist, based on worship of Dionysus, a god of fertility.

Among the common themes in mystery religions are impending cataclysm, safety and eventual salvation for the chosen, and the appearance of a savior. The coming catastrophe will destroy the world, and only members of the correct religion will be allowed to escape from their current unhappy prison-like existence where their lives are the sport of the gods. A young king will come, bringing spring and summer and he will save the Earth that winter has made cold and lifeless. There will also be a woman, a fertility goddess, who is both a mother (fertile) and a virgin. The saved will join in an ultimate union with their savior in a kingdom of heaven on Earth. To become one of the chosen, an individual must undergo initiation rites, take part in various rituals carried out in strict secrecy, and make a substantial financial donation to the religion.

New mystery religions continue to make appearances from time to time. In about the year 815 by the Roman calendar (or 60 CE), word begins to spread of a relatively new Jewish sect that is based on the mystery of the death and redemption of a man named Jesus, from the city of Nazareth. Members of this Jewish sect believe that the young king, the savior, has already come to Earth in the form of the man Jesus, that Jesus was executed by the Romans, and that he subsequently disappeared from the place of his internment. They believe that this savior will return to Earth to rule after the coming apocalypse. The primary advocate for this Jewish sect is a man named Paul from the city of Tarsus. Under Paul's leadership, this new sect experiences a slow but steady growth (Fredriksen, 1988).

AFTER ROME

For centuries, Roman polytheistic "paganism" (as it is called by later Christian writers) tolerates religious diversity, just as the Greeks had done. New peoples with different sets of beliefs are simply assimilated into Roman culture. However, by the 4th century of the Common Era, this changes with the increasing power of the growing Jewish sect, now called Christianity. For the Christians, there is only one right way to believe. Thus, as the Christians become increasingly powerful in the Roman world, tolerance for other faiths disappears, and the Empire is torn apart by bloody battles between peoples of different faiths. By about the 6th century, after waves of violence, the Christians triumph and the public practice of other faiths is destroyed. By that time, the center of the Roman Empire has already been moved far from Rome.

In 312, the Roman general Constantine defeats his rivals and takes over as Emperor of the Roman Empire. In 330, he moves the capital of the Empire to his homeland and renames its principal city Constantinople. He takes with him as many of the writings of Greek philosophers as he can gather. These serve as the philosophical foundation for a new culture that outlasts any in the West since Egypt.

The city of Constantinople and its surrounding empire, Byzantium, remain at the center of religious and cultural life in the West for centuries. Whatever progress occurs in Europe in medical and psychological thought during this time occurs in Byzantium. As Byzantium interacts economically and militarily with its Arabic neighbors to the south, the Greek influence passes to Islamic philosophers. Thus, Islamic philosophers have an advantage over their European counterparts in Rome because they have access to many more Greek texts, including the works of Galen and Aristotle.

THE EARLY MIDDLE AGES IN EUROPE

Rome continues to be weakened by a variety of pressures. These include a continuing influx of tribes from all over western and northern Europe; a bankrupt economy where money has disappeared and transactions have reverted to a barter system; a population sent into precipitous decline through civil war, disease, and famine; and a serious disruption of the familiar class structure (Bark, 1958). In the face of these pressures, those who remain in Rome search for ways to restore the glory and social stability of the old Roman Empire. Stoicism becomes the official state philosophy of Rome during the early centuries of the Common Era. Another popular philosophy is Neo-Platonism, so called because this philosophy draws some of its originating ideas from the writings of Plato.

Neo-Platonism

Neo-Platonism borrows liberally from Platonic philosophy but also adds much that would most likely seem quite foreign to Plato.

The Essential Duality of the Human

Neo-Platonic philosophy begins with an assumption that a person is not a single entity but is both a material body and a separate spiritual soul. Similarly, the world itself is material but is an inferior copy of a perfect spiritual realm. The material world is of interest only because it can occasionally provide signs or clues about the spiritual realm.

The material body of a human is created from earth, is in a constant state of decay and corruption, and is only a temporary abode for the soul, which is imprisoned within the material body. The soul is released at the time of the physical death of the material body and then travels to and dwells in the spiritual realm.

True Knowledge

According to Neo-Platonic philosophy, sensory observations of the material world are unreliable. In fact, sensory systems only provide illusions of reality; they actually interfere with gaining true knowledge. True knowledge is revealed only when one is free of sensory distractions. True knowledge is revealed in dreams, trances, sudden insights, and intense inner experiences, not through observation, nor through reason.

Augustinian Doctrines of Christianity

The goal of early Christian theologians was to encourage the growth of Christianity by finding ways to bring divergent sets of beliefs together into a single faith. Many theologians contributed to the effort to win new converts. Their work is relevant to the history of psychology because their ideas shape epistemology in the West for at least the next 1,000 years.

Among these theologians is Augustine of Hippo in North Africa, who begins his writings after Rome is finally sacked in 455, not long after Christianity is declared legal in Rome. Instead of bringing the kingdom of heaven to Earth and reunifying Rome, it appears to many that conversion to Christianity has caused the absolute destruction of Rome. Augustine is thus sometimes described as a "Christian apologist" because his first efforts are directed at explaining why Rome falls at the same time that Christianity is adopted by Roman leaders. Building on the work of many others, Augustine articulates a theological position and integrates many divergent belief systems into one. He turns a simple faith in the teachings of an obscure Jewish sect into Christianity, which becomes a power, a worldview, and a dominating system of thought that influences the history of psychology in profound ways.

Augustinian Ontology and Epistemology

For Christian ontology, the one god (now God) is what is real. What man needs to know about the material world is that God created it. According to Augustine, man does not need to know anything about nature except that God created it. God created the heavens and the Earth, and God placed man, the paragon of His creation, at the center of the universe.

When, therefore, you ask what we should believe in matters of religion, the answer is to be found not by exploring of the nature of things, as was done by those whom the Greeks call physicists. Nor need we be fearful if a Christian should fail to know some things about the force and number of the elements: about the motion and order and eclipses of the stars; about the form of the heavens; about the species and natures of animals, plants, stones, fountains, mountains; about the reaches of space and time, about the signs of approaching storms, and a thousand-and-one things which these men discovered or thought they had discovered. For even they, excelling by their great genius, burning with the love of research and free to indulge in it, investigating some things by the aid of human conjecture and searching out others by means of historical research, have not found out all things. And so as to their vaunted discoveries, these more often are opinion than certain knowledge.

For the Christian, it is enough to believe that the cause of all created things, in heaven or on earth, whether visible or invisible, is none other than the goodness of the Creator, who is the one and true God. Further, the Christian believes that nothing exists save God himself and what comes from him.

(Augustine, 420/1947, p. 19)

For the Church fathers, or clerics, man knows only by interpreting revelations from God, especially the Scriptures, and through the faith that is granted to believers. The Scriptures are written in Latin, and only clerics can read. They alone receive divine revelation because only they live sufficiently spiritual lives. A spiritual life is conducted by engaging in meditation and other forms of intense introspection.

Before he comes to these conclusions, Augustine lives a life of debauchery and skepticism. He wonders if there is anything that he can really believe. Eventually, using logical introspection, he concludes that he must at least believe in his own existence as a thinker because he can doubt his own existence. Having come to believe in his own existence and in the existence of the one omnipotent God through reason and introspection, Augustine writes that others must have faith in his word because God is revealed to him (Augustine), to other church fathers, and through religious rituals.

Free Will and Salvation

Augustine develops a religious doctrine focused on the struggle between the material human body that is part of nature and the spiritual human soul that is part of the divine. The body seeks to persuade man to do evil but the soul can help man to do good. God is omnipotent but He grants men knowledge of right and wrong and free will to choose between them. Evil exists in the world because men choose evil. When men choose good, they are rewarded in an afterlife, but when men choose evil, they suffer guilt. Thus, man's behavior is controlled by internal feelings of virtue and guilt. The Romanesque stone carving shown in Fig. 2.1 adorns a cathedral in Burgundy, France. Preoccupation with punishment and redemption tormented Europeans of the early Middle Ages.

Religious Doctrine and Misogyny

Misogyny is codified in the doctrines of many religions and philosophies. Both Greek and Roman cultures are intensely patriarchal, and men are more likely to

FIG. 2.1. *The Weighing of the Souls of the Damned* (Gislebertus, ca. 1100; photo courtesy of John R. Benham).

be educated; therefore, the writings and teachings that survive are more likely to be written by men. Thus, as Christian doctrine is formalized in the early Church, women are blamed for bringing sin and misery into the world through the "fall from grace" in the Garden of Eden and for seducing men away from spiritual pursuits.

The Legend of Pandora

The god Prometheus steals fire from the heavens and gives it as a gift to mortal humans. This infuriates Zeus, who asks Hephaestus, a patron god of tradesworkers, to create the first woman. Zeus names this first woman Pandora. The name Pandora means "all-giving" in Greek, so the gods bestow all of their choicest gifts on her and place these in an earthenware jar. Like most women, Pandora is insatiably curious, and she cannot resist opening the jar to peer inside. But when she does, all of the gifts from the gods begin to fly out. Before she can close the lid, nearly all of the gifts have flown. Only one gift remains, and that is Hope, the lid having been shut before she could escape. That is why, in the face of all earthly evils, hope is the only blessing left to humankind.

IMPLICATIONS OF RELIGIOUS THOUGHT
FOR PSYCHOLOGY

The connections between Augustinian theological doctrines and psychology are numerous. Many of the assumptions made in the Western world about thoughts, feelings, and behaviors are based on these early Christian doctrines.

Free will versus determinism. **Free will** *is the notion that behavior varies as a function of individuals' choices uninfluenced by biology, experience, situation, or any other cause.* **Determinism** *is the belief that behavior is not freely chosen but is caused. Augustine suggested that behavior is caused in part by desires to avoid feeling guilty and desires to seek out the pleasure of feeling virtuous. This notion of internal motivators for behavior is threaded throughout the history of psychology and also raises some interesting questions about the limits of free will within Christian doctrines.*

✓ Stop and think.

Just how free is our will if God establishes absolute rights and wrongs, then punishes and rewards behavior with feelings of guilt and virtue?

The mind–body problem. Coming to believe that there is an aspect of the person that is not part of the physical body creates a new set of questions having to do with the relationship between these parts. For many philosophies, the immaterial aspect is the part of the human that thinks, remembers, or has intentions and is called the intellect or the mind. For religions, the aspect of the human that transcends the physical is the soul. In either case, the mind–body problem is the question about how a nonmaterial aspect of the human interacts with a material aspect. How and where does that interaction occur, and what is the mechanism by which that happens?

✓ **Stop and think.**

If thoughts are immaterial, how can they be made into neurochemical changes in the brain, and how can changing the neurochemistry of the brain, as with modern antidepressants, change thoughts?

The nature-versus-nurture question. According to Christian doctrine, the innate knowledge of right and wrong is what makes humans accountable for their behavior. If right and wrong have to be learned, then individuals might commit a wrong simply because they had never learned the difference. How could persons then be held accountable for their behavior? Questions about innate knowledge are referred to as the "nature-versus-nurture" debate, and these questions present philosophers and psychologists with many interesting problems for many centuries.

The relationship between human and nonhuman animals. A hierarchy that places the human above nature, as does Christian doctrine, separates humans from nature and from all other animals. In this way of believing, men are no longer part of nature but are in conflict with nature as in "man against the elements." Nature, nonhuman animals, slaves, women, and children come under the dominion of man in Judaic, Christian, and Islamic monotheistic religions. Placing a transcendent and divine soul in man makes him qualitatively different from and superior to all other animals. This idea influences Western perspectives about relationships between humans and nature, between humans and nonhuman animals, between human males and females, and even between Western humans and all other groups of humans. In Greek culture, women and slaves are "less than" citizens through some accident of nature or failing of virtue—the Greek concept of virtue being equivalent to something like courage in battle. In early Christian doctrine, women and slaves are created as lesser creatures by God. They thus fall below men in the hierarchy and should be regarded accordingly.

A Period of Intellectual Stagnation

Although Greek philosophy is respected throughout the era of the Roman Empire, after the collapse of Rome, the admiration for such intellectualism disappears, and persecutions against philosophers and scholars by religious leaders are more common. For example, in 415, at the library in Alexandria, a celebrated female mathematician, astronomer, and Neo-Platonic philosopher, Hypatia, is dragged into a place of worship by Christian monks during Lent, beaten, hacked into pieces with oystershells while still alive, and then burned. The monks are acting on orders from Cyril, the Bishop of Alexandria. In addition to her intellectual achievements,

Hypatia's offenses include an unwillingness to convert to Christianity. Neo-Platonic philosophic influences are seen in her use of music therapy to treat mental illness. These are regarded by Cyril as heresy against Christian beliefs. A large part of the collection of manuscripts in the library is also burned at about this time. The remainder of the collection is destroyed in 646, when Islamic armies invade the city.

⏱ The Times

When thinking about the philosophy of the Greek Classical period, it is important to keep in mind that this culture is intensely patriarchal and an-drocentric. When the Greek philosophers talk about "the virtuous man," or ask "why do men behave the way they do," they are really talking about men. In fact, they are really talking only about free, economically privileged men. Women, children through the age of adolescence, the elderly, tradesworkers, servants, the poor, the crippled, and slaves are not allowed a vote in the ruling of any city, are not given ritual burials, and are not considered citizens.

Although the Western world shows admiration for Classical Greek culture, philosophy, literature, and politics, more disturbing aspects, such as slavery and the place of women in Greek society, are ignored, even though these aspects were also important in shaping the Classical worldview. The continuum of sexual practices acceptable for males in Classical Greek culture, where upper-class men are expected to respond at different times in their lives to both men and women, seem especially disturbing to many Westerners. Interestingly, there is no such noun as "homosexual" in the ancient Greek language, and there is also no noun for "heterosexual." Thus, the modern practice of placing men into categories based on whom they are having sex with is meaningless in that ancient culture (Dover, 1978). Although the distinction might seem important today, one has to wonder if these sexual practices influenced the development of philosophical or psychological thought in Classical Greece or why some in the present day assume that they must have.

The patriarchy comes to power with the establishment of permanent cities, private ownership of land and other property, and the resulting interest in identifying paternity of offspring. This emphasis on preserving biological bloodlines is one factor causing men to restrict and control the freedom and behavior of women. In the Greek cities, for example, a typical upper-class household includes the man of the house, a wife who seldom leaves the confines of the women's quarters in the inner house, sons and daughters, and a small collection of household slaves (Keuls, 1985). In lower-class families, where cultural practices like having to provide a dowry make female children an economic drain, girl infants are often sold into prostitution or slavery, left at the temple to serve as concubines for the priests, or abandoned on a hillside to die (Mireaux, 1959).

During this era, slavery is widely practiced throughout the Middle East and around the Mediterranean. Slaves are occasionally acquired from far-distant lands, including parts of Africa, but more often they are the women and children of vanquished enemies or former citizens who have fallen into debt (Lerner, 1986). Slaves are considered to be property and have no legal status. During Roman times, life for most people is a matter of hand-to-mouth subsistence-level farming, but for upper-class Romans in centers of population, standards of living are relatively high. They enjoy such amenities as indoor plumbing, a wide selection of foods, and, for the men, leisure time provided by large numbers of slaves.

3

From an Age of Spirits to Humanism: How Many Angels Can Dance on the Head of a Pin?

This chapter takes us to European cultures that followed the fall of Rome and illustrates that many Western assumptions about thoughts, feelings, and behaviors originate in the theology and philosophy of the Middle Ages in Europe. The consequences of using trust in cultural and religious beliefs as the way to know about nature are also examined. At the beginning of the Renaissance, humanistic philosophies make their entrance.

PHILOSOPHY IN THE MIDDLE EAST

Nearly all of Classical Greek and Roman philosophy is lost to the West after the sacking of Rome and the burning of the great library at Alexandria in the 4th and 5th centuries. The writings that do survive are those that are carried by Constantine to the new Christian Byzantine capital and those brought to the Arabic peninsula by scholars fleeing the fighting in Alexandria.

Byzantine Influences

During this same period, Byzantium, like Rome, is a Christian city in which Classical Greek philosophy is used to support and defend Christian doctrines (Loverance, 1988). The primary contribution Byzantium makes to natural philosophy is to preserve the work of Classical philosophers so that when Byzantium comes into contact with the Islamic world, beginning in the 7th century, these Greek works are transmitted to Islamic philosophers.

At least one Byzantine physician, Poseidonus, of the 4th century, does make significant and unique contributions to later psychology. He reports in detail the effects of brain damage, an indication that he understands the localization of specific brain functions (Gross, 1998). Galen previously identified the front of the brain as the location of mental faculties, but Poseidonus finds that lesions in the front of the brain impair imagination, lesions in the rear impair memory, and lesions in the middle produce deficits in reasoning. It is not until several centuries later that Western medicine and psychology are influenced by these findings.

Islamic Religion and Philosophy

In the 7th century, the Islamic religion begins to be organized around the teachings of Mohamet, a prophet from Mecca born in about 570. Islam quickly becomes a political, economic, and military power, as well as a religious influence throughout the Arab region. Over the next 400 years, Islam becomes the state religion of the area from Spain through North Africa, eastward to Persia, and comes into increasing conflict with Christians to the north and the west.

Like Judaism and Christianity, the Islamic religion is monotheistic. Practitioners, called Muslims, believe that their god, Allah, is a god of reward and retribution, omnipotent, omniscient, and grants free will to humans. Muslims believe that Mohamet, like Jesus, was a prophet sent by Allah to bring important messages to humans. In fact, Muslims regard Mohamet as simply the last in a succession of prophets that includes Jesus (Fakhry, 1983). In its early centuries, Islam is more tolerant of religious and cultural diversity than are Christians of this era, but both relentlessly persecute those who continue to believe in Greek and Roman gods and goddesses. Mohamet preaches compassion and mercy for the downtrodden and brotherhood and equality among men. But once formalized into a written doctrine, the Islamic religion, like Judaism and Christianity, becomes uncompromisingly patriarchal and condones numerous discriminatory practices toward women (Lerner, 1986).

Until about 1100, Islamic religion supports the development of a natural philosophy and the observational study of nature based primarily on Classical Greek and Roman philosophy and medicine. Medical and anatomical information gathered in Alexandria is available to Islamic philosophers. Indian culture influences Islamic philosophy through writings such as the ancient Upanishads, composed between 800 and 600 BCE. These are dialogs, much like those of Plato, discussing how best to live and addressing other psychological questions. Indian physicians believe, for example, that although disease results primarily from supernatural powers, it may also be related to poor sanitation or an imbalance of bodily humors. Mental health is also considered to be associated with a refusal to control desires and emotions.

These Indian beliefs about factors that influence health and personality eventually became part of early Islamic natural philosophy (Fakhry, 1983).

Natural Philosophy in Islamic Thought

Islamic natural philosophy begins with the Greek philosophers whose works are regarded as precious treasures. These writings are eagerly sought and translated into Arabic, particularly those of Aristotle and Galen, and form the foundation for Islamic observation and description of nature. Medicine, in particular, is praised in the Islamic religious text, the Koran, as an art that brings one closer to Allah.

Medicine

During the Middle Ages, Islamic medical practitioners rely more on naturalistic explanations than do European physicians, who accept many supernatural explanations. Adopting Galen's methods of observation and description can be productive of new knowledge, but one of Islam's most progressive naturalists and physicians, Abu Bakr al-Razi, points out that simply adopting Galen's writings as an authoritative source of truth may not be fruitful. That is, al-Razi asserts, although it may be appealing and easier to accept the word of an acknowledged authority like Galen, if the authority is wrong, the treatment will probably not be effective. In spite of an atmosphere of growing religious constraints on freedom to conduct medical research in the 10th century, the nonconformist al-Razi also attacks a variety of superstitious religious beliefs about illness and health, including the idea of miracles and miracle cures. He is not the first, nor the last, to note that people often prefer answers that make them feel happy over answers that are factually true. Legitimate treatments often take time to show positive effects, and al-Razi suggests that this is why many people prefer faith healers whose effects, although illusory and transitory, are often dramatic and immediate. In addition to several treatises on astronomy, philosophy, and religion, al-Razi's writings include careful descriptions of diseases and, remarkable for the time, discussions about the relationship between hygiene and disease. Based on Pythagorean and Platonic thought, al-Razi's treatments for both physical and mental illnesses include calming music, healthy diet, and relaxing baths to restore balance and even some chemical remedies. Individuals suffering from "**melancholia**," another name for depression, are encouraged to engage their minds with distracting and complex games like chess (Davidson, 1992). Although al-Razi's reputation as a free thinker and challenger of religious doctrine survives, only a few scraps of his writing do. Most of his works are lost, as both Islamic and Christian religious fundamentalists become more powerful in the later Middle Ages.

Psychology

Nowhere is the influence of Classical Greek philosophers on Islamic culture more evident than in the writings of Abu 'Ali al-Husain Ibn Sina. Ibn Sina interprets and elaborates Aristotle's theory of the three psyches and attempts to conform Greek philosophy to Islamic theology. Ibn Sina's thoughts about psychology evolve initially from Neo-Platonic influences coming directly from the scholars at Alexandria. In Ibn Sina's religious interpretation, Aristotle's three psyches take on a hierarchical form such that vegetative and sensitive psyches make humans physical, earth-bound, and animalistic, and the rational psyche makes humans god-like. The five **corporeal** or bodily senses make humans like animals and the ability to reason makes humans like Allah. In Western ideologies, the physical senses through which information about particular objects is obtained make man animal-like, but rational thought about universal concepts makes man god-like. For Judaic and Christian ideologies, the soul is associated with the body, but is also separate and independent, capable of transcendence. In early Islamic ideologies, the soul is located in the body, specifically in the brain.

Islamic philosophers and physicians of this era, including Ibn Sina, remain unconvinced about the **transmigration** of the soul, the movement of the soul from one body to another. Instead, they continue to believe as Classical Greek philosophers did that reason and breath leave the body at death but that no aspect of the human travels on to some metaphysical plane of existence. The rational soul is immortal only in the sense that rational thought itself, like a mathematical principle, does not die (Ivry, 1974).

The contribution Ibn Sina makes to Islamic psychology is based primarily on an earlier Arabic interpretation of Aristotle's *Metaphysics*, written by Muhammad b. Tarkhan al-Farabi, who is more original than Ibn Sina but less easily understood (Goodman, 1992). Ibn Sina elaborates Aristotle's psyches into a number of mental faculties, places them in a hierarchy, and identifies the specific brain structures in which the faculties of the sensitive psyche are located. Neither Ibn Sina nor al-Farabi are able to verify their theories with observational evidence because later Islamic religion forbids human dissection. Their works survive as texts in medical schools until the 16th century in Europe (Rahman, 1952).

Both Ibn Sina and al-Farabi focus their psychologies on the study of thinking. Most mental faculties are attributed to the sensitive soul, with reason alone reserved for the rational soul. This early Islamic psychology includes an aspect of thinking called "potential reason." Potential reason includes a **faculty**, or special mental power, of prophecy. According to Islamic philosophers, the mental faculty of prophecy is available to humans as a consequence of the omniscience and omnipresence of Allah. Because Allah is omniscient, all events everywhere at all times are knowable, although most people do not exercise this aspect of the rational faculty. However, some people do reason well enough to be aware of future or distant events. They demonstrate prophecy either by foretelling future events or by describing events that occur at a distance (Fakhry, 1983; Davidson, 1992). In this way, Ibn Sina and al-Farabi provide a rationalistic account of the popular belief in precognition and clairvoyance.

Islamic faculty psychology continues to influences Western thought far into the Middle Ages. The hierarchical structure of mental faculties, for example, is one significant aspect of Islamic thought that survives the transition to European philosophy.

THE HIGH MIDDLE AGES IN EUROPE

The Search for Stability

In Europe, nostalgia for the great days of the Roman Empire begins in the moments of its earliest decline. Longing for some real or imagined past when life was easier, safer, more comfortable, and more stable seems to be a part of the human condition. In the years from about 400 to 1400 of the Common Era, each new political or military leader who emerges gains strength by making promises to deliver safety and stability.

In 768, Charles the Great, better known as Charlemagne, is crowned king of the Franks, one of the largest and most powerful tribes in Europe. Among Charlemagne's most noteworthy accomplishments is the establishment of schools throughout his kingdom. Since the time of the fall of Rome at the end of the 4th century, literacy has been restricted to members of the clergy. When Charlemagne decrees the establishment of abbey schools at monasteries, he makes education and literacy available to many more.

The teachers at abbey schools are Roman Christian monks, some of whom gain recognition as gifted teachers. Aspiring scholars come from all over Europe to study with them. Eventually, long after Charlemagne, these communities of scholars develop into what are called universities. These universities are not established to train people for employment in some field or to educate them for the workforce, but to provide opportunities to study theology and philosophy. The University of Paris, for example, is established in the 12th century for the purpose of gathering clerical scholars together so that they may interpret Scripture and critique and rewrite Classical Greek philosophy so that it conforms to Church doctrine. Bringing scholars together at these universities allows for the kind of critical, rational thought that is expressed through skepticism, questioning, the weighing and sifting of evidence, and lively debate (Kemp, 1996). This is the origin of the modern university and the purpose for which universities are established.

The reign of Charlemagne also sees the reestablishment of criminal law, so that violence for the sake of profit incurs a penalty, and some semblance of a more stable society emerges. More monasteries and village churches are built, and there begins to be a more orderly rhythm to people's lives. The Sabbath is recognized, although time cannot often be spared to observe it as a day of rest. The local church bells ring out the canonical hours that divide the day into time periods, and measured time begins to take on a significance that it has not had in human culture prior to this period. Agricultural innovations, including the iron plow and the harness for draft animals, result in increased crop yields. There is a decrease in crop loss due to marauders. Hence, people are better fed, infant mortality decreases, and fertility and life expectancy increase.

The Power of the Roman Church

The Roman Christian Church grows slowly in power and wealth throughout the Middle Ages, although the principles by which the Church functions and its doctrines remain relatively fluid through the 11th century. Its remarkable growth in economic power derives partly from the sale of clerical positions in the Church hierarchy. Church members are also able to purchase promises of redemption by buying printed prayers called indulgences. If enough indulgences are purchased to cover one's sins, entry into Heaven is assured. In addition to receiving cash donations, the Church is also deeded large tracts of land by rich noblemen on their deathbeds, in efforts to purchase salvation.

Doctrines and Heresies

In 1096, Pope Urban II preaches the first Holy Crusade to Judea to reclaim the land of Jesus's birth from the Islamic and Jewish infidels who live there. Among the spoils acquired by the West during the Crusades are many of the writings of Greek Classical philosophers, including many of Aristotle's works. The recovery of these writings throws into question certain Church doctrines and highlights existing dissention among the clergy as to official religious practices. This then instigates the development of formal written doctrines and religious ritual. It is at this time, for example, that the **Eucharist**, the ritualized sacrifice and eating of the body and blood of Christ, becomes a part of official Christian religious practice.

As religious doctrine is written down and agreed on by Church authorities, it becomes **orthodoxy**, or the right way to think and believe. Other forms of worship and other belief systems are defined as **heterodoxies**, or wrong ways to think and believe. Wrong belief systems are considered heresies, even if they, too, are based on the teachings of Jesus and define themselves as Christian.

SCHOLASTICISM

During the 12th and 13th centuries, Aristotle's philosophical works concerning psychological questions become available to Christian clerics in the West. These clerics, referred to as **Scholastics**, attempt to interpret the writings of Classical

Greek philosophers so that they support the more mystical Roman Christian orthodoxy. Aristotle's naturalistic approach to psychological questions proves especially vexing to the Scholastics who, after initially hailing these newly available
philosophical writings, later declare them to be pagan heresies and attempt to
destroy them (Weinberg, 1964).

Eventually, however, ways are found to make Aristotle's naturalism conform
to the Church's supernatural doctrine. The Scholastics' efforts are made easier because they are working with Islamic translations and interpretations of Aristotle's
writings that have already been made to appear to support Islamic and Eastern
Christian religious doctrines. The epistemological questions that the Scholastics
consider about what humans can know and how they come to know can be organized into several issues, all of which have direct application to the study of human
behavior.

The Problem of Knowledge

According to Augustine, who is introduced in the previous chapter, God is the only
truth humans can know, and the way to know God is through trust in revelation,
Scripture, and church authorities. Scholastic clerics do not doubt Augustine's assertions, but, bowing to pressure from an increasingly educated population, they
seek a more complete answer to epistemological questions.

✓ Stop and think.
How could you use logic to support the argument that God exists?

For example, the monk Anselm offers rational thought as an additional way to
know God. He puts forward a logical argument to prove that God is real, which
says that because the human mind can think about or conceive of a being powerful
enough to create and rule over everything, then that being must truly exist. Thus,
rational thought becomes a support for faith in God. Writing at about the same
time, Peter Lombard, also an Augustinian monk, argues even more strongly for
the use of reason and also for the use of observation of God's works in the world
to know God. These 11th-century monks thus set the stage for the arrival new
epistemologies in Western thought in the 13th century (Potts, 1980).

Realism Versus Nominalism

Scholastics also broaden the question from whether it is true that men can really
know God to wondering if men can really know anything at all. What is real? The
Scholastics, however, approach the issue from an entirely different worldview than
that of the early Greek physicists. For example, Plato argued that the forms, or
universals, were real, but some Scholastics wonder if universals are real things or

simply names that are given to classes of things. Maybe the names do not represent anything real. Believing that universals are real is called **realism**. Believing that universals are just names given to sets of particular instances is called **nominalism**.

As you think about this issue, you might be comfortable enough accepting only particular instances of cats as real and you might find the notion of a universal form, catness, to be a rather foreign idea. But what about something like justice?

✓ **Stop and think.**

Is justice a real thing, or is it a name given to a set of particular instances of just behavior?

Similarly, what is intelligence? Is intelligence a real thing, or is it simply the name given to a set of behaviors or characteristics? In the Middle Ages, some Scholastics argue that universals are real, and others argue that they are merely sets of instances that have been given a name. Because these sets have been given names, they can seem to represent something with an independent reality. But those may only be names, or, as the Scholastic monk Roscelin would say, only *flatus vocis*, puffs of air made when the name is spoken.

✓ **Stop and think.**

Are there other things that are believed to be real because they have a name?

By What Method May We Know?

Throughout the Middle Ages, questions about how humans can know God continue to be debated by the Scholastics, with several arguing against the Church doctrine that faith, revelation, and authority are the only ways to know God. The monk Peter Abelard suggests, for example, that if God is really omnipotent, omnipresent, and omniscient, then all ways of acquiring knowledge would lead to knowledge of God and no method of inquiry could lead to doubt. Several later Scholastic clerics make similar arguments. The Dominican monk Roger Bacon outlines moving arguments in support of using mathematics and what he calls **experimental science**, the observational study of nature, as keys to understanding and knowing God. Both Bacon and Robert Grosseteste, another monk, propose and conduct scientific-like studies of light and its role in optics as avenues by which the light of God may be better understood. These clerics argue that the Church should encourage, not discourage, the use of reason and even observation of the natural world as equally valid ways to know God (Burke, 1962).

Roger Bacon identifies four causes of human ignorance and error that prevent men from receiving the benefits of divine wisdom. First is what Bacon sees as an unjustified reliance on authorities, although he makes it clear that he is not talking about Church authority. Second is the human tendency to remain a slave to habits, traditions, and customs, even in the face of contradictory evidence. Third is what Bacon calls popular prejudice that blinds us to other evidence. He is speaking here about the ways in which humans are predisposed to think, including the desire to maintain social cohesion by going along with the opinions of others no matter how ill-informed they may be. And finally, Bacon says, conceit and overconfidence in our own knowledge and ability to reason cause us to remain ignorant (Burke, 1962).

In making these arguments, Abelard, Bacon, and many others create an atmosphere for the continued questioning of Church authority and doctrine. Their goal is to demonstrate that all ways of knowing will lead to knowledge of God, but the eventual effect is to open debate and doubt about the authority of the Church. To Church authorities, these arguments create an atmosphere of doubt in faith and skepticism about Church doctrine, which is considered a sin. For this reason, many of these clerics are punished. Most of Abelard's writings are burned, and he dies on his way to appeal to the Pope after being condemned by Church authorities. Roger Bacon is imprisoned for his heresies and very nearly excommunicated.

Summary of Scholastic Thought

Scholastic thought in the 13th century may be usefully summarized by examining the thoughts of the Dominican monk Thomas Aquinas (ca. 1225–1274). Aquinas is convinced that Aristotelian naturalistic philosophy is correct, but for the Church, this naturalism veers dangerously away from orthodoxy. When the Scholastics are confronted with Aristotle's apparent heresy, they respond with a doctrine of "double truth." One truth, they contend, is based on reason, and this is the truth of the natural world. The other truth, equally valid, is based on revelation and is the truth of Church orthodoxy (Russell, 1945).

Aquinas sets about to reconcile these two truths and to resolve the epistemological questions raised by Scholastic theologians about whether one can know God through observation and reason or only through faith. The resolution he proposes is that, because God created everything, God also created the natural world, including humans. In the same way that one can come to know an artist by examining the works created by that artist, one can also come to know God by examining God's creations in the natural world. And the natural way to study the natural world is through observation and reason. Aquinas argues that the spirit of man is interdependent with the matter, or body, so that knowing about both are equally valid ways to know God.

The theological system organized by Aquinas has important implications for religion and religious practice, but there are three reasons that his work is relevant to a history of psychology. First is his success in persuading Church authorities that observation and the description of nature should be encouraged rather than disallowed. This is important for the progress of all domains of natural philosophy, as well as for the study of human and animal behavior. Second, because Aquinas has great interest in human psychology, he studies and writes about Aristotelian concepts of biopsychology. In doing so, his work furthers the inclusion of psychology among the other natural sciences that emerge in the following centuries, thus helping to make those biopsychological concepts available today. Finally, Aquinas speculates about human motivation and suggests that humans are motivated by desire. He argues that humans are motivated by desires for what is not good for them. Thus, humans do wrong, not because they are evil, but because they are weak and unable to resist desire, even when they know their actions are wrong (Russell, 1945).

The Consequences of Scholasticism

In many ways, Scholastic debates about Church doctrine have the opposite of the desired effect. The very idea that the doctrine can be debated at all is itself an example. The Scholastics' intent is to strengthen Church doctrine, but the result demonstrates that it is possible to debate and question the doctrine. By successfully arguing that the Church should allow for the study of nature as a way to know God, the Scholastics demonstrate that those doctrines can be changed. This is contrary to the Church's assertion that doctrine represents God's wisdom revealed to the authorities. Unfortunately for the Scholastics, in 1277, the Church condemns the synthesis proposed by Aquinas and forces the separation of philosophy, the study of the natural world, from theology, the study of God.

The failure of the Scholastics' attempted synthesis is articulated well in the 14th-century works of Marsiglio, a monk at the University of Padua in Italy, and by William, his protégé and a Dominican monk from Ockham in England. Marsiglio de Padua and William of Ockham conclude that nature provides only circumstantial evidence, but no direct evidence for the existence of God. These monks argue that God must be known through faith alone. The same may be said of human will or the transcendent soul. If one accepts Church doctrine, then one might well believe that will and soul are real, but without faith in Church doctrine, there is no evidence in nature for the existence of free will or of a transcendent soul. In spite of their steadfast assertion of faith, both Marsiglio de Padua and William of Ockham are excommunicated from the Church. They only manage to avoid the ultimate penalty for challenging Church doctrine by taking refuge in the court of Roman Emperor Louis IV, who is at war with the Pope. There they remain under the protection of the Emperor for the last years of their lives.

William of Ockham is best remembered for the doctrine of **parsimony**, the assertion that explanations that utilize the fewest assumptions are the most likely to be true. Because assumptions are, by definition, beliefs for which there is no evidence, it stands to reason that when attempting to explain a phenomenon, the explanation for which there is direct observational evidence is more likely to be true than an explanation that requires assumptions. The argument that one should accept the explanation that requires the fewest assumptions is referred to as **Ockham's razor**.

THE BLACK DEATH

Widespread famine and diseases like smallpox are still common in Europe through-out this period. Then, in 1348, the bubonic plague sweeps across Europe from seaports in Italy. Called the Black Death because in its final stages it darkens the skin of its victims, the virus is carried by fleas living on the blood of infected ro-dents. The population of rodents explodes in the decades just prior to 1348 because Christian monks preach that cats are agents of witchcraft, and millions of cats are killed.

Demographic estimates are difficult to make for this period, but it is generally agreed that at least 30% to 40% of the population of Europe dies between 1348 and 1350 (Cantor, 2001). In some locations, death rates are even higher. Normal burial practices are impossible to maintain, and in some cases, entire villages have to be abandoned because of the number of decaying bodies left unburied. Civic life breaks down, the planting and harvesting of crops is disrupted, and care for domestic animals and even for human infants and children becomes haphazard as families disintegrate. After 1350, the bubonic plague returns again and again every few years with little warning and no understanding as to its cause.

A Psychology of Disaster

Those who are left behind find a variety of ways to cope in the world that remains. Some people adopt a stoic philosophy and carry on their normal lives by accepting whatever happens as the will of God. Great acts of heroism occur as some try to give comfort and care to the dying and others expend great effort in burying the dead. Still others give up all hope and try to blot out the terror around them by drinking heavily and engaging in other acts of reckless abandon.

For all, the biggest question is why. What has caused this terrible disaster? Many believe it is the will of God and that God is punishing them. This explanation is undermined by the fact that Christians, even very devout Christians, are dying too, including Christians who spend their days nursing the sick.

✓ **Stop and think.**
Could you explain in your own words what causes disease? Would your explanation sound plausible to someone who does not know about germs?

The Church's official position is that nonbelievers are to blame. In the search for scapegoats, the burden eventually falls most heavily on the Jews. Late in the previous century, Jews in England and in the region today called France were forced to convert to Christianity and to abandon their land and businesses or be killed. In the years of the plague and for several years after, throughout Europe, hundreds of thousands of Jews are driven from their homes or killed, including those who had already converted to Christianity. Sometimes, nothing more than a rumor that the Black Death is in the next village is enough to cause the villagers to kill whole families of Jews living near them. *In the face of seemingly inexplicable disasters, the first human impulse seems to be to fall back on authority and to find someone to blame and punish.*

Challenging the Church

At a time when Church doctrines and clerical practices are beginning to be questioned and even criticized by a few, the fact that Christian clerics die in the plague only adds to the growing doubt about the adequacy of the authorities. In the 14th century, an atmosphere of doubt encourages the willingness to question and challenge Church authority. In addition to doubts about Church doctrine, Christians are critical of the sinful behavior and sexual misconduct of many clerics, outraged by the great wealth generated through the sale of Church offices and indulgences, and convinced that the Church is inventing bogus miracles to increase its power and economic clout.

HUMANISM: A NEW FOCUS

Disease and Famine

One reaction to the plague is a shift away from concern about the afterlife to interest in the present and heightened curiosity about the immediate human experience. When combined with other economic and social developments, these changes in intellectual interests give birth to the cultural movement in the West called **humanism**.

From the Hereafter to the Here and Now

Throughout the Middle Ages, life for most people is difficult, violent, and quite likely to come to a miserable but mercifully early end. Christians are encouraged to hope for a better life in the hereafter. But something about the devastating 14th century turns this focus around. The change begins first in Italy and later moves throughout Europe. By the 15th and 16th centuries, people are becoming more interested in their present earthly lives, in attaining pleasure, maximizing happiness, and understanding the human experience. Perhaps it seems as though death will come to us all soon enough, and thus we had best enjoy the life we have been given while we still have it (Tuchman, 1978).

The Workings of the Body

As a part of the concern with the present, the study of the human body resumes in ways that have not been seen since the times of Galen. By the 16th century, the study of anatomy and medicine is reborn. Scholars at universities in many parts of Europe are training doctors, performing dissections, and conducting experiments to try to understand the workings of human and nonhuman animal bodies.

Concepts of the Mechanical

There is a flurry of mechanical inventions at this time. Levers and pulleys are put to work to raise and carry loads. Water-, wind-, and heat-propelled turbines drive gears to operate mills and turn all sorts of engines.

When the increasing interest in the workings of the body is combined with the accumulating understanding of mechanical principles, a new way of thinking about the body is born: the body as machine. This mechanistic conception of the body comes to have a significant impact on the study of psychology in the centuries that follow.

Secular Powers Grow Stronger

From the 12th to the 16th centuries, **secular** powers, those not associated with the Church or a religion, become more powerful, and the legal, economic, and political powers of the Church decline. For close to 1,000 years in Europe, the Church held almost unlimited power and set the intellectual agenda. Kings, emperors, feudal lords, and other secular political powers were always thorns in the side or even outright threats to Church authority. However, by the time of the 16th century, especially around the region now called Italy, these powers become institutionalized in the political forms of city/states and become economically capable of mounting a credible challenge to the Church.

Small villages grow into larger settlements, as unlanded individuals move to population centers. People begin to practice trades like ironwork, carpentry, and cabinetmaking. Crafts- and tradesworkers gain more control over their lives and begin to demand more respect. Organizations of craftspeople form into guilds to establish standards for quality and fair prices for their products, and to train apprentices in the trades.

A NEW WAY OF KNOWING

By the end of the 14th century, trust in Church authorities was no longer the only way to know. Epistemology began to change in important and profound ways and took on some of the reliance on observation and experience that those in the 21st century will recognize as familiar. But this age of the spirit left its imprint on Western philosophy and later, psychology. Many of the assumptions that have influenced the study of psychology are inherited from this time in history.

Inherited Assumptions

The following assumptions will sound familiar. They became part of the official religious canon only a few hundred years ago, are still very much a part of Western culture, and still influence many present-day answers to psychology's questions.

The Essential Duality Is Real

It is assumed that there are two parts to the human: spirit and body. This duality also applies to the universe so that the universe consists of an observable natural realm and an unobservable supernatural realm. The human consists of an observable material body that is part of nature and an unobservable spiritual aspect that is supernatural, that is divine, and that separates humans from nature.

The Spiritual Is More Worthy of Study

Although nature is real, it is worthy of study only because it provides clues to reveal the supernatural. For psychology, the spiritual aspect of the human is the domain of study. The actions of the body are interesting only insofar as they reveal the unobservable spiritual aspect that causes those actions. Internal unobservable motivators of behavior are assumed to exist and are more important to understand than the behaviors or any external motivators originating in nature.

The Personal Is Private

The internal, spiritual aspect of the human is unique to each person and is private, unknown, and unknowable to any other. Because this spiritual aspect motivates behavior, humans have free will.

Epistemology for a New Age

In the late 13th century, the study of nature through observation is sanctioned by the Church, but only because nature reveals the supernatural. By the 16th century, the observational study of nature is conducted to understand nature. This transition in epistemologies is a slow one and fraught with many setbacks. Humans' preferred ways of coming to believe, such as simple explanations with high face validity, continually interfere with these new ways of knowing.

FROM CERTAINTY TO DOUBT
IN THE WEST

We enter the late 14th century just as the Black Death has plunged Europe once again into economic despair and widespread famine. The Hundred Years' War between England and France will rage on until 1453, further disrupting life in Northern Europe and depleting resources. In spite of these adversities, people in this region eventually recover. Economic and agricultural advances are made, and increasingly efficient forms of ship-building and navigation come into use.

During the 14th through 16th centuries, technological developments allow European explorers to come into extensive contact with peoples in many parts of the world. Economic, political, and religious concerns also spur geographic exploration and discovery.

The Certainty of Trust

For hundreds of years in the West, the Roman Christian Church provides some semblance of order. For those living in misery, there is the promise of salvation in the afterlife, a spiritual refuge. For those fearing for their safety or living in poverty, the Church sometimes provides a place of physical refuge, or at least a stable physical presence in changing times. For those wishing to explore philosophical and intellectual issues, the Church defines the scope of inquiry and eventually the limits of the discourse. For those seeking answers to existential questions about the meaning and purpose of life, the Church provides simple, unshakable answers and a refuge from doubt, fear, and confusion. There is certainty and thus security and comfort in coming to believe through trust.

✓ **Stop and think.**
What possible harm could come from having trust?

The Costs of Trust

There are many benefits to basing one's beliefs on trust, especially during difficult times when certainty is most ardently desired. But there are also costs because coming to believe based on trust alone does not leave room for questions. The answers must be accepted as given.

Trust Requires Obedience

An epistemology based on trust requires obedience to that belief system, no matter how difficult or painful that might be. If your authorities say that you must sacrifice your first-born child, you have no recourse, and because a sacrifice is not really a sacrifice if you do not give up something dear to you, that sacrifice is painful.

If trust requires that believers kill those who hold different beliefs, then that is what is to be done without question or further explanation. Although most wars have almost certainly been fought over economic and political considerations, war is often justified and perpetuated based on differing trust-based belief systems. For example, when Christian Crusaders reach Jerusalem in 1099, they slaughter nearly everyone in the city of every other faith, including the children. *The English and the Irish have been at war with one another over differing interpretations of Christian doctrine almost incessantly since the reign of King Henry VIII in 1534. Even today, Christians and Muslims are at war in many parts of the world, Muslims and Jews are at war in Palestine, Catholic Christians are at war with Protestant Christians in Ireland, and quasireligious wars go on in many other places as well. All of this warfare is justified by belief systems based on trust.*

To question a belief system built on trust is to demonstrate a lack of trust. After all, if one is questioning, one must not have sufficient trust. Certainty is granted only to those who are able to dismiss all doubt and never question their belief system.

✓ Stop and think.
If having trust means never questioning your beliefs, how do you know they are true?

Trust Can Be an Intellectual Dead End

By its very definition, trust does not allow for questions or require justification. The goal of Scholastic theologians in the 13th century is not to justify their faith, but to more fully understand the sources of their faith. Scholastics' questions are limited to knowing God. Some of them try to assimilate questions about nature, but the goal is always to strengthen faith in God.

Change Is Not Valued

Beliefs based on trust are unchanging and considered timeless. Thus, progress or improvement is meaningless. The ancient Egyptians enjoyed a stable and unchanging culture for at least 3,000 years using this strategy. The ancient Chinese also enjoyed a highly developed and stable culture for more than 2,000 years (Murphy & Murphy, 1968). But Western culture is diverse, made up of many different groups with many different belief systems. By the 14th century, Western belief systems are becoming more fluid. In this era, Western epistemology entertains more questions and undergoes significant change over time.

Life in Europe in the 14th century offers ample room for improvement, so people are motivated to seek better lives. Sometimes doing so requires questioning Christian Church dogma and revealing that some beliefs based on trust are not borne out by the observation of events in nature.

CRACKS IN THE FOUNDATION OF FAITH

For 14th- and 15th-century skeptical minds, Church doctrine leaves room for doubt. The Church may say that the natural world is only an illusory copy of an eternal and transcendent spiritual reality, but it is hard not to experience nature as real. The promise that good behavior will be rewarded in an afterlife may be appealing, but seeing that all around you greedy and evil people are rewarded in this life is hard. The Church may tell you that you are insignificant, that God speaks only to a chosen few, and that your relationship with God is best mediated through the power of Church authorities and the ritual and drama of Church liturgy. But if you are indeed responsible for your own actions, then it only seems right that you should also be able to communicate directly with God. If the purpose of life is to serve God, is the exercise of the many creative gifts you have been given not also a way to serve God?

Individualism

The most salient theme of the 15th and 16th centuries in Western intellectual thought is the relatively novel idea of the importance and centrality of the individual. Plato thought about universals, like the form human, rather than particular humans. The Church focuses on God and life in the hereafter rather than focusing on present lives here and now. After surviving the Black Death and the subsequent breakdown of feudal society, philosophers begin to be interested in the present lives of humans, not as a way to know God but as a way to know the human experience. The reasons for this rise in individualism are myriad, but they include religious, political, and economic transformations.

A Personal Relationship With God

There are many obvious discrepancies between the founding doctrines of Christianity and the rituals, practices, power, and wealth of the Roman Christian Church in the 14th century. Even within the Church, these discrepancies lead to widespread dissention that culminates when the Augustinian monk Martin Luther nails his 95 theses to the door of the church in Wittenberg in 1517. The sale of indulgences is particularly disturbing to Luther, whose goal is to reform the practices of the Roman Church. Luther believes that individuals should be held personally responsible for their sinful transgressions and that the Church should not mediate between the sinner and God's judgment by granting absolution, especially not for payment.

Others before Luther also argued that each individual should seek a personal relationship with God. Francis of Assisi, for example, advocated meditation and private prayer over Church ritual, and John Wyclif urged that all people should read the Bible and decide for themselves what it says. But Luther's particular target is the Church's practice of promising that it can deliver divine forgiveness and salvation in return for money or land. He protests that only God can forgive sin, and therefore those who sin should not seek absolution from the Church no matter what they are able to pay. Sinners should instead pray privately for forgiveness from God and be prepared to suffer eternal damnation in hell. In Luther's adamant and uncompromising message, he preaches that belief in Christian principles is essential if one expects to be saved.

Unfortunately for Luther, he has chosen as his target the one Church practice that is the most lucrative and also affords the Church the most power over its members. For this, he is accused of heresy and is excommunicated from the Church. But the idea that individuals remain personally accountable for their sins and should seek a personal relationship with God catches fire, especially in Germany, where Luther's protests eventually become a Protestant movement and lead inexorably to a schism in the Roman Church.

The Political and Economic Individual

The idea of the individual as a political entity is reawakened as people move from serfdom, in which they are virtually enslaved to a feudal landholder, to independence as skilled tradesworkers in the newly born cities. Instead of going to war to protect the feudal lord and his lands, individuals begin to think of themselves as citizens of a particular city and are willing to go to war to protect their city as an extension of their own personal interests. As citizens having responsibility for the governing of the city, individuals take an interest in city policy, city planning, and the defense of the city. Not since Classical Greek times has the individual been so responsible for the life of the city.

Similarly, the idea of capitalism or the accumulation of assets is conceived as individuals become the source of their own capital through work and the exercise of their skills. Serfs work to increase the lord's capital, but independent citizens of the city work to produce their own assets.

✓ **Stop and think.**
Are there costs to the individual of living in an individualistic culture rather than a collectivist culture?

Humanism

Tied closely with the theme of individualism is the idea that humans should be at the center of human thought. The Scholastic assertion that all philosophical thought and creative energies should be focused on understanding God is displaced in the 15th and 16th centuries by the desire to explore nature for the sake of understanding nature and by fascination with the human experience and the place of humans in nature. This new focus is called humanism.

The Nature of the Human Mind

Humanists argue that if men are at the center of God's creation, and if men have been given dominion over nature, then it is essential to understand the true nature of what it means to be human. The Church teaches that men are at the midpoint between God and inanimate matter, standing just below angels in the hierarchy. Although Scholastic theologians discuss and debate questions about how angels think, humanist philosophers are concerned with how men think, asking questions such as, "Is there just one divine truth, or does each man have a different perspective on truth?"

✓ **Stop and think.**
Is there a difference between truth and opinion?

The Potential for Improvement

What puts men into their exalted place in the divine hierarchy is that they have rational and transcendent minds. That makes them god-like. Other animals behave in a mechanical way as a consequence of being driven by their natures and are thus not capable of improvement. Angels, on the other hand, are already perfect and therefore have no need for improvement. Men alone are in need of and capable of improvement. Men are able to change because they possess a spark of the divine. Thus, they are capable of changing for the better, improving, and making progress. In this era of humanistic philosophy, the new idea appears that one need not settle for the station or fate into which one is born, but can work to "better" oneself.

As one person is able to improve, so then are all, and therefore society as a whole improves. An infectious sense of optimism is born in this era. Now that the intellectual shackles of Scholasticism are broken and humans begin to explore the mysteries of nature and the human experience, there is belief in the human power to understand using god-like rational minds.

The Centrality of Human Perspective

This idea that the human experience is central spreads to many aspects of Western culture, at least in Italy where this movement begins. This period in Western history is named the Renaissance by later 19th-century scholars.

Art

In the fine arts, religious themes depicting scenes from Biblical stories have dominated for centuries. In this new era of humanism, painters adopt secular themes, showing ordinary people in the rich detail of everyday situations. They illustrate folk stories and create portraits of wealthy patrons. Leonardo da Vinci, for example, paints religious scenes but also sculpts and paints the human figure with careful attention to anatomical detail.

This is the period in Western art when perspective appears. Previously, figures and scenes were shown as flat objects against a flat background, as God might have seen them. During the Renaissance, the perspective is brought to earth and scenes begin to be shown as humans might actually see them, receding into the background.

Music

Musical expression also moves away from religious themes and begins to adopt and elaborate on folk songs and what is called street music. This music is played on instruments that are relatively easy to make and to play so that ordinary people can participate in making music.

Literature

The same transition occurs in the popular literature of the time and is dramatically illustrated by comparing Dante's *Divine Comedy*, completed in 1321, with Boccacio's *Decameron*, completed in 1353. The *Divine Comedy* describes the various levels of purgatory and hell, exemplifying a religious theme. Boccacio's bawdy and raucous *Decameron,* on the other hand, is a story about a group of pilgrims who leave the city to escape the plague and the all-too-human tales they tell one another as they wait in exile until it is safe to return to the city.

In the 13th century, skepticism toward Church dogma begins to be voiced, and by the 14th and 15th centuries, there is a transition in philosophy away from the spiritual toward the earthly, human, and secular. By the 16th century, there is a renewed sense of wonder in nature, discoveries in the workings of nature, and an explosion in creative thought and expression. Although humans crave stability and certainty, some philosophers suggest that the spirit of discovery and creativity in the West in the 16th century is born of and fostered by skepticism and the inevitable instability that follows (Russell, 1945).

SKEPTICISM RETURNS

Just as Church authorities have feared, doubts about theological dogma ignite a new wave of skepticism that ultimately undermines the influence, power, and wealth of the Roman Christian Church. But the skepticism of this era also stems from economic and political pressures. As feudal society declines, cities and towns grow, a new middle class of tradesworkers appears, and skepticism extends beyond Church dogma to nearly every aspect of life in 16th-century Europe.

A Skeptical Perspective

One of the most influential writers of the era, and one whose thoughts illustrate this new wave of skepticism, is French nobleman Michel de Montaigne (1533–1592). Montaigne's works are published in the last half of the 16th century. He questions the very possibility of ever reaching certain knowledge. He revives the Greek philosophers' concerns that even observations of nature cannot represent true knowledge because the natural world is in a constant state of change. Montaigne attacks accepted doctrines, such as the medieval understandings of Greek philosophy, and even newer humanistic ideas about the centrality of man. He takes particular issue with religious assertions and the common popular belief that humans are above other animals in some teleological hierarchy and are therefore closer to God, better able to reason and communicate, and capable of greater happiness through the use of rational thought (Frame, 1965).

Montaigne's Skepticism

Presumption is our natural and original malady. The most vulnerable and frail of all creatures is man, and at the same time, the most arrogant. He feels and sees himself lodged here, amid the mire and dung of the world, nailed and riveted to the worst, the deadest, and the most stagnant part of the universe, on the lowest story of the house and farthest from the vault of heaven, with the animals of the worst condition of the three (those that walk, those that fly, those that swim), and in his imagination, he goes planting himself above the circle of the moon and bringing the sky down beneath his feet. It is by the vanity of this same imagination that he equals himself to God, attributes to himself divine characteristics, picks himself out and separates himself from the horde of other creatures, carves out their shares to his fellows and companions the animals, and distributes among them such portions of faculties and powers as he sees fit. How does he know, by the force of his intelligence, the secret internal stirrings of animals? By what comparison between them and us does he infer the stupidity that he attributes to them?

> When I play with my cat, who knows if I am not a pastime to her more than she is to me? We entertain each other with reciprocal monkey tricks. If I have my time to begin or refuse, so has she hers. . . .
>
> This defect that hinders communication between them and us, why is it not just as much ours as theirs? It is a matter of guesswork whose fault it is that we do not understand one another; for we do not understand them any more than they do us. By this same reasoning they may consider us beasts, as we consider them. . . . We must notice the parity there is between us. We have some mediocre understanding of their meaning; so do they of ours, in about the same degree. They flatter us, threaten us, and implore us, and we them. (Montaigne, 1580/1958, pp. 330–331)

The Discomfort of Doubt

The problem with skepticism is that, although it brings into question beliefs that may be wrong, it does so at the expense of the stability gained by certainty. Doubting unseats stability. This may eventually lead to more correct beliefs, but, in and of itself, doubt is not progressive. Montaigne's skepticism, for example, leads him to be very pessimistic about the plight of humans. Other writers of his era recognize that what is needed is an alternative epistemology, a new way of finding what is real and what is true, a new method for establishing certainty and, it is hoped, stability.

EMPIRICAL DISCOVERY: TWO STEPS FORWARD

The epistemological philosophy that advocates experience as a foundation for belief is called **empiricism**, possibly named after the Classical Greek philosopher, Sextus Empiricus. Empiricus was a Skeptic whose writings were recovered by the West in 1562 and then influenced skeptical thought in the 16th century.

Empiricism and rationalism are not mutually exclusive because both empirical and rational philosophers accept and use elements of the other in formulating beliefs. The hope is that empiricism informed by rationalism will yield beliefs that are not just opinions but truths, and that will finally provide the certainty that is so anxiously sought.

Human Potential

By the 16th century, Church authorities have told individuals for 1,000 years that God has put them where He wants them to be, gives them everything He wants them to have, and causes the events that He wants them to experience. During the Renaissance, the idea arises that humans have the power to challenge fate and change their lives. The **zeitgeist** (the spirit of the times) changes, and the idea of progress, of the potential for improvement begins to take hold. Pessimism about this earthly life and the focus on an afterlife wanes, and a new spirit of optimism grows, based on the power of humans to observe and know the world of nature in which they live. For 1,000 years, prayers have been offered as a means of avoiding natural calamities. Sometimes prayers are answered and sometimes not. For thousands of years before that, sacrifices are offered along with prayers, but those seem to be answered in more or less random ways as well. By the 16th century, some are suggesting that by knowing nature and by having a better understanding of the place of humans in nature, humans might be able to improve their lives by their own active efforts.

Medicine

After decades of devastating plagues in which the clergy are as likely to die as anyone, people begin again to take an interest in natural causes of disease. As religious strictures loosen, a new era of descriptive medicine is born. Scholars at medical universities in Italy begin to conduct human dissections and find evidence in their observations that some previous beliefs are false. One such scholar is Andreas Vesalius of Padua, who publishes a medical text based on his anatomical studies in which he refutes many of the beliefs handed down from Galen.

Among the long-held beliefs dismissed by Vesalius is the idea that thought originates in the ventricles of the brain and that this is where the human soul resides. His argument is based on his dissections, which show that many nonhuman animals have ventricles very similar to those found in humans, yet only human animals have souls: "Such are the inventions of those who never look into our maker's ingenuity in the building of the human body (Vesalius, 1543/1952, p. 6). In Fig. 3.1 Vesalius illustrates a classic psychological paradox—the human brain contemplating itself.

The belief that the ventricles of the brain have important functions in human thought arises from the fact that these structures are readily identifiable in dissection. In Vesalius' time, it is believed that the cerebral cortex serves primarily either as a protective covering, a kind of rind, over the more important ventricles located along the brain stem, or, as conjectured by Vesalius, as a structure to allow the blood vessels to bring nutrients to the ventricles. The study of the cerebral cortex itself does not really begin until the 17th century, when technological advances in microscopy allow for the direct study of neural cells (Gross, 1998).

Human Nature

Speculation about the nature of human nature is reinvigorated in 15th- and 16th-century humanistic philosophies. Significant technological improvements in printing make these speculations available to many people throughout Europe.

FIG. 3.1. *De Humani Corporis Fabrica* (Vesalius, 1543/1952; photo courtesy of Francis A. Countway Library of Medicine).

Social/Political Psychology

Most of the interest in human nature in this era concerns how people interact with and influence one another in groups. Niccolò Machiavelli (1469–1527), for example, an Italian bureaucrat, publishes *The Prince* in 1532, a text in which he provides guidelines for how best to take over, subjugate, and rule groups of people. His guidelines, based on his observations and descriptions of human behavior, suggest that most people can easily be manipulated to behave as a leader wishes, even against their own best interests. To achieve this goal, the leader must only exploit the people's desire for self-preservation and their need to maintain social cohesion. In other words, to lead, a leader must instill fear and then create a vocal minority that agrees with him. Machiavelli points out that individual human behavior is malleable and that effective social organization may come from exploiting the weaknesses inherent in how the human mind processes information. He argues that religion, morality, and the law are institutions that can be used by an astute leader much in the same way that armies are used to gain control over people.

Machiavelli is condemned by the Roman Christian Church, his works are placed on the Church's Index of Forbidden Books, and he is accused of being influenced by the devil. This is not surprising when one considers that among his most controversial observations are those concerning the ways in which religion is used to invoke obedience and control and to obtain desired political ends.

Individual Differences

Other philosophers of this era focus on individual psychology. In 1538, Juan Luis Vives (1492–1540) of Spain publishes what eventually becomes a very influential book, based on his observations and thoughts about human behavior. Vives discusses the effects of emotions on behavior and suggests that emotions can cause changes in the bodily humors. His ideas presage notions of reciprocal relationships between physiological and psychological states that suggest a physiological basis for psychological states.

Thoughts and Feelings

Vives believes that emotions also play a role in forming associations in memory, so that experiences that occur in conjunction with intense emotions tend to be associated with those emotions in memory, and later those same emotions may elicit memories of the experiences. Thus, Vives points out the importance of what is now called the learning environment. He supports education for all, including women, and emphasizes the importance of individualizing instruction for each student. Similarly, Julius Scaliger (1484–1558), an Italian physician of the same era, speculates that emotions and muscles are associated with memories so that subsequent experiences not only elicit memories but emotional and muscular responses as well.

The notions that experiences are remembered in both mind and body, and that movements of the body can elicit thoughts about previous experience, add to growing ideas about the ways in which human behavior is like the functioning of a machine. Although these ideas are not original in this era, the zeitgeist supports their exposition at this time. As a result, Vives' book becomes very popular and influences French mathematician and philosopher René Descartes and other later philosophers.

Evidence

Many of these ideas derive from ancient authorities and philosophies. The conviction that there are bodily humors that influence physical health and mental well-being is a persistent idea, for example, with no evidence to support it beyond the word of authorities and widespread belief.

These ideas are also based on unstructured observations that are associated in ways that make logical sense. Although these observations are conducted by learned individuals, their methods are still the casual, unstructured, and untested methods of folk psychology. This method yields descriptive speculations that are supported mostly by face validity. However, even strong face validity is not sufficient evidence; for example, the sun appears to rotate around the Earth, but that does not make it true. An epistemological method that can be relied on and that provides more substantive evidence is needed.

AND ONE STEP BACK: THE CHURCH REACTS

Throughout Christendom, pressures are increasing to reform the corrupt practices of the Roman Christian Church and its powerful and wealthy leadership. Several alternative Christian religions are winning followers, including the Protestants. Ancient Teutonic fertility cults are reappearing as rural peoples move from mountain enclaves into the new cities, doubts are rampant about the piety of Jews who have been forced to convert to Christianity, and observations of nature are leading to confusion about the veracity of many Church teachings. The Church responds by making some changes in practice and a few changes in doctrine, but the strongest Church reaction is to engage in an intense and deadly campaign to eliminate dissenters. This campaign begins with the Inquisition against the Jews in Spain in the 13th century and spreads throughout Europe for more than 300 years (Russell, 1972). There is no way to estimate the number of individuals persecuted and killed by this movement during this period.

THE CERTAINTY OF MATHEMATICS

There is one source of certainty, mathematics, that is spiritual and transcendent, and also earthly, scientific, and observable in nature. Certainty in mathematical concepts is found throughout written Western history beginning with the Egyptians, in Pythagorean thought and Platonic philosophy, cited in Augustine, and revered by Aquinas. The truth of mathematics is evident in observation and in reason, and even the most skeptical philosopher can accept the universal truth of mathematics. Thus, if a proposition can be proven using mathematics, if a question can be addressed using numbers, the answer arrived at will be that much more likely to be accepted and believed. This is as true in the 16th century as it is today.

Belief in the truth of mathematics means that questions should be posed in terms that are measurable. As Galileo Galilei (1564–1642) points out in the 17th century, there are really two worlds. There is the natural world of physical reality where things have shape, size, and weight, and there is the subjective world of sensory experience where things have reality only insofar as they are experienced by a sensing animal. The size and weight of a rose are objectively measurable, but its fragrance, the intensity and variation of its color, and the degree of its beauty are qualities that are judged by subjective opinion.

Hence I think that these tastes, odors, colors, and so on are no more than mere names so far as the object in which we place them is concerned, and that they reside only in the consciousness. Hence if the living creature were removed, all these qualities would be wiped away and annihilated. (Galileo, 1623/1957, p. 274)

The significance of this distinction for psychology is that the subject matter of psychology has to do with qualities that are not measurable but are subjective qualities of sense and thought. Galileo asserts, as many others have since, that science is the study of objective and measurable physical reality, implying that psychology, by its very definition as the study of thoughts, feelings, and behaviors, can never be a science.

REVEALED TRUTH IN NATURE

During the 15th, 16th, and 17th centuries, scholars in the West observe nature for answers to questions about natural phenomena, strictly for the purpose of understanding nature, not to discover clues about the supernatural. *Nature must be understood by observation informed by reason, and the supernatural must be understood by trust. The conflicts that remain between trust and observation, both in these centuries and today, concern disagreements about the boundary where nature ends and the supernatural begins. This distinction remains for psychology because of the lingering assumption that human thoughts, feelings, and behaviors originate in some aspect of the human that transcends nature.*

Cosmology

The confusion between trust and observation in these centuries is exemplified in the work of the Polish natural philosopher Nicolai Copernicus (1473–1543). Copernicus delays publishing his **heliocentric** theory of the universe until just before his death in 1543. This is because Copernicus' religious beliefs that the sun is at the center of the universe violate Church doctrines of an Earth-centered universe. Another example is Giordano Bruno (1548–1600), a follower of Copernican theory. Bruno teaches heliocentrics and argues that the universe is infinite, has many suns and many planets orbiting other suns. He also argues for the possibility that intelligent life exists elsewhere in the universe. Bruno travels to Italy in hopes of convincing the Pope of his beliefs. Instead, he is interrogated by the Inquisition, judged a religious heretic, and burned at the stake because of his refusal to recant his beliefs.

Copernican heliocentricism is based on trust rather than observation and is not much better at predicting astronomical events than the Greek philosopher Ptolemy's ancient **geocentric**, or Earth-centered, theory on which Church doctrine is based. Copernicus' theory is a case of a belief based on trust that coincidentally happens to be true about nature. A successor in the study of heliocentric cosmology is Johannes Kepler (1571–1630). For Kepler, actual observations serve only as supporting evidence for his religious faith in heliocentricism. Kepler makes mathematical calculations of his observations of the movements of bodies in the sky, proving that the sun is indeed at the center of the solar system and demonstrating that elliptical models, rather than circular models, fit his observations of the orbits of planets around the sun.

Other concepts about nature also make their appearance at about this time. For example, the idea that everything in the universe is made up of tiny particles of matter is resurrected, and this atomistic theory of the material universe eventually becomes a foundational belief in natural philosophy. The assumption that the universe operates by a set of mechanical laws that can be mathematically calculated also gradually grows into a model for examining all of nature.

Teleology and Natural Causes

The discovery of natural forces like gravity illustrates a distinction between teleology and naturalism. **Naturalism** is the belief, supported by systematic and replicable observations, that nature is governed by a set of causes. In contrast, teleology is the belief that nature is governed by design and that events in nature happen because they are meant to happen according to the design. In other words, a teleological belief system asserts that events in nature happen not as a consequence of causes, but for a purpose. The natural human fondness for teleologies likely results from the fact that significant events are more likely to be noticed by humans, because humans see patterns even where they may not exist, and because humans are likely to judge erroneously the probability of events in which they already believe. People seem prone to believe in a cosmic or divine plan. Finding that events in nature happen as a consequence of causal laws seems disappointingly mechanical, makes human lives and needs tangential to natural forces, and makes it more difficult to maintain teleological beliefs in purpose and design.

As natural causes for natural events are found in the 16th century, beliefs about supernatural powers and about the central place of humans in the universe become harder to hold. Thus, learning that the sun, not the Earth, is at the center of the solar system and that the Earth and other objects in space move as they do because of natural forces challenges human beliefs in divine plans. Religious doctrines that causal powers reside with God alone are threatened by this growing reliance on naturalistic explanations for events in nature.

Psychological and Theological Consequences

If the sun, not the Earth, is at the center of the universe, then humans are not at the center of the universe and everything does not literally revolve around us. But how could it be that the universe was not designed specifically for us and for our use? If there are other suns and other planets, possibly even other people, how can humans justify a belief that they are God's chosen and favorite creation? If our god is just our god, and other people on other planets have other gods, which is the one true god? As sailors begin geographic exploration, other people with many other gods are being found even here on Earth.

Gradually, as heliocentricism becomes accepted and some of the laws of nature that govern the physical universe are discovered, human understanding about our place in the universe changes dramatically, and God seems to withdraw and not be as close in a daily way. The events of everyday life are explained more parsimoniously by the laws of nature. God seems more like a creator who set everything in motion but may no longer be present daily and may intervene only occasionally in the form of miracles. Have we been abandoned in this mechanical universe by a now-absent God?

In this era, mind is defined as a nonmaterial aspect of the human; therefore, natural philosophy has nothing to say about mind. As long as psychological questions are about individual subjective thoughts and not about the observable physical universe, there is no place for psychology in natural philosophy.

⏱ The Times

Europe is still heavily forested during the period from about 500 to 1348, and sudden death seems to lurk behind every tree. All kinds of wild and dangerous animals lie in wait, especially bear, wild boar, and the wolves of Red-Riding-Hood fame. Babies and children are common prey for wild animals, especially during times of drought and famine when, like in the story of Hansel and Gretel, parents intentionally abandon some children deep in the forest so there will be more food for the others. In the frequent years of famine, up to 10% of the population dies. Visions, probably hallucinations caused by the effects of hunger or food poisoning, are common. Even when food is available, it consists mainly of grains, so that "Give us this day our daily bread" is a serious and heartfelt prayer.

Homes are small, dark, cold, damp, and often made of earth. Most people stay outside as much as possible, going indoors at night for safety from predators. Without heat or windows, nor candles for light, houses are a perfect breeding ground for disease. Epidemics of smallpox, dysentery, malaria, and respiratory infections regularly sweep through whole villages.

The average lifespan is about 21 years for people who are comparatively wealthy, like the feudal lords and their families, but for ordinary folks, it is even shorter. Among the well-off, one half of all babies die in the 1st year of life. It is not unusual for a man to have four or five wives in his short lifetime, losing several to death associated with childbirth. Violence is a common occurrence, as a percentage of the population makes a living by killing and stealing from neighbors.

People living under these pressures are understandably naive and credulous, believing that they are at the mercy of mysterious supernatural forces, including evil spirits, sorcerers, and witches who lurk around every corner. They search for signs in nature of what the future may hold and seek salvation from this earthly hell. The Christian saints are believed to possess supernatural powers and the ability, if so disposed, to deliver this salvation. It is widely believed that even conversion to Christianity is not sufficient to ensure salvation. Nevertheless, not willing to take any chances, many do convert to Christianity, and the wealthy make generous financial donations to the local saints and to the Church.

Perhaps unintentionally, however, these promises of salvation also promote many other superstitious beliefs. For example, the idea that the natural earthly world is only a reflection of the perfect eternal reality beyond suggests that the natural world might provide "signs" of that eternal reality. Recall that humans tend to make assumptions about design in nature, look for cause and effect, and see patterns where none may exist. These tendencies caused people in the early Middle Ages to look for such signs. They believe that the lines etched in the palm of the hand, birthmarks, the location of the stars at the time of birth, or the pattern of tea leaves at the bottom of a cup reveal something important and valid about the future.

During this time, slavery is still practiced in Europe, as it is in most of the rest of the world, and, as is also universally true, the slaves are more likely to be women. In England, about 10% of the population entered in the "Domesday Book" of 1086 are slaves. Male criminals and debtors are killed or sold as field slaves. Their wives and children become field or house slaves, and younger women who are landless, uneducated, and otherwise unable to provide for themselves are sold and used as prostitutes.

War follows on war throughout this period in Europe. From smaller local conflicts to the Hundred Years' War between France and England, what few resources are available are often squandered in bloody battles over territory.

Education, even at a rudimentary level, is available only to a select few, and most people's lives are not much different from those of their parents. Toward the end of this era, the study of nature begins to yield technological developments and advances in medicine, but again, those are available only to a few. For example, as European medical knowledge moves beyond the wisdom of the ancients, and as male doctors are trained at universities, women are moved out of their traditional roles as midwives. Childbirth, which had been a part of everyday life attended to by midwives and friends of the mother, now becomes a medical condition requiring the attention of male doctors. This change, however, is not accompanied by a decrease in either maternal or infant mortality, and childbirth is still a very dangerous undertaking.

The Renaissance spreads, and by the 16th century, nearly all of Europe begins to recover from successions of plague and famine. Intellectual thought is evident again, although vastly altered from the theological philosophies of the 14th century. The West is finally ready for the emergence of a new way of knowing.

4

The Birth of Science: Is There Anything You Cannot Doubt?

In this chapter, the birth of science as a new way of knowing is discussed, and the place of Descartes' rational philosophy in this new epistemology is explored. Important developments in the methods of early science and statistics are covered, as well as the answers to psychological questions offered by philosophers and politicians during this period. We seek to understand why mathematics and science come to have such power in the West. Even as the revolution in scientific, philosophic, and intellectual thought proceeds during the 17th and 18th centuries, both science and philosophy become, for a time, the servants of frightening religious ends. Finally, at the end of the 17th century the principles of Newtonian science are articulated.

REVOLUTION IS IN THE AIR

Ontological Revolution

For many centuries before the 16th, the cosmos was a mysterious and wondrous place ruled by a grand hierarchy with a fearful and all-powerful God at its head. Supernatural beings surrounded us, and signs and symbols revealed the unseen spiritual realm to those who would see. Our worldview was a profoundly spiritual one in which the physical body and spiritual being were united. Western peoples believe that their experiences in and perceptions of this world represent reality, so that if something is perceived to be present, such as a mirage in the desert, then it really is present. As the 16th century closes, important changes begin to occur in what is believed to be real.

During the next centuries, the world is increasingly viewed as mechanical and mathematical. The symbols of mysticism retreat as nature becomes like a machine, made of matter not spirit, and subject to predictable natural laws, not the whims of spirits. The realization dawns more clearly that the universe exists independently of human needs and concerns. Even our own natures become strangely divided as the material body separates from the spiritual soul. Opinions begin to be recognized as only subjective and not necessarily reflections of objective reality.

As a consequence, it becomes harder to have trust in supernatural beneficence granted through devotion and prayer. A simple but systematic observation of the events in nature reveals that wishing rarely (if ever) influences objective reality. At the same time, observations of nature bring new knowledge about the workings of nature, so that people are less subject to nature's devastating vagaries. God is becoming more distant, but humans can make life better through their own efforts, and further improvement is expected through the use of reason and the systematic observation of nature.

Epistemological Revolution

Changes in what is believed to be true are driven by changes in epistemology. After 2,000 years of believing only through faith and authority, people in the West begin again to rely on observations of nature informed by rational and independent thought. Although Scholastics like Aquinas try to maintain a synthesis between coming to believe by trust and coming to believe by observation, this attempt fails. The new epistemology dictates that the supernatural must be known through trust only, and nature may be known through observation. This is not a sudden transition, nor is it final, especially when it comes to understanding the dual aspect of the human, who is part natural and part spiritual.

A NEW WAY OF KNOWING

In 1574, when 13-year-old Francis Bacon (1561–1626) enters Trinity College, Oxford, the curriculum consists exclusively of the study of Aristotle's writing as interpreted through Scholastic theology. Even in Oxford's very Protestant venue, Aquinas' interpretation of "The Philosopher" (Aristotle) is the basis of all that is known and all that will ever be known. Once they have studied a Scholastically translated Aristotle and have mastered the art of logical discourse, students will know what is known and be able to engage in the study of knowledge.

False Idols of Knowledge

Bacon, like many adolescents, rebels against the traditional wisdom of his elders and sets out on a path that carries him, and much of Western philosophy, to a new method for seeking knowledge. As Bacon describes in his book, *Novum Organum*, published in about 1605, human reason is subject to various weaknesses that lead to beliefs that may not be true. A new method must be devised that will reveal the truth in spite of human propensities to believe untruths. Bacon suggests that these weaknesses in reason have led to the worship of false idols of knowledge in the same way that heretical religions might lead to the worship of false idols of faith.

Idols of the Theater

For example, people make false idols of the actors they have placed on center stage: the authorities and Classical philosophers. People too readily accept what is taught by authorities, without asking for evidence or proof.

Idols of the Marketplace

People also make false idols of the language used to conduct commerce or to engage in logical rational argument. Language, which is used to explain and transmit knowledge, can have different meanings for different people. But people tend to assume that everyone means the same thing when using the same words. Bacon suggests that when the results of observations are put into writing, each word should have a fixed meaning.

Idols of the Cave

People make false idols of their own opinions, mistaking opinions for truths and believing that their own opinions are true for all people. According to Bacon, personal opinions arise from individual biological predispositions in physiology or psychology, past experiences, and differing educational backgrounds. Thus, these opinions are specific to each individual. True knowledge should be sought collectively by pooling observations and sharing interpretations among observers. In this way, the weaknesses that cause people to believe that their personal opinion represents truth may be overcome.

Idols of the Tribe

Finally, people make false idols of perceptions that result from weaknesses inherent in the entire tribe of human minds. Bacon is especially critical of the tendency of the human mind to see patterns where there are none; to assume design; to be impatient to find quick, simple, cause-and-effect answers; and to be unduly influenced by strong emotions.

✓ **Stop and think.**
Can you think of a recent example in which one or more of these idols
have interfered with good critical thinking?

Because of these weaknesses of human intellect, because people worship false
idols of knowledge that lead away from truth, Bacon says a new method for seeking
truth is needed, one that will help overcome these weaknesses of intellect. He points
out that a right method is like a right path and that a very swift runner, if set on a
wrong path, will only use swiftness to move more and more quickly away from the
truth. But even a slow runner will eventually reach the right place if traveling on
the right path. The following four major themes are identified in Bacon's proposal
of a new method.

Knowledge Is Power

Having knowledge about nature can give us power, not to have dominion over
nature, not to control nature, but to alter our relationship with nature. Bacon believes that knowledge about nature will better the human condition. When reading
the Scholastics, students are encouraged to study nature for the purpose of contemplating its relationship to the divine, but Bacon points out that this spiritual
contemplation has done nothing to protect humans from ignorance about the workings of nature. Instead, the study of nature should be put into the service of making
humans less helpless and less passive in the face of nature. Knowing the truth gives
us the power to alter our relationship with the thing known, and thus the goal of
knowledge should be to help us alter our fate.

For Bacon, knowledge of nature must always be sought in charity and humility.
Knowledge of nature must be sought for the purpose of alleviating human suffering
and enhancing the quality of life for all living creatures. This knowledge should
never be used to acquire private gain but should always be shared freely and used
for the greater good. And humans must remain humble in the face of nature,
recognizing that "nature can only be commanded by being obeyed." If humans
try to impose their own designs and schemes on nature, they will remain forever
helpless. False knowledge may make people feel powerful for a time, but nature
will never be dominated by mere humans.

Philosophy Must Be Divorced
From Religion

Bacon reserves his most ardent criticism for Scholastic theologians who have,
he says, caused us to confuse natural philosophy with religion to the detriment
of both. Instead of learning from the patient and humble observation of God's
actual creation, humans are too likely to assume that there is a design, such as

"everything happens for a reason." Human minds impose design and purpose on nature, arrogantly come to believe that this human-invented design is genuine, and fail to examine God's actual creation:

> Against [the corruption of philosophy by mixing it up with superstition and theology] we must use the greatest caution; for the apotheosis of error is the greatest evil of all, and when folly is worshipped, it is, as it were, a plague spot upon the understanding. Yet, some of the moderns have indulged this folly, with such consummate inconsiderateness, that they have endeavored to build a system of natural philosophy on the first chapter of Genesis, the book of Job, and other parts of Scripture; seeking thus the dead amongst the living. And this folly is the more to be prevented and restrained, because not only fantastical philosophy but heretical religion spring from the absurd mixture of matters divine and human. It is, therefore, most wise soberly to render unto faith the things that are faith's. (Bacon, 1605/1859, p. 351)

Begin With Inductive Reason

As Bacon sees it, the right method for acquiring true knowledge is to start by assuming that nothing is known. If it is possible to begin with a mind clear of all prior assumptions, then observations will not be shaped and biased by what is already believed to be true.

Once the mind is cleared, careful observations of the actual things in nature may be conducted, always letting nature be in command by remaining open to observing what nature reveals, one small piece at a time. After enough observations have been conducted, some general conclusions may be drawn about the objects of those observations. This general conclusion should then be tested against further observations to ascertain if it applies in all instances. The goal should be to draw larger and larger conclusions, testing through observation at each level, until some basic law of nature is arrived at that applies across all instances.

> Doctor Watson: "This is indeed a mystery. What do you imagine that it means?"
>
> Sherlock Holmes: "I have no data yet. It is a capital mistake to theorize before one has data. Insensibly one begins to twist facts to suit theories, instead of theories to suit facts."
>
> (Conan Doyle, 1900, pp. 6–7)

Natural Philosophy Must Be Dynamic, Cooperative, and Cumulative

Natural philosophy must be dynamic, or always open to change. This dynamic aspect of the study of nature, *what is today called science*, is an essential but often misunderstood component of the method. Religions assert that there are absolute and sacred truths that are universal and unchanging across all time. But for Bacon's study of nature, *and for scientists since*, generalizations about nature must always remain subject to further observation and future change.

The study of nature must also be a cooperative venture, one that uses the contributions of many diverse minds. It is through the cooperation of many individuals conducting observations and suggesting possible generalizations, Bacon believes, that the personal biases called the "idols of the cave" may be overcome.

Finally, natural philosophy must be cumulative, so that higher and higher levels of generalization are continually sought. In this way, human understanding of the general principles underlying nature becomes deeper and more complete.

For Bacon, and for science in general, the proper method for understanding nature is one that overcomes the natural weaknesses in human reason and has the potential to create a new relationship between humans and nature. This technique produces verifiable and serviceable truths about nature, not based on the word of authorities, not through magical and sudden revelations, but through methodical and patient observations:

> Again, the reason science works so well is partly that built-in error-correcting machinery. There are no forbidden questions in science, no matters too sensitive or delicate to be probed, no sacred truths. That openness to new ideas, combined with the most rigorous, skeptical scrutiny of all ideas, sifts the wheat from the chaff. It makes no difference how smart, august, or beloved you are. You must prove your case in the face of determined, expert criticism. Diversity and debate are valued. Opinions are encouraged to contend—substantively and in depth. (Sagan, 1996, p. 31)

THE PHYSICAL UNIVERSE

Just over 20 years after Francis Bacon's death, the Oxford Experimental Science Club is founded in 1648 for the purpose of furthering Bacon's new way of knowing about the physical universe. Even without sophisticated means of observation and measurement, members of this club explore questions such as the physical nature of the moon and factors that might influence the power of humans to someday travel in space (Purver, 1967). Natural philosophers of the 17th century study nature by observing and describing nature and only for the purpose of knowing about nature. Divine revelation and philosophical speculation are abandoned in favor of the empirical methods articulated by Galileo Galilei, Francis Bacon, and others. These empirical techniques yield more valid and reliable information about the physical universe than has ever resulted from revelation or speculation.

The scope of what makes up the physical universe is defined in this era by what Galileo calls the primary qualities. Everything that can be measured, everything that has shape, size, or weight, is considered part of the physical universe. Thus, everything in the physical universe can be experienced by human sensory systems and also has a reality that transcends individual sensory experiences. For example, two people weighing the same banana on the same scales should find the same weight each time if the device is reliable. The weight of the banana transcends individual sensory systems and is thus a part of the physical universe.

✓ **Stop and think.**
What gets left out if one must consider as important only that which can be observed and measured?

At the end of the 17th century, there are aspects of reality that are not regarded as part of the physical universe but are important to the questions of psychology. Among these are the spiritual aspects of the human, including the will, soul, mind, or spark of the divine. These are secondary qualities: the subjective aspects of reality, like beauty, that cannot be measured. The secondary qualities are part of sensory experience, but they do not transcend individual experience. The smell, taste, and color of a banana are secondary qualities. Each individual may taste the banana but may or may not agree with others that the banana tastes good. And even if all agree that a banana tastes good, what is meant by that? How good is good? Is the good taste of a banana a quality inherent in the banana or is it dependent on taste perception, so that taste happens only in the eater's mouth? Secondary qualities are real but they are not, according to natural philosophy in the 17th century, part of the physical universe. To the degree that psychology is the study of subjective secondary qualities, it is not considered part of the physical universe either. Thus, the questions of psychology are not studied using the same methods that are used to study the physical universe.

THE ROLE OF MEASUREMENT

Studying only the primary qualities encourages confidence in numerical findings. How much do bananas weigh? If this banana weighs 120 grams, but another banana weighs 130 grams, which is more representative of the weight of bananas? Other questions could be asked about the range of weights within which bananas fall and about where, within this range, this particular banana falls. The numerical results transcend the opinion of any one individual mind. The weight of bananas may appear to have little to do with psychology, but some 18th-century natural philosophers do try to weigh the soul, for example, by weighing a dying person just before and after death. Noting that the weight does not change when death occurs, they do not conclude that there is no soul. Instead, they conclude that the soul must not weigh anything, thus illustrating that preexisting beliefs can influence conclusions about what is observed.

Trust in the transcendent truth of numbers can leave humans vulnerable to various kinds of statistical tricks if good critical thinking skills are not used or the basic laws of probability are misunderstood. For example, a mathematical statement can appear to be authoritative when it is really only substituting mathematical terms for ordinary words. Or sometimes a variable is chosen for study only because it is measurable, not because it is predictive or interesting. Sometimes what is measurable is studied in an effort to understand the immeasurable.

Knowledge and Opinion

Although statistics can be used to cause confusion, their use still helps overcome the false idols of knowledge. Throughout this journey through Western thought, humans have been concerned with degrees of certainty, have usually recognized that some things are more certain than others, and have nearly always accepted that mathematical truths are the most certain truths of all (Cowles, 1989). Thus, in the 17th century, signs in the physical universe are measured in the search for certain knowledge.

Degrees of Certainty

Some observable signs in the physical universe do indicate the state or presence of something else that may be less observable or measurable. In other words, some signs are reliable indicators about the state or presence of something unobservable. For example, skin temperature and swollen lymph glands are outward signs indicating something about the presence of illness, whereas no matter how skilled the reader, tea leaves in the bottom of a cup are not related to the state or presence of anything. Because some signs actually do indicate the state or presence of something else, it becomes important to discriminate between those signs that do reliably predict and those that do not.

Scientia and Opinio

The Latin term for certain knowledge is **scientia.** By the 17th century, certain knowledge is obtained through demonstration. There are the "high sciences" of astronomy and physics, in which aspects of the physical universe are demonstrable using measurable primary qualities. Signs in the high sciences are readily measurable and highly certain. There are other branches of inquiry in which the degree of certainty is less. What is known in these areas is, in Latin, **opinio**, not certain knowledge, but probable knowledge, or opinion. Opinions are those assertions that are made by authorities or by the testimony of judges. The branches of inquiry in which states or relationships are known by reading the less measurable signs are the "low sciences," such as alchemy or medicine. In the low sciences, the signs are read and opinio is rendered, but measurement is not possible and knowledge is less certain. In this era, psychology does not even achieve the status of a low science. In Fig. 4.1, alchemists measure the signs of their science.

FIG. 4.1. *The Alchymist*, by Pietro Longhi (1661; Pignatti, 1968, plate no. 176).

In the low sciences, there is confusion between the new scientific epistemology and the traditional belief in authorities. What distinguishes scientia from opinio is the method by which belief is derived. For scientia, it is demonstration. For opinio, the method is the word of authorities or judges who know how to read the signs in nature: the magicians, sorcerers, witches, physicians, and those to whom God has chosen to reveal the secrets of nature. Some people are more skilled readers of signs, and they become the authorities or the judges. Some signs are also more **valid**, or objectively true, than others. Will you get sick and die? The lines on your palm may reveal the answer, but the pallor of your face and the temperature of your skin are more valid signs. Signs are not certain, but they render an opinion more probable.

The ability to read these kinds of signs is eventually transformed into the practice of medicine. And the reading of signs is what physicians do to diagnose and treat disease, both physical and mental. *In the present day these are called symptoms, but in the 17th century, they are called signs.*

Signs as Evidence

The frequency with which a sign accurately predicts an outcome is a measure of its validity. In science, signs with a very high probability of being valid are referred to as evidence. Valid observable evidence accurately predicts outcomes. Those speculations that are supported by evidence are more likely to be true "scientia" and not just "opinio."

Discriminating between what constitutes evidence and what does not remains as difficult a task in the present day as it was in the early days of science. Although many of the readers of signs make predictions that are no better than chance, palm readers being an example, some learn to exploit weaknesses in human reason and make people believe that what they offer is evidence. Recognizing that the human mind sees patterns where none exist or that people are more likely to believe what they want to be true, those readers can easily trick us into paying good money for useless services.

Reasons to Measure

Humans are vulnerable to a variety of statistics-related mistakes in thinking that can lead to beliefs for which there is no evidence. Measuring the reliability of the signs and thus establishing evidence can help to overcome these mistaken beliefs and the fears that follow. For example, the careful measurement of the outcomes on all occasions when success is wished for can help overcome the human tendency to remember those occasions when wishing is associated with success and to forget those when it is not.

Overcoming the Idols of the Cave

The careful observation of signs, including measuring wherever possible, helps to overcome the tendency to believe that what is already known is what is true. It was measurement of the observed bodies in space that made it clear that the sun does not circle the Earth, even though it looks as though the sun moves across the sky. If two objects, one heavy, one light, are dropped from the top of a tower, it seems certain that the heavy object will fall faster and land first. But just as surely, measurement shows that this is not the case.

Overcoming the Inability to Estimate Probability

Weaknesses in estimating probability can be exploited in a variety of ways. Those who are not skilled at understanding the numerical odds of a future event are more likely to risk more than they can afford to lose. Not being able to estimate probability makes judging risk versus benefit more difficult. Wise decisions are harder to make about everyday issues, such as whether or not to buy insurance, the likelihood of winning the lottery, or judging if one is likely to become a victim of crime. Measuring helps to overcome the inability to estimate probability correctly (Hacking, 1975).

Overcoming Fears About Chaos

Often, nature and the gods can seem capricious and chaotic. One year the plague sweeps through town, so people move to the country. The next year, floods wipe out the new country home. One year crops are plentiful, the next they are not. Fears about the capriciousness of nature are even reflected in cosmogenic myths, in which deities achieve their place of prominence and authority by first conquering the forces of chaos in nature. Measurement is another way to help to calm human fears about the apparent randomness of nature.

Uses of Measurement

Sampling

By 1700, several concepts about measurement are understood, even in the low sciences. For example, it is understood that where it is not possible to measure every instance, predictions may be made by measuring a sample of instances. How many times must a rock be observed falling when dropped before one might be willing to predict that the next time the rock is dropped it will fall?

How will you die? What is the best way to know the most likely causes of death? If a list of all causes of death for the last week is published, you could select a sample of these lists and count how many people died from each cause. But how many lists must be sampled before making a statement about the most likely causes of death? Enough lists must be sampled to avoid having a single unusual list cause an incorrect prediction. For example, a terrible fire claiming many lives during 1 week would cause an overestimation of the risk of dying in a fire. The lists chosen as the sample must also accurately represent the whole population about which you wish to predict. For example, to predict the likelihood of death from particular causes in the city of London, one must make certain that the lists show all possible causes of death, that they include all of London, and that they do not count areas outside of London. If the sample is representative, it is possible to predict for a whole population. This opens up new phenomena to examination through measurement. Anything where measuring every instance would be too cumbersome or even impossible can be studied by examining a representative sample.

Divining Patterns in Nature to Estimate Risk

In the late 17th century, John Graunt, an English haberdasher (hatmaker), was concerned that most people worried a great deal about dying from causes that were not really very likely to kill them. He understood that numerical data could be used to "divine" patterns in the past that might shed light on the future. He used data from the "Bill of Mortality" published each week, which listed the causes of deaths in London the previous week. After examining the lists published between 1604 and 1661, he determined from what causes people were most likely to die. His conclusion: "Whereas many persons live in great fear, and apprehension of some of the more formidable, and notorious diseases following; I shall onely set down how many died of each: that the respective numbers, being compared with the Total, those persons may the better understand the hazard they are in." (Graunt, 1662/1975, p. 31)

RATIONALISM AS ANOTHER
WAY OF KNOWING

By the early 17th century in the West, philosophers accept that, to understand nature and what is physical, observations of nature must be conducted, whereas the supernatural or metaphysical will be revealed only through trust. In which domain does the human belong? Are humans purely natural, or is there also a spark of the divine, the supernatural? If humans are purely natural, then observations should eventually reveal everything about human thoughts, feelings, and behaviors, but if humans are partly supernatural, then another method, another way of coming to believe, another epistemology for the study of humans must be found. In the 17th century, French mathematician and philosopher, René Descartes (1596–1650) offers **rationalism**, the use of reason and logical argument, as this alternative epistemology.

✓ Stop and think.
Which are humans: natural animals or supernatural beings?

Rationalist approaches to the study of nature and humans are proposed because of several weaknesses in Bacon's inductive empirical approach. These weaknesses include common failures in human perception, like seeing mirages in the desert.

For Descartes, rationalism is seen as a way to improve on perceptions, rather than as an alternative to empirical study.

Antiauthoritarian

Rationalistic philosophers, especially Descartes, reject Scholastic philosophy's reliance on authorities for understanding nature. Like Bacon, Descartes is unhappy to find that the philosophy taught at the university consists of the study of Aristotle's philosophy and Aquinas' theology and that any other way of seeking knowledge is not just discouraged, but in this era of increasing accusations of heresy, may even be persecuted. Both Descartes and Bacon agree that the study of Aristotle will only get one as far as Aristotle got, but no further.

Skepticism and Naturalism Are Dangerous

At the same time, Descartes is a devout Catholic. He is disturbed by skeptical philosophies like those offered by Montaigne and by empirical philosophies that regard humans as purely natural and mechanical. Skepticism may be potentially productive of new and creative ideas, but it is also disruptive to the social order and disturbing to individual happiness. Allowing people to seek and accept truth on their own terms leads to a kind of intellectual anarchy that may prove dangerous to the entire social order.

For example, in this era, skeptical and naturalistic conceptions are threatening well-established beliefs in the divine hierarchy. As observations in nature reveal amazing physical similarities between human and nonhuman animals, questions arise about the assumption that humans are closer to God or more god-like than other animals. Believing that humans are like animals gives rise to doubts in the belief that humans have a transcendent soul and animals do not. What is the soul, and where is it located? Religious rationalists like Descartes seek certainty, but they insist on a certainty that preserves the human soul and thus confirms theological authority.

At the same time, rationalist conclusions must be compatible with the growing movement for empirical study. Rational approaches to science argue that pure inductive fact gathering is useless without a guiding hypothesis that helps determine which observations to conduct. A hypothesis is derived from reasoned thought about the subject at hand. Observations can then be conducted to confirm the hypothesis.

THE RATIONAL METHOD

The rational method involves using observations combined with logical argument to arrive at a certain conclusion. The first step is to establish premises. If these are true, and the conclusion follows logically from these premises, then the conclusion is certain. The premises of a logical argument are assumed to be true. The classic example of a logical syllogism is this:

> All men are mortal.
> Socrates is a man.
> Therefore, Socrates is mortal.

Introspection

Because logical argument or reason is necessarily conducted in the mind, an examination or observation of one's own knowledge is conducted to determine correct premises. Thus, in a rational argument, introspection is considered a form of observation. In the same way that sight provides information about the external world, introspection provides information about the internal world. One of the problems with relying on introspection as a research tool is that each person's introspection is likely to lead to different observations, making unifying generalizations difficult to reach.

Weaknesses in Human Reason

Like empiricists who are aware that sensory experience of objective reality is altered by human perceptual processes, rationalists are aware that humans commit systematic kinds of errors in reasoning. To help standardize the knowledge gathered from introspection, Descartes proposes four rules to control for these weaknesses in reason and thus attain certainty.

1. Whatever is concluded as certain must be so clearly true and so logically sound as to allow for no reason for doubt.
2. A problem should first be divided into the smallest possible units before attempts are made to solve it.
3. These smallest possible units should then be ordered from the simplest to the most complex.
4. Although these units describe the problem completely, they only describe specifics, but the conclusions drawn should be general.

According to Descartes, if these rules are followed in each analysis, illogical conclusions may be avoided and certain knowledge may be achieved.

✓ **Stop and think.**
Can you think of anything that is so clearly true and so logically sound as to allow for no doubt?

The Rational Process

Begin in Doubt

Both empiricists and rationalists agree that if true knowledge is desired, all assumptions and previously learned beliefs must be cleared from the mind. Each premise must then be examined carefully before it is accepted to determine if it can, in any way, be doubted. For example, Descartes begins by examining everything that he believes to be true and can find almost no belief that cannot be doubted. Can he doubt that God exists? Yes, this devout Catholic concludes, this is a belief that can be doubted. Can he doubt that he himself exists? Yes, he concludes, he can certainly doubt that his body exists. He can doubt that his sensory organs and the information they provide are real. All of this may simply be an illusion.

Resolve Doubt

In Descartes' analysis, there are some beliefs that are so clearly true and logically sound that there is no reason to doubt them. Descartes considers beliefs of this nature to be innate. To build a body of knowledge, one must begin with these innate truths. Even if Descartes can doubt that all of his actions, experiences, and even his body are real, he cannot doubt that he is doubting. Therefore, he must exist, if only as a doubter. This is both clearly true, and it is also logically sound. Because doubting is a form of thinking, Descartes concludes that because he is thinking, he must exist, if only as a thinker—cogito ergo sum in Latin.

Build a Logical Sequence

Once established as true, premises may then be used to construct a logical sequence of argument that leads to further truths. For example, having concluded that he exists as a thinker, Descartes goes on to argue that the existence of God may be established through logical argument as well. According to Descartes' logic, the fact that humans are able to conceive of a God who is omnipotent, even though omnipotence is not a part of the human experience, is evidence that an omnipotent God must exist. How else would humans have conceived the concept of omnipotence? In this way, logical arguments are constructed with conclusions that may, or may not, be tested by observation.

Conduct Observations to Confirm

For rationalists, whereas observations are used to help establish premises, the proper place of observations and experiments is to confirm conclusions arrived at through logical argument. Thus, rationalists suggest that conclusions reached through reason and supported by observations are superior to conclusions reached only through observations inductively tied together into reasonable generalizations.

RATIONAL CONCLUSIONS

By establishing the existence of mind, Descartes has defined and proven the existence of an aspect of the human that is distinct from the body. No one can doubt the existence of human reason and thought. No matter what observations empiricists may make about the physical human body, human reason still transcends nature. Furthermore, because only humans think about their own thoughts, only humans possess this immaterial and transcendent aspect. According to Descartes, other animals may think, but they do not think about their own thoughts, and therefore they do not possess souls. Souls in the form of minds live on after the material body dies and will be rewarded or punished in the afterlife. Thus, the Church's power to provide salvation is maintained. In this way, Descartes' philosophy supports and preserves the authority of the Church.

Trust Sensory Information

Echoing Aquinas but using logical deduction to arrive at the same conclusion, Descartes argues that because God exists, is perfect, and would not deceive us, sensory experiences can usually be trusted. Even so, sensory experiences must be clearly represented in consciousness to be considered certain, and any discrepancy between sensory experience and rational explanation should be resolved in favor of reason.

Innate Ideas

Descartes goes on to conclude that there are other ideas that are also innate. For example, although there is no place in the material world where there is perfect unity, the mind can conceive of unity; therefore, the ability to think about unity must not derive from sensory experiences in this material world but must be innate. Similarly, ideas of infinity and mathematical concepts like those used in geometry must also be innate. Descartes is not concerned with providing evidence that these ideas are innate; his argument is that they are so clearly true and so logically sound as to allow for no reason for doubt (Descartes, 1641/1986).

Mechanism

Mechanical devices are becoming an important part of the landscape in 17th-century Europe as time-keeping devices, as labor-saving machinery, and even as entertainment. For example, Descartes is fascinated with the mechanical moving statues of gods and goddesses in the grottoes under the Royal Gardens at Saint-Germain. It is even rumored that he names his daughter Francine after the Francini brothers who construct the statues in 1634 (Gaukroger, 1995). The statues are operated hydraulically by pressure plates buried just below the surface in the pathways. Stepping on the plates causes water to flow through hidden pipes and turns on the mechanical figurines as one walks through the garden. Like others in this era, Descartes sees many parallels between mechanical systems and living bodies.

Nerve Transmission

Descartes proposes a theory of nerve transmission in living beings that works much the same way as the mechanical figures in the garden (Gross, 1998). Hollow nerves carry "animal spirits" to structures in the brain where the spirits are transferred to response circuits, triggering muscular responses. All of this can occur in the complete absence of conscious thought. In this way, behavior is mechanical, and the body can be thought of as an "earthen machine."

Human Soul

Human nervous and muscular systems function much like those of other animals. It is the human soul that allows for thinking about experiences and behaviors. So although animals behave the way their machines are built to function, the soul allows humans to reason about and choose behavior. Because the soul is nonmaterial, it does not exist in space as a multidimensional object. Descartes argues that it must be something like a single point.

✓ **Stop and think.**
How could something nonmaterial, like a thought, get translated into something material, like a body behaving?

Arguing that the human soul causes human behavior requires an explanation about how exactly this nonmaterial soul could cause a material body to act. This is the **mind–body problem** and a question that confounds both philosophers and physiologists. Descartes proposes a solution. He decides that the translation from thought to action occurs inside the brain and that there must be a structure in the brain responsible for this function. This structure would serve as the receiving station for the thought from the nonmaterial soul and would then translate the thought into action in the material body. It would also receive sensory information from the body, change that into a nonmaterial form, and then transmit it to the soul for use in choosing a response.

Descartes reasons that this structure would be present in the human brain but not in other animals. Because human sensory systems generally provide two impressions of experience (two eyes, two ears, etc.), but thoughts are only one impression, there should only be one structure in the brain where this translation occurs. He then conducts dissections on a variety of animals, including on human brains obtained from autopsies. He observes that only humans have a pineal gland and finds only one pineal gland in human brains. As a result of his observations, he identifies the pineal gland as the organ where the nonmaterial soul communicates with the material body.

Descartes is wrong, of course, on a number of counts. For example, nonhuman animals do possess pineal glands. This is an instance where Descartes' rationalism might have benefited from some additional empirical observation. *The question about how the actions of the material body are translated into the thoughts of the nonmaterial soul remains with us today.*

THE CONSEQUENCES OF RATIONALISM

Descartes' philosophical rationalism has a number of important consequences for the history of science and psychology. One of the most important is the idea that the truth about psychological matters may not need to be observable or measurable if it can be established rationally. In fact, to the degree that the study of psychology is the study of a nonmaterial and thinking soul, certain truth about psychology may only be accessible through rationalism according to Descartes.

From this point forward, the term *mind* is considered more appropriate than the term *soul* when discussing psychological questions:

> Thus because probably men in the earliest times did not distinguish in us that principle in virtue of which we are nourished, grow, and perform all those operations which are common to us with the brutes apart from any thought, . . . they called both by the single name soul. But I, perceiving that the principle by which we are nourished is wholly distinct from that by means of which we think, have declared that the name soul when used for both is equivocal; and I say that, when soul is taken to mean the primary actuality or chief essence of man, it must be understood to apply only to that principle by which we think, and I have called it by the name mind as often as possible in order to avoid ambiguity; for I consider the mind as not as part of the soul but as the whole of the soul which thinks. (Descartes, 1641, as cited in Watson, 1979, p. 13)

Even the mind, however, still lies outside the realm of the empirically observable and measurable. In this era, the study of human experience, including human perceptions, thoughts, and feelings, remains firmly rooted in philosophical speculation.

Although rationalism as articulated by Descartes is not incompatible with empiricism, observations and experience play entirely different roles in each of these approaches. Philosophers of science today still argue over whether the practice of science lives up to its Baconian ideal of fact-gathering observations unbiased by hypothesized expectations or whether rationally derived hypotheses are not just commonly used but are even necessary to help define the scope of observations undertaken (Kuhn, 1970; Popper, 1968). Even though new students of science are often taught that science begins in unbiased wonder, rarely do scientists conduct observations without expectations, usually worded as hypotheses, about what will be observed and found.

In the West, both empiricism and rationalism take their places on the intellectual stage only about 400 years before the present day. This is not much time in terms of intellectual development. Thus, the models of psychology that emerge in the 17th century are familiar to us in the present day. For example, the origin of more modern studies of stimulus–response relationships lie in Descartes' conception of "earthen machines," sensing and responding to the environment without conscious intervention.

Even more striking is Descartes' assertion that the human is dualistic. The human body is physical and part of nature, but human thought is metaphysical and so is not part of nature. This assumption of duality is referred to in following centuries as Cartesian science. Furthermore, the study of the body should be left to those who study nature, and the study of the mind should be a different discipline altogether. The latter assumption justifies the discipline of psychology. It also returns the nonmeasurable secondary qualities to a legitimate place in science, at least for a while. Descartes claims that he has defined a science of the study of secondary qualities. That science of the secondary qualities eventually becomes psychology.

A CASE STUDY:
THE ENLIGHTENED MIND AND 300 YEARS OF WITCH PERSECUTION

Magic, Science, and Religion

From its earliest origins, science is inextricably bound up with religion and magic (Dampier, 1948). Because humans are predisposed to making superstitious assumptions, beliefs in supernatural powers are common. From a time before history, some have earned a living by promising to invoke the supernatural powers in our behalf. Healers combine a carefully acquired knowledge of the medicinal effects of plants with incantations designed to activate and exploit human biases in reasoning, often achieve dramatic results, and occasionally even effect cures. Soothsayers invoke supernatural powers and foretell the future, maintaining their credibility by taking advantage of all-too-common human misunderstandings about the laws of probability.

Magic

Concepts of good magic and evil magic, or the ability of humans to call on the powers of the supernatural, have been present in Western thought since at least

Roman times. Good magic has beneficial effects, such as a cure from disease, an abundant crop, or a healthy live birth. Evil magic has evil consequences, and in Roman law, damage done through the use of evil magic is as prosecutable as is damage that is done through a physical act. All magic, both good and evil, is achieved through supernatural intervention.

By the 15th and 16th centuries, a distinction is made between natural magic and supernatural magic. Supernatural magic enlists supernatural powers to achieve its ends, but there is also a kind of natural magic that is embodied in the properties of nature. Magnetism, for example, is thought of as a magical power that allows some stones to effect movement in certain other objects and is thus a form of natural magic. Natural magic invokes only powers in nature. In this era, however, most people still believe that all magic, supernatural or natural, requires the intervention of deities or demons, and most people are thus very distrustful of the new study of the powers in nature.

Demons

Widespread beliefs in the daily presence and activity of good and evil supernatural powers, including Christian saints, forest spirits, and mischievous demons of all kinds, add to the confusion among magic, religion, and science. Christian beliefs in an evil supernatural power stem originally from Jewish tales of evil deities, and those have their origins in even more ancient Near Eastern supernatural powers of fertility and death. When Europe comes into contact with Eastern Christianity in the 12th century, these beliefs in a powerful supernatural deity of evil, second only to God in its ability to intervene in the lives of humans, become an important component of Western Christian thought. After the fall of Constantinople in 1453, when Western Christianity comes into contact with Eastern Christianity, beliefs in demons and the devil blossom in a Western world ripe for these ideas.

Irrational Thought Reigns

There are some circumstances that seem most likely to call forth human tendencies to accept, use, and promote irrational thinking. Among these are unstable economic, political, or religious times. The 16th through the 18th centuries in the West see instability in all of these areas. Serfs who have survived for generations by farming move off the land and into cities, the feudal order disintegrates, secular political structures threaten the authority of the Church, and the Church is torn by reform and revolution from within. Beliefs in how best to live, in the rewards to be received in a heavenly afterlife, and in the Church's power to deliver that salvation, are shaken.

Moreover, rational, critical thought does not seem to come naturally to humans, even in the best of times. As belief in the power of evil grows in the West during these centuries, superstitious beliefs abound. Illnesses, crop failures, and all sorts of calamities are thought to be the work of evil demons. Arguments between friends, marital incompatibility, and lust are caused by demons jealous of human relationships. Epileptic fits, delusions, and especially behaviors today associated with mental illness are considered evidence of demonic possession. Furthermore, demonic possession is believed to be caused by sinful behavior. If human behavior is caused by human thought, and human thought derives from the soul, it is not such a leap to believe that deviant behavior is caused by a soul that has gone astray. These wandering souls have joined forces with the devil. They have become demons or witches, and they have the ability to call forth other demons to do their bidding. Like the good supernatural powers, these evil demons may also take on human or animal form (Ginzburg, 1985).

Of course, not all of the enthusiasm for the witch persecutions during this era comes from irrational beliefs. Because anyone may accuse anyone else of demonic possession, many accusations are motivated by personal, economic, political, and especially religious ends. Those accused as religious heretics by the Church are among those most likely to be executed as witches. No one is much concerned that innocent and pious individuals may be falsely accused, because everyone knows that God protects the innocent and would not let them be accused. Property belonging to convicted witches is claimed by the accusers, political enemies can be deposed simply by accusing them of witchery, interpersonal animosities are permanently resolved, and religious authority is strengthened. As men move into practicing the art of medicine, women serving as midwives become targets of the accusation of witchcraft (Clark, 1997). Once accused, denying that one is a witch is used as evidence to substantiate the charge. Admitting that one is indeed possessed does not help either, as that will only hasten one's trip to the stake, although when asked to name co-conspirators, at least one doomed but resourceful confessor names all of the court officials as agents of the devil (Russell, 1980).

Pope Innocent VIII authorizes two Dominican monks to serve as inquisitors in witch trials, and in 1486, they publish *The Witches' Hammer*, or *Malleus Maleficarum*, a manual about how to recognize, bring to trial, and "save" those who have willingly "abandoned themselves to devils." According to this widely read and very influential book, demons may manipulate the thoughts of innocent humans and cause them to act in evil ways. Demons may cause infertility, impotence, loss of sensory or motor abilities, mental confusion, insomnia, sleepwalking, or sudden death. Therefore, any form of emotional or psychological disturbance is taken as evidence of consorting with demons. Acting as agents of the devil, witches and their animal companions can cause evil by a malevolent stare or even a sideways glance.

In descriptions that sound remarkably like stories of alien abductions from our own times, the transcripts of witch trials include accounts of being removed from bed, carried through walls, and whisked through the air to distant locations. They tell stories of creatures that disturb sleep by sitting on one's chest, cause nightmares of suffocation and falling, suck blood, steal children, and sexually molest and impregnate their victims.

Scientific Evidence Against Witches

If proof were ever needed that a little knowledge is a dangerous thing, one of the earliest uses of the new, empirical method is to identify and establish the guilt of those accused of witchcraft. *Among the most common false beliefs about science is that observations of nature can be used to reveal the supernatural. When people do not understand what constitutes scientific evidence, they are more likely to succumb to the irrational claims of pseudoscience.* Pseudoscience is an area of study that claims to be scientific, but produces no evidence based on the methods of science. Sixteenth-century pseudoscience takes the form of observational and experimental tests to identify those possessed by demons.

The Pricking Test

It is believed that demons enter through the skin and the area where entry has occurred will be insensitive to pricks of a pin and less likely to bleed. Those accused are thus subjected to pricking all over their bodies. If a site is found that is less sensitive than others, that is evidence that a demon has entered. Demons also hide themselves in the hair, especially pubic hair, so the bodies of the accused are shaven, eliminating these hiding places. This also reveals birthmarks, scars, moles, or warts, all of which are signs of possession.

The Weeping Test

Because witches are the agents of evil, they are not moved by accounts of the suffering of Christ on the cross or other sad stories and are thus less likely than the innocent to shed tears. It is recommended that this test be used with caution, however, as witches are sometimes able to shed false tears or to smear their faces with spittle so that they appear to be crying.

The Floating Test

For the floating test, the accused witch should be shaven, tied wrists to ankles, and then pushed to the center of a deep pool or pond by men wielding long sticks. Because the soul has weight, if she still possesses her soul, she will sink and fail to resurface, proving that she is innocent of the charges. If she continues to float when the sticks are removed, that is proof that her soul has been taken by the devil, and she should be removed from the pool and burned.

These observational tests are used to identify and convict those who have allowed the devil to enter their material bodies and take control of their spiritual souls. The execution of a witch is conducted so that the demons may be driven from her body and her soul may be saved. Officials are reluctant to sentence a witch to death, however, until she has confessed. Therefore, once she is identified, she is tortured until a confession is extracted, although about 10% of those who are killed persist "in denying their guilt to the moment of death" (Russell, 1980).

The best estimates are that as many as 750,000 people are executed for heresy or witchcraft (Thomas, 1971). The vast majority of them are women, and most are older women (Russell, 1972; Clark, 1997). They die a horrible death. They are tortured and then usually shackled to a stake and burned alive while family and former friends watch with the full approval of religious authorities. "The Comtian view that human thought has progressed from magic to religion to science is now thoroughly discredited, for the three have often been indistinguishable, and in any event varying degrees of sophistication in each have been found at all levels of society from the primitive to the modern" (Russell, 1972, p. 7).

PARADIGM FOR A NEW AGE

By the end of the 17th century, the practice of science is transforming the land-scape of Western intellectual thought. As has been true in the past, this change in epistemology is triggered by skepticism. Seventeenth-century Western skepticism is based on the rejection of Scholastic epistemology. For more than 200 years, skeptical voices have grown stronger and asked more disturbing questions.

This latest wave of skepticism is profoundly different from those that have gone before. Instead of a **nihilistic** tearing down of belief systems, this new skepticism challenges thinkers to construct a new belief system. This new way of knowing will be one that everyone can understand and help build, one that reflects personal and immediate experiences, and one that genuinely helps humans to cope with the awesome powers of the natural world. The new skepticism is directed not at asserting certain truth, but at embracing doubt as an integral part of its new way of knowing.*This new way of coming to believe is referred to by present-day philosopher Thomas Kuhn as the scientific paradigm (Kuhn, 1970).*

The Scientific Paradigm

According to Kuhn, a paradigm is a shared worldview or way of looking at and understanding a body of knowledge. A paradigm is a global theoretical framework through which to view and experience the physical or social environment. Part of the purpose of a paradigm is to facilitate interactions and communication among individuals in the group. Paradigms begin with a set of shared assumptions that suggest both specific questions and a definition of the methods to be used in the search for answers.

The Assumptions of a Paradigm

By definition, assumptions are never tested. Thus, it might be reasonable to suppose that before adopting assumptions on which to found a paradigm, great care would be taken to assure their truth, but often this is not the case. The shared assumptions that found paradigms are very often the sort of "truths" arrived at intuitively. They can be simple, cause-and-effect explanations that feature personal experiences and are compatible with existing beliefs. For example, the Scholastic paradigm began with the assumption that this planet and everything on it was created for the occupation and use of humans by a supernatural entity called God.

The Questions of a Paradigm

The shared assumptions of a paradigm also give rise to a set of questions to be explored. Thus, the questions explored within a paradigm are not all of the possible questions, but only those that make sense to explore within the context of the assumptions. For example, Scholastic questions were ones about how God may be known, what human duties to God are, what sin is, what will is, and if the soul is transcendent. Scholastics did not ask about the relationship between humans and animals because their assumption was that everything in the world had been provided by God for the use of humans.

The Methods of a Paradigm

The assumptions also suggest the methods used to find answers. It is through the use of common methods that interaction and communication is made possible. To return to Scholastics as our example, if the spiritual realm is the only one that really exists, and the most important question is to know God, then the way to find the answer is to seek divine revelation. Reading and discussing the wisdom that has been revealed to others and that has been received in the form of Scriptures, the writings of Classical philosophers, and the revelations of early Church Fathers, are also acceptable methods by which to know God.

The Strengths and Weakness of Paradigms

Paradigms facilitate the search for knowledge by defining the boundaries of what is already known, specifying the questions to be explored, and establishing the ground rules for conducting the search. Without first setting these parameters, no collective and cooperative search for knowledge could be conducted.

On the other hand, paradigms necessarily limit the worldview. As indicated earlier, questions that lie outside the boundaries of the assumptions are not explored, and potentially illuminating methods based on different sets of assumptions are not utilized. Finally, the assumptions on which paradigms are founded are never tested. If the assumptions are not true, then the entire enterprise is wasted. Because each person is immersed in the paradigms of their own time and culture, entire lifetimes may be spent convinced of a false set of beliefs.

✓ Stop and think.
How can paradigms be changed?

Why and How Paradigms Change

*Paradigms do change, although change is usually a very slow and potentially uncomfortable process. Paradigms change when the truth of the founding assumptions is repeatedly and credibly challenged. It is only when there is strong and undeniable evidence that the assumptions are almost certainly false that a paradigm begins to change. The evidence that an assumption is false arises not from tests of that assumption, because assumptions are not tested, but instead from what are called anomalies. An **anomaly** is a piece of evidence that violates one or more of the assumptions of the paradigm. For example, 16th-century Christian Church doctrine asserted that God has placed Earth at the center of the universe. However, astronomers of this period realized that their observations were inconsistent with this assumption of geocentricity, that the Earth was at the center. Instead, their observations were more consistent with heliocentricity. These observations were anomalies; they violated the assumptions of the Scholastic paradigm. Most of the time, the individuals who uncover and point out anomalies are ignored or discredited. But if the anomaly appears again and again, as did these astronomical observations, they become more difficult to ignore.*

More than 100 years after these 17th-century observations are made, and after repeated observations by many astronomers, the authority of the Church is successfully challenged with regard to this issue. The real significance of this anomaly, of course, is that it throws into doubt all of the assertions contained within Church doctrine. If the Church Fathers are wrong about this founding assumption of the medieval paradigm that places humans at the center of God's creation, what else might they be wrong about? How is it possible that Church Fathers could interpret the Holy Scriptures so incorrectly? Is the Bible to be interpreted only metaphorically and not literally? How is one to know what to think if one cannot trust Church authorities?

The Principles of Newtonian Science

From about 1680 onward, much of the credit for advancement in understanding the laws that govern the physical universe is given to the English physicist, mathematician, and alchemist, Isaac Newton (1642–1727). And because from that time until recently most of science is conducted using the principles of discovery articulated by Newton, for the next 2 centuries, Western science is called Newtonian science.
The principles of Newtonian science begin with an assumption that, although God created the universe, He does not actively intervene to influence events in the universe. Therefore, natural causes must be found to explain events in the universe. The will of God should not be used as an explanation for natural events no matter how implausible a natural cause may seem. According to Newton, the following five assumptions should be made when conducting science:

1. The physical universe is governed by natural laws, so all explanations for events in the physical universe must be based on these laws and nothing else.

2. There are four basic components of natural laws, and everything in the physical universe can be explained in terms of these four components:
   (a) matter, existing at a point in space and having mass;
   (b) absolute space, consisting of immovable points;
   (c) absolute time, consisting of moments that flow equably without regard to anything else; and
   (d) motion, which is caused by force.

The explanations that science offers for any event in the physical universe must be stated in terms of interactions among these four components of natural law.

3. No teleological explanations may be offered. That is, there is to be no assumption of purpose in the laws of nature.
4. Scientific explanations should use as few assumptions as possible to explain events in the physical universe. Only those causes that are necessary and sufficient should be accepted, removing all philosophic and religious dogma and all unnecessary assumptions from the practice of science.
5. Humans must always recognize that, although the laws of nature are absolute across all time and space, human understanding of those laws is incomplete. Humanly generated scientific knowledge is, therefore, always provisional and open to further correction. This is because of human ignorance, not because of any variability in the laws of nature.

THE GOALS OF SCIENTIFIC STUDY

Validity. This new epistemology should yield knowledge about nature that is free from bias. The solutions to nature's mysteries are not to be found down blind alleys of prejudice that lead to confusion, destruction, and death at the hand of the awesome forces of nature. Scientific findings are to be objective and not tainted by any of Francis Bacon's idols of false knowledge. That is, scientific findings will not be biased by cultural or religious assumptions, the unfounded opinions of authorities, or political motives. Scientific findings should not be subject to linguistic confusion, rhetorical tricks, personal prejudices, or emotional reactions. By engaging in direct observations of natural phenomena, and then organizing those observations using logic, scientists hope to come as close to true knowledge about nature as is possible for humans.

Reliability. By sharing scientific methods and findings, others will be able to conduct their own observations of similar phenomena and thus establish the reliability of the findings. Establishing reliability allows the generalizing of findings to similar situations.

Public results. Findings are shared in public meetings and by publishing in scholarly journals. As early as 1560 in Italy, then spreading throughout Western Europe, small groups of men meet informally to discuss their observations of nature. In 1660, the Royal Society of London for the Promotion of Natural Knowledge is founded, and chartered by Charles II in 1662. The Royal Society begins publishing *Philosophical Transactions* in 1665 to share the findings of its members. Across Western Europe, scientific societies organize and begin publishing journals. Although women are often active participants in collecting and analyzing data, financing scientific studies, and writing up the results of scientific observations, they are not permitted to join or be present at the meetings of these new scientific societies.

Practical results. Although not a primary goal of the new empirical science, it is hoped that a greater understanding of nature will allow humans to be less subject to its negative effects. Even the most pious and devout die in plagues, along with the wicked, raising doubt that spiritual causes are to blame for illness. Even in cities and towns where none of the usual scapegoats are found—no Jews, no gypsies, and few witches—plagues still take their toll. Eventually, the practice of systematically collecting empirical observations begins to reveal patterns that are useful in helping to understand the true cause of disease, not so much so that humans can control nature, but so that its devastating effects may be avoided. Important and helpful discoveries are made in physics, chemistry, medicine, biology, and botany.

THE MODERN SCIENTIFIC PARADIGM

The scientific paradigm of the 19th and 20th centuries owes its allegiance to these 16th- and 17th-century beginnings. From the assumptions that found the paradigm to its skeptical methods, present-day science is Bacon's new way of knowing, Descartes' rationalism, and Newton's science.

Scientific Assumptions

*Like all paradigms, the new epistemology is founded on assumptions. Besides assuming that sensory experiences are valid and trustworthy, the scientific paradigm also assumes that everything in the physical universe is made of matter, a belief labeled **materialism** by 19th-century philosophers. Furthermore, because the physical universe is made of matter, all events in the physical universe must be caused or determined by matter acting on matter.*

Materialism

Assuming that everything in the physical universe is made of matter leaves the spiritual aspects of the universe intact and permits scientific inquiry without calling into question religious belief systems. Separating the spiritual from the material creates a division between religion and natural philosophy that allows for the pursuit of knowledge into the laws that govern the physical universe. Assuming materialism allows for the study of these laws through observation and measurement. After more than 1,000 years of religious doctrines against the study of nature, by 1700, the beliefs of Greek physicists like Thales and Democritus returned. Natural philosophers began again trying to identify the matter that makes up the physical universe.

Determinism

A second assumption of science is that all events in the physical universe are determined by matter acting on matter according to rational laws. According to 18th-century philosophers, God is rational, and because humans were created in His image, humans are also rational. The physical universe is thus designed and governed according to rational principles, and humans are capable of understanding the laws that govern nature using their God-given rational minds and sensory systems.

The laws of nature dictate its design and function in the same way that mechanical principles determine the functioning of machines. In 1628, William Harvey published his findings that the blood in living bodies does not ebb and flow the way the ocean tides do, as was previously thought, but instead circulates throughout the system, pumped by the heart, which operates in the same way as a mechanical pump. Determinism is the assumption that everything that happens in the physical universe is determined by these kinds of mechanistic natural laws. Assuming that matter acts on matter in ways determined by the laws of nature eliminates spiritual causes from the physical universe. That is, those who employ the new empirical epistemology in the study of nature no longer accept explanations that rely on unseen or immeasurable supernatural forces. Rocks do not fall to the ground when dropped because they feel companionship with the earth and wish to rejoin it, as Aristotle suggested. Instead, there is assumed to be some observable and measurable force that causes rocks to fall when dropped. The task of the new way of knowing was to find that natural cause.

Scientific Questions

Assuming that the physical universe is made of matter means that there is nothing in the physical universe that cannot be observed and potentially understood by humans. Thus, this new epistemology could be used to study everything in nature. In contrast, assuming that knowledge can only be acquired through trust creates an epistemological dead end. Beyond agreeing that spiritual forces work in mysterious ways, humans can know nothing more about them. But assuming that humans are capable of experiencing and understanding all of nature removes the shackles of supernaturalism. The 18th century explodes with new scientific knowledge.

Nature is no less mysterious than it ever was, but it is a mystery that all are able to experience and invited to explore and help solve.

Scientific Methods

The methods for conducting empirical research are determined by the assumptions of the scientific paradigm. Scientists seek to understand the physical universe by observing and experiencing nature. These observations are conducted systematically, are measured rather than merely described, and are shared in such a way that invites scrutiny and skepticism. By conducting systematic and measured observations, nature will be understood as it really is and not as human minds perceive it or wish it to be.

At all stages in the scientific endeavor, the spirit of skepticism is kept alive. No finding is ever considered proof of anything, as nature is always open to further investigation. Instead, the findings of science are stated in terms of probability, so that there is always room for further study. In this way, coming to believe through the methods of science is profoundly different than coming to believe through trust or logical argument.

⊕ The Times

The 16th-century Reformation of the Roman Catholic Church leads to a century of religious wars in Europe. The Thirty Years' War, pitting one faction of Christians against another, is only one of many wars that rage throughout this era. The witch craze is another measure of the power that charges of heresy have to destroy lives and even whole communities.

Poverty is the primary fact of life for most people, as war, famine, and plague continue to ravage Europe. Most people live in tiny huts with their extended family, work hard on the land year round, and eat nothing but bread and thin soups day in and day out. Toward the end of this era in Europe, feudal patterns of land ownership begin to disappear, and the wealthier classes look to other prospects for exploiting resources. Among these are settlements in the New World. These are established initially for the purpose of providing saleable resources to European markets but prove disappointing until about the mid-18th century, when it is discovered that tobacco grows well in the New World.

From the early 17th century on, the universe is increasingly viewed as mechanistic. Machines help to control nature, and even humans are thought of as biological machines governed by the sometimes discernible laws of nature. Although a part of nature, humans are also capable of understanding nature.

5

Philosophical Answers to Psychological Questions: If a Tree Falls in the Forest and There Is No One Around to Hear It, Does It Make a Sound?

This chapter explores 18th-century approaches to the questions of psychology. Because human mind is thought to transcend the physical universe, the rational and speculative methods of philosophy are used to study these questions. Various perspectives are explored, including rational, empirical, and romantic philosophies. In the meantime, progress continues in understanding the physical universe through science. By the early 19th century, the intellectual world is ready for theories of evolution based on observational evidence and the application of those theories to psychology's questions.

PHILOSOPHERS AND PHILOSOPHIES OF THE HUMAN

During the 18th century, attempts to understand human thoughts, feelings, behaviors, and relationships with others are not made by scientists, but by philosophers, artists, poets, and novelists. Until well into the 19th century, no empirical methods for the study of human mind are developed. Therefore, philosophy is the main method that is used to answer psychological questions, rather than science.

Some philosophers emphasize the role of experience in shaping knowledge, motivation, and relationships. Others suggest that psychological characteristics are a result of rational thought and the desire to achieve goals. Regardless of

118

whether a philosopher assumes that behavior is motivated more by past experience or by rational thought, the philosophical method is speculation. Speculations are then supported with logical argument and casual observations. These are the only methods available to philosophers of psychology in these centuries. Several of the philosophers discussed in the next section are acquainted with one another, and most read the written works of the others. They are the intellectual and educated elite of their time; their writings and ideas are influential among their peers and have remained so to the present day.

The Women

Before going further, it should be noted that, although a few individual fathers permit their daughters to be educated in the privacy of their homes, women are not admitted into any major institutions of higher education in Europe or North America until about 1850. A few intellectuals argue that women should be educated. For example, Mary Wollstonecraft (1759–1797), a British author best known for her book *A Vindication of the Rights of Woman* (1792), says that women should be given access to higher education, but only for the purpose of making them into better mothers.

Some women participate in philosophical and intellectual discussions, but male publishers will not print their writings, and women's influence is thus not felt outside their own circles (Bridenthal, Koonz, & Stuard, 1987; Cooney, 1996). As a result, the work explored here will only be that of a few men who influenced psychological thought among the intellectual elite in this era. *Before beginning, let's reacquaint ourselves with the questions of psychology:*

Why do other people behave the way they do?
How can I get other people to do what I want them to do?
How much of what happens to me can I control?
Can I be happier, and, if so, how?
What is the best way to live?

The Selfish Motive

...and which is worst of all, continual fear and danger of violent death; and the life of man, solitary, poor, nasty, brutish, and short.

(Hobbes, 1651/1958, p. 107)

Born prematurely along the southern cliffs of England amidst the confusion of the Spanish war against England, Thomas Hobbes (1588–1679) develops one of the most cynical philosophies of human nature. He believes that humans are each driven by a constant fear of violence at the hands of others and by the desire to get what is needed to survive. People spend their lives gathering as many resources as possible and arming themselves against the attacks of others, always fearing that others have more resources and more effective weapons. So for Hobbes, humans, like other animals, are motivated by two basic emotions, fear and desire; are concerned first with their own survival; and are willing to take from others without regard for the needs of the others. Thus, people always behave the way they do out of self-interest, and all people are driven by these same motives.

Hobbes bases his beliefs partly on his own experience of fearfulness. He readily admits to a great many fears, including an almost overwhelming fear of the dark. Given that humans are predisposed to see evidence that supports what they already believe to be true, it is not surprising that the very fearful Hobbes develops a philosophy that assumes selfish and fearful motives and then sees ample evidence to support his beliefs.

Government is the only way to prevent humans from living in a constant state of violence, according to Hobbes. To reduce their own fear and to prevent a cycle of increasing interpersonal violence, people join together in a social contract to form a government. Hobbes decides that an absolute monarchy, meaning the rule of an all-powerful king, is the proper form of government. If people live in awe of, and under the rules of, a monarch, and if institutions of government are established to enforce social rules, only then, Hobbes believes, can humans live together and work productively.

Hobbes' writings represent one of the earliest articulations of a belief that has become foundational in modern Western cultures: that of the motivating power of self-interest. After Hobbes, it is common for political and psychological thought in the West to be based on this belief that humans behave almost exclusively out of self-interest. Although it is possible to construe much of human behavior as motivated by self-interest, there is little empirical support and much evidence that does not support this belief (Miller, 1999; Wallach & Wallach, 1983).

A contemporary of both Francis Bacon and Galileo, Hobbes attempts to bring a materialist philosophy to the study of the human. In the same way that Galileo studies the material in the skies, Hobbes advocates for the study of the material that drives human thoughts, feelings, and behaviors. He regards emotions as resulting from the movement of matter, the motion in some internal substance in the head, which either helps or hinders the achievement of some desired goal. Thus, humans are motivated by the desire to seek pleasure and avoid pain caused by the motion of a material substance in the head. Like Descartes, Hobbes views human psychology in mechanical terms, so that human thoughts, feelings, and behaviors are seen as a result of the laws of nature applied to the material, biological, human machine.

Also like Descartes, Hobbes speculates about how objects and events in the world are transformed into perceptions and thoughts. He concludes that it is the motion of matter that causes perceptions. External objects cause the motion of matter in the eyes, which in turn causes the motion of matter in the brain. It is thus motion that causes thoughts. Furthermore, the motion of some matter in one part of the brain may cause the motion of nearby matter, thus causing thoughts about related objects or events (Herbert, 1989).

Because of these speculations, Hobbes is identified as an early **associationist**, or believer that knowledge about the world is acquired by associating new information with previously experienced objects and events. Hobbes' philosophy is based partly on a few structured observations he conducts to establish an empirical basis for his ideas. Thus, Hobbes provides a philosophy that justifies later empirical measures of psychological phenomena.

The Blank Slate

John Locke (1632–1704) is an English philosopher and medical doctor who earns his degrees at Oxford University. He bases his philosophical speculations on the assumption that humans begin life as blank slates, or in Latin, **tabula rasa**. According to Locke, humans are born with a variety of faculties or mental abilities but without the knowledge of ideas or facts. This is a radical departure from earlier Scholastic assumptions that humans have innate knowledge, for example, of the difference between right and wrong. This is also a departure from Cartesian rationalism and the assumption that the mind is innately stocked with a wealth of ideas. As evidence in support of his principle of the blank slate, Locke offers observations of young children and those he calls idiots, pointing out that if humans are born with any ideas, then those ideas should be known by everyone, including children. But if children, who have not yet learned, or idiots, who do not have the ability to learn, do not know these ideas, then, Locke says, that is evidence that these ideas must be learned. Observations of children make it clear that they often do not have the kinds of ideas that Cartesians insist are innate. Therefore, the evidence proves that Cartesian rationalism is wrong, according to Locke's observations.

Experience

According to Locke, experience forms the basis of most ideas, and experience has two sources. The first is sensory experience of the physical world. The second is reflection, or the operations of the mind as experience is thought about and sensations are associated together. Thus, humans begin with a blank slate and then learn by sensing the physical world and thinking about and associating sensory experiences. Locke recognizes that there are natural abilities and biases that are sometimes difficult to overcome but maintains that education and experience shape character (Axtell, 1968).

For Locke, wrong ideas originate from incorrect associations. In the mind, two events occurring closely together in time and space become associated together. Although the simultaneous occurrence of these events may be purely coincidental, people come to think of them as causally related to one another. Because wrong ideas originate from incorrect associations, Locke believes that wrong ideas can be corrected simply by demonstrating more correct associations.

Influenced by Galileo and others of his peers, Locke distinguishes between primary and secondary qualities. Unlike Galileo, Locke suggests that both are important parts of the human experience and thus worthy of study. Locke fashions a philosophy of the human that emphasizes mechanical principles of sensory experience and the association of those experiences through reflection.

Moral Responsibility

In suggesting that nothing is known innately, Locke brings into question the basis of Western Christian morality. If individuals commit a wrongdoing, but do so only because they have not learned otherwise, then it becomes the failure of the teacher that is responsible for the wrongdoing and not the action of the uneducated individual. Thus, Locke's philosophy appears to eliminate personal responsibility. Locke's response is that if individual responsibility is decreased in his philosophy, it is only because social responsibility is increased. If the wrongdoer is less personally responsible, that is only because society is more responsible. If experience is primary in shaping individual psychology, then it is incumbent on all of us to take responsibility for the shaping of individuals' experiences.

✓ **Stop and think.**
How much responsibility should individuals bear for their behavior if they have never been taught right from wrong?

Education

Locke is concerned with the treatment, education, and training of children. Although he never marries and has no children of his own, he advises that children need a proper diet without too much sugar, lots of fresh air, plenty of sleep, and a good share of physical exercise. Most importantly, children need education and, as a society, all should take responsibility for seeing that children are properly educated. Locke emphasizes rewards and a positive and affectionate relationship between teacher and child as the most effective way for children to learn. At the same time, Locke suggests that if we expect hardy citizens, we should begin by hardening children. Children should sleep on hard surfaces, not soft beds; they should engage in rigorous physical conditioning; and crying or other emotional displays should not be tolerated (Locke, 1693/1989).

The Wild Boy of Aveyron

Early in the morning on January 8, 1800, a naked and dirty boy of about 12 years of age approaches a small village in Aveyron, a province in southern France. He appears to have lived alone in the woods for quite some time and has learned to feed himself on roots and whatever else he can find. It is likely that his family could not care for him and so abandoned him in the woods. This sounds very cruel, as of course it is, but the abandonment of children a family cannot care for has been practiced among humans since before history. Remember the story of Hansel and Gretel, abandoned in the woods by their stepmother?

News of this boy makes its way to Paris within a few days of his capture, where it comes to the attention of medical doctors and natural philosophers. They are anxious to observe the boy and study his behavior. Here is an opportunity to discover what sort of a creature a human would be if deprived of the influences of human culture—a chance to explore the differences, if any, between human animals and nonhuman animals. Most importantly for philosophers, this is a chance to explore whether moral behavior must be learned or is an innate characteristic of humans.

By this time in Western history, world travels have revealed the existence of many different types of primates, many of which bear some resemblance to humans. In fact, in Indonesia, an animal has been found that seems to be a bridge between animals and humans. Called the orangoutang (forestman), this creature walks upright, hunts like a human, and communicates with its fellows.

The wild boy of Aveyron is named Victor by the villagers and is brought to Paris. Over the course of the next several years, a young physician, Jean-Marc-Gaspard Itard, attempts to teach Victor to speak, to dress properly, and to behave as a morally upright young gentleman. But the efforts come to naught. Victor either runs or trots but never walks in a normal gait, and when he wishes to run fast, he drops to a position using his hands as well as his feet. Although he is capable of making sounds, he never learns to talk or even communicate about anything other than his immediate physical needs.

His moral education is no more successful, as described here in Dr. Itard's diary:

> I wanted to know if this child of nature would be content with his share if I put him with another person and gave them each an equal proportion of the same food—if he would respect that of his neighbor as property not belonging to him. But nothing of the sort transpired; he has no idea of property, wants everything for himself alone, because he thinks only of himself. (as cited in Lane, 1976, p. 43)

Victor does apparently experience human-like emotions. He grows sad after the death of his guardian's husband and demonstrates awareness that the man will not return by removing his place setting at the table. Eventually however, Victor's education is abandoned. He returns to the forest whenever he can escape, and a decade later, he is found in the woods again, fearful, half-wild, and still unable to speak (Lane, 1976).

Everything Is God

Born of Portuguese Jewish parents who are forced by the Spanish Inquisition to take refuge in Amsterdam, Baruch Spinoza (1632–1677) develops a rational theology and philosophy that he believes is better suited to an era of naturalistic explanations than any of the established religious faiths of the late 17th century. He begins by rejecting epistemologies based on revelation and religious doctrine. At the same time, he also warns against too much reliance on sensory information as a way of knowing truth. His personal theology and philosophy are built on arguments that he views as logical, but which offend nearly every intellectual and theologian of his time. All of Spinoza's books are placed on the Church's Index of Forbidden Books. By the end of his life, he is ostracized from his Jewish congregation and also excommunicated from the Catholic Church.

Early in his career, Spinoza is enamored of Cartesian rationalism, but he is bothered by Descartes' dualism. Why, wonders Spinoza, should there be two distinct realms, the spiritual and the worldly, the mind and the body, God and nature? Instead, he suggests, there is really just one realm. The spiritual and the worldly are two aspects of the same universe. The mind and the body are different aspects of the human. God is the same as nature.

God Is Nature

Spinoza's theology is called **pantheism**, which is the belief that God is present everywhere and at all times because everything is God. There is no division between God and nature because God is nature and God is nothing more than nature. Spinoza suggests that it is the human imagination that turns God into a human-like form and gives God human characteristics, like the need for companionship, a gender, or emotions like love and anger. Spinoza offers a new view of God for the new, empirical epistemology, arguing that now that humans are beginning to understand nature, they will no longer need to rely on ancient myths of a human-like God.

By denying that God is part of some other spiritual dimension, Spinoza must then also deny the existence of spiritual demons. In his time, the kinds of behaviors symptomatic of mental illness are commonly attributed to the will of God or to the intervention of demons. Spinoza denies the existence of supernatural gods or demons, insisting that whatever causes the distress of the mentally ill must be natural and not the result of supernatural intervention. He thus advocates for more humanitarian treatment of the mentally ill and lays the groundwork for later medical interventions in the treatment of mental illness.

Mind Is Body

Similarly, Spinoza argues that there is no mind separate from body, but they are simply two aspects of the human. A mental event may be described as a nonmaterial thought or as the action of matter in the brain, but those are simply two different ways of talking about the same event. Because there are two ways of talking about it does not make it two different events (Spinoza, 1677/1985). Thus, Spinoza eliminates the mind–body problem by denying that they are separate things. This also allows him to deny Descartes' theory of the pineal gland as the place where the spiritual mind interacts with the physical body.

✓ **Stop and think.**
What evidence exists that there are aspects of mind that transcend brain?

Spinoza's assertion that the mind or soul is actually part of the physical body has important implications for psychology. If human thought is the consequence of matter acting on matter, then the study of thought is really the study of observable and measurable matter. This makes thought a primary quality and turns psychology into a study of primary qualities. If human thought is a consequence of matter acting on matter, then it is subject to the laws of nature. The characteristics of human thought thus reside in the matter that makes up the human brain.

No Personal Immortality

If there is no spiritual realm but all is nature, then when the body dies, the matter that makes up the mind will transform into some other kind of matter, just as the body does. Thus, although the matter itself transcends death, there is no spiritual aspect of the human that lives on, and all religious promises of heavenly reward are illusion. This logical consequence of Spinoza's philosophy is profound and accounts for many of his problems with established religions. Ultimately, his denial of immortality causes his ideas to be rejected by both theologians and philosophers.

No Free Will

Equally disturbing is Spinoza's argument that all human behavior is determined by causes arising from the action of matter acting on matter. Spinoza agrees that it is very hard to identify the causes that determine behavior but insists that ignorance of the causes is no reason to conclude that human behavior must be freely willed.

What many find upsetting about Spinoza's doctrine of determinism is the elimination of a sense of personal freedom. But, Spinoza argues, what is lost is only an illusion anyway, the illusion of free will. What is gained is the real freedom that lies in coming to understand better the laws in nature that govern human thoughts, feelings, and behaviors. Having arrived at his theology through logical argument, Spinoza then goes on to advocate for observation as the way to know nature. Logic is a good way to engage in philosophy, he suggests, but logic may not be a good way to study nature because nature may not be logical.

Self-Preservation

Observation reveals that every life form seeks to preserve its own existence. Thus, Spinoza concludes, self-preservation is the master motive that determines all thoughts, feelings, and behaviors, including those of humans. That which helps in survival is good, and that which threatens survival is evil. Spinoza distinguishes between passions, which are intense feelings uncontrolled by rational thought, and emotions, which are feelings harnessed by reason. Passions reduce the possibility of survival, whereas emotions enhance survival. The greatest good, or highest pleasure, comes from a clear understanding of the laws of nature (God), and thus human survival is most enhanced by the observational study of nature embodied in the careful practice of science.

Religious Skepticism

"It is indeed an opinion strangely prevailing amongst men, that houses, mountains, rivers, and in a word all sensible objects, have an existence, natural or real, distinct from their being perceived by the understanding" (Berkeley, 1710/1920, p. 31).

Along with many of his colleagues, the philosopher and Anglican bishop George Berkeley (1685–1753) becomes concerned with what he sees as a dangerous movement toward materialism. For Berkeley, the inevitable conclusion of materialism is the loss of faith in anything spiritual, including not just human soul, but even God. Berkeley's philosophical goal is to attack materialism at its very foundation: the assertion that matter is the only reality.

Recall Locke's belief that primary qualities reside in material objects and are thus independent of perception; they exist whether or not anyone is currently perceiving them because they are properties of matter itself. Secondary qualities, on the other hand, reside in the perceiver and thus do not exist unless they are being perceived. Both primary and secondary qualities are perceived, but secondary qualities exist only in perceptions. Beginning from this materialist conclusion, Berkeley points out that even primary qualities are known only through perception. The weight, shape, or size of an object, for example, is known only as it is seen, touched, measured, and so on. What this means to Berkeley is that there is no real distinction between primary and secondary qualities. All qualities of all objects are known only through perceptions, and thus, he concludes, if perception is the basis of all reality, it is possible that objects may exist only when they are being perceived. Berkeley calls into question the material reality of anything.

Berkeley's detractors ask how it could be that when perceiving objects, humans are also able to perceive that the objects are at some certain distance away. That is, if the object itself does not really exist but is only a perception, why are those objects perceived in three dimensions, and why is space observed between the object and the perceiver? Why should depth be a quality of the perception of objects that have no material reality?

Others object that Berkeley's assertion that there is no material reality, only perception, violates all common sense—things do exist. And with this, Berkeley has no argument. Objects do exist, but they exist only because they are being perceived. Objects exist, according to Berkeley, because at all times and in all places, objects are perceived by God.

✓ Stop and think.

If a tree falls in the forest, but there is no one around to hear it, does the tree make a sound?

Nature and Mind

Scottish philosopher David Hume (1711–1776) asserts the primacy of the study of the human mind, declaring that no science can reliably precede the science of the human mind because all scientific study is conducted by and through the human mind. He is linked with the British empiricists who precede him, Hobbes, Locke, and Berkeley, because of his assertion that experience is the primary shaper of ideas. Hume believes that what can be known about the world is only what can be perceived and that, absent experience, there is no knowledge (Hume 1739–1740/1878).

Taking a materialist perspective in his philosophy, Hume points out that, like other animals, the human body is designed to be capable of perceiving those parts of the natural world that are necessary for continued survival. The knowledge that humans have through perception is the only knowledge humans can have, but that knowledge so accurately reflects what is encountered in the world that it enables humans to survive. Hume's philosophy about the natural biological bases of human behavior leads him to speculate about the possibility of conducting studies with peoples from other parts of the world and even with other animals. The goal for Hume and his contemporaries in conducting these kinds of comparative studies is to learn more about what distinguishes White European males from all other inhabitants of the planet. Their comparisons lead European philosophers of this era to conclude that they and their peers are mentally superior to all others.

Laws of Association

Hume shares the view that association is the principle by which elements of perception adhere to one another. Association results in learning and the forming of complex ideas. Hume suggests that there are three laws governing how simple elements of perception are associated together into ideas. First, he says, those perceptions that resemble or are like one another are associated together in the law of resemblance. Second, those perceptions that take place together in time and space are associated in the law of contiguity. Finally, those perceptions that occur in regular sequence are associated in the law of causality.

Causality

Hume expresses some controversial ideas about cause and effect. He suggests that the human belief that two events are related causally is only an accident of human perceptual capacities. In other words, human perceptual systems operate in such a way that when two events meet the following criteria, the belief then follows that A must cause B.

Event A and Event B occur closely together in time and/or space.

Event A precedes Event B.

Event B occurs only when preceded by Event A.

Humans come to believe that A causes B because this is a human habit, the word Hume uses to designate human biological predispositions. Causality is an idea humans get when events are associated together in this way. So the idea that one event causes the other is only an accidental and illusory relationship. Thus, Hume suggests that the idea that cause exists in the universe may be an artifact of how the human perceptual system works and not an accurate representation of what is true in the universe. Hume is not necessarily saying that cause and effect do not exist in the universe, only that the human assumption of cause and effect is a belief based on perceptions. Like all beliefs, cause is only more or less probable, based on the strength of the evidence.

✓ Stop and think.

Why do you think Hume is accused of being an atheist for suggesting that cause is only an artifact of human habits?

The Self

Hume also offers a disturbing idea about another cherished notion, that of the unified and coherent self. He asserts that the self is really only a series of perceptions. Memories of how we felt and behaved in the past are associated together, and the resulting complex idea is thought of as a self. But what is called the self is still only a complex idea built out of a series of experiences, not a real, independently existing thing.

> ✓ **Stop and think.**
> Try to describe your "self" without listing a series of perceptions, experiences, and memories.

The Passions

Hume argues that passion is the primary motivator of behavior. Human passions constitute human nature, and they are established by human physiology. Furthermore, as each individual experiences the world, some experiences become associated with pleasant feelings and some with unpleasant feelings. Those experiences that have been associated with pleasure are sought out in the future, and those that have been associated with pain or discomfort are avoided. This philosophy is referred to as **hedonism**. Hume is arguing that behavior derives from past associations with pleasure or pain. In other words, behavior derives from learning and not from the exercise of free choice. Hume is thus another philosopher who denies the existence of free will.

Appearance Is Truth

Influential as a rationalist philosopher, the Scotsman Thomas Reid (1710–1796) takes a commonsense approach to understanding reality. Unlike Berkeley, Reid asserts that physical reality exists independently of anyone's perception. Furthermore, physical reality exists in very much the same form as it is experienced in sensory perceptions. In support of this argument, Reid points out that even those who say they do not know for certain that their senses accurately reflect reality still behave as though they do. They step around posts rather than trying to walk through them, they avoid stepping in puddles, and generally they behave as though they trust the information provided by their senses. If they did not do so, if they routinely walked into posts and behaved as though they did not trust or had "lost their senses," we would declare them "mad" and lock them away, if only for their own safety.

Not only is reality accurately sensed, but Reid also suggests that the conscious experience of physical reality is not built up out of the basic elements of sensation associated together by rational thought. Instead, conscious experience is comprised of meaningful wholes perceived immediately as they are in physical reality. This is in contrast to associationistic philosophies, like those of another Scotsman, James Mill, who believes that complex ideas, like the idea of a rose for example, comes to consciousness first as perceptions of the basic elements: shapes, lines, colors, smells, and textures. Eventually, those basic elements are associated together into a perception of the whole rose. This happens only after the basic elements have appeared contiguously several times. Reid rejects this idea and says that the conscious experience of roses, and of the rest of the world, consists of meaningful wholes perceived immediately as they are in physical reality (Campbell & Skinner, 1982).

Reid points out that if perceptions of reality were built out of some basic elements of sensory experience associated into meaningful wholes through the use of reason, then most people would never perceive reality because "the greatest part of men hardly ever learn to reason" (Reid, 1785/1969).

Categories of Thought

As a professor of philosophy in Germany in the late 18th century, Immanuel Kant (1724–1804) is influential in philosophy, and many of his ideas bear directly on questions considered later by psychologists. Kant himself admits that his inquiries into psychological questions are instigated by Hume's assertion that humans only have subjective knowledge of the world based entirely on sensory impressions. For Kant, this is an unsatisfactory epistemology, and he sets out to establish for himself what it is that humans can know and how it is that they come to know.

Innate Categories of Thought

Kant asserts that knowledge of the world begins with sensory impressions, but the experiences of the senses are then organized into categories of thought by an active mind. For example, visual impressions are organized using the category of space, so that some objects are perceived as near, whereas others are perceived as far away. Time represents another category of thought. Sensory experiences are organized as having occurred at some time in the past, presently, or anticipated to occur in the future. Other categories of thought include possible or impossible events and perceptions of cause and effect. Kant considers all of these categories of thought to be innate. The human mind actively organizes sensory experiences in these ways without having learned to do so, but simply because this is the way mind works.

The Categorical Imperative and Morality

From his assertion that humans are impelled to categorize sensory experience, Kant goes on to build a system of morality. Religions encourage moral behavior by threatening punishment or promising reward. Philosophers, who believe ideas are shaped by experience, suggest that moral behavior is shaped by seeking pleasure and avoiding pain. Morality results from this hedonistic principle because all individuals should behave so as to maximize the most good for the most people.

Kant's system of morality rests instead on the idea that humans are impelled to behave morally by an innate understanding that each of us should choose behavior that we would want others to choose if they found themselves in a similar situation. Thus, although making different choices is possible, humans know innately that they should behave according to the categorical imperative, treating others as they themselves would like to be treated.

Kant goes on to acknowledge that the idea of moral responsibility is meaningless without assuming a belief in free will. He cannot prove the existence of free will, does not attempt to do so, and makes no claim that free will actually does exist. He only asserts that, for moral responsibility to have any meaning, humans must believe that they have free will. According to Kant's logic, it is enough that humans believe they are free to choose.

The Phenomena and the Noumena

Kant agrees with the empiricists that observation is the proper way to study nature. He calls those aspects of reality that are known through sensory experience the **phenomena**. The actual objects of reality he calls the **noumena**. The phenomena are our perceptions of reality, and the noumena are the actual objects of reality. Because humans can only experience nature through perception, they can never know the noumena, only the phenomena (Kant, 1781/1927).

Psychology Cannot Be a Science

In Kant's time, psychology is defined as the introspective analysis of the mind. Defined thusly, psychology could never be studied experimentally for two reasons. First, although the mind exists in time, it does not exist in space, and things that do not exist in space can never be measured. Because the basis of experimental science is the systematic observation and measurement of the physical universe, an analysis of something that cannot be measured must lie forever outside the realm of scientific study.

✓ **Stop and think.**
Where, in space, is a thought?

Second, science requires observation, and Kant argues that the mind cannot be observed introspectively because it will not stop to be examined. Even if it would, the very act of observing it introspectively changes it. Thus, philosophers are left forever to speculate about the mind. Kant does suggest that, although the why of behavior can never be studied empirically, scientists could and should attempt to study the how of behavior. Furthermore, a sort of a science of the mind might be developed by examining the products of the mind as manifested in culture. Through such study, scientists may hope someday to predict and control human behavior in the same way that they are learning to predict and control other aspects of nature.

Summary of Philosophical Speculation

A common assumption of most of these philosophical approaches to understanding the human experience is that thought is not part of the physical universe and thus cannot be studied empirically. Even John Locke, who asserts that the questions of psychology will someday be subject to the scientific method, still maintains that the mind is not made of matter.

Although there is nothing resembling a scientific psychology during the 17th and 18th centuries, clearly these philosophers are considering psychological questions. Thus, the philosophical questions that are raised in the 18th century begin to lay the foundation for the scientific study of psychology in the centuries that follow.

ROMANTIC REBELLIONS

The seeds of a cultural perspective known as **romanticism** are sown during the 18th century, in opposition to rational and empirical philosophy. Most of those engaged in the romantic movement are writers and artists, but some are also philosophers. These individuals regard intense emotion as the most important motivator of behavior and what brings meaning to human experience. Romanticism is both an outgrowth of, and a rebellion against, mechanical empiricism and cold, impersonal rationalism.

Eighteenth-century romantic philosophers oppose authority in all forms, from religious and political powers to traditional philosophical thought. They also oppose scientific empiricism, materialism, and systematic observation as the way to gain knowledge of nature. For romantic philosophers, there are true feelings hidden behind the observable and measurable, and these are what bring meaning to human experience. This mysterious realm of intense feeling is not accessible through scientific observation but through literature and art.

Literature

Throughout human history, inquiries into psychological matters are often conducted by telling stories about people's lives. Thus, the literature, theater, and art of any era represent attempts to understand the human experience. Sixteenth- and 17th-century Western literature consists of poetry and plays, much as it has since Babylonian times. The literature of this era explores the human condition by telling stories about the lives of individuals, but does not attempt to explain, either systematically or in general, why people behave the way they do: "Out, out, brief candle! Life is but a walking shadow, a poor player that struts and frets his hour upon the stage and then is heard no more" (Shakespeare, 1623/1969, p. 1133).

By the 18th century, a new form of literature, the novel, appears in the West. In writing these fictional stories, novelists teach people how to live better lives by showing them the consequences of misconduct or virtue. The novels are directed at the newly emerging middle classes and tell stories about why people think, feel, and behave the way they do; about relationships between people; and even about the nature of mind. Thus, they address psychological questions but not by conducting scientific or philosophic inquiries. Instead, literature and theater engage in a kind of folk psychology.

In the middle of the 18th century, romantic thinkers begin to influence literature with the introduction of a form called the Gothic novel. Gothic stories are set in remote and desolate surroundings, have macabre and intensely emotional themes, and tell tales about hidden and mysterious aspects of human experience. These novels reflect romantic notions that life cannot be fully understood without first recognizing the place of intense emotions in motivating behavior. Both reason and experience create a thin veneer over more basic but hidden human nature, which is rooted most deeply in fear, desire, and the wish to be thought of well. The novel *Dr. Frankenstein*, written in 1818 by Mary Shelley (who is 18 at the time she writes the story), is an example of this Gothic genre. Dr. Frankenstein steals body parts from cadavers to create an outwardly revolting creature. But the monster's hidden character is emotional, caring, and has the potential to be loving, thus illustrating the contrast that can exist between outward appearance and inward reality.

Romantic Psychologies

Romantic ideas influence the development of psychology in many ways. Ideas about hidden motivators of behavior and the importance of emotion are found in romantic philosophers' emphasis on emotions, creativity, spontaneity, and free will and are an important influence on 19th-century philosophical psychology. The philosopher Arthur Schopenhauer (1788–1860), for example, publishes *The World as Will and Idea* in 1818, in which he argues that the only reality is a universal, immaterial, and unmeasurable will to survive. Schopenhauer and other German romantic philosophers assert that emotions are not made of matter, cannot be measured, and are irrational. Thus, thoughts, feelings, and behaviors are not determined by the laws of nature but are spontaneous, so that the will is free. Some find comfort in these ideas, but others find them disturbing. If it is true that there is an immaterial will that is spontaneous, not measurable, and not bound by the laws of nature, then there are no laws that govern thoughts, feelings, and behaviors, and there can never be a science of psychology.

Some of Sigmund Freud's ideas come out of this romantic tradition, as do many ideas embodied in humanistic psychology. Romantic themes emerge again and again in psychology through the next 200 years.

SCIENTIFIC PROGRESS

By the early 19th century, science is revealing secrets of nature and leading to developments that will have profoundly beneficial effects on human life. Science is not only describing nature but also predicting and sometimes even controlling nature. Astronomers can now predict eclipses, and medical researchers are developing vaccines that prevent some illnesses. Related developments in technology are making life longer, more pleasant, and less frightening for many in the West.

The idea is growing that all of nature might be explained in terms of matter and material forces. Religious authorities still find this idea disturbing, believing that the benefits of science come at too great a cost. Materialism seems to eliminate God or at least remove God from everyday life. The growing importance and even authority of science is undermining the political, social, and economic power that has been held for centuries by religious authorities. Theories about the physical universe no longer conform to religious doctrine. The physical sciences also begin to separate themselves from philosophy and from the methods of philosophical speculation. Furthermore, the search for meaning is not a part of science. The methods of science can provide answers about how the universe works and how humans have come to be, but science must leave questions about why the universe exists and the meaning of human existence to the domains of philosophy, art, literature, and religion.

Throughout the 19th century, there are advances in understanding the laws of nature. In spite of occasional humbling mistakes, the scientific outlook is positive and optimistic. It seems as though there are no limits to the human understanding of nature if research proceeds by using the careful methods of science.

Although psychological characteristics seem inaccessible to the experimental methods of the natural sciences, that changes toward the end of the 19th century. For this reason, scientific developments in many domains, but especially physics, chemistry, and biology, have relevance for the history of psychology.

Physics and Chemistry

The physical universe is readily explained as atoms of matter. Chemistry is the study of the ways in which atoms of matter can be combined. A variety of different "elements" or kinds of atoms of matter are discovered. The modern Periodic Table of Elements begins to take shape. Philosophers have long assumed that there must be different kinds of energy. By the 19th century, physicists learn that there is only one kind of energy, and the suspicion grows that even energy might be made of atoms of matter (Dampier, 1948).

The sciences of physics and chemistry are combined early in the 19th century to build a battery that produces electricity. For the first time, scientists make a direct connection between a material substance, chemicals, and a force, magnetism, to produce another force, electricity. Along with others, German physicist, anatomist, and physiologist Hermann von Helmholtz (1821–1894) concludes that if matter is composed of atoms, then electricity must also be composed of atom-like particles. If matter can be used to produce energy, then matter and energy must, on some basic level, be very much alike.

It is established that, although matter may alter its state from a solid to a liquid to a gas, it does not change in amount. The amount of matter is conserved, and this can be shown by its weight. This is called the conservation of matter.

By 1840, it is known that energy can be converted from one type to another. The power of falling water, the heat generated by fire, or an electrical current, can all be turned into the force needed to turn gears (Cohen, 1985). Thus, in 1847, von Helmholtz gives a general account of the principle of the conservation of energy (Koenigsberger, 1965). This principle states that nature contains a fixed amount of energy, which can be transformed but not added to or subtracted from. In other words, in any closed system, energy is conserved. Energy is a measurable quantity, and in a closed system, which the universe is presumed to be, the total amount of energy remains constant.

By the 19th century, light is understood to be either particles or waves, a form of energy, and subject to the same principle of conservation as all energy. To maintain consistency in what is known at the time about physics, and because of the way that light travels in waves, it becomes necessary to postulate the existence of a rigid substance that light travels on or through. So instead of "atoms and the void," most physicists of this era agree that there must be another substance, which they call the aether. The aether is unobservable but is everywhere that space is and, except for its rigidity, behaves the way that space behaves. The theory of the aether persists throughout the 19th century and is only abandoned during the early 20th century when the laws of physics and the nature of "the void" are more fully understood.

In spite of its eventual abandonment, the theory of the aether suggests that there may be real but unobservable forces in nature that influence how observable matter behaves. From here it is no great leap to a theory that there may be real aspects of the human that, although unobservable and unmeasurable, still influence human behavior (Kantor, 1963–1969).

Relevance to Psychology

These developments in the physical sciences have direct relevance for understanding human thoughts, feelings, and behaviors. The same principles that are proving so productive in physics and chemistry may apply to the processes of the human mind as well. If, as John Locke asserts, the mind is like a blank slate at birth, how are experiences in the physical world translated into mental events and then into observable patterns of behavior? Associationists assert that our primary sensory experience of an object is of the basic elements. These basic elements are analogous to the atoms of matter in the physical universe or the elements in chemistry. Associationists hold that the basic elements of perception are bound together by laws of association, much like gravity binds atoms of matter, to form complex thoughts and patterns of behavior.

> ✓ **Stop and think.**
> Can you explain exactly how a sensory experience becomes a thought?

Biology's Connections With Psychology

Biology is the study of living organisms. Thus, throughout history, the study of human thoughts, feelings, and behaviors is inextricably bound up with biology. Through most of the 19th century, biologists, anatomists, and physiologists share several goals. Among these is the desire to understand the force that causes living things to live. These scientists also take on the philosophers' search for a metaphysical soul, or "ghost in the machine" (Ryle, 1949). The difference between philosophical searches for the soul and biological, anatomical, or physiological searches is the new method, the empirical scientific method of systematic observation and experiment.

Understanding Life

With advances in optical technology, such as the development of the microscope, comes the discovery of the basic unit of all life forms, the cell, first observed in the 17th century. From the simplest organisms observed in pond water to the most complex life forms, all are constructed from single cells. The generation and reproduction of cells results in the beginning of life, and the death of cells spells the death of organisms. Thus, the cell serves as the basic building block of life. As such, the cell becomes the biological equivalent of the atom in physics, the element in chemistry, and the basic mental element in psychology. These analogies between domains make nature seem to fit together into a simple and yet elegant pattern, and foster even greater confidence in the truth and reliability of the scientific study of nature.

Vitalism

Throughout history, the seemingly spontaneous nature of thoughts, feelings, and behaviors, as well as the very appearance of life itself, have given rise to and supported a variety of mystical assumptions about vitalistic "life forces" and "psychic energies." These forces are proposed to explain how living things differ from nonliving things. During the 17th and 18th centuries, the science of biology is established as the study of living things. By the early 19th century, the search to find and understand the vitalistic life-force has become a major goal for biologists.

> ✓ **Stop and think.**
> What is the relationship between a soul and a mind?

The Ghost in the Machine

The philosophical problem of the relationship between the mind and the body has undergone numerous transformations through the course of history. During the Classical Greek and Roman era, it was believed that rational thoughts came from a mysterious rational soul, but personality and emotions were a consequence of physiology. It was the balance of the humors that determined personality type, mood, energy level, desire for sleep, and so on. Thus, many psychological characteristics resulted from physical characteristics.

During the early Christian era in the West, the body was viewed as "mere flesh," despicable and worthless, a prison in which the soul was trapped and a burden that tempted the soul away from the divine. The mind was caught between the earthly body and the divine soul. Humans were given free will by God and could thus use the mind to choose between pursuing physical pleasures and contemplating the divine.

By the 19th century, the body is viewed as a machine that serves the soul. The mind is the part of the human that links the material body with the immaterial soul. Still, confusion remains as to how the mind mediates between the mechanical body and the divine soul. Philosophers and physiologists alike devote themselves to the study of the interactions among sensory experiences, perceptions, emotions, and behaviors.

Some of the same principles that are transforming science and the understanding of nature are reflected in other aspects of Western culture in the 19th century as well. Associationistic ideas that complex thoughts are built up out of collections of simple basic elements of perception are reflected, for example, in the 19th-century style of painting called pointillism. Pointillism is the use of tiny dots of color, associated together, to give the impression of a scene. Pointillism is illustrated by the work of Georges Seurat (1859–1891), shown in Fig. 5.1.

PHILOSOPHICAL PSYCHOLOGY

Political Science and Economics

As has been true since the time of Machiavelli, Plato, and even before, philosophers still speculate about how best to organize groups of people under political and economic systems. Their inquiries are thus closely related by topic, if not always by method, to psychology. Eighteenth- and 19th-century political theories,

FIG. 5.1. *Sunday Afternoon on the Island of La Grande Jatte*, by Georges Seurat (1886; photo courtesy of the Art Institute of Chicago).

in particular, have important influences on the early development of psychology. For example, the political and economic philosophy called **utilitarianism** grows out of the belief that humans are motivated by the desire to maximize pleasure.

The philosophers Jeremy Bentham (1748–1832), James Mill (1773–1836), and his son John Stuart Mill (1806–1873) are usually credited with developing the philosophy of politics and ethics known as utilitarianism. The general principle of utilitarianism is the belief that the rightness of any political, economic, or judicial system should be judged by the social consequences of adopting that system. The amount of human happiness or suffering generated by the adoption of a system determines its utility. In the same way that individual humans are said to be motivated to seek pleasure and avoid pain, political systems should be judged by how much good is generated for how many people.

✓ **Stop and think.**

Which economic system, capitalism or communism, might generate the greatest good for the largest number of people?

Although similar ideas have been articulated in the West at least since the time of the Epicureans in Rome, utilitarianism is proposed in the 18th century by Bentham in response to an existing judicial system that he sees as based only on intuition and retribution. In Bentham's view, wrongdoers are being sentenced based only on feelings of revulsion for the crime and the desire to seek revenge. Bentham proposes, instead, a system of justice in which punishments for certain types of crimes would be spelled out in advance and would be based on the social consequences of the criminal act. Thus, a political leader who forms an alliance with an enemy of the state would be judged more harshly than one who has a love affair while in office. Wealthy individuals who embezzle money from companies would be judged more harshly than parents who steal food to feed their children. This system of justice specifically rejects the idea that some actions are wrong independent of their consequences. *A utilitarian in the present day might argue, for example, that the private use of recreational drugs should be considered a crime only if there are negative social consequences. So whereas getting in a car and driving after the use of a drug would be a crime, the use of the drug in the privacy of one's home would not.*

✓ **Stop and think.**
Are considerations of pleasure and pain really what motivates humans to act in certain ways and not others?

Human Nature

French Naturalism

During the 18th century, a philosophy of human nature built on the work of René Descartes arises in France. Referred to as **naturalism**, this philosophy is exemplified in the writings of Julien Offray de La Mettrie (1709–1751), a physician and philosopher. French naturalism is based on the assumption that the laws of nature apply to humans just as they do in the rest of the physical world. Thus, understanding thoughts, feelings, and behaviors requires understanding the laws of nature as they apply to humans. In his book (entitled in English, *Man a Machine* (1748/1912), La Mettrie asserts that humans are just like machines. Therefore, the concept of soul is "but an empty word" used to explain the origins of thoughts, feelings, and behaviors that are not yet fully understood. In support of his contention that human behavior is mechanistic and bound by the laws of nature, La Mettrie points out that various influences on the physical body, like drugs, disease, and fatigue, can also influence thoughts and feelings. His point is that the mind must not be independent of body because if it were, no such interactions would be observed. If mind is body, then nonhuman animals also have a mind. La Mettrie suggests that apes might be taught language in the same way that deaf humans are taught to communicate and might be made into "little gentlemen" if provided with the right education.

Positivism

Positivism is the assertion that only those aspects of the universe that can be publicly observed can be known for certain. When it comes to the study of human nature, positivism is most often associated with the work of an otherwise obscure French political and social activist, Auguste Comte (1797–1857). In 1855, his six volumes of positivist philosophy are published in English. In these, he argues that science should be applied to the study of the human, but only to those aspects of the human that can be observed and measured. Thus, positivism equates the knowable with the observable. According to Comte, there are two types of statements. One type of statement refers to the objects of sense, and that is a scientific statement. Any other type of statement is nonsense. All sciences, including a science of human nature, should adhere to the method of observation. In the order of the degree to which their conclusions can be publicly observed and thus known, Comte arranges the sciences in the following hierarchy:

Mathematics
Astronomy
Physics
Chemistry
Physiology and Biology
Sociology

The last science in the hierarchy, sociology, is the science of human social nature proposed by Comte. He argues that societies can be ranked in three stages based on how people in those societies explain events in nature. The three stages are the theological stage, metaphysical stage, and scientific stage. People in societies in the theological stage believe that events in nature, such as floods, illnesses, or bountiful harvests, are caused by the intervention of supernatural beings, gods, angels, demons, and devils. A society progresses to the metaphysical stage when its people begin to believe that events in nature are caused by unseen powers or forces, like psychic energy, and are part of some cosmic teleological design or purpose. A society only progresses to the final scientific stage when its people begin to believe that events in nature are caused by the observable laws of nature. Floods are caused by warmer ocean waters, illnesses are caused by germs, and bountiful harvests are caused by adequate rain, good soil, and the right crops. Comte proposes sociology as the study of how different human societies compare in terms of the stages in which they are currently operating. This comparative sociology is as close as a positivist could ever hope to get to understanding human nature.

Psychology does not fit into Comte's hierarchy of the sciences. He is disdainful of the psychology of his era, which is the introspective study of an unseen soul. What philosophers call consciousness, Comte refers to as a collection of sensations and nothing more. He points out that, even after thousands of years of introspection, not one single fact about consciousness is known. Comte, like many others, concludes that, because science is the study of that which is publicly observable and psychology is the study of the private and unseen soul, psychology will never be a science and will thus remain forever nonsense (Comte, 1855/1974).

NATURAL HISTORY AND PSYCHOLOGY

Like psychology, other disciplines, such as geology, geography, natural history, and anthropology, begin to take shape during this era. The focus of this research is to understand nature and the place of humans in it.

Early Evolutionary Theory

Theories that life forms currently found on Earth have gradually changed from earlier forms have been around since the time of the early Greeks. These theories are based on observable evidence, such as fossils, but have little influence in Western thought until the mid-19th century. Plato and Aristotle denied the possibility of the evolution of life forms, and early Christian doctrine asserted that God had created all existing life forms in their present state. The idea that life forms had changed since the time of their creation implied to pre-19th century Christians that God's first creations had somehow been imperfect. A literal interpretation of the Biblical story of Earth's earliest days tells of a cataclysmic beginning and, once creation is complete, an unchanging Earth, even in the face of natural forces. Well into the 19th century, it is seriously argued that fossils are not evidence of now-extinct life forms but, instead, are objects hidden in the ground by God (or evil demons) to test our religious faith (Dampier, 1948).

During the 17th and 18th centuries in the West, an alternative doctrine called transformism was suggested to explain the fossil evidence. **Transformism** was the idea that life forms currently found on Earth were not created in their present form by God, but emerged from primordial matter as a result of the laws of nature and evolved slowly into those that are present today. The idea of transformism was expressed in the cosmogenic stories of many cultures throughout the world but was suppressed in the Christian West from the time of Augustine.

By the 19th century, the growing science of geology uncovers more and better fossil evidence of the prior existence of species not currently found, as well as evidence for the gradual transformation of some species from one to another. This evidence is problematic for at least two reasons. First, this fossil record provides evidence that violates Church doctrine. Second, and more importantly for scientists, this evidence requires some explanation. How could it have come to be that an animal as large as a horse, and in the form of a horse, was once a much smaller animal and a very different looking animal, although still undeniably a horse?

✓ **Stop and think.**
Imagine that you do not know anything about genes or about natural selection. Can you think of a way to explain how and why species have changed over time?

By the middle of the 19th century, the evidence is undeniable that life forms have changed over time. One explanation that is offered is the idea that characteristics that are acquired during a lifetime are somehow passed along to the offspring. Furthermore, if each individual strives to become stronger, smarter, and more skilled, and those acquired characteristics are passed on to offspring, gradually, over time, that family will become better and better. This popular theory of the inheritance of acquired characteristics is attributed to French naturalist and botanist Jean Lamarck (1744–1829) and is referred to as Larmarckian evolution. Larmarck's idea, based on the fossil record, is that the characteristics of life forms change as the characteristics needed for survival change. For example, if the sources of food on dry land disappear, but there is still plenty to eat in the water, some life forms on land will learn to swim and adapt to living in an aquatic environment. Because these organisms have learned to swim, their offspring will be born with the ability to swim. Thus, Larmarck's theory of evolution relies on the transmission of acquired characteristics.

This theory has high face validity, that is, not only does it appear to fit the available evidence, but it also seems likely to be true. However, the theory of the inheritance of acquired characteristics is labeled as blasphemous because it contradicts Church doctrine. What's more, Larmarck's theory seems to require that life forms have had eons of time in which to adapt to these changing environments. Using Scriptural references, earlier theologians had calculated that only 4,004 years had elapsed between the creation of the Earth and the birth of Jesus. In 1778, the French naturalist George-Louis LeClerc, known better as Comte de Buffon (1707–1788), used geological evidence to argue that Earth had been created about 75,000 years ago. In neither case was this enough time to explain the very gradual changes in life forms that are revealed in the fossils. It is not until 1833 that geological evidence is published establishing that the Earth is significantly older than previously believed.

Once the actual age of the Earth is understood, Larmarckian evolution becomes a widely accepted explanation for the changes in species across time. Early in his career, even the naturalist Charles Darwin accepts the theory of the inheritance of acquired characteristics. As Larmarckian evolution becomes more widely known and more popular, it begins to be used to explain social as well as biological phenomena.

Sociology and Evolution

The chief proponent of the application of Lamarckian theory to the social world in the mid-19th century is English philosopher Herbert Spencer (1820–1903). Spencer has no formal education in philosophy or any of the sciences, although he is a voracious reader. He also writes and, because his ideas have popular appeal, is widely read. For Spencer, evolution is the unifying principle for all branches of knowledge. With no evidence to support his ideas, Spencer makes several assertions, many of which have profoundly influenced psychology. For example, Spencer argues that evolution leads species to attain greater and greater degrees of complexity. Furthermore, greater intelligence derives from a more complex nervous system. Thus, it is clear (to Spencer) that because "civilized man has also a more complex or heterogeneous nervous system than uncivilized man" (Spencer, 1880, p. 341), civilized man will also be uniformly more intelligent. These beliefs increase the interest in comparing human psychological characteristics with those of other animals, measuring intellectual differences between Europeans and other peoples, and measuring individual differences between Europeans. These beliefs also influence the study of infant and child development.

Another of Spencer's influential hypotheses is his explanation of the origins of behavior. Like earlier philosophers of hedonism, Spencer argues that when a behavior is followed by a pleasant or successful outcome, the behavior will tend to be repeated, but when behavior is followed by an unpleasant or unsuccessful outcome it will tend not to be repeated. Because the philosopher Alexander Bain writes something very similar at about the same time, this comes to be called the **Spencer–Bain principle**. For Spencer, this principle explains association and is the basis of learning for all animals. The only difference between species, according to this idea, is a quantitative difference in the number of associations each species is able to make. Species with highly complex nervous systems will be able to make many more associations than those with simpler nervous systems. Furthermore, the Spencer–Bain principle holds across all species, meaning that scientists can make interesting and important discoveries about learning in humans by studying the process in "simpler" species. Also, it makes no difference whether the learning is happening in a laboratory or in the animal's natural environment; the principle remains the same across all learning environments. *These assumptions are what allow for psychology's program of laboratory research using rats in the 20th century.*

The Spencer–Bain principle also suggests that the process of forming associations is utilitarian. That is, associations serve useful purposes for the individual by shaping more and more successful behaviors over time. *Assuming that psychological characteristics, like association, serve useful functions in helping individuals to adapt provides the foundation for later 20th-century functionalist psychology.*

Social Darwinism

Francis Bacon warned 3 centuries ago that people have a tendency to believe those things that they want to believe, even when there is no evidence to support those beliefs. And nowhere is that tendency better exemplified than in the application of Larmarck's evolutionary theory and Spencer's philosophical speculation to the set of beliefs that is referred to as "social Darwinism." Social Darwinism is the popular, but mistaken, notion that it is possible to apply the principles of biological evolution to sociological phenomena. In founding his sociology, or the formal study of societies, Spencer argues that the same principles used to explain how strong species get better over time whereas weak species die out can be applied to societies. And, by applying those same principles to the process of learning, it is also possible to explain why one strong individual thrives whereas a weaker one only gets weaker. Businessmen and leaders of industry in the West believe in and support Spencer's ideas because they seem to provide a scientific justification for the cutthroat economic practices and policies that have allowed those men to succeed in a competitive market environment. Good businessmen have succeeded because they are stronger and deserve to succeed.

Many of Spencer's assertions have a powerful influence on popular thought in the 19th century and even today. Nevertheless, it is important to remember that, even though many of these ideas have high face validity and support much of what many people would like to believe to be true, Spencer provides only casual observations to support his assumptions. Later, scientists must search for supporting evidence, but many of those who follow Spencer begin by assuming that his assertions are true, so that many of those assertions are not tested for decades.

Natural Selection

This is the most significant problem with the Lamarckian theory of evolution: It is based on untested assumptions. In 1858, armed with the evidence of the real age of the Earth and after collecting the necessary evidence, but working independently, British naturalists Alfred Russell Wallace (1823–1913) and Charles Darwin (1809–1882) jointly present the data that establish the principles of natural selection. These principles propose laws in nature that cause life forms to change:

1. As the economist Thomas Malthus had established in 1798, living organisms tend to produce more offspring than can be supported by the environment. Thus, there is a constant struggle for access to insufficient resources.
2. There is variation among members of a species, so that each member of the species has slightly different characteristics than every other member.
3. Those individuals that exhibit characteristics that allow them to gain access to more of the resources survive and go on to successfully reproduce and fill every available niche in the environment.

So far, these principles are not much different from those proposed by Lamarck. The difference comes when Wallace and Darwin add the final piece.

4. It is the successful variations, not acquired characteristics, that are transmitted to offspring.

Those physical variations that just happen to provide an advantage in gaining resources in that environment appear in the next generation only because individuals with those characteristics are more likely to reproduce. Neither Wallace nor Darwin is able to provide any convincing explanation of the mechanism that allows those variations to be transmitted to the offspring. It is not until the work of Augustinian monk Johann Gregor Mendel (1822–1884) becomes widely known early in the next century that anyone understands the role played by genes in influencing individual differences within a species and the variations among species.

Relevance for Psychology

These principles of natural selection come to have a significant impact on psychology over the next several decades. To begin with, the brain is an organ that has evolved along with all of the other organs. To the degree that mental activity is a consequence of brain function, thoughts, feelings, and behaviors can be understood as the result of the same evolutionary pressures that have shaped the rest of human physiology. So, for example, in the same way that there is a perceptual preference for simple, symmetrical visual patterns, humans also have a tendency toward becoming overweight under conditions of abundant high-caloric resources. Shared emotional responses, cognitive mechanisms, and motivational biases are presumed to arise from these same evolutionary pressures. Today, the study of possible evolutionary pressures on thoughts, feelings, and behaviors is called sociobiology, or more recently, evolutionary psychology. But the idea that human behaviors and mental faculties have been modified over time by the principles of natural selection is not a new one. Darwin himself proposed this idea (Richards, 1982), even before the publication of his book, The Expression of Emotions in Man and Animals, *in 1872. In this book, Darwin illustrates similar emotional states in a human and a chimpanzee (see Fig. 5.2).*

Ideas about evolution, and especially the evolution of the mind, are also influential in the rise of comparative psychology. In the 19th century, comparative psychology is founded on the assumption that all animals, including all "races" of humans, are distributed along a continuum of evolution. This continuum is arranged so that those creatures closest to the Earth are considered the least evolved and those closest to God (Caucasoid, upper-middle class, educated, northern European, male humans) are considered the most fully evolved.

Finally, the relevance of the principles of natural selection for psychology is manifested in later schools of psychology. For example, the concept of learning is of

A

B

FIG. 5.2. Emotional states in man and animal. Charles Darwin's illustration of similar mental states in (A) a human and (B) a chimpanzee (Darwin, 1872/1896, pp. 141, 180).

primary importance in behaviorism, and many behaviorists share the assumption that not just behaviors, but thoughts and feelings as well, come into existence and persist when they are reinforced by the surrounding environment. Thus, in the same way that species-typical human psychology exists as a result of successful adaptations to the environment evolved over eons, the psychological characteristics of individuals are also shaped over a lifetime by learning. The roots of functionalism, behaviorism, comparative psychology, and evolutionary psychology are found in these principles of natural selection.

⊕ The Times

In the 18th century, humans wrest more control over their own lives as they learn to predict and control nature. Not just nature, but totalitarian religious authority and despotic political rulers are dethroned from their control over the lives of ordinary humans. Revolutions occur in the New World and in France, as individual freedom is sought, at least for a few. Political, economic, and intellectual power is maintained in the hands of privileged White European land-owning men, and is exercised as though it is a right. Slavery of the poor and of people of other races is still widely practiced throughout Europe and the Americas. Women are not educated, and many live in conditions little different from those of slaves. People who are weak, the poor, the sick, and the mentally ill are relegated to the margins of society, persecuted, and despised.

The Western paradigm for seeking truth about the physical universe becomes empirical and scientific. The physical universe is assumed to be made of matter and governed by a few laws in nature. At the same time, God becomes more distant. Instead of creating each rock, each tree, each creature, each living thing, just as it is found, God has created matter, put into place the laws that govern how matter acts on matter, and now seems to have gone away. Slowly, the distance that develops between God and humans begins to influence the way that people think about their relationships with others, their understanding of themselves, and their beliefs and feelings about their place in the universe.

6

Physiological to Experimental Psychology: Can Consciousness Be Inspected?

The purpose of this chapter is to explore how the use of the Scientific Method and the passion for measurement begins to influence the study of consciousness in the early 19th century in the West. The growth of scientific theory and knowledge in several domains will be examined along with the transitions from philosophical psychology to physiology and then to experimental psychology. By mid-century, the study of psychology is taking many directions. As a discipline, psychology seems to be becoming more divided. Some psychologists reject science, whereas others pursue anatomical studies and still others measure relationships between physiological and psychological functioning.

PHYSIOLOGICAL PSYCHOLOGY

The Story of the Two Astronomers

At Greenwich in 1796, the astronomer Maskelyne, as every psychologist knows, dismissed Kinnebrook, his assistant, because Kinnebrook observed the times of stellar transmits almost a second later than he did. Maskelyne was convinced that all through 1794 there had been no discrepancy between the two of them. Then in August, 1795, Kinnebrook was found to be recording times about half a second later than Maskelyne. His attention was called to the "error," and it would seem that he must have striven to correct it. Nevertheless, it increased during the succeeding months until, in January, 1796, it had become about eight tenths of a second. Then Maskelyne dismissed him. The error was serious, for upon such observations depended the calibration of the clock, and upon the clock depended all other observations of place and time. (Boring, 1957, pp. 134–135)

The problem for astronomers is to achieve consistency in their observations because of the importance their measures have for navigating ships at sea, calibrating clocks, and studying astronomy. Finding differences in recording times between individual astronomers introduces an unwelcome element of inconsistency, but raises interesting questions for all scientists, especially for those who study the mind. For example, how can a study of objective reality be conducted at all if reality can only be known through unreliable human observations? Equally of interest and concern are questions about how and why individual differences in observation occur and if human observations can be adjusted so as to accurately measure objective reality. Astronomers attempt to solve the problem by determining a **personal equation** for each observer, a factor used to equate observations across individual observers. For later students of the mind, the personal equation becomes the study of individual differences in reaction time.

> ✓ **Stop and think.**
> If subjective experience is not a direct reflection of reality, how does it differ?

Beginning in the 19th century, the process by which the physical world becomes transformed into thoughts begins to be explored scientifically. The questions about psychology do not change, but the method for finding answers does. Instead of relying on trust or the word of authorities and instead of coming to conclusions through reason, speculation, and argument, answers are sought through systematic observations and measurement of nature. In psychology, observations are conducted on sensory and nervous systems in both human and nonhuman animals.

Experimental psychology conducted in the last half of the 19th century has important roots in the scientific studies of animal physiology conducted during the first half of the century, mostly in German laboratories, but in France, Italy, and Spain as well. German universities are state-supported during this time and are thus less constrained by religious authorities than in most other countries in Europe. Researchers and scholars are provided with funding and equipment for experimental research, and they are given the freedom needed to pursue the questions that interest them without interference from those who disagree with their methods.

Vitalism and the Study of the Human

Although philosophers have speculated for centuries about mechanical determinants of thoughts and behaviors, those ideas are no more popular in the early 19th century than they were for the Greeks. The search continues for the mysterious and metaphysical force that begins and directs life and that is the "self" that continues on after the physical death of the body. The conviction that there must be such a force is so strong that the conviction alone seems to constitute sufficient evidence for its existence. Although it is generally acknowledged that the actions of all other forms of life are directed by mechanical principles, the study of human physiology is largely directed toward finding the vital soul.

Respiration and Digestion

Among the physiological functions that seem to be directed by a soul are involuntary behaviors, such as breathing and digesting food. In Greek and Roman times, the belief was that vital spirits were present in the air and drawn into living bodies through the process of respiration. In support of this idea, for example, Galen points out that fire needs air to burn and that, like living beings, fire dies if deprived of air. This is why the Greek word psyche, the "breath of life," is translated by early Christian theologians as "soul" and interpreted as a vitalistic spark of a divine spirit that gives life.

During the 19th century, the discovery is made that turning food into nutrients and then into energy is a purely chemical process. In the middle of the century, the chemical, and thus material, basis of respiration also comes to be understood. These findings link the study of the physical sciences to the biological sciences and begin the blurring of the distinction between organic and inorganic matter.

✓ **Stop and think.**

What does distinguish living things from nonliving things? What do all living things do that no nonliving thing does?

Reproduction

Another physiological function that seems to have ties to some mysterious force is the process of the reproduction of life. Throughout history, there has been much speculation about how new life begins. With the invention of the microscope, it becomes possible for the first time to see individual cells. In the 17th century, Antonie van Leeuwenhoek (1632–1723) uses a microscope to see human spermatozoa (sperm cells) for the first time. Philosophers speculate that sperm cells contain a **homunculus**, or fully formed human in miniature, which is planted into the uterus. The uterus is nothing more than a vessel in which the homunculus gains size and weight until it is ready to be born. By the 19th century, with the coming of microscopic biology, the chemical and thus material bases of fertilization and germination are better understood (Kantor, 1963–1969). Thus, empirical observations of developing organisms during the 19th century reveal the inorganic, or chemical, basis of life. Speculations about vitalism are eliminated from biology, and biology is transformed to the study of matter and the mechanics of natural laws. In spite of this, theories about vital forces continue to influence early 19th-century speculation about the human mind.

Electricity and Magnetism as the Vital Force

Probably because they can mysteriously influence objects across empty space, both electricity and magnetism are mistaken for vitalistic forces, sometimes, quite literally, the spark of life. This perception is exploited by Mary Shelley, who has Dr. Frankenstein use the electricity generated by a thunderstorm to bring his monster to life. Late in the 18th century, the discovery is made that nerves in organic tissue communicate through electricity and that electrical stimulation can trigger muscular responses. In this era, a variety of physical and mental ailments are attributed to the need for electricity to boost the vitalistic force, thus providing increased energy. In Fig. 6.1, a patient receives electrical current through his bare feet to cure a headache in a common 19th-century procedure.

Mesmerism

The mystery of magnetism has inspired "miracle cures" since the earliest days of physiology. Mesmerism is good example of this phenomenon. In 1766, Franz Anton Mesmer (1734–1815) graduates from the University of Vienna Medical School after completing his dissertation about planetary influences on human physiology. He develops an interest in magnets and begins to use them in treating his patients with, he believes, some degree of success. Later, he decides that his own body generates sufficient magnetism, so that instead of using magnets he can effect cures and place his female patients into altered states of consciousness simply by waving his hands over them and pressing down on an unidentified body part he calls the "ovarium." In Mesmer's view, his work provides evidence that mind influences body.

Later practitioners of scientific experiments in hypnotism suggest that their ability to induce altered states of consciousness in subjects by the application of magnetic energy is clear evidence that consciousness itself is made only of matter. During the early years of the 19th century, there are no distinct lines between what might be science and what might not be, and Mesmerism is a good example of the resulting confusion (Winter, 1997). Although Mesmer is ridiculed by many of his

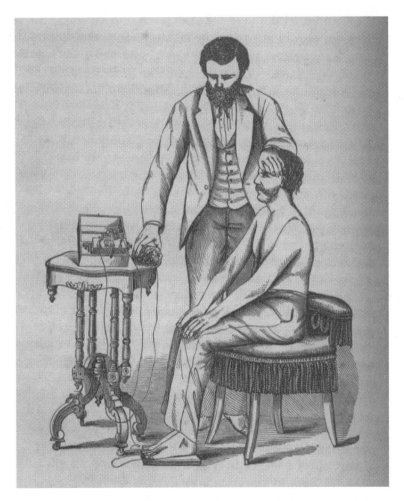

FIG. 6.1.   Electrical curing (Beard & Rockwell, 1871, p. 192).

contemporaries, his work is carried on by a few of his followers. The influence of Mesmer's work can be seen in 19th- and early 20th-century approaches to psychotherapy that use hypnotism and trance states to effect their cures.

Neurophysiology

Built from associations of cells, powered by the functioning of a pump-like heart and circulatory system, and working by the pulleys and levers of muscles and bones, Descartes' and earlier philosophers' mechanical human reappears in the study of physiology in the early 19th century. Popular culture reflects this in Offenbach's opera, *Tales of Hoffman*. The protagonist Hoffman falls in love with Olympia, the perfect woman, who later turns out to be only an automaton operated by springs (Offenbach, 1881/1959).

Microscopic observation has long revealed that earlier theories about the nerves as hollow tubes through which some substance travels were incorrect. As the following quotation shows, the theory that nerves carry information by vibration is also not compatible with the evidence:

> We are informed by anatomists, that although the two coats which inclose a nerve, and which it derives from the coats of the brain, are tough and elastic, yet the nerve itself has a very small degree of consistence, being almost like marrow. It has, however, a fibrous texture, and may be divided and sub-divided, till its fibres escape our senses; and as we know so very little about the texture of the nerves, there is great room left for those who choose to indulge themselves in conjecture.
>
> The ancients conjectured that the nervous fibres are fine tubes, filled with a very subtile spirit or vapour, which they called *animal spirits*; that the brain is a gland, by which the animal spirits are secreted from the finer part of the blood, and their continual waste repaired; and that it is by these animal spirits that the nerves perform their functions. Des Cartes has shewn how, by these animal spirits going and returning in the nerves, muscular motion, perception, memory, and imagination, are effected. All this he has described as distinctly as if he had been an eye-witness of all those operations. But it happens that the tubular structure of the nerves was never perceived by the human eye, nor shewn by the nicest injections; and all that has been said about animal spirits, through more than fifteen centuries, is mere conjecture.
>
> Dr. Briggs, who was Sir Isaac Newton's master in anatomy, was the first, as far as I know, who advanced a new system concerning the nerves. He conceived them to be solid filaments of prodigious tenuity; and this opinion, as it accords better with observation, seems to have been more generally received since his time. As to the matter of performing their office, Dr. Briggs thought that, like musical cords they have vibrations differing according to their length and tension. They seem, however, very unfit for this purpose, on account of their want of tenacity, their moisture, and being through their whole length in contact with moist substances; so that although Dr. Briggs wrote a book upon this system, called *Nova Visionis Theoria*, it seems not to have been much followed. (Reid, 1785/1969, p. 84)

> ✓ **Stop and think.**
> How do the nerves transmit their information to the brain?

The means by which information is carried from the sensory organs to the brain remains a mystery in the early 19th century. By midcentury, physiologists are trying to understand the neurological bases of perception, and it is through the medium of this physiological research that psychology as a science eventually emerges from philosophy.

The work of the German physiologist Franz Gall (1758–1828) serves as an example of this transition from philosophical speculation to the experimental study of the brain. Trained as an anatomist, Gall begins his study of the brain in an effort to substantiate the theological claim that objects in the physical universe are translated into mental events through faculties of the mind. According to this perspective, mental faculties are given by God, and "each faculty makes manifest a God-given correlation between mental and physical processes" (Reed, 1997, p. 28). Philosophers, on the other hand, are uncomfortable with the notion of an immaterial mind being divided. Gall takes an empirical approach to the question.

Early in his career, Gall makes significant contributions to understanding brain functioning. He is among those who identify the brain as an organ that carries out specific bodily functions. Just as the stomach is an organ that digests and the lungs are organs that breathe, the brain is the organ that thinks. Gall recognizes that the cerebral cortex is not a rind, or protective covering, for the lower structures of the brain, as was previously believed, but has important intellectual and emotional functions of its own. Further, based on the evidence from brain dissections, he comes to believe that the various intellectual and emotional faculties of the mind are localized in specific parts of the cortex, so that the cortex is really a set of several organs, each with specific functions. In Gall's view, the mind and brain are related to one another in that the brain is the tool of the mind, but he still thinks of the mind as something metaphysical and thus independent of the brain.

Because intellectual and emotional functions occur in physical organs of the body, Gall believes that these psychological functions should be observable and measurable. If this is true, then at least some aspects of the mind become primary qualities. Thus, there may finally be a way out of philosophical speculation about mind and a beginning to a science of the mind.

To many, Gall's work seems to imply that psychological functions may be like other physiological functions, such as digestion or respiration. This suggests that it is the functioning of organs, not a freely willing soul that causes thoughts, feelings, and behaviors. This threatens the Christian doctrine of free will, and Gall's work is denounced by theologians as well as by his colleagues. His lectures are banned in some countries as a threat to religion and morality, and his book, published in 1819, is placed on the Roman Catholic Church's Index of Forbidden Books.

Gall speculates that cortical organs can be developed through intellectual exercise in the same way that heart muscle may be developed through physical exercise. This suggests that the relative size of these organs both determines and is determined by the degree to which those faculties are used. Furthermore, the size of these organs differs from one individual to another, and this difference explains personality differences. Thus, Gall is among the first to propose the importance of individual differences in brain functioning and the relationship between those differences and variations in personality.

This recognition of the importance of individual differences gives rise to the comparative study of brains. The brains and skulls of many different animals and of humans from a variety of races and geographic locations begin to be compared with one another. Not surprisingly, these early comparative studies find evidence that Caucasian Western European males of the educated upper classes have larger brains and thus more fully developed intellectual faculties than any other humans.

Phrenology and Pseudoscience

Gall asserts that differences in the size of cortical organs might be determined by examining the shape of the head. Nineteenth-century science is always looking for ways to observe and measure, and these individual differences in head size and shape prove to be irresistible objects of measurement. Gall calls his new technique cranioscopy, but much to his consternation, his colleague Johann C. Spurzheim (1776–1832) quickly renames the technique **phrenology**, which means the science of the mind, and popularizes its practice throughout Europe and North America.

Scientific observations comparing skull size and shape to underlying cortical structures soon show that Gall's ideas are false (Gross, 1998). However, the idea has widespread public appeal. In the West, there is intense interest in trying to understand human motivation and personality differences and in being able to predict and possibly control psychological characteristics. Phrenology seems to offer a powerful tool toward achieving those ends. The size and shape of the skull presents easily accessible, observable, measurable, and highly personal evidence. The idea that the organs of the brain shape the outside of the skull is simple and easily understood, contains strong elements of cause and effect, and has high face validity. Even more importantly for those living in the 19th-century era of scientific progress, phrenology seems like science. Thus, phrenology becomes wildly popular among the general public and remains so even until the early 20th century.

Evidence for and Against the Localization of Brain Function

Gall's ideas about the localization of brain function stimulate research into relationships between brain injuries and specific psychological deficits. By 1848, it is known that damage in the front part of the brain often results in language deficits. This is an indication that there is a specific location for language functions. Then, in April 1861, French physician Paul Broca (1824–1880) presents a case study in which he observes a language deficit in a living patient and later, after the patient's death, locates the damaged part of the brain that caused the deficit. This work thus supports the contention that specific functions of the mind are conducted in specific locations in the brain. The real significance of Broca's work lies in his demonstration that a whole function, that of language production, is localized in a specific part of the brain.

However, there is also support for the contrary belief that the cortex functions in a more unitary way and not as a set of discrete organs. The French physiologist, Jean-Pierre Flourens (1794–1867), provides experimental evidence to support a more limited model of localization. Over several years, Flourens conducts a series of vivisection (live dissection) experiments on the effects on behavior of brain lesions, mostly in birds. He observes that the site of the lesion is mostly irrelevant because a lesion almost anywhere in the cortex results in devastating effects on behavior. The evidence from these studies leads to his conclusion that the cortex functions in a holistic or unitary way, with only limited localization of function (Gross, 1998). This conclusion is also in keeping with Flourens' philosophical and theological convictions. He is a Cartesian dualist who views the soul as residing in the cerebral hemispheres and believes that, because the soul is unitary, the functions of the cerebral hemispheres must also be unitary.

The Sensory System

✓ **Stop and think.**
Do visual perceptions happen immediately, as soon as the eyes are opened, or does it take some time for the images to reach the brain?

At about this same time, two laboratories, one in England headed by Charles Bell (1774–1842) and one in France headed by François Magendie (1783–1855), publish evidence that there is more than one kind of nerve cell. These researchers independently establish that there are sensory nerves that carry impulses from the sensory organs to the brain and motor nerves that carry impulses from the brain to the muscles of the motor system. This discovery is called the **Bell–Magendie law**.

The functioning of sensory and nervous systems seems like the place to begin to explore questions about how reality is transformed into subjective experience. How do the various sensory systems receive information, and how and where is that information transmitted to motor nerves?

The first modern physiological laboratory is established by Czech physiologist J. E. Purkinje (1787–1869) at the University of Breslau, in Poland. He conducts research on the nerves and organs of vision between 1823 and 1850. Within a few years, German universities follow with their own laboratories.

This is not to suggest that physiologists have given up the notion of an immaterial human mind, only that nervous and sensory systems are increasingly viewed as material and measurable. For example, one of the earliest professors of physiology with whom many others study, Johannes Müller (1801–1858), believes that even human organs are endowed with a vital nonmaterial force that coordinates their operations. Many of Müller's students, however, reject these vitalistic convictions.

Hermann von Helmholtz, mentioned earlier in connection with the principle of the conservation of energy, is one of Müller's students. Helmholtz rejects physiological vitalism. Helmholtz believes instead that all aspects of physiology are material and operate according to laws in nature. He is trained as a surgeon, but is inclined toward physics, and he eventually extends the principle of conservation to living organisms. Helmholtz states that the amount of energy consumed by organisms is equal to the amount of energy expended by them. He thus applies a law governing the physical universe to the biological universe and contributes to the movement toward blurring the distinction between living and nonliving matter.

Like other physiologists of the era, Helmholtz conducts experimental research on living organisms. In 1850, his findings on the rate of nerve conduction are published, demonstrating that when a nerve in a frog's leg is stimulated, it takes a measurable amount of time for the muscle to respond. After further study, he concludes that nerve conduction travels at the rate of 90 feet per second. According to Boring (1957, p. 42), "This established the disturbing idea that to move your finger voluntarily was not an act of mind in itself, but was a later event caused by a previous act of mind." Helmholtz's findings also refute Professor Müller's conviction that nerve transmission travels at the speed of light.

✓ **Stop and think.**
What implications does this have for the theory of mind as will?

Helmholtz also finds significant differences between individuals in their reactions to sensory stimulation, but it is not until much later in the century that these differences are explored. Helmholtz himself concludes that because reaction time varies among individuals, it must be an unreliable measure of physiological functioning and abandons this line of research.

The Tactile Senses

The study of the tactile senses does not receive the same attention in the 19th century as does vision and audition, where the main question concerns how visual and auditory information in the physical world is transmitted to the sensory nerves. No similar transmitting mechanism is needed for tactile sensations because the physical stimuli causing them act directly on the nerves of the skin. However, the German physiologist Ernst Weber (1795–1878), who publishes his most important works in 1834 and 1846, devotes almost his entire career to the experimental study of the tactile senses. He studies both the external sense of touch and something he calls common sensibility, defined as internal physical sensations, like pain and muscle movement. In his investigations, Weber begins by noting that the external sense of touch is made up of a combination of pressure, temperature, and location. Commonly, the experience of pressure and location would seem to be indistinguishable, so that pressure applied to a finger is experienced as both a pressure and a location. Similarly, pressure applied to two different fingers at the same time is experienced as two pressures at two locations. But, Weber asks, what about when two fingers are touched together? This is experienced as two pressures but only one location. It is this kind of experience that leads Weber to conclude that pressure and location are separate aspects of the sense of touch.

Weber also conducts research into the "two-point threshold." This involves placing two stimuli on the skin so close together that the subject identifies only one location, then moving the stimuli in a series of steps further and further apart until the subject reports feeling two locations. When this distinction is made, the two-point threshold has been reached. Weber discovers that the threshold for the perception of two points varies on different parts of the body, meaning that some places on the skin are more sensitive to tactile stimulation than others. The degree of perceived weight also varies with different parts of the body, as does the capacity for discrimination between temperatures. These differences lead Weber to conclude that sensitivity to touch is determined by the density of nerve fibers, and the density of nerve endings varies on different parts of the skin.

Weber is also interested in the conscious experience of differences between closely related stimuli. For example, he presents research subjects with two weights, one in each hand, systematically varies the relationships between the weights, and asks the subjects to report their perception of the weights. He explores the point at which subjects are able to discern a difference between the weights. How much more must the weight in one hand be than the weight in the other before the subject will report feeling a difference? The point at which the subject will report a difference Weber calls the "just noticeable difference" (jnd). He is then able to identify a mathematical relationship between changes in the weights and perceptions of those changes. The smallest perceptible difference between two weights is not absolute—the same for each difference—but is a relative difference between the weights. An increase of only a gram over the standard weight will be perceived if the standard weight is 40 grams or less. But if the standard weight is more than 40 grams, an increase of only a gram will not be perceived at all. This ratio of 1:40 holds across all variations in standard weights. In finding this ratio, Weber brings mathematical relationships to the study of psychological experience and provides a foundation for the further systematic study of such relationships. Weber's studies may be described as true psychological research because he is measuring conscious experience (Brauns, 1997).

Vision

From the time of Aristotle, people believed that visual sensation was a result of tiny copies of the physical object being transmitted to the eye. By the mid-19th century, it is understood that the nerve fibers of the retina respond in a patterned way to visible patterns encountered in the environment. In this way, conscious experience results from the patterned responses of nerve fibers in the retina. The question about how physical sensations are transformed into mental events is thus moved closer to the brain, although there is as yet no understanding about how patterned electrical responses on the retina become conscious thoughts.

✓ Stop and think.

Why is only one image seen when there are two retinas, each transmitting a different image to the brain?

For example, consider the case of the ability to perceive how close or far away an object is using only visual sensation. Helmholtz points out that the brain actually receives two images, one from each retina. Gradually, he says, the ability to coordinate these two images into a single one is learned. This learned ability then becomes unconscious. An unconscious inference of depth is made from comparisons of the two images and the angles at which they are received. Thus, Helmholtz concludes, depth perception is an innate consequence of the way in which the visual system is built and the way that unconsciousness functions.

There are also theories about how color vision functions. Johannes Müller argues that there are specific nerves responding to specific types of stimulation, such as visual nerves that respond to light and auditory nerves that respond to sound. The research of Thomas Young (1773–1829) provides evidence that there are three types of substances on the back of the eye, each chemically sensitive to different wave lengths of light. Helmholtz applies his theory of specific nerve fibers to conclude that, instead of substances, there are three types of nerve fibers on the retina. All of these ideas are combined into the **Young–Helmholtz** theory of color vision. This theory states that color vision is a result of three types of receptors, each responsive to different wavelengths of light.

This theory provides a structural explanation for a vision deficit like color-blindness. If a person cannot see red, it must be that the nerve fibers sensitive to that wavelength of light are missing or inoperative. As is also true in research on language functions, this method of coming to understand how a system must operate by examining cases in which there is a deficit has been and still is a very important method in psychological research.

The time has come when the many striking discoveries of the Physiologists relative to the nervous system should find a recognized place in the Science of Mind, I have devoted a separate chapter to the Physiology of the Brain and Nerves. (Bain, 1885, page iii)

Audition

Physiologists also try to identify the specific structures or nerve fibers that account for hearing and for the hearing of different pitches. Helmholtz, for example, speculates that, just as a piano string will vibrate in response to an external source of sound waves of the same frequency to which the string is tuned, there may be specific nerve fibers in the ear that vibrate in response to specific sound waves. Later researchers explore these questions more fully.

Taste and Smell

The senses of taste and smell do not receive any significant attention until late in the 19th century. Smell, in particular, remains baffling throughout this period because the mechanisms by which smell is perceived are not obvious. Aristotle's theory was that smells result from tiny copies of the object of perception traveling through space to the sensory organ. Although this idea is discredited with regard to visual images, it persists about smells. Some classification systems of smells and tastes are proposed, but the aspects of the physical stimuli that cause the sensations, and the physiological structures that produce the perceptions of taste and smell, remain mysterious.

Physiological Conclusions

The match between what is physically present and what is consciously experienced is often not good. Discrepancies between the physical and the mental can be explained in terms of two factors. The first is the operation of the sensory receptor system. The second is what Helmholtz calls the unconscious inferences of the observer. According to Helmholtz, these inferences are learned, complex, and difficult, if not impossible to measure. It takes more than 100 years before many psychologists begin to acknowledge the powerful role played by unconscious processes in perception.

Psychophysics

As long as consciousness remains impossible to measure and psychology is the study of consciousness, there can never be a science of psychology. The task of those studying consciousness in the 19th century, then, is to find ways to measure. Psychophysics is the first effort to systematically measure relationships between the external physical world and the internal world of consciousness. Gustav Theodor Fechner (1801–1887) reasons in 1858–1860 that if a systematic relationship can be found between known changes in physical stimuli and changes in the conscious experience of those stimuli, that would be a measure of consciousness. These kinds of discriminations are similar to those explored by Weber in his laboratory.

Fechner wants to measure relationships between the physical or objective world and the mental or subjective world. He is interested in the relationship between physical stimuli and both the underlying physiological mechanism of sensation and the subjective experience. The interest in physiological sensations becomes a part of physiological study, whereas the subjective or conscious experience becomes the province of psychology. Aside from his career as a physicist and scientist, Fechner is something of a mystic, fascinated with a spiritual reality, and interested in finding connections between the physical and the metaphysical. He is described as a panpsychic (Boring, 1957), believing that everything that is physical has a soul, including inanimate objects.

Following Weber's work, Fechner finds that weights varied systematically are perceived in systematic ways, but not in a one-to-one ratio. Instead, weights varied geometrically are perceived arithmetically. This relationship is stated mathematically as:

$$S = k \log R$$

What this formula means is that, for conscious experience S (mental sensation) to change arithmetically, the stimulus magnitude R must change geometrically. This is more complex than Weber's ratio and extended to other sensory modalities. Fechner has found a mathematical formula that explains a systematic relationship between physical objects and conscious experience. A part of consciousness has thus been measured, demonstrating that a science of consciousness may be possible after all. Psychophysics is a first step in the transition of the study of thoughts, feelings, and behaviors from philosophical speculation to science. Those who follow build on these foundations supplied by physiologists.

ROMANTIC IDEAS

In the mid-19th century, those who ponder the questions of psychology take many paths. Many, including writers, artists, philosophers, and even some scientists such as Fechner, continue to believe that the human experience cannot be fully understood through the methods of science alone. The thesis that true knowledge about an objective reality can be achieved only through systematic observation and measurement is attacked from a variety of perspectives. Both Catholic and Protestant religious authorities assert the insignificance of human knowledge against that of the divine. Romantic thinkers view emotion, intuition, and other subjective ways of coming to believe as superior to observation and experience.

Art and Literature

Romantic ideas pervade the cultural life of the 19th century. Early 19th-century literature explores beauty, love, and sensual pleasures. This is the era of exciting and romantic novels, such as Jane Austen's *Sense and Sensibility* and *The Three Musketeers* by Alexandré Dumas.

Romantics assert that there are aspects of a beautiful sunset, a piece of heartrending music, or a delicious meal that cannot be measured. Similarly, these romantic expressions explore aspects of the human experience that cannot be measured. The creators of these works and those who read and view them are exploring human thoughts, feelings, and behaviors.

Exploring is not the same as explaining, however, and the distinction is an important one. Nineteenth-century romantics are content to explore and describe the human experience, whereas scientists seek to explain and answer questions. Thus, when studying the human experience, both the methods and goals of the humanities differ categorically from those of science.

Romantic Philosophy

The distinction between science and philosophy remains a fuzzy one, because many scientists espouse philosophies and are influenced by philosophers. The distinction between philosophy and science is exemplified by the writings of Dr. Mises, a pseudonym created by Fechner to express his more mystical and philosophic views. Dr. Mises writes of his beliefs that everything in the universe, including the universe itself, has consciousness. Fechner himself believes that there is unity between science and philosophy, but his creation of Dr. Mises illustrates the growing distrust philosophers have of the narrowness of science and the concern that scientists have with what they see as the vague and abstract nature of philosophy.

Like their counterparts in the humanities, romantic philosophers emphasize the intuitive or emotional aspects of human experience over the rational mind. They argue that there are aspects of human nature and human experience that are not observable to others and cannot be reduced to measurable phenomena. They assert that humans are not primarily rational but are motivated first by emotions. Human behavior is often motivated by irrational emotions, like the desire to continue surviving, even in situations where the more rational thing might be to die.

According to the philosopher Schopenhauer, the most intelligent humans become quite adept at surviving. Having met their survival needs, these people become bored. The only way to escape this boredom is in the pursuit of interests not related to survival, such as art, music, poetry, or philosophy.

Nineteenth-century romantic philosophy is a short-lived movement, culminating with the writer and philosopher Friedrich Nietzsche (1844–1900) later in the century. However, romantic philosophy does influence scientific psychology. Wilhelm Wundt, for example, often described as the founder of modern psychology, gives the preeminent place in his psychological theories to volitional motivation, which is the desire to act to achieve some goal. Sigmund Freud claimed to have come to his conclusions independently, yet the connections between Freud, Schopenhauer, and Nietzsche are undeniable. For example, Schopenhauer, writing 50 years before Freud, argues that human behavior is motivated by irrational forces, much like Freud's later idea of the "id." Schopenhauer also argues that the will actively represses ideas that might cause insanity if allowed to become conscious, presaging Freud's ideas about repression and defense mechanisms. Also, Schopenhauer calls the human will the wellspring of culture because it forces humans to pursue art, poetry, and philosophy to escape the tyranny of irrational forces. Freud calls this process sublimation. Similarly, Nietzsche argues that basic human nature, which is irrational, must be controlled and modified by rationality. These romantic ideas are mirrored in many aspects of Freud's psychoanalytic theory. Finally, Freud, Schopenhauer, and Nietzsche are all accurately described as unusually pessimistic about human nature.

> Hope is the result of confusing the desire that something should take place with the probability that it will. Perhaps no man is free from this folly of the heart, which deranges the intellect's correct appreciation of probability to such an extent that, if the chances are a thousand to one against it, yet the event is thought a likely one. Still in spite of this, a sudden misfortune is like a death stroke, whilst a hope that is always disappointed and still never dies, is like death by prolonged torture. (Schopenhauer, 1844/1942, p. 45)

In many ways, both Schopenhauer's and Nietzsche's ideas form bridges between speculation and empiricism, and thus between philosophy and science. Schopenhauer claims, for example, that all of his psychological theories are derived from the observation of human behavior. He urges philosophers and scientists to interpret the world as it really is and is constant in his appeals that conclusions should be based on personal experience. He does not want to be a "conjuror of ideas" like other philosophers (Schopenhauer, 1841–1852/1994, p. viii). Like his scientific contemporaries, Schopenhauer rejects a philosophy of abstract ideas in favor of one based on observation and experience.

For his part, Nietzsche accepts the evidence of science while at the same time arguing that the knowledge that science is uncovering has taken meaning from human lives. Rationalist philosophers and scientists, for example, have killed God by providing natural explanations for natural phenomena. Evolutionary theory is "true but deadly," having placed us not at the top of some hierarchy of life but alongside all of the other animals on Earth in an evolutionary sense (Golomb, 1989).

Hard Times

The 19th century's passion for measurement for the purpose of ascertaining "facts" is satirized by Charles Dickens in his 1854 novel, *Hard Times*. Here, we are introduced to Mr. Gradgrind, "a man of realities. A man of facts and calculations. A man who proceeds upon the principle that two and two are four and nothing over" (p. 16). Grangrind approaches all questions "with a rule and a pair of scales, and the multiplication table always in his pocket, sir, ready to weigh and measure any parcel of human nature, and tell you exactly what it comes to" (p. 16). He argues that life is "a mere question of figures, a case of simple arithmetic" (p. 16). To his children's teacher he asserts, "Teach these boys and girls nothing but Facts. Facts alone are wanted in life. Plant nothing else, and root out everything else. You can only form the minds of reasoning animals upon Facts: nothing else will ever be of any service to them. This is the principle on which I bring up my own children" (p. 15). And yet, in spite of Gradgrind's careful bringing up of his own children to seek out only measurable facts, they insist on sneaking away to watch the antics of a traveling circus, a fancy that Gradgrind can find no way to comprehend. (adapted from Dickens, 1854/1987)

The Rejection of a Science of Consciousness

> ✓ **Stop and think.**
> If only matter is observable, can consciousness be studied by observation?
> If it can, does that mean that consciousness is made of matter?

Suggesting that consciousness can be studied by observation implies that consciousness is as material as all other aspects of nature. An early 19th-century philosopher Johann Herbart (1776–1841), for example, suggests that there may eventually be a mathematics of consciousness (Leary, 1978). If consciousness can be explained as matter acting on matter, then where is the nonmaterial and transcendent human will? Trying to imagine that consciousness is nothing more than matter in motion violates the human intuitive sense of a self that is distinct from the material body. Imagining that others may, by the simple observation of matter, be able to peer inside the supposed private domain of others' minds makes many people uncomfortable. Through most of the mid-19th century, it is accepted, even by many scientists, that human consciousness will never be observable and that questions about consciousness must remain forever the province of speculation.

Spiritualism and the Occult

In 1850, in upstate New York, a movement called Spiritualism appears and spreads rapidly throughout the United States and Europe. Spiritualism is the belief that it is possible to communicate with the spirits of animals and people who have died. These spirits might be the self, a will, the mind, or even some mysterious nonphysical form of energy (Porter, 1972). This notion of a type of energy that is psychic, rather than physical, is expressed in the writings of Johann Herbart. He argues that thoughts and ideas have a force or energy of their own, and it is this energy, rather than laws of association, that cause ideas to attract one another to form complex ideas. According to Spiritualists, psychic energy transcends physical death. Only very special people, called mediums, have the power to perceive this type of energy and mediate between the living and the dead.

Communication with the dead becomes popular among a wide variety of people (Conan Doyle, 1930). In the United States alone, millions of people spend millions of dollars to visit mediums and attend seances. Some of the most learned scholars and prominent individuals in the country are among those attending Spiritualist performances and professing to hold Spiritualist beliefs (Moore, 1977; Marshall & Wendt, 1980; Coon, 2002). As the movement spreads, prominent scholars associated with the study of psychology take differing positions on Spiritualist beliefs. Wilhelm Wundt and G. Stanley Hall, discussed in succeeding chapters, attack Spritualism, whereas the philosopher and psychologist William James comes under attack for his interest in Spiritualism (Coon, 2002).

Historians offer a variety of explanations for the appearance and popularity of Spiritualism at this time in history. Often, it is assumed that Spiritualism is a rejection of the growing presence and power of science and technology, but there is not much evidence to support this argument. Spiritualism is not a rejection of science, but "thought of itself as an empirical, scientific attempt to prove the real existence of that other realm" (Moore, 1977, p. 7). Nineteenth-century Spiritualists are typically well educated, often even antireligious, and usually firm believers that science is the only reliable way to gain true knowledge (Moore, 1977).

By the 19th century, science and technology are producing their own miracles, like vaccines and locomotives, and turning them into everyday experiences. Technological miracles, like the telegraph, allow for communication in real time with people who are very far away, even across the ocean. It is no great leap to imagine that someday technology will allow for communication with the dead (Coon, 2002). What a comfort to be able to believe that a loved one lives on, even after death, in another realm and can be contacted almost as easily as sending a telegram.

Spiritualism withers almost as quickly as it appears. Many mediums are exposed as frauds and hucksters, producing their illusions by using common magic tricks, such as hidden mirrors and accomplices in adjacent rooms. Their tricks are perpetrated on people who want very much to believe, as Francis Bacon warned might happen. When the methods of scientific testing are brought to bear on Spiritualist claims, no evidence is found of contact with any nonphysical realm.

STRUCTURE AND FUNCTION: MEASURING MIND

As 19th-century physiologists observe and measure relationships between reality and consciousness, anatomists and physicians weigh and measure the structures of the brain. At the same time, naturalists look for ways to explore the evolutionary origins of mind.

The Origin of Human Mind

When applied to living organisms, the principle of the conservation of energy eliminates the foundations of vitalism. By mid-19th century, biologists understand that life arises not from some mysterious life-force but from combinations of chemicals under favorable conditions. Darwinian principles of evolution by natural selection, now widely accepted, provide explanations for the physical characteristics of all life forms.

One problem with accepting evolution in the animal kingdom is the unavoidable conclusion that humans have also evolved from some different life form. Particularly unacceptable is the idea that humans have evolved from something like present-day chimpanzees or gorillas. In other words, humans are not some special case endowed by their creator with certain inalienable rights and abilities that no other animal has or is capable of having. Instead, humans are just another form of life. Thus, although humans may have taken dominion over all other animals, they are not given that right by a divine creator. This conclusion violates religious doctrines and is demeaning and dehumanizing.

> ✓ **Stop and think.**
> What does it mean to suggest that the mind is subject to the principles of natural selection?

A related problem has to do with accounting for human mind using the same principles of natural selection that account for the evolution of physical structures. If mind is merely a function of physical structures in the brain that have evolved over time, does this mean that other animals also have minds? This becomes a central question for psychologists over the next several decades.

Comparative Psychology

Recognizing the evolutionary links between humans and other animals increases interest in **comparative psychology**, which is the study of the psychological characteristics of animals of all kinds, both human and nonhuman. In the 19th century, it is widely believed that nonhuman animals are less highly evolved than humans. Thus, in this era, comparative psychology is studied because of the belief that human thoughts, feelings, and behaviors may be understood by examining those characteristics in "less highly evolved," or "less complex," species. The underlying assumption is that both physical and psychological characteristics have evolved.

Evolutionary ideas also give rise to the comparative study of humans. Anthropologists and many others of this era believe that humans with different skin colors and physical characteristics actually belong to distinct species of humans.

Furthermore, these different species of humans can be ranked in terms of their level of evolution, with those claiming origins in northern Europe being ranked as the most highly evolved.

It should be noted that the idea that some animals are more highly evolved than others, including that some humans are more highly evolved than others, is not supported by the principles of natural selection, nor by anything that Charles Darwin wrote or said about evolution. These beliefs arise out of a preexisting Western worldview that certain people of northern European descent are superior to all other peoples. These beliefs provided the philosophical foundation for slavery, as well as for many other forms of Western imperialism and the exploitation of other peoples around the world. In the late 19th century, scientific support for these beliefs is sought and, in one of science's more embarrassing chapters, found.

Mental Measurement

Although most 19th-century physiologists, anatomists, and philosophers of nature hold firmly to the conviction that the human mind transcends mere matter, they nevertheless struggle to find some aspect of consciousness that can be measured. One clear difference between one human consciousness and another is intellectual capacity. Some people achieve more than others within a particular cultural definition of achievement. Some people become learned, articulate, and renowned university professors, whereas others merely cook and clean. Some people make a great deal of money, whereas others barely eke out a living. If these differing levels of achievement are due primarily to differences in intellectual capacity, then it would be interesting to be able to measure intellectual capacity. The anatomists who attempt to answer this question begin with three convictions. First, they share the widespread Western belief that there are at least four, or maybe five, distinct races of humans. Second, they are convinced that brain size is directly related to intellectual capacity. And third, they believe that of these distinct races of humans, males of northern European descent have the largest intellectual capacity.

All scientists in every era begin their investigations from within particular paradigms that shape the questions they ask and the methods they use to answer those questions. It would be easy to dismiss the work of the 19th-century physiologists who begin their work measuring intellectual capacity with these three erroneous convictions. However, simply dismissing this work on those grounds might further blind us to how preexisting worldviews influence the science of psychology, even as it is conducted in the present day. Better to examine psychology's whole history than to avoid those aspects that current paradigms find unacceptable.

Racial Distinctions

Based on encounters with cultures around the globe, the four distinct races or species of humans identified by anthropologists are Caucasians, American Indians,

Asians, and Africans. Later, others add Malaysians as a fifth. In both cases, humans are thought to have originated from a single northern European prototype, the Caucasoid male, named after a mountain range in Russia, where the most beautiful people are said to live and from where human life is first believed to have originated (Gould, 1996). Thus, all other humans are degenerations of the ideal type.

✓ **Stop and think.**
Are individuals with bigger brains smarter than those with smaller brains?

Brain Size and Intellectual Capacity

The assumption that intellectual capacity is related to brain size is a natural one to make. The idea is simple and has good face validity. Nineteenth-century anatomists have access to data that would refute such an assumption; for example, they know that elephants and blue whales have larger brains than humans. They even know that brain size is really a function of body size, so that individuals with bigger bodies also usually have bigger brains. In spite of this, many ignore these data and maintain the conviction that brain size is directly related to intellectual capacity.

Northern European Male Superiority

Many of these upper-class northern European males also believe that, as a group, they possess a superior intellectual capacity to any other race of humans, superior even to the women of their own group. After all, no other group has as well-developed a culture, as productive an economy, nor as superior a civilization as has been created in the West. Although women have sometimes achieved great things, and it is often recognized that they have been educationally disadvantaged, still, as a group, the achievements of women pale in comparison with those of men.

Some conclude that, because women and people of other races have lesser abilities, they should play lesser roles in society. Others argue that, even though these other people are lesser, they deserve the same rights as the superior group. But nearly all agree that women and people of other races are inferior (Gould, 1996). To be sure, they do have important roles to play. For example, they are unsurpassed at providing for the needs of the superior group. If it can be established by scientific evidence that these other groups do indeed have less intellectual capacity, then it will be clear to all that the supporting roles they play are destined by nature itself. Thus, measuring intellectual capacity becomes an important goal.

> ✓ **Stop and think.**
> How would you measure brain size?

Measuring Brain Size

Attempts are made to measure brain size and to make comparisons across gender, race, socioeconomic status, occupation, and lifestyle. To establish the expected superiority in Caucasian male brain size, anatomists like French physician Paul Broca use a variety of techniques, such as the actual weighing of dead brains removed during autopsy. They also try measuring the skulls of people still living. Neither of these techniques provides reliable evidence of a difference in brain size between groups. Eventually, anatomists settle on measuring the capacity of empty skulls, collected from graves and medical schools, as the best way to determine brain size. These skulls are filled with birdseed or lead shot, and the amount of seed or shot that can be fitted into the skull is weighed.

After collecting data from a variety of sources, anatomists decide that their hypothesis is supported. Educated upper-class Caucasian males do indeed have the largest brains. Women's brains are equal in size to men's when the difference in body size between women and men is corrected for, but, Broca argues, there is no need to make this correction in the data, nor to conclude that women's brains are equal to men's brains because:

> ... we must not forget that women are, on the average, a little less intelligent than men, a difference which we should not exaggerate but which is, nonetheless, real. We are therefore permitted to suppose that the relatively small size of the female brain depends in part upon her physical inferiority and in part on her intellectual inferiority. (Broca, 1861, p. 153, as cited in Gould, 1996)

*Today a number of irregularities with these 19th-century attempts to measure brain size are recognized. For example, in cases where group differences were found, the researchers were aware of which group each skull belonged to before they began their measurements. Thus, if they expected to find that one skull held more than another, it was not hard to find ways to fit more into that one. This is why researchers should be **blind** to the variables and hypotheses during data collection. Also, although a program of research is always begun with a hypothesis, the goal in science is supposed to be to test the hypothesis in whatever way will be required to prove it wrong, not to prove it right. That is why the **null hypothesis** is tested for, which is the hypothesis that there are no differences between groups. Today, blind and **double-blind** (meaning that both those who collect the data and the participants are unaware of the hypothesis) designs are used, tests are made* *for the null hypothesis, and students are required to study experimental research methods during their earliest undergraduate training.*

Statistics and Mental Measurement

The role played by statistics in 19th-century mental measurements can be illustrated by the work of Francis Galton (1822–1911), a cousin of Charles Darwin. Galton, like many of his contemporaries, has a passion for measuring. He measures variables like the weather, fingerprints, and psychological variables like the effectiveness of prayer, perceptions of beauty, or degree of boredom. Charles Darwin emphasizes the importance of variations among individuals in the process of natural selection, and after reading Darwin's *On the Origin of Species by Means of Natural Selection*, published in 1859, Galton becomes fascinated with measuring these differences. He sets up a laboratory to measure every conceivable difference among individuals, from head circumference and socioeconomic status to sensory sensitivity. He collects data from more than 17,000 participants, amassing a huge set of data on individual differences *that has not even yet been fully analyzed.* As Galton makes comparisons among these many measurements, for example, by comparing arm length with leg length, he develops a measure he calls the co-relation. Among the co-relations Galton explores in his data are relationships between the sexes on a number of variables. *Most psychology students today are familiar with Pearson's* r, *a measure of* **correlation** *developed by a follower and student of Galton's, Karl Pearson (1857–1936).*

Galton assumes that intellectual capacity is a consequence of sensory acuity, not brain size, that is, the better the sense of hearing or the better the ability to see, the higher the intellectual capacity. This is why he includes sensory acuity among the measures that he makes. Because sensory acuity is an inherited physical characteristic, Galton and others naturally conclude that intellectual capacity is also an inherited characteristic and not subject to the effects of learning and interactions with the environment. If intellectual capacity is an inherited characteristic and those who are brighter rise to higher levels of eminence in society, then it stands to reason that eminence should run in families. To explore this question, Galton examines lists of people who have achieved some degree of recognition. He discovers that it is common to see multiple members of the same family reaching higher levels of eminence (Galton, 1869). His own family is a good example of this, with his grandfather, Erasmus Darwin, being a recognized biologist; his cousin, Charles Darwin, the naturalist; and, of course, Galton himself. In examining the records to establish that eminence runs in families, Galton is conducting what is referred to as **archival research**, in which data are collected from the historical record.

In a further effort to understand the origins of intellectual capacity and achievement, Galton also develops a questionnaire and distributes it to 200 of his fellow scientists, initiating the use of **survey research** in psychology. In the title of the book reporting the results of this survey, *English Men of Science: Their Nature* *and Nurture* (1874), Galton gives a name to an area of inquiry that proves historically important to psychology. The study of the relative importance of inherited characteristics and learning, and relationships between the two, is referred to as **nature versus nurture**. Galton notes that most of the scientists surveyed said they had been interested in science "for as long as they could remember," supporting his belief that intellectual capacity is inherited. Eventually, Galton decides that, although the potential for high intelligence is inherited, it is only fully developed in the proper kind of environment.

To further explore relationships between nature and nurture, Galton collects data from **monozygotic** (identical, or single-egg) and **dizygotic** (fraternal, or separate-egg) twins, some raised together and some in different homes. He finds that identical twins are more similar to each other than are fraternal twins, even when the identical twins are raised apart. This adds evidence to his conviction about the importance of inherited characteristics.

In his passion to measure the naturally occurring individual differences that are both the raw material for and the products of natural selection, Galton brings psychological research closer to its present-day form in a variety of important ways. He measures psychological variables widely regarded in the 19th century as unmeasurable. For example, he measures how much his colleagues "fidget" at scientific meetings, arguing that this is a measure of boredom. In measuring an aspect of consciousness, Galton is participating in experimental psychology, just appearing in the latter half of the 19th century in German laboratories.

EXPLORING THE CONTENTS OF CONSCIOUSNESS

Examining and measuring the anatomy of the brain may be one way to bring the methods of science to bear on the questions of psychology, but in the mid-19th-century physiologists, following in the tradition of Weber and Fechner, advocate a different approach. They are more concerned with finding ways to measure the contents of consciousness than with the anatomy of the brain.

✓ Stop and think.
Why do you have the thoughts you have? Why those thoughts and not others?

Because the consciousness of others cannot be observed, mind must be inferred only through the subjective testimony of introspection (Daston, 1982). The mind directs thoughts and behaviors and makes individuals responsible for their choices. Thus, the search for mind is closely tied with Christian religious doctrines. In fact, in the 19th century, these studies are referred to as "moral philosophy." On the other hand, if mind is not metaphysical but is instead as material as the rest of our physiology, what, if anything, is free will? Are attention and volition empirical questions or ethical questions?

✓ **Stop and think.**

How does suggesting that free will is a physiological question, and not a moral one, threaten the traditional foundations of ethics and Western law?

Some of psychology's questions lead to testable hypotheses. For example, associationists say that humans begin life with a consciousness that is like a blank slate. Sensory systems then provide a variety of experiences that, through repeated exposures, become meaningful basic elements of perception. The laws of association then explain how these basic elements of perception are slowly assembled together into complex thoughts and ideas.

If associationism explains where thoughts come from, then understanding consciousness becomes a matter of first understanding how the sensory systems work to provide those simple sensations. Then the laws of association that allow simple sensations to be built into complex thoughts must be understood. Thus, during the last half of the 19th century, studies of how sensory systems work are brought together with philosophies about how complex ideas are built up. The new discipline of science that emerges is psychology, defined as the study of consciousness through the methods of natural science.

German Experimental Psychology

✓ **Stop and think.**

Can consciousness ever be inspected?

Within German universities, a few individuals begin to believe that consciousness can be measured. Among these is Wilhelm Wundt (1832–1920), who holds a chair in philosophy at the University of Leipzig in Germany. Trained as a medical doctor, Wundt knows about Fechner's work in psychophysics, has studied physiology under Müller at the University of Berlin and served as a research assistant for Helmholtz for 8 years. Wundt teaches courses, including one called Psychology as a Natural Science, even before accepting the position at Leipzig. He believes that consciousness can be studied by using many of the scientific methods learned while conducting physiological research. Although consciousness itself may not be observable, Wundt believes that conscious functioning might be measured. For example, one might observe and describe how much time is required to complete various mental tasks.

Wundt calls his technique "experimental introspection." For Wundt, psychological study has two goals. The first is to discover the basic elements of consciousness (sensations), and the second is to discover the laws of association that govern how those basic elements are combined into perceptions, thoughts, and complex ideas.

More in agreement with Lamarck's theory of the inheritance of acquired characteristics than with what he sees as Darwin's very passive theory of natural selection, Wundt views all animals, including humans, as actively striving to adapt successfully to their environments. Thus, the basic elements of consciousness are combined into complex thoughts for the purpose of achieving some desired goal that will enhance adaptation. Because this is a willful effort directed toward a goal, Wundt calls his theory of psychology "voluntarism." By this, he does not mean to imply that behavior is freely willed. He only means that, driven by some biological need, humans actively and even creatively engage in behaviors that are intended to help fulfill that need.

On the strength of his conviction, but with little support from his university, in 1879, Wundt sets aside some space in which to conduct the kinds of studies in standardized introspection that he believes will be useful (Bringmann, Voss, & Ungerer, 1997). *Although others set up psychology laboratories elsewhere, both in Europe and the United States, Wundt is traditionally credited with the formal founding of the discipline of experimental psychology.*

The model established for experimental psychology in Leipzig would hardly be recognizable to present-day students of psychology. To overcome objections to introspection as a scientific method, Wundt advocates the method of standardized introspection. This makes the role of the observer as central to the method, as in astronomy and all other sciences. The observer *(in today's language, the subject or participant)* must know how to observe and what to observer, whereas the experimental manipulator is only there to ensure that the conditions for observation are right (Fuchs & Milar, 2003). Thus, the issue of individual differences in reliability of observations and the astronomers' personal equation becomes a critically important question for psychologists.

In Wundt's laboratories, research is conducted collaboratively among many students. To amass sufficient reaction time data to draw meaningful conclusions, students sometimes serve as observers and sometimes as the manipulators of the stimuli. Because he is a trained observer, Wundt's own reactions to the experimental stimuli are often collected. Unlike the physiologists alone in their laboratories, dissecting and testing dead or dying specimens, these students of psychology are cooperatively observing and measuring one another's reactions to answer their hypotheses. A major goal is to explain consciousness on the basis of underlying mental functions, such as attention. The objects of attention explain, in part, the contents of consciousness. Wundt's laboratory is a lively place, and by 1897, experimental psychology has expanded at Leipzig to fill an entire building. The questions of psychology also quickly come to differ from those of physiology. Whereas physiological studies continue to focus on how the various sensory systems operate, psychological questions begin to be more about attentions and other mental functions.

Wundt believes that experiments alone will never provide a full understanding of human consciousness. A second explanation for consciousness lies in examining aggregate human behavior in the context of culture and the various forces working to drive human evolution. For example, Wundt believes that language and its role in shaping consciousness can only be understood through studies of cultural contexts, such as those conducted by anthropologists. He believes that understanding these influences are also necessary if we are to fully understand consciousness and motivation (Wundt, 1916). Most of his later career and writings are focused on these interests.

In addition to having established a laboratory, Wundt holds a place in the history of psychology by virtue of his perseverance, organizational skills, and the sheer volume of his work. During the 45 years that he holds an academic position at Leipzig, from 1875 to 1920, he supervises 186 doctoral dissertations by students from countries all over the Western world and publishes more than 491 books, journal articles, book chapters, lectures, and reviews (Wundt, 1927). In 1881, he establishes psychology's first academic journal, *Philosophical Studies*, as a forum for his students' papers. The movement toward the scientific study of the questions of psychology is already "in the air" at the end of the 19th century, but would most likely not have proceeded so rapidly without the energy and direction of Wilhelm Wundt. Although most of his students eventually adopt theoretical perspectives divergent from his, there is no argument that Wundt's career has had a powerful influence on shaping present-day Western psychology.

Experimental Psychology Outside of Germany

At the University of St. Petersburg, the Russian physiologist Ivan Sechenov (1829–1905) also advocates coming to understand psychology through the use of the methods of natural science, not surprisingly because he, like Wundt, worked with and studied under Müller and Helmholtz. In his book *Reflexes of the Brain*, published in 1863, Sechenov argues that consciousness does not represent a metaphysical soul, but results from muscular and material movements (Yaroschevskii, 1982). *Reflexes of the Brain* is banned by the Catholic government of Russia, and Sechenov's influence on 19th- and early 20th-century Western psychology is thus limited (Frolov, 1937).

At Cambridge University in England, an attempt is made to promote experimental psychology as a discipline in 1877 and to establish a laboratory there. But the University Senate turns down the proposal on the grounds that it would "insult religion by putting the human soul in a pair of scales" (University College London, 2004). England is one of the last Western countries to institute the formal study of experimental psychology.

European-type physiological psychology travels rapidly to North America, where it finds fertile ground in a more pragmatic and less religiously dogmatic intellectual environment. In 1875, the philosopher William James (1842–1910) establishes a teaching laboratory at Harvard University after traveling to Germany to hear the lectures of Wundt and others. Experimental psychology in North America takes on a very different character than that in Europe, more concerned with function than structure and with practical applications over purely academic questions.

Unconscious Mind

Both ordinary daily experience and the experimental study of consciousness leads to the belief that there must be another aspect of mind beyond consciousness. For example, it is possible to respond to hearing one's own name spoken while still asleep. Dreams can often only be called into conscious awareness with difficulty later. Under hypnosis, memories can be retrieved that are not available to consciousness. In experimental studies, people are influenced by stimuli, even though the exposure is so brief that they insist they have no memory of them (Marcel, 1983).

To the 19th-century scholar, these kinds of experiences suggest the existence of two minds, one conscious and one unconscious. Even Fechner's psychophysics suggest the existence of unconscious mental processing. If mind is soul, and there is more than one mind, which of these minds is soul? Is soul the conscious and rational mind or the largely unconscious mind? Is the unconscious mind also rational, or do the roots of irrational thoughts and behaviors lie somewhere in its dark mysteries? Questions like these haunt physicians and psychologists of the late 19th century, like Sigmund Freud. Along with the loosening of religious grip on intellectual concerns, these questions may help account for the declining focus toward the end of the century on psychology as the study of the human soul. Like a prism with many sides, psychology is a discipline with many facets as it moves into the next century.

⊕   **The Times**

The early 19th century sees the Industrial Revolution beginning with the machine production of textiles followed by the mass production of a wide variety of consumer goods. Machine industry provides jobs and creates a middle class, which provides the market for these goods. By midcentury, there have been many improvements in the daily lives of ordinary people.

For almost the first time in human history, many people can afford more than one set of clothes. Famine is no longer a constant threat, and instead of day after day of potatoes and bread, ordinary people can enjoy an occasional fruit or vegetable and maybe even a little meat.

There are downsides to this revolution as well. These include not just the terrible air and water pollution, or the mind-numbing and even life-threatening nature of the jobs in the factories, but also the psychological consequences of this new kind of life. Men, women, and even children provide the power that makes the factories run, so people are literally part of the machine. Humans have become cog-like parts of the industrial machine. Work lives are separated from personal lives, and jobs become less about the completion of meaningful projects and more just the means to get money. Late in the century, the exploitation of the working classes collides with political ideas of individual freedom and explodes into movements to organize workers into unions.

The 19th century also sees a phenomenal expansion in systems of transportation. New railroads carry the raw materials needed by industry and deliver the finished goods. Steamships ferry people to new jobs while trolleys and omnibuses move them around the growing cities. Families who have never been more than walking distance from home and each other suddenly find themselves scattered and living days' or even weeks' travel away. A massive network of new communication technologies begins to emerge. Radio messages travel across the ocean, and the telegraph and telephone are invented and come into widespread use by the end of the century. In midcentury, huge rotary presses are publishing daily papers.

European powers continue to claim territories and colonies throughout the world, taking over and occupying previously independent peoples in the political and economic movement referred to as imperialism. These occupied territories become increasingly impoverished while providing the resources needed to supply Western industry and sustain the increasingly rich standard of living in the West. The slave trade is active, bringing mostly people of color to take agricultural jobs in the rapidly industrializing West and enslaving workers in Western colonies as well. It is not until 1848 in Britain and 1868 in the United States that slavery in the home countries is outlawed.

Seven hundred years after the establishment of universities in the West, the first women are admitted. In 1837, Oberlin College in Ohio admits women to study with men, the first institution of higher learning in the country to do so. But as late as 1868, there are still only four women's colleges in the United States authorized to grant the bachelor's degree (Sklar, 1971). Women are actively fighting for the same rights as men throughout the 19th century. These include the right to own property, the right to divorce, the right to make decisions about their children's lives, the right not to be treated as property, the right not to be legally beaten and raped by their husbands, the right to an equal education, the right to equal job opportunities and pay, and the right to vote in national elections. Women are granted the right to vote in Germany at the conclusion of World War I in 1919, in the United States in 1920, in Italy in 1925, in England in 1928, in Spain in 1933, and not until 1945 in France.

7

A Divided Discipline: What Is the Function of Mind?

In this chapter, we explore the differing sets of assumptions about the origins, nature, and functions of psychological characteristics that divide scholars in the final quarter of the 19th century. These differing assumptions lead to different questions and diverse approaches to the study of psychology. Prominent among these approaches is the study of those individuals who exhibit behavior indicative of disturbances in thought, the mentally ill. Later in the chapter, the influences of Western culture on psychology are examined as the new science embarks on its journey across the Atlantic, where a uniquely North American landscape of empirical psychology is discovered.

DIVISIONS CREATED BY IDEAS

By the end of the 19th century, most who call themselves psychologists are united by allegiance to empirical scientific methods. They adhere to the methods of standardized observation and experimentation that have proven so successful in the other sciences. Even though united by methods, these psychologists typically adopt one of three sets of differing assumptions about what motivates thoughts, feelings, and behaviors. These sets of assumptions shape the intellectual landscape of psychology at the end of the 19th century.

Elementalism

Among these is an **elementalist** psychology based on the assumption that conscious mind is made up of basic mental elements associated together. Elementalists embrace positivistic research methods. They conduct careful, systematic observations of mental operations and experiment with manipulations of stimuli. They hope to reveal important and previously little understood characteristics of the basic mental elements and to uncover the laws by which the elements are combined or associated into complex thoughts. A few elementalist researchers, notably Wundt, prefer research methods that, they argue, preserve more of the environment or context. Wundt, for example, is concerned that isolating variables of interest away from the context in which they ordinarily occur will not result in useful knowledge.

Holism

Taking into account the context in which an organism functions forms the basis of another major influence on psychology at the turn of the century. **Holism**, or dynamic psychology, is the perspective that any real understanding of psychological characteristics must take into consideration the whole organism or person in interaction with a whole environment. The person is imbedded in a network of dynamic or constantly changing interactions. Holistic psychologists also recognize the possibility that thoughts, feelings, and behaviors may be caused by both conscious and unconscious motivators. According to dynamic psychology, the whole being, both conscious and unconscious, in constant interaction with the environment, is what determines thoughts, feelings, and behaviors. Mind is constantly changing in response to changing needs and the changing environment. Empirical research methods are used in holistic approaches to psychology, primarily to provide the evidence needed to support intuitions and rationally derived principles.

Evolutionary Principles

The principles of natural selection are embraced by many psychologists and become a third major influence on the development of psychology as a science. The assumption is that useful explanations for thoughts, feelings, and behaviors lie in understanding better the context in which humans evolved as a species. For example, in the late 19th century, Northern Europeans commonly believe that they are more peaceful than other ethnic groups. This conviction is based on the belief that these other groups are not as fully evolved.

Those who favor evolutionary assumptions collect anecdotal observations of animal behavior and then draw comparisons between those and human behavior. These researchers are often accused of attributing human characteristics to nonhuman animals, or **anthropomorphizing**. Darwin himself points out, however, that attributing certain characteristics, like conscious thought, only to humans is also a kind of anthropomorphizing (Darwin, 1916).

As the various domains of psychology are considered through the remainder of this journey, the intellectual paths of elementalism, holism, and evolutionary principles will often be encountered.

PSYCHOLOGY FOLLOWS MANY PATHS

On the next part of this journey through the history of Western psychology, several different paths will be explored, all of which lead from the late 19th century to the discipline recognized in the present day as psychology. At its beginning, the science of psychology has a slightly different focus in each country in which it is studied. As seen in the previous chapter, experimental psychology first begins to appear during this era, led in large part by the establishment of research laboratories at German universities. German students usually attend German universities, read journals published in German, and typically follow the interests inspired by their German professors. The same is true for French students, English students, and eventually for students in North America as well.

The focus on experimental psychology predominates in Germany for many years. Late 19th-century German elementalist interest in the contents of consciousness influences all of Western psychology as students from many other countries study in German universities and take what they have learned home with them.

In France, the medical profession influences the institutional treatment of the mentally ill, and this becomes a focus for French psychologists. These French psychologists are reputed to be more interested in providing therapy and in clinical applications of psychological study than they are in laboratory experiments (Goldstein, 1987).

As the British Empire expands its colonial holdings throughout the world, British philosophers and naturalists pursue their interests in comparing all of the various forms of life encountered in their travels. Thus, for many years, British psychology has a comparative focus and claims roots in the earlier work of philosophers like Alexander Bain and Herbert Spencer.

Russian physiologists and physicians follow a different path, strongly influenced by materialist philosophies and by the work of German physiologists like Müller and Helmholtz. It is only after the turn of the century that the findings of Russian physiological psychologists become important to the development of Western psychology.

These geographic or cultural differences in psychology are by no means absolute. French researchers like Théodule Ribot (1835–1916) engage in the experimental study of psychology, and Germans like Johann Langermann (1768–1832) are concerned with the treatment of the mentally ill. Italian, Danish, and Swiss scholars and psychologists are also active in both experimental and therapeutic psychologies.

The Study of Consciousness

The principal proponents of the elementalist paradigm in psychology are the Germans. The legacy of the empirical study of human consciousness that grows out of Wundt's laboratory at Leipzig is far-reaching.

Structuralism and Titchener

Only a few of the students coming out of the German universities continue to study the basic mental elements and the laws of association that so fascinated Wilhelm Wundt early in his career. Among those who do pursue elementalist assumptions is Edward Bradford Titchener (1867–1927), a British student who receives his doctorate at Leipzig in 1892. Titchener then returns to England, where he hopes to continue his experimental study of psychology. Finding, to his dismay, that universities in England oppose experimental psychology, Titchener reluctantly accepts a position at Cornell University in New York State. Here, James Angell (1869–1949), an American who also studied at Leipzig, has recently established a laboratory for the experimental study of psychology. Titchener spends the remainder of his life in the United States. He is often thought of as Wundt's only loyal disciple, but as his career progresses, even his work moves away from Wundt's more holistic concern with the contents and operations of consciousness.

Titchener's work is designed to illuminate the nature of the basic elements of consciousness and the mechanisms or laws of association by which complex thoughts are formed. He does not share Wundt's willingness to try to explain consciousness, saying instead that consciousness can only be described, not explained. Titchener also does not accept Wundt's idea that consciousness is shaped by concepts, like attention, that cannot be further broken down. He believes instead that consciousness is made up only of basic elements associated together. He assumes that eventually the physiological bases of both the elements and the mechanisms of association will be discovered and described (Leahey, 1981). Titchener calls his search for the functions and structures of mind **structuralism**.

Titchener employs the same methods of standardized and controlled introspection in his laboratories that he learned as a graduate student in Leipzig. The difference between observations in physics and those in psychology is that conscious mind is both the subject of observation and also the observer. Thus, in psychology the observation is called introspection, rather than inspection. In all other regards, structuralists believe, the scientific investigation of psychology should be conducted using exactly the same methods used in any other study of nature. Just as in chemistry, psychologists should attempt to isolate the basic elements, vary them systematically so as to understand how they are related, and be able to replicate the same findings when the experiments are repeated. The structuralists believe that the only way to gain a true understanding of how consciousness is structured is by following these methods.

Titchener is convinced that this type of investigation will make it possible to arrange "the mental elements precisely as the chemist classifies his elementary substances" (Titchener, 1912, p. 49). The basic mental elements consist of all sensory experiences, images (ideas, memories, and thoughts), and affections (emotions). These basic mental elements vary along the dimensions of quality, intensity, clearness, and duration. Structuralism is the attempt to identify and measure these basic mental elements and their attributes and to understand how those elements combine to produce complex conscious thought. Structuralists are not opposed to attempts to understand the functions of consciousness, but they believe that hypothesizing about the functions of consciousness before the structures of consciousness are understood will lead to beliefs that structures exist for the purpose of performing some function, that is, that function precedes structure. "There is, further, the danger that, if function is studied before structure has been fully elucidated, the student may fall into that acceptance of teleological explanation which is fatal to scientific advance" (Titchener, 1898, p. 453).

Over his years at Cornell, Titchener admits many students to graduate study in his laboratory, including many women. For example, his first doctoral student is Margaret Floy Washburn, an animal psychologist whose work is discussed later in this chapter. Titchener is one of very few psychologists to accept women into graduate study in the late 19th century. Almost half of his graduate students are women, and more women complete their doctoral studies with him than with any other psychologist of the time.

A few of Titchener's students continue to pursue the structuralist paradigm in their careers, but by the early 20th century, elementalist questions are considered irrelevant by many North American psychologists. Introspective research about the basic elements of consciousness and the laws by which those elements are combined diminishes after Titchener's death in 1927.

The Imageless Element

Other students from the laboratory at Leipzig take the search for the elements of consciousness in different directions. Oswald Külpe (1862–1915), for example, a graduate from Leipzig who accepts a position at the University of Würzburg in Germany, begins to believe that conscious thought might not always be a result of the combination of sensations, images, or affections. Instead, he suggests, thought might occur even in the absence of any image at all. This might happen, as Külpe and other researchers demonstrate, when people are asked to judge the relative weight of two objects. Most people have no difficulty making the judgment, but when asked to describe the elements of thought experienced while making the judgment, most people are unable to provide any description. Külpe and his colleagues suggest that thought processes like judging are a previously unidentified basic process of consciousness they call "imageless thought."

✓ **Stop and think.**
Can you think a thought that is not accompanied by a mental image?

Holistic Consciousness

The legacy of the laboratory at Leipzig is not limited to those who continue the program of research that originates there. Psychologies that oppose elementalist theories and ideas are equally a part of that legacy. Although just as concerned with the contents of consciousness, some psychologists are skeptical that psychological characteristics can be explained by laws governing how basic elements are combined. They argue that making that assumption makes humans more like machines than like freely willing, morally responsible people. For example, Franz Brentano (1838–1917), at the University of Vienna, suggests that consciousness operates in a more holistic manner by carrying out whole "acts" of thought, like judging, visualizing images, or experiencing emotions and desires. These psychological acts are intentional, not mechanical. They are not automatic but are directed at achieving some purpose. Thus, Brentano asks questions about how consciousness helps humans to function in the world and not about basic elements and laws of association (Baumgartner & Baumgartner, 1997; Brentano, 1874/1981).

Unconscious Motivation

Other late 19th-century researchers of mind oppose the elementalist paradigm because of its focus on conscious mind alone as the motivator of behavior. These psychologists argue that this leaves too many thoughts, feelings, and behaviors unexplained. Like romantic philosophers, they argue that it often feels as though emotions have more to do with motivating behavior than does rational thought.

> The heart has its reasons which reason cannot know.
> (Blaise Pascal, Pensées IV)

In the late 19th century, psychologists increasingly look for unconscious motivators of thoughts, feelings, and behaviors. These nonconscious motivators might be other aspects of mind, so that mind is actually made up of both conscious and nonconscious minds, or the motivators might be something widely viewed as something entirely different from mind, such as emotion.

Comparative Psychology

In 1872, Darwin publishes *The Expression of the Emotions in Man and Animals*, in which he argues that emotion has been selected for during the evolution of both human and nonhuman animals because the ability to express emotion has survival value. For example, the feeling of fear in a life-threatening situation may facilitate adaptive responses, such as fleeing the situation. The facial expression of fear may communicate the need to flee to one's companions. Similarly, thinking, reasoning, and problem solving also might increase an organism's chances of survival in difficult situations. In the same way that certain physical characteristics aid survival in particular environments, psychological characteristics also facilitate survival and reproduction.

This idea is evident in the work of Francis Galton, who suggests that psychological characteristics are as measurable as physical ones and as subject to the laws of inheritance (McClearn, 1991). Darwin also argues in 1859 in *On the Origin of Species* that characteristics that have been selected for during evolution will show continuity across all species. This idea is misrepresented by others to mean that humans are more highly evolved than other animals, primarily by Spencer, but also by Wundt. The implication is that the history of the evolution of, human mind can be traced by examining the less evolved minds of other animals. This may explain why the study of animal mind becomes popular at this point in the history of psychology.

The Anecdotal Method

Darwin's friend and fellow naturalist, Canadian George Romanes (1848–1894), is among those who pursue the study of animal mind late in the 19th century. Romanes collects hundreds of anecdotes about interesting and amazing animal behaviors from which he infers intelligence and complex emotions in nonhuman animals. In 1882, he publishes *Animal Intelligence*, which is a collection of these descriptions of animal behavior. For example, he has collected stories about scorpions that sting themselves to death when surrounded by fire. He then speculates that the scorpions experience despair at finding themselves in such dire straits and decide to commit suicide rather than face burning to death.

Romanes' first book is only descriptive and is a first step in coming to understand mind, both human and nonhuman. He publishes two more books, *Mental Evolution in Animals* in 1884 and *Mental Evolution in Man* in 1888, both of which explicate the methods he proposes for the study of human and nonhuman mind. Romanes names his study comparative psychology and describes it as the study of similarities and differences in psychological characteristics across species. He likens comparative psychology to the already existing field of comparative anatomy in physiology.

Unfortunately for Romanes and for the subsequent study of animal mind, most of the attention is directed at his first book, made up mostly of anecdotal descriptions. He is attacked from two directions. First, he is accused of drawing conclusions about the causes of behavior from the anecdotes he describes. Because in this first book he only describes behavior and conducts no controlled experimental study, he is attacked for drawing causal conclusions from descriptive data. Second, he is accused of anthropomorphizing. The scorpion stinging itself out of despair is behaving as a human might in similar circumstances. Theologians, in particular, are disturbed by the growing interest in attributing higher level abstract thought to nonhuman animals. They are concerned about comparisons that seem either to elevate nonhuman animals to the level of humans or to lower humans to the level of all other animals.

✓ **Stop and think.**

If nonhuman animals think, do they have free will? Do they also have souls?

How Should Animal Mind Be Studied?

In response to these objections, other students of animal mind clarify the field and suggest more scientific methods. Fellow British scientist C. Lloyd Morgan (1852–1936), for example, believes animal mind is an important area of study but reminds scientists to be careful of how they interpret animal behavior: "In no case is an animal activity to be interpreted as the outcome of the exercise of a higher psychical faculty, if it can be fairly interpreted as the outcome of the exercise of one which stands lower in the psychological scale" (Morgan, 1904, p. 59).

Morgan then gives an example of what he means. While teaching in South Africa, Morgan has the opportunity to observe the behavior of scorpions himself. He notes that Romanes' description that some scorpions sting themselves to death when surrounded by fire is accurate, but it may not be accurate to conclude that scorpions experience despair and intentionally kill themselves. Morgan suggests that instead of a higher faculty, such as a complex emotion like despair, scorpion behavior may be explained in terms of a lower faculty, such as a reflex—stinging— that is exercised more or less automatically in threatening situations.

Given the state of technology in the late 19th century, the study of any mind, human or nonhuman, is limited to either introspection in the case of one's own mind or inference in the case of the minds of others. Morgan points out that there are really two kinds of inferences that can be made when studying the minds of others. The first is **projective inference**, in which one's own mental experiences are projected onto the other. Thus, we can imagine the despair we might feel on finding ourselves surrounded by fire, knowing that we will inevitably burn to death. In such circumstances, and with means of a quick and painless death readily at hand, we might indeed commit suicide. But to conclude that these feelings are also the subjective experience of the scorpion is a projective inference.

There is a scientifically valid way to make inferences about the minds of others, and this is what Morgan calls **objective inference**. An objective inference is one that infers only those mental powers that may be verified by public observation and measurement. Thus, objective inferences may be drawn about an animal's perceptual capabilities or its capacity to attend to stimuli. For example, do scorpions have the ability to recognize and retreat from fire? This testable objective inference is potentially informative in the study of animal mind. As a further illustration of the need to avoid projective inferences when describing animal mind, Morgan offers the following story of how his terrier learned to open the gate and escape from the yard.

Story of Tony, the Fox Terrier

Tony, when he wanted to go out into the road, used to put his head under the latch of the gate, lift it, and wait for the gate to swing open. Now an observer of the dog's intelligent action might well suppose that he clearly perceived how the end in view was to be gained, and the most appropriate means for effecting his purpose. Once more, therefore, I must draw attention to the canon of interpretation adopted at the outset of our inquiries concerning minds other than ours, namely, that in no case is an animal activity to be interpreted in terms of higher psychological processes, if it can be fairly interpreted in terms of processes which stand lower in the scale of psychological evolution and development. The question is therefore whether Tony's behavior can be fairly explained without his forming any conception of the relation of the means employed to the end attained. It appears to me that it can. I watched the development of the habit. The latch of the gate is at a level just above the reach of Tony's head. When the latch is lifted, the gate swings open by its own weight. When Tony was put out of the front door, he naturally wanted to get out into the road, where there was often much to interest him. He ran up and down the fence, and put his head out between the iron bars, now here, now there, now elsewhere, keenly gazing into the road. He did not specially look out or near the gate, nor did he seem to be trying to get out. He appeared only to be looking restlessly and wistfully at the familiar road. At length it so happened that he put his head beneath the latch. The latch was thus lifted. He withdrew his head and began to look out elsewhere, when he noticed that the gate was swinging open, and out he bolted. After that, gradually he went, after less frequent poking of

> his head in the wrong place, to the opening from which the latch could be lifted. But it took him nearly three weeks, before he went at once and without hesitation to the right place and put his head without any ineffectual fumbling beneath the latch. Why did he take so long? I think partly because there was so little connection between gazing out into the road and getting out into the road. He did not, at first at any rate, seem to do the former in order to effect the latter. The relation between means and end did not appear to take form in his mind, even subconsciously as means to the end. And I take it that he never had the faintest notion of how or why looking out just there came to mean walking forth into the road. (adapted from Morgan, 1904, pp. 292–293)

Comparative psychologists bring positivistic experimental methods to their study of animal mind. The American psychologist Margaret Floy Washburn (1871–1939), the first woman to receive a PhD in psychology, makes major contributions to the experimental study of animal mind. For example, she establishes that fish have the ability to perceive color and uses experimental methods to explore other questions about perception, attention, and consciousness in nonhuman animals. In 1908, she publishes *The Animal Mind*, which becomes the standard textbook for comparative psychology for many decades.

> ✓ **Stop and think.**
> What really distinguishes human animals from nonhuman animals? Is there anything that any normal human can do that no other animal does?

Washburn points out that the only way anyone can attempt to understand the subjective experiences of another is through inference from behavior. We each infer that others experience similar thoughts and emotions as our own by observing their behaviors. This is why we often infer that nonhuman animals also experience similar thoughts and emotions. For example, from their behavior we infer that nonhuman animals must at least experience emotions like fear or even anger:

> ✓ **Stop and think.**
> What must the experience of emotion be like for a nonhuman animal?

We speak, for example, of an "angry" wasp. Anger, in our own experience, is largely composed of sensations of quickened heart beat, of altered breathing, of muscular tension, of increased blood pressure in the head and face. The circulation of a wasp is fundamentally different from that of any vertebrate. The wasp does not breathe through lungs, it wears its skeleton on the outside, and it has muscles attached to the

inside of the skeleton. What is anger like in the wasp's consciousness? We can form
no adequate idea of it. (Washburn, 1908/1936, p. 3)

The common goal pursued by early comparative psychologists is to explain and
understand animal mind, but for a variety of reasons, others reject the very idea
of animal mind. They point out that animal mind must always be inferred from
watching animal behavior. Thus, parsimony requires giving up the assumption of
animal mind. Of course, as Washburn and many others have suggested, skepticism
requires that any mind other than one's own must be inferred by observing behavior.
Thus, parsimony would also require giving up assumptions of any mind other than
our own.

Because it is always necessary to infer mind in others from their behavior, the
possibility always exists that there is no mind there. Early in the 20th century,
some psychologists reject inferences about the existence of animal mind. They
argue that scientific explanations for the behavior of others, including animals,
can be found in behavior alone. The major paradigm of early 20th-century North
American psychology called behaviorism originates in part from the rejection of
comparative psychology's study of animal mind.

The Development of Human Mind

Many of the same forces that lead to an interest in animal mind also result in
an increased interest in comparing the psychological characteristics and development of infants and young children with those of adults. In particular, beliefs in
something called recapitulation drives the interest in studying early development.
Recapitulation is the 19th-century theory that, during prenatal development and
even after birth, the human goes through each successive stage of evolution experienced as the human species evolved. So it is believed that, early in prenatal
development, the human embryo is a fish, later mammalian, and at birth like a
primitive human. Thus, by studying infants and young children, one might come
to better understand the processes by which adults have become fully human.

The earliest systematic observations of development in infancy in the West are
conducted by the German physician Adolf Kußmaul (1822–1902). The results of
his carefully conducted experiments on the sensory and perceptual capabilities of
infants are published in his book *Investigations of the Mental Life of Newborn
Human Children* in German in 1859. On the basis of his experiments, Kußmaul
concludes that Aristotle's findings attributing significant abilities to young infants
are more compatible with the experimental results than are John Locke's, who
theorizes that infants are born as blank slates with few abilities. For example,
Kußmaul finds that within a few hours of birth, even before they have been fed
anything, infants show distinctive facial expressions to sweet and bitter tastes, that
these expressions are specific to each taste, and that they are the same expressions
seen when adults experience the same tastes. Thus, infants do not exhibit one
vague response that gradually differentiates when associations are formed, as is

commonly assumed. Instead, they exhibit specific unlearned responses to a large range of stimuli.

Kußmaul's findings are published in English in 1863 and are later used by others who also conduct observations of early development. For example, Charles Darwin, not only a noted naturalist, but also a devoted father, carefully observes and then publishes notes on his son's early development. William Preyer (1841–1878) publishes *The Mind of the Child* in 1882. Milicent Shinn (1858–1940), the first woman to earn a PhD in psychology from the University of California (Clemens, 1998), publishes a detailed diary of one infant's physical and mental development as her doctoral dissertation in 1898. This work is reissued for the lay audience in 1900 as *The Biography of a Baby* (Stevens & Gardner, 1982).

American psychologist G. Stanley Hall (1844–1924) is usually credited with founding the scientific study of child development, despite the fact that these other studies are published long before his and he conducts very little science himself. Hall's work in developmental psychology is concerned primarily with the education of young children. For example, early in his career, he uses questionnaire and interview techniques to collect data about what young children just entering kindergarten know about the world. He concludes that 5-year-old children do not know much. What is referred to as child study eventually becomes a popular field in North America, one that is relatively open to study for women scholars, and one that has a variety of clinical and other applications.

Physiological Psychology

As seen earlier, Russian physiologist Ivan Sechenov's work is influenced by his studies in Helmholtz's laboratory in Berlin, by Spencer's philosophy, and by ideas about the evolutionary bases of what Sechenov calls "psychical" faculties. His research supports the belief that the evolution of sensory organs was accompanied by the evolution of psychological characteristics (Frolov, 1937). This belief leads Sechenov to conclude that psychological phenomena can be studied and will best be understood not through introspection, but in terms of the physiological functioning of the brain and nervous system. For Sechenov, consciousness is not a mysterious inner spirit that directs behavior but, instead, both thoughts and behavior are caused by external events:

> Let us then enter the world of phenomena engendered by the functioning of the brain. It is generally said that this world embraces the entire psychical life; few people can be found now who would not accept this idea with greater or lesser reservations. The differences in the views of the various schools consist merely in the fact that some regard the brain as the organ of the spirit, thus divorcing the latter from the former, while others declare that the spirit is the product of the functioning of the brain. Not being philosophers, we shall not discuss these differences here. (Sechenov, 1863/1965, pp. 2–3)

> ✓ **Stop and think.**
> If thoughts cause behavior, then what causes thoughts?

Using a variety of nonhuman animals, Sechenov demonstrates that even reflexes can be inhibited in a variety of ways. Sometimes, this inhibition of reflexive response occurs because of some external or physiological event that is not under conscious control. Other times, it is possible to exert volitional control over a reflex, such as when you stop yourself from sneezing. Sechenov also demonstrates that reflexive responses are not always directly related to the intensity of the stimulation. Inhibition explains this discrepancy. Sechenov views development, particularly human development, as a process of learning to inhibit and thus control reflexive behaviors. In other words, Sechenov argues, thoughts are nothing more than reflexive responses to external stimulation, just as are behaviors. In fact, behaviors are reflexive responses with motor activity exhibited, and thoughts are reflexive responses with motor activity (behaviors) inhibited (Brozek, 1972).

Prior to this explanation of inhibitory processes, it was hard to understand how all behavior might be explained in terms only of physiological reflexes. But Sechenov's demonstration of the inhibition of reflexes provides a physiological explanation for why behavior appears to be so complex. In his book, originally titled *An Attempt to Bring Physiological Bases Into Mental Processes*, Sechenov seeks to explain how all thoughts and behaviors can be reduced to the expression or inhibition of physiological reflexes in the cortex, eliminating the need for a directing mind.

These ideas are considered subversive of faith and religious beliefs. To avoid offending those with strong religious beliefs, the censor at the University of St. Petersburg requires Sechenov to change the title of his book so that it sounds more technical and uninteresting (Boakes, 1984). In 1863, *Reflexes of the Brain* is published. In spite of the name change, Sechenov's work is banned and has little influence in the West until the mid-20th century. It is not until after the Russian Revolution in 1917 that his writings are revived and his work goes on to influence other Russian scientists, including Ivan Pavlov (1849–1936) and Vladimir Bekhterev (1857–1927).

At the turn of the century, the Russian physician and physiologist Ivan Pavlov is deeply immersed in his research on the functioning of the digestive system. In 1904, he receives the Nobel Prize for the development of surgical techniques and for contributions to the understanding of digestion. Pavlov is unimpressed with the introspective methods of psychologists and convinced that psychology could never be an objective science. Pavlov's work on animal physiology does eventually come to have a powerful influence on the science of psychology, as becomes clear when our path crosses Pavlov's again later on this journey.

Medical Psychology

The workings of the human mind, conscious or unconscious, are mysterious and never more so than when the mind seems to malfunction, or even vanish completely, leaving its former owner to suffer in lunacy or madness. Even here, however, the movement of Western intellectual thought toward objective observation, description, and measurement begins to override religious doctrines about the influence of demons or punishment by God.

MADNESS

The recognition of mental malfunctioning is not new in the 19th century. Various forms of psychological and behavioral dysfunction are noted in the earliest medical writings. Throughout most of Western history, little distinction is made between those with limited intellectual capacity and individuals whose views of reality differ dramatically from most others'. Until very late in the 19th century, both of these populations are treated in a similar manner. Even in the early days of institutionalization, these people are often housed in the same asylums and sometimes on the same wards. Similarly, for most of this time, little distinction is made between those with what are called neurotic symptoms and those suffering from the complete break with reality referred to today as psychosis.

Early Explanations

Folk ψ

Long after the natural causes for many physical illnesses begin to be identified, religious doctrine, philosophical speculation, and the assumptions of folk psychology shape understandings about the causes of mental differences.

Ancient Assumptions

Greek and Roman physicians describe a variety of mental differences, including depression, mania, paranoia, and schizophrenia, as well as noticeable differences in intellectual capacity. They also suggest causes for these conditions related to imbalances in the bodily "humors" or sometimes resulting from the interventions of gods, demons, or other supernatural powers. Cures are also recommended based on the assumptions about cause. When the cause is presumed to be biological, such as an imbalance in the humors, the cure is a physical one. Rest, a balanced diet, massage, soothing music, and healthy living are prescribed to return the humors to their proper balance, just as in the case of a physical illness. When the cause is presumed to be supernatural, the cure involves making the proper supplications to the gods. Assumptions about madness being caused by supernatural powers are shared by ancients throughout the world (Howells, 1975).

The Medieval View

If reason is what distinguishes humans from other animals, then those who have lost their reason are like animals (Scull, 1993). Furthermore, the Christian doctrine of free will holds that each mind is "free and responsible for its own states and acts" (Boring, 1957, p. 694). Thus, the mad have been deprived of their reason by God (Scull, 1993), or they are choosing to behave inappropriately. If the mad are believed to be suffering from demonic possession or divine retribution, they are very likely to be persecuted and even executed as witches. Untold thousands of the insane, mostly women, but also some men and children, are convicted of witchcraft and burned at the stake during this era (Russell, 1972).

Some families seek out magical cures, and a few exorcisms are attempted to drive demons away. In most cases, though, treatment consists of prayer or physical punishment. In fact, the Bible reports that God encourages the stoning to death of those who are possessed by spirits (Lev. 20:27; Miller, 1975). *Even in the present day, the doctrine of free will continues to influence many assumptions about a variety of mental states and about the individual's ability to control thoughts and behavior (Seligman, 1994).*

Enlightened Lunacy

By the middle of the 16th century in the West, the term **insanity** is used to describe those whose thoughts, feelings, and behaviors are significantly different from those of most other people. These individuals are believed to be suffering, experiencing disordered states of mind, and even "mad" from unrestrained emotions.

What Life Is Like for the Mad

Prior to the 18th century, individual families are responsible for the care of family members with any kind of illness, including insanity. Kept locked away from the public eye, the insane are chained in back rooms, in holes dug in the dirt floors of the family hovel, or staked behind the house day and night, in good weather or bad, *just as they are today in undeveloped parts of the world*. The insane who have no family live in the streets in the company of and indistinguishable from other indigents and common criminals (Scull, 1993). They wander the countryside, making a living by begging or stealing, and often becoming the victims of violent crime. They move into large urban areas during the Industrial Revolution, joining farming families forced off of their land as large agricultural enterprises grow.

Speculations About Causes and Cures

By the 18th century, speculation begins about natural causes of madness. Astrological influences, imbalances among the humors, or a combination of these may be blamed (MacDonald, 1981). The moon is presumed to cause an episodic type of madness known as "lunacy," that waxes and wanes with the phases of the moon. People are warned not to allow the light of the full moon to fall on their heads and faces during sleep, lest they succumb to lunacy.

Modern Madness

The insane begin to be moved from family homes and streets into "mad houses." At first, these mad houses are simply private homes where the proprietor, called a "mad doctor," takes responsibility for as many individuals as can be kept on the premises. Mad doctors usually have no medical training, do nothing except provide minimal custodial care for the inhabitants, and are not subject to any kind of oversight or regulation. Mad doctoring could be a very lucrative business, as anxious as most families are to keep their insane relatives out of sight (Scull, 1993).

Institutions Appear

The first institution in the West to house the insane is established in 1247 in Bethlem, England, later acquiring its colloquial name "Bedlam" (Digby, 1985). Until the 18th century, Bedlam is one of only a few such institutions. Although Christian doctrines include charity for those in need, insanity is believed to be a punishment sent by God. So for hundreds of years, very few Christian congregations provide any aid for the insane. As religious institutions lose their authority during the 17th and 18th centuries, however, and secular powers grow, other charitable and political powers begin to assume responsibility for those in need, including the insane (Scull, McKenzie, & Hervey, 1996).

The real growth in the establishment of institutions for the insane and those of diminished mental capacity occurs during the late 18th century, so that by 1850, many more are housed in institutions than with their families or on the streets. The new middle class in the West has the money to pay for a variety of services, including for the care of an insane family member. As the 19th century goes on, more and more people are confined to institutions. Public facilities paid for with tax dollars are established in England and in several countries in the West (Scull, 1993).

In the late 18th century, large "asylums," "almshouses," and "workhouses" are established by local governments to house landless indigents, the mentally deficient, and the insane. Gradually, the mad begin to be separated out as a distinct population from other poor folks. Asylums house only a fraction of the insane, but they quickly become overcrowded, understaffed, filthy, dangerous, and ridden with vermin and disease. Some historians argue that the conditions in the institutions for the insane are not much different from the conditions of any of the workhouses for the poor. Nevertheless, descriptions made by some of the thousands of curious people who pay a small fee to visit Bedlam and similar institutions suggest that the conditions are nothing short of appalling.

Inside the Mad House

Imagine yourself as a resident of a damp, crumbling, cold stone ward in Bedlam in the mid-18th century, infested with rats. If you are lucky enough to have any clothing at all, it is made from something like burlap, scratchy and uncomfortable, with no undergarments provided. On a good day, you will be brought a small bowl of watery cereal a couple of times, enough to keep you alive, but not enough to prevent disease and never enough to fill you. All day, you are chained to the wall, strapped in a restraint, or manacled to one or more of your fellow prisoners. Dirty straw serves as both bedding and latrine. Because there are only two or three keepers for over 100 of the insane and no one to work the night or weekend shifts, you are locked in wooden cribs at mid-afternoon and left there until mid-morning the next day with no food, water, or way to relieve yourself. Routinely, you are whipped or beaten to drive the sinfulness out of you and cure you of madness. Drugs are administered to many of you that cause violent vomiting or worse, and you are left to sit in the mess. The screaming, moaning, and hysterical laughter of your companions is rarely interrupted. All the while, curious visitors pay your keepers for the privilege of being allowed to wander through the ward to laugh at the amusing spectacle presented by you unfortunate creatures (Scull, 1993).

As if that is not frightening enough, imagine that anyone can be declared insane and locked up in such an institution. As late as 1851, for example, statutes are being passed in the United States to allow that married women can be committed to asylums "at the request of the husband" with no other evidence of insanity required (Szasz, 1970).

Tye them Keeper in a Tether,

Let them stare and stink together;

Both are apt to be unruly,

Lash them daily, lash them duly,

Though 'tis hopeless to reclaim them,

Scorpion rods perhaps may tame them.
    (Swift, 1736/1966, pp. 835–836)

The insane are still seen in this era as more like animals than humans because they have been deprived of reason, the very thing that makes them human. The reign of King George III from 1760 until 1820 in England brings particular interest to the question of madness. *Although it is clear today that King George III was suffering from an intermittent form of a metabolic disorder, porphyria,* during his reign, he is believed to be mad. By 1810, he becomes completely incapable of logical thought. The plight of King George III brings madness into the public eye and raises new questions about the causes of insanity.

Two thousand years after Greek assertions of physical causes, biology again is identified as a possible cause of insanity in the 18th century. Discoveries about the natural causes of physical illness in medical science, empiricist notions about the importance of learning in shaping our thoughts and behaviors, and positivist faith in scientific progress each play a role in bringing the methods of science to bear on questions about mental differences. In 1716, masturbation and "involuntary nocturnal emissions" are suggested as causes for mental illness (Szasz, 1970). This idea has widespread appeal and is a popular theory well into the 20th century. No effort is spared in preventing children from masturbating. Sermons are preached in churches, parents are urged to lecture their children on the evils of "abusing themselves," and mechanical devices to prevent children from engaging in such acts while asleep are widely advertised. In the late 18th century, Anton Mesmer asserts that madness is caused by the misalignment of the animal magnetic forces in the body. He recommends magnetic treatments to bring these forces back into the proper alignment. His followers continue to offer mesmeric, hypnotic, and magnetic cures for various mental states, *even today*.

Early 19th-century physiological assumptions about the causes of some kinds of madness also include the belief, held by ancient Egyptians and written about by the Greek physician Hippocrates, that **"hysteria"** is caused by the wandering of the uterus (hyster) inside the body or by disturbances in the uterus. Hysteria is characterized by paralysis in various parts of the body, the loss of sensation or disturbances in sight or hearing, severe headaches, palpitations of the heart, abdominal pain, or even a stubborn cough (Alexander & Selesnick, 1966). Because of its cause, hysteria is thought to be a uniquely female affliction. The Greeks recommended vaginal fumigation to bring the uterus back into position and proper function and advocated marriage and regular heterosexual activity as a cure. Late in the 19th century, the cause of hysteria is expanded to include malfunctions in the ovaries and genitalia, and surgery to remove the diseased organs is recommended as a cure. As a result of this belief among the (almost exclusively) male medical profession, thousands of women in the United States and Europe are operated on to remove their ovaries, and many more have their clitorises removed as well (Knoff, 1970; Lerman, 1996).

Assumptions are still made about balancing the bodily humors in mild cases. One treatment often recommended includes the then-common technique of "bleeding" to drain excess fluid. For example, the physician Benjamin Rush (1745–1813), remembered today as a signer of the Declaration of Independence, believes that deranged thoughts result from high blood pressure in the brain and advocates bleeding as a cure. Cold-water treatments are thought to cool the blood and thus reduce the fever that is causing the madness. Rush also invents a "tranquilizing chair" to treat even the most incurable of the mad:

> I have contrived a chair . . . to assist in curing madness. It binds and confines every part of the body. By keeping the trunk erect it lessens the impetus of blood toward the brain. By preventing the muscles from acting, it reduces the force and frequency of the pulse, and the position of the head and feet favors the easy application of cold water or ice to the former and warm water to the latter. Its effects have been truly delightful to me. It acts as a sedative to the tongue and temper as well as to the blood vessels. In twenty-four, twelve, six, and in some cases four hours, the most refractory patients have been composed. I have called it a Tranquillizer. (1810, as cited in Butterfield, 1951, p. 1052; Rush, 1811)

Placement in a swinging chair also becomes a popular treatment for the institutionalized insane. The chair can be whirled about violently, and the direction changed suddenly, eventually resulting in an "instant discharge of the contents of the stomach, bowels, and bladder, in quick succession" (Burrows, 1976).

Some treatments are directed toward restoring reason. Various kinds of restraints (*similar to the present-day "straitjacket"*) are used. These help the mad regain control during passionate outbursts. A variety of methods for inducing fear are also used, either by startling the patient with a sudden fright or by "staring down" the patient. Water treatments, such as a near-drowning or pouring a steady stream of water on the head while the patient is tied securely in position, are popular. If the mad think and behave the way they do because of having formed incorrect associations, as suggested by John Locke 200 years before, then treatment should involve clearing the slate and having them form new associations. Many doctors who use Rush's Tranquillizing Chair attribute its success to the breaking of learned associations and restoring the individual to the "blank slate" so that new and more appropriate associations may be taught (Burrows, 1976).

The Reformers

In Catholic countries, especially Spain, France, and Italy, there is another tradition of care for the insane. Here, Catholic orders of nursing sisters have been providing humane institutional care and treatment for the insane since the 16th century. These orders emphasize that the insane should be treated with gentle kindness and patience. Talking to the insane to console and comfort them, sympathizing with them, encouraging them about the future, and ministering to their spiritual as well as physical needs are widely used to treat the mad and found to be effective (Jackson, 1999). In Italy, asylum physician Vincenzio Chiarugi (1759–ca. 1820) recommends a form of "moral therapy" in the treatment of depression that involves talking with patients about their problems: "It will be necessary in cases of true melancholia especially to promote and encourage hope, which is completely opposite to sadness and fear" (Chiarugi, 1793/1987, p. 137).

As modern medical practice appears in the West, and biological explanations for madness come to be more widely accepted (Scull, 1993), conflicts begin to arise between religious traditions and medical physicians (Goldstein, 1987). French physicians, like Pierre Cabanis (1757–1808) and his friend Philippe Pinel (1745–1826), advocate "moral treatment" of the insane. Their treatments are derived from observations in hospitals for the insane operated by the Catholic orders and also from Pinel's observation of the wife of the administrator at Bicêtre asylum, who calms "maniacs" with only words of consolation (Shorter, 1997). Pinel recommends similar kinds of talking therapies to the ones he has seen the Catholic sisters practicing with their patients. Because he writes and publishes, and because his training as a physician and his status as an upper-class man give him credibility among the powerful men of the era, Pinel's work is recognized by his peers. *He is remembered in present-day history texts as one of the first to recommend the humane treatment of the insane and the reform of institutional practice, whereas the Catholic nursing sisters and the wife of the hospital administrator from whom his ideas originate are mostly forgotten.*

Late in the 18th century, a movement begins to improve the lives of residents of large institutions for the insane in England. Driven mostly by reformers associated with the Religious Society of Friends (Quakers), this movement grows in influence throughout the early part of the 19th century. The York Retreat, where humane treatments are employed, is founded by Quakers in 1796. Treatments are based on the Quaker belief that kindness, attention, and persuasion will return lost reason to the insane (Digby, 1985). The York Retreat becomes the model for at least half of the private mental hospitals created in the United States in the first quarter of the 19th century (Grob, 1994). Inmates are more often released from their chains, although still likely to be restrained with devices like straitjackets. Hygiene, staffing, and diet are improved. Beating and whipping are replaced by other forms of treatment.

In the United States, Dorothea Lynde Dix (1802–1887) of Massachusetts is credited with the establishment of more humane institutions for the care of the insane and the mentally deficient, and reform in the treatment of these individuals (Viney, 1996). Although in frail health herself, Dix devotes her life to improving the lives of the insane. She travels, writes, and testifies on their behalf, and she successfully lobbies state legislatures, Congress, and the governments of several other countries. In the United States, Benjamin Rush, who is often also considered a reformer, urges that the insane be released from their chains; be allowed fresh air, sunshine, and exercise; and not be put on display for the amusement of others. As a result of the efforts of Dix and other reformers, for a time during the 19th century, conditions do improve. However, overcrowding becomes a serious problem later in the century as the numbers of insane individuals increase dramatically.

Science and Insanity

As the insane are gathered together and housed in larger numbers, scientists establish classification systems and research the causes of insanity. Pinel and French neurologist Jean-Martin Charcot (1825–1893) pursue clinical interests in individual differences, emotions, and personality. Charcot's students include the French testing psychologist Alfred Binet, the American philosopher and psychologist William James, and the Viennese neurologist Sigmund Freud. Russian asylum doctor Sergei Korsakoff (1853–1900) notes the chronic memory loss and psychosis that result from the overconsumption of alcohol, and Karl Wernicke (1848–1905), a German professor of psychiatry, lists other psychological consequences of alcoholism.

Changes in the care of the mentally ill in the West follow what is often the pattern in science: first description, then prediction, and then attempts at control. Early reforms in the care of the mentally ill are accompanied by the description of cases, and then by the classification of types of mental illness. Hypotheses about probable causes are proposed. Finally, treatments are devised based on the hypothesized causes.

Increase in Numbers

The 19th century sees a dramatic increase in the number of mentally ill throughout the West. This increase is attributed to three causes. First, more of the mentally ill appear as they are moved from family care to institutional care. Second, a worldwide epidemic of syphilis beginning early in the century results in large numbers of (mostly) men with degenerative forms of mental illness. The third reason for the increase in the number of mentally ill is the increased use of alcohol. There is a sharp rise across this period in the numbers of people, again mostly men, suffering from the forms of mental illness associated with chronic alcohol use (Shorter, 1997).

Classification

Both mild mental illnesses, such as anxiety or mild depression, and more serious psychoses are of concern in the 19th century, but little is understood about either. In 1883, the German physician Emil Kraepelin (1856–1926) publishes a classification system for the identification and treatment of the mentally ill. This occurs at the same time that medical doctors are developing classification systems for the diagnosis and treatment of physical illnesses. Prior to this time, health and illness were viewed as integral to an individual's character. But during this era, illness begins to be viewed as a result of a condition that can be isolated from the person. Thus, medicine becomes the treatment of conditions and not of people (Burke, 1985).

Kraepelin classifies mental illnesses according to the presumed cause of the illness, the degree of involvement of the brain and nervous system, the observed symptoms, and the recommended treatments. In the last edition of his classification system, published in 1899, Kraepelin divides psychotic illnesses that have no known organic cause into two broad categories. The illnesses characterized by disturbances in emotions or mood he labels "manic-depressive psychoses," and he predicts that these patients will recover with the proper treatment. The psychotic illnesses characterized by little or no emotion or mood are labeled "dementia praecox," and Kraepelin predicts that these patients will most likely not recover. Kraepelin provides a set of diagnostic criteria for each affliction. Among the symptoms seen in those suffering from dementia praecox are hallucinations, which he describes to help physicians recognize the disorder:

> By far the most frequent are hallucinations of hearing. At the beginning these are usually simple noises, rustling, buzzing, ringing in the ears, tolling of bells ("death knell"), knocking, moving of tables, cracking of whips, trumpets, yodel, singing, weeping of children, whistling, blowing, chirping, "shooting and death-rattle"; the bed echoes with shots; the "Wild Hunt" makes an uproar; Satan roars under the bed. (Kraepelin, 1911/1971, p. 7)

During this period, the belief that mental illness results from the intervention of supernatural powers continues to decline, and the belief that physical disease is at the root of insanity grows. By the late 19th century, psychoses are usually assumed to arise from brain disease or degeneration. Thus, mental illness becomes medicalized, and treatment comes under the authority of medical doctors, neurologists, and alienists, a new specialty for the treatment of those alienated from their reason. Supernatural explanations for mild mental illnesses, on the other hand, are replaced by explanations having to do with weaknesses of will or some other character flaw on the part of the afflicted individual.

Treatment

In this era, treatments for the mentally ill are often based on the idea that restoring a person to more normal functioning requires allowing them to gradually relearn to use their rational powers of mind and thus regain the will to overcome their irrational emotions. Patients are removed from their restrictions and given more responsibilities as they demonstrate the ability to maintain control over their emotions.

For many, this more humane treatment results in dramatic improvements in behavior. Unchained and treated like reasonable people, many exhibit more rational behavior. Pinel suggests that mild mental illness may be caused by psychological factors (Pinel, 1801/1962). For example, the confusion and stress induced by poor living conditions and the illogical or irrational thoughts caused by chaotic surroundings might cause mental illness. Alienists who are trained to help people who have been alienated in some way from their rational selves begin to work with the mentally ill, first in France and later throughout the West. But this treatment does not work for everyone, and even some of those who exhibit signs of recovery for a time later seem to fall back into depression or mania. These failures of moral therapy spur the search for better explanations and treatments.

Although Mesmer's ideas about magnetic treatment are discredited, they never fully disappear. Particularly in France, followers of Mesmer continue to practice "magnetism" (Shorter, 1997) and claim some success in the treatment of neurotics. For example, Marquis de Puységur (1751–1825) discovers that after being "magnetized" into a peaceful trance, people respond to his suggestions and follow his commands. For example, if they are told that they feel pain, they report that they do indeed feel pain. If told that they do not feel pain, they not only report no pain, but they also do not respond even when pricked with pins. In a "magnetized" state, people can even be induced to exhibit symptoms very similar to those seen in mental illness. If the symptoms of mental illness can be induced in normal people through "magnetism," some doctors wonder if those same symptoms can be relieved by magnetism in the genuinely mentally ill.

✓ Stop and think.
If symptoms of mental illness can be induced through magnetism, could those symptoms also be cured that way?

In the 1880s, hypnotism, a more modern form of "magnetism," is revived by the French medical community. This revival takes two very divergent paths. The neurologist Jean-Martin Charcot believes that hypnotizability is a sign of a weakened nervous system and evidence of a neurotic disorder. People who are easily hypnotized are neurotics. He argues that hypnosis can be used only to diagnose nervous disease. Opposing this view is Hippolyte Bernheim (1837–1919), an internist, who argues that hypnotizability is not a sign of disease because even normal people can be hypnotized. He believes that mental disease is sometimes a consequence of suggestion. Because suggestion can cause mental illness, it might also be used to cure mental illness. Patients could be hypnotized, and physicians could suggest that patients recover from symptoms. Later, Bernheim decides that nonhypnotic suggestion from an influential doctor, that is, the doctor simply talking with the patient, is just as effective for some patients, marking the beginning of modern psychotherapy (Shorter, 1997).

More and more attention is focused on disorders of the nervous system, defined as the nerves, nervous fluids, and nervous energy. Overactive nerves, a depletion of nervous fluids, or an exhaustion of nervous energy can lead to neuroses. Nervous exhaustion is presumed not to be either hereditary or contagious. By accepting this diagnosis, families can avoid the stigma of degeneration, and individuals can escape charges of being weak-willed. Having an organic nervous disease is seen as far preferable to madness and significantly less likely to get one confined to a dreaded asylum. "True!—nervous—very, very dreadfully nervous I had been and am, but why will you say that I am mad?" (Poe, 1842/1992, p. 657).

There is increasing interest in the late 19th century in physical treatments, particularly for the nervous system. Another medical specialist appears, the neurologist, who is trained to treat disorders of the nervous system. These treatments include electrical stimulation of the body designed to spark life back into an inactive nervous system. Patients who complain of lethargy or depression have their nervous systems re-energized by the application of electrical stimulation to various parts of their bodies. Electrotherapeutics is very popular in the mid-19th century for all manner of nervous disorders (Beard & Rockwell, 1871) and keeps alive the ancient Greek tradition of physiological treatments for illness (Stone, 1997).

Also beginning in midcentury, then increasing dramatically toward the end of the century, "water treatments" are sought for mild nervous ailments. Especially in France, spas provide curative mineral waters for the treatment of nervous symptoms, and people travel to these spas from all over Europe. In addition to drinking the water, neurotics bathe in it and are offered other forms of "hydrotherapy," including cold showers and douches. By the end of the century, French spas are treating 300,000 to 400,000 visitors a year, providing cures at healthy profits for spa owners and the doctors who prescribe the treatments (Shorter, 1997).

Unfortunately, even by the end of the 19th century, the medical treatment of all forms of mental illness has proven mostly ineffective. No form of treatment is found to consistently cure any condition or reliably reduce symptoms. Those patients who do recover probably owe their recovery to spontaneous remission rather than to anything doctors have done for them (Howells, 1975).

EMPIRICAL PSYCHOLOGY: A UNIQUELY NORTH AMERICAN BLEND

Although Wundt, in Germany, is given credit as the founder of modern experimental psychology, the science is also growing in importance in North America. For example, G. Stanley Hall receives his doctorate in philosophy from Harvard in 1878, but because his topic is related to those explored in experimental psychology, Hall is often credited with having received the first doctorate in the United States in psychology. Hall establishes and maintains an active graduate program in psychology at Clark University from 1888 until his death in 1924 and promotes the study of psychology as a science. In fact, from 1893 until at least 1898, most of the graduate degrees awarded in psychology in the United States are awarded to students from Hall's program.

Among the doctoral candidates Hall accepts is Francis C. Sumner (1895–1954), an African American student who has applied to other universities in the United States but never been admitted. In June 1920, Sumner becomes the first African American to earn a doctorate in psychology. He goes on to found a graduate program in psychology at Howard University in Washington, D.C., where he provides graduate opportunities for many other African Americans. Despite of his own achievements, Sumner repeatedly expresses the opinion, controversial even at the time, that nearly all other African Americans should receive only vocational training (Sawyer, 2000).

By 1895, there are dozens of laboratories of experimental psychology at universities across North America and thousands of experimental, clinical, developmental, physiological, comparative, and other types of psychologists engaging in the scientific pursuit of answers to questions about thoughts, feelings, and behaviors. A few of the "brass instruments" typically found in a turn-of-the-century psychological laboratory are shown in Fig. 7.1. These include "a sonometer [center] and a few tuning forks for audition [lower left], a color-mixer [upper right] and Wheatstone stereoscope for vision [upper left], and stop watch [lower center] for time measurements."

The Women

Personal Struggles

It is not until the mid-19th century that women are admitted to higher education in the United States, and even through the end of the century, there are many fewer places where women are able to obtain a college degree than there are for White men. To address the problem, several women's colleges are established at about the same time colleges are being established for Americans of African descent (Pifer, 1973). Both women's colleges and colleges for African Americans are smaller, significantly less prestigious, and not as well funded as institutions open to White men. As women increasingly seek higher education and begin to compete intellectually with men, concerns begin to be raised about the effects of such rigorous study on the delicate health of upper- and middle-class White women. Fears are voiced regarding possible detrimental consequences for the reproductive capacity and inclination for marriage of educated women and about their increasing economic independence (Winter, 1998). Hall, for example, argues in his influential textbook on adolescent development that intellectually oriented women become "functionally castrated," rendering them unsuitable as wives and mothers (Hall, 1907).

The movement of women into graduate study is slow. For example, in the United States, doctoral degrees in several fields of study are offered after the Civil War, beginning at Johns Hopkins University in 1876. By 1890, there are 3,382 graduate students enrolled in these programs. Only 409 of these students are women, however (Scarborough & Furumoto, 1987).

FIG. 7.1. Brass instruments (Sanford, 1893, p. 436, as cited in Popplestone & McPherson, 1994, p. 16; photo courtesy of the Archives of the History of American Psychology–The University of Akron).

It is not until the 1890s that graduate programs are offered in psychology. In these programs, students are trained to conduct rigorous experimental research and to be scholars and professors of psychology. Yet, very few of these new graduate schools in psychology are open to women, and even those that allow women to attend classes often will not grant them degrees, even after they have completed all of the required coursework. For example, William James at Harvard University admits Mary Calkins to his courses in the 1890s, and she completes all of the coursework required for the PhD. Although her professors enthusiastically recommend her, Harvard authorities refuse to grant her the degree because she is a woman (Calkins, 1961; Scarborough & Furumoto, 1987).

Despite the obstacles, the experimental work being conducted by the women who are able to find a place in the graduate study of psychology is similar to that being conducted by the men. For example, mathematician and physiological psychologist Christine Ladd-Franklin (1847–1930) at Johns Hopkins and later at Columbia University researches and publishes on visual perception and makes major contributions to understanding the process of color sensation (O'Connell & Russo, 1990).

Professional Lives

After completing graduate study, the challenges for women in psychology only increase. Finding an academic position is difficult, especially for those who, although fully qualified, have been denied the degree. In many cases, finding a position commensurate with their training proves impossible, and women leave the field. Some accept positions as teachers in secondary schools, and some of the more fortunate find academic positions in women's colleges or as part-time instructors at universities. Throughout the early part of the 20th century, it is considered unseemly for an upper- or middle-class White woman to be employed outside the home after marrying. Therefore, to hold onto even part-time academic positions, these women must forgo marriage.

Most of the women who are employed in academia are hired by the few women's colleges that exist (Woody, 1929/1966). Here, they find significantly heavier teaching loads than at the universities where only men are employed. The laboratories for conducting research at women's colleges, if they exist at all, are smaller and less well equipped. And because there are no graduate programs at these universities, there are no graduate students to train. With no students to carry on their work and reputations, women psychologists' contributions and ideas are less likely to continue on to influence new generations of scholars.

In 1904, E. B. Titchener organizes a new professional meeting of psychologists called The Experimentalists. This group holds regular meetings at different graduate universities. Here, the latest in experimental work is presented and discussed, and graduate students can be introduced into the discipline. Titchener and the other men forming this organization specifically exclude women from membership or participation (Furumoto, 1988). Apologists for Titchener and his friends argue that women are excluded from these meetings because the men would be smoking. In a letter written in 1912 challenging The Experimentalists' policy of excluding women, Christine Ladd-Franklin says, "Have your smokers separated if you like," goes on to inform them that "I for one always smoke when I am in fashionable society," and concludes by reminding them that "a scientific meeting is a public affair" and should thus not exclude women who are fellow scientists (as cited in Scarborough & Furumoto, 1987, p. 125).

Despite these criticisms, The Experimentalists continue to exclude women until 1929, 2 years after Titchener's death. For many years after this, women are still not well represented among its members. Exclusion from professional organizations of scientists has continuing repercussions for the careers of women. It is often in just such organizations that graduate students are recognized and meet those who are in positions to further their careers. For example, a young John Watson, later credited as the founder of behaviorism, first comes to the attention of established scholars at the meetings of The Experimentalists (Larson & Sullivan, 1965). At the same time that Watson is being introduced and mentored into the field, it is rumored that women graduate students resort to hiding under the tables to hear the proceedings (Scarborough & Furumoto, 1987).

Forced out of mainstream experimental work after the turn of the century and denied university positions and research facilities, many women trained in psychology move into clinical and applied work instead (Capshew & Laszlo, 1986; Furumoto, 1987; Koppes, 1997; Milar, 2000; Stevens & Gardner, 1982). Thus, in the early decades of the 20th century, women are more likely to make major contributions in the fields of clinical, developmental, and testing psychology than in experimental research.

Functionalism

When psychology makes the journey across the Atlantic to North America, both its questions and its methods take on a uniquely American flavor, reflecting the political, economic, social, and cultural values of the late 19th century in the United States and Canada. In this rapidly industrializing part of the world, the values of business and industry become the values of the culture. Without a heritage of either strong religious powers or secular authority (a monarch), the values of business and industry dominate political and cultural ethics. Americans are pragmatic, seeking practical answers to questions about how to produce more products at lower costs and maximize profits. The questions of psychology are important only if the answers will have some practical application. Basic research is seen as irrelevant. What is relevant is applied research that will help to solve problems of human conduct and explain the functions that consciousness serves. This set of values is called **functionalism**.

Higher Mental Functions

While structuralists are concentrating on the basic mental elements, functionalists are more concerned with how whole minds function to help organisms adapt to their environments. Functionalists assume that consciousness exists for the purpose of helping organisms to survive and adapt to the physical world. They understand the importance of experimental control, but they also want to understand higher mental processes, such as learning, memory, problem solving, motivation, emotion, the formation and maintenance of beliefs, and concepts of a self. The goal is to find a way to understand these higher processes using experimental methods.

After reading Wundt's assertion that it will never be possible to study higher mental processes experimentally, the German philosopher Hermann Ebbinghaus (1850–1909) decides to find a way. He rejects philosophical speculation as a productive way to study consciousness and argues that psychology must be conducted scientifically if it is to provide valid information. He selects memory as a higher function that he will study experimentally. He embarks on an experimental research program designed to study how and why memories are formed and what is more or less likely to be remembered.

Ebbinghaus maintains strict experimental controls in his studies of memory. For example, in his studies of verbal memory, he recognizes that if his subjects have had some prior exposure to a stimulus word, they will be more likely to remember that word in the experimental situation. For that reason, he uses "nonsense" syllables instead of real words. He also carefully measures his results and is thus one of the first to present quantitative data on higher mental functions. Other researchers also conduct experimental studies of memory. For example, American Mary Whiton Calkins (1863–1930), who establishes one of the early psychology laboratories in North America, uses what she calls the "paired associates" technique. She discovers that a numeral is better remembered if it is presented along with a color. She also finds that pairing the numeral with a vivid rather than a neutral color makes it even more likely to be remembered.

Ebbinghaus also argues that basic research is distinguished from applied research only by the context (Postman, 1973). Basic research is conducted just to know why or how, whereas applied research is done for the purpose of solving some problem. So, Ebbinghaus concludes, what is learned in basic research may have application later, if the context changes, and sometimes research conducted to solve a problem results in a new understanding of the process being investigated. Thus, the line dividing scholarly pursuits driven by pure curiosity from practical research done to provide solutions is not a distinct one.

Pragmatic American Functionalism

Until late in the 19th century, the psychology taught in universities in North America is a form of "moral philosophy" grounded in the philosophical and theological search for the human soul. This is because these universities are founded by churches, some Catholic but mostly Protestant.

Theories of evolution also influence psychology in North America. The principles that have so eloquently explained biological evolution are adopted by American functionalists and applied to a variety of domains, from economics, politics, philosophy, and science in general to the science of psychology. For example, when applied in business, these principles mean that the businesses that survive are the ones that are stronger and better. Thus, an economic system should be designed to ensure that businesses that are stronger will survive and prosper and any business practice, no matter how ruthless, should be judged only by how that business prospers.

Pragmatism intersects with psychology in defining the questions that are considered important. American pragmatic psychologists seek solutions to practical problems. Pragmatism also intersects with philosophy and psychology in defining the nature of reality. For pragmatists, how well an idea works or how adequately a concept explains an experience or observation is one measure of its validity. If, for example, believing that life is good increases happiness and leads to a more satisfying life, then the belief that life is good is a valid one. William James argues that the truth of an idea is not inherent in the idea. Instead, an idea is made true by events. "You can say of it either that 'it is useful because it is true' or that 'it is true because it is useful.' Both these phrases mean exactly the same thing" (James, 1907/1948, pp. 161–162).

Rejection of Elementalism

Except for Titchener, who is an immigrant from across the Atlantic, and a few students he influences, North American psychology rejects elementalism as not useful. The experimental study of the structures of consciousness makes the mind seem static or unchanging, and makes human thought and behavior seem mechanical. To the Americans, structuralists' questions about the contents of consciousness are less important than functionalists' questions about the purposes served by mind.

The New Psychology

North American psychology retains the empirical approach so important in European psychology. In 1885, Hall refers to this empirical approach to the study of mental functions as the "**new psychology**," to distinguish it from the older moral philosophy (Hall, 1885). Thus, this uniquely American blend is a psychology that is practical, that seeks to understand function, and that is discovered through empirical study.

The Methods of Functionalism

The application of empirical methods requires breaking the problem of consciousness down into small enough pieces to examine experimentally. Without doing that, there is too much danger of finding only the evidence that supports what is already believed, seeing patterns where there are none, falsely assuming causation, or any of the other errors in thinking to which humans are all too prone. The problem for American functionalists is that the functions of mind are less easily broken down and experimentally manipulated than are sensations or reaction times.

For philosopher William James and psychologist G. Stanley Hall, the solution is to redefine empiricism. Instead of experimental manipulation, they define empiricism broadly as all aspects of experience, including experience that is not publicly observable (Viney, 2001). James especially believes that scientists must remain open to the possibility that all experience, both objective and subjective, may reveal aspects of individual reality, so that the contents of consciousness include both kinds of experience.

A good example of the rejection of elementalism and the functionalist's definition of empiricism is William James' philosophy with regard to the nature of consciousness. James argues that consciousness is not made up of discrete elements associated together, but is instead a constantly flowing dynamic stream of thoughts, all connected with and dependent on those coming before and after. The strongest evidence in support of this idea is that this is how consciousness is experienced: as a flowing stream of thought. James' empiricism does not necessarily require measurable experimental evidence to support its contentions, but it does require logical coherence and the evidence of experience.

As to the contents of the stream of consciousness, James' arguments are strictly functional. From a vast array of incoming sensory information, attention selects based on "consequential utility," mirroring biological principles of natural selection (Leary, 1992). Thus, what is in consciousness are ideas that are or may be useful. This notion influences many psychologists who follow.

The Heart Rejects Determinism

Recall that the scientific search for the laws that govern nature requires first the assumption of materialism. The inevitable conclusion, then, is that whatever happens in the universe is determined by how matter interacts with matter. Translated into psychology, what this means is that thoughts, feelings, and behaviors can be reduced to matter and are determined by matter acting on matter. A scientific psychology is the search for the laws that govern the matter that makes up thoughts, feelings, and behavior.

The problem with this is that, intuitively, most people feel that they have an internal will, a directing consciousness, or "a ghost in the machine." Thus, the idea that what feels like freely willed choices are really matter acting on matter is disturbing and makes some people uncomfortable with scientific psychology.

As the story goes, William James is disturbed by this deterministic account of psychology. In fact, on recognizing the conclusion of determinism that must be drawn from materialism, James falls into a deep depression. Coming to believe that he has no free will, he finds himself feeling hopeless and unable to work for weeks. After reading the work of French philosopher Charles Renouvier, James decides that it is the belief that he has no free will that has made him so depressed. Therefore, he must change this belief. He makes his first act of free will the choice to believe in free will. James is better able to function in his professional life after making this choice (Fancher, 1996). This story illustrates the functionalist attitude that the evidence of subjective experience and the utility of an idea can be enough to establish its validity. It also shows why James is often described as the founder of American functionalism in psychology. "We cannot live or think at all without some degree of faith. Faith is synonymous with working hypothesis. The only difference is that while some hypotheses can be refuted in five minutes, others may defy ages" (James, 1896/1956, p. 95).

Interestingly for the student of psychology, James' choice to believe in free will applies only to his personal life. In his professional life as a scientist, he continues to advocate a methodological form of determinism. That is, when doing science, a psychologist must assume that thoughts, feelings, and behaviors are caused, and psychology is the search for those determining causes.

✓ **Stop and think.**

Is the existence of free will an empirical question? If free will exists, what are its limits (if any)?

William James has great influence over psychology in North America at the turn of the last century. He writes a textbook, *The Principles of Psychology*, that is used in psychology courses across North America for many decades. His philosophical speculations about the nature of consciousness, the self, habits, and emotions form the central questions for many research programs in the field. But James himself becomes disillusioned with psychology. It is alleged that he refers to it in later years as a "nasty little science" (Heidbreder, 1933, p. 155). Eventually, he returns to the formal study of philosophy.

The Limits of Introspection

In the early years of the 20th century in North America, psychology turns away from James' form of empiricism toward experimental science. Comparative psychologists are accused of anthropomorphizing (Dewsbury, 1992). The narrative and descriptive methods of "child study" suffer from a lack of adequate controls (Zenderland, 1988). Introspective methods reveal much, but are limited. Introspection can reveal only our own minds, whereas the minds of others can be known only through inference. By the early 20th century, most psychologists in North America accept only objective methods in the search for explanations for psychological characteristics.

🕐 **The Times**

At the turn from the 19th to the 20th century, North Americans are committed to the path of modernism. Modernists believe that the natural world can be understood and even controlled through the application of scientific methods. By 1900, public education becomes compulsory in the United States, in the belief that the continued progress of a scientific society requires that everyone be able at least to read and write.

Astronomers find and name the eighth planet in our solar system, Neptune. Physicists discover that the atom is not indivisible but is made up of even smaller particles of matter. Electrical and magnetic fields are found, certain kinds of cathode rays are discovered to penetrate skin and tissue, resulting in "X-rays," and radioactivity, named by Marie Curie, is found to generate electricity.

Technological marvels rival religious miracles. In 1903, Wilbur and Orville Wright get an airplane off the ground. Although Morse code remains the most common means of instantaneous long distance communication, passenger and freight trains are traveling at 60 miles an hour on over 200,000 miles of track in the United States. Automobiles with internal combustion engines are beginning to appear in urban areas where there are roads.

Since midcentury, chemists have been able to create organic substances from inorganic chemicals. Thus, it appears that life is not some special exception to the laws of nature that govern the rest of the universe but is also a consequence of matter acting on matter.

At the same time, humans remain at the mercy of many of nature's powers. In 1906, a major earthquake in San Francisco kills over 3,000 people. In 1918, an epidemic of influenza sweeps around the world, killing more than 20 million people, including 675,000 in the United States. In 1900, the median life span in the United States is only 47 years. Clearly, modernity still has a long way to go.

8

A Science of Behavior: Is Consciousness a Myth?

This chapter begins with an exploration of the transition in psychology from the introspective study of mental events to behaviorism and the description of observable behavior in the first few decades of the 20th century. The intensive study of relationships between physiology and psychology are covered, including the application of biology's principles of natural selection to psychological characteristics. In this context, the history of the testing movement is explored in a variety of domains. The impact of ideas about psychology at the turn of the century on popular culture and the future direction of psychology as both an academic and an applied discipline are also examined.

THE LANDSCAPE CHANGES

On entering the 20th century, it is clear that the landscape of psychology is undergoing dramatic changes. In fact, the very scope of what psychology is in the West is being redefined. From the study of a transcendent and immaterial psyche, psychological studies are beginning to focus on observable behavior. Although this may seem somewhat limiting, there are good reasons for this transition. Let's explore some of these reasons.

Elementalism and Evolution

Elementalist theories of consciousness regard learning as the primary source of thoughts and feelings among all animals. Even domestic and circus animals can be taught a variety of behaviors through association. All organisms seem to learn in the same way, by forming associations between sensory experiences. It also does not matter where the learning is occurring: The principles of learning remain the same. Learning can be studied by observing instances of learning in real-world settings, but learning can also be studied in the more controlled environment of a laboratory.

Also, it seems that more complex animals are capable of forming more complex associations. It is widely believed, for example, that humans are the most complex animals and that humans are capable of the highest level of thought, as evidenced by civilization itself. Therefore, the only important mental difference among species is a quantitative difference, or one of measurable complexity. The mind of any other animal is just like a human mind, just less complex. Thus, animal learning can be used as a model to understand the more complex learning that takes place in the human mind. The process of forming associations and the capacity for complex thinking result from physiological differences in the structure and functioning of human and animal brains. As a consequence of these assumptions, the major theories of learning that appear in early 20th-century Western psychology are derived from the study of learning in animals.

An illustration of early attempts to reduce learning to a simple level is the doctoral dissertation research presented by Edward L. Thorndike (1874–1949) at Columbia University. Thorndike places food-deprived cats into cages, called puzzle boxes. The cats can only escape by stepping on a flat lever. He then measures how long it takes the cats to escape. Thorndike finds a good deal of variation across cats, and across trials, but for each cat, the time to escape gradually becomes shorter and shorter. Each cat begins by engaging in many random movements, clawing and scratching inside the cage, before accidentally stepping on the lever that causes the cage to open. As they are placed again and again in the cage, they engage in fewer and fewer random movements, more quickly happen upon the lever, and escape from the cage in less time. Thus, the behavior of Thorndike's cats is much like that of Morgan's fox terrier, Tony.

By the beginning of the 20th century, significant advances have been made in understanding the physiology of the brain. The brains and nervous systems of many animals have been dissected, researchers have experimented with the intentional creation of lesions in the brains of animals, and the results of accidental lesions in human brains have been studied. The work of various scientists, including Italian physician Camillio Golgi (1843–1926), Spanish neurologist Santiago Ramon y Cajal (1852–1934), and German anatomist Wilhelm Waldeyer (1836–1921), extends cell theory to the brain itself. These scientists demonstrate that the brain is made up of a vast collection of individual neurons connected in some way to one another. Later in his career, Thorndike develops a physiological explanation for association. He suggests that associations occur when new connections are established between neurons in the brain.

Thorndike proposes two laws of learning to explain the gradual elimination of random movements when the cat is placed in the cage (Thorndike, 1898).

The Law of Exercise or Repetition

The more often an association, meaning a neural connection, is practiced, the stronger it becomes. Similarly, the longer a neural connection remains unused, the weaker the connection becomes.

The Law of Effect

If an association is followed by pleasure, satisfaction, or reward, it will be strengthened and will be more likely to reoccur. If an association is followed, instead, by pain, punishment, or annoyance, it will be weakened and will be less likely to reoccur. Thus, learning is determined by its consequences.

Most comparative psychologists in the early 20th century do not believe that animals escaping from puzzle boxes are thinking about how to solve the problem and get out. Instead, the animals are engaging in random movements, called "trials," and making many unsuccessful responses, called "errors," before successfully escaping. Thus, animals are not capable of thinking about how to solve problems; they are only engaging in "trial-and-error" learning.

✓ **Stop and think.**
What do you think about the ability of nonhuman animals to solve problems?

All of this research on animal learning and animal mind must be conducted by observing the behavior of animals. Whereas psychologists who conduct introspective studies with humans can talk with their subjects, the psychologists who study animals can only draw inferences about animal mind from watching animal behavior. The need to infer mind from the observation of behavior is part of what gives rise to behaviorism in the early decades of the 20th century.

From Introspection to Experimentation

Recall that Wundt assumes, along with many philosophers down through the ages, that thoughts, feelings, and behaviors originate in one of two ways. First, there are physical experiences, the elements of sensation, and the forces in nature that form the contents of consciousness. Wundt calls these physical causes. Second, there are mental forces that direct attention, and there are unique and creative ways that each individual synthesizes physical sensations and gives value and meaning to experience. Wundt calls these the psychical causes (Wundt, 1897/1969).

This dualistic explanation for thoughts, feelings, and behaviors is rejected as metaphysical by succeeding generations of psychologists, people like Ebbinghaus and Titchener. These people want to turn psychology into a natural science defined in the same positivistic terms as physics and the other natural sciences. Doing this will require abandoning Wundt's emphasis on the dynamic nature of psychological processes and accepting, instead, the study of sensory processes and the mechanics of association. Observation of behavior must be conducted rather than introspection about mental forces. Defining psychology in the same terms as physics means that the task of psychologists should be to describe only that which is publicly observable and accept only the most parsimonious explanation of the relationships seen among observations that is consistent with the evidence. "Ah, that is metaphysical speculation, and like most metaphysical speculations has little reference at all to the actual facts of real life, as we know them" (Wilde, 1899/1992).

Wundt argues that although the physical causes are open to experimental investigation, the psychical causes are not. The "new" psychologists insist that the proper method for explaining thoughts, feelings, and behaviors is through experimentation. Even complex mental phenomena can be explained only to the degree that those processes can be defined in terms of behaviors and thus made subject to experimental investigation. Any knowledge not acquired in this way should be considered mere speculation and fantasy, just as it is in physics.

✓ **Stop and think.**
Is mind real or only an idea?

The new psychologists argue that there are no mental forces independent of nature, no psychical causes qualitatively different from physical causes, no experiencer independent of the experience. So-called psychical causes, they say, are mere metaphysics, driven by the human desire to set ourselves above nature. Such speculations about mental forces have no place in psychology. To suggest that there is an experiencer that is independent of the experience is not parsimonious. What Wundt calls the experiencer is not a real thing, but only the name given to associations of sensations. Recall that the empiricist philosopher David Hume suggested this when he said that the experience of personal agency is illusory or just a comfortable way to understand the combination of certain sensations. According to Hume, the self as agent has no place in scientific psychology. Titchener echoes Hume when he says that the idea of a "knower" is merely a convenient fiction that refers to certain combinations of sensations, and he points out: "Our own position has been that mind and body, the subject-matter of psychology and the subject-matter of physiology, are simply two aspects of the same world of experience. They cannot influence each other, because they are not separate and independent things" (Titchener, 1912, p. 13).

Instead of having two kinds of experience, mental and physical, the mental is only a result of the physical. The task of psychology, therefore, is to explain the mechanics of how mental phenomena depend on physical processes.

In reply, Wundt argues that if it is true that there is nothing but physical causality, nothing but the biological organism, this reduces or subordinates psychology to biology: "If knowledge of all of reality devolves upon natural science ... then psychology finds its work done before it has started with it" (Wundt, as cited in Danziger, 1979, p. 211).

According to Wundt, the psychical causes give value and meaning to experience. The problem for new psychologists is that value and meaning have no place in natural science. For example, the biologist describes what is observed in nature, but does not assign meaning to what is observed. If psychology is to be a natural science, the positivists argue, then it must also avoid making judgments about value or meaning. Those kinds of judgments should be left to the humanities, art, literature, music, and philosophy.

By the second decade of the 20th century, positivistic values have replaced mentalistic notions in Western psychology. Ebbinghaus' nonsense syllables, for example, are chosen on the basis of having no value or meaning. Titchener even provides a positivistic theory of meaning based on the context of experience. Titchener's idea is that the phenomenon that has been referred to as "purpose" or what Wundt calls "will" is only a matter of learned "habit mechanisms," and value is a matter of "preferential response," based on past experiences. Although Titchener himself would likely have objected, others later suggest that Titchener's context theory of meaning and his emphasis on controlled laboratory methods facilitate the emergence of the next paradigm for Western psychology, behaviorism (Tweney, 1997).

PHYSIOLOGICAL BASES
FOR PSYCHOLOGY

By the 20th century, the movement is under way to turn psychology into a natural science. The underlying assumption of this movement is that thoughts, feelings, and behaviors originate in and are determined by the physiology of the material body. The research methods employed are observation and measurement, just as are used in the other natural sciences.

If the content of consciousness is made up of sensory experiences, then the goal of psychology should be to observe, measure, and describe the functioning of the various sensory systems and the transformation of sensory experience into meaningful perceptions. Fechner's methods of psychophysics have been refined

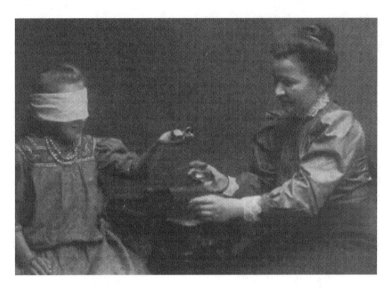

FIG. 8.1.   Experimenter and subject in weight-judging experiment
(reprinted from *A Pictorial History of Psychology* by H. Brauns
et al., copyright 1997, with a permission from Quintessence Publishing Co., Inc., p. 99).

and are used in psychology laboratories throughout the West to measure perception
in all sensory modalities. These are the psychophysical methods.

1. *Just noticeable differences (jnd).* The experimenter adjusts the magnitude
    of the stimulus in incremental steps until the subject reports a difference.
    The goal is to identify the range of stimuli that are perceived as equal to the
    standard.
2. *Method of constant stimuli.* The experimenter presents pairs of stimuli, one
    being a standard and the other varying in magnitude at each presentation. The
    subject reports whether the varied stimulus appears greater than, less than,
    or equal to the standard. *This same type of test is used today in optometrists'
    offices.*
3. *Method of adjustment.* The subject adjusts the stimulus to bring it above
    or below threshold or to a level that matches a standard. A typical weight-
    judging experiment is illustrated in Fig. 8.1.

The Physiology of Vision

The physical organs of vision are dissected to understand their structure, and
psychophysical studies are also under way to explain the transformation of physical
visual stimuli into visual perceptions. Introduced earlier, the study of the perception

of color provides a good example of efforts to understand how a material body can create mental events.

Modern studies of the perception of color begin in the 17th century using prisms. Isaac Newton is usually given credit for noting that light rays can be broken into colors and for pointing out that color does not reside in the rays, but comes instead from something in the perceiver. In the early 19th century, researchers find that all colors can be derived from three standard wavelengths of light: red, green, and blue. The English physicist Thomas Young concludes that there must be three different types of cells in the retina responsive to these three wavelengths (Helmholtz, 1856–1866/1961).

Christine Ladd-Franklin suggests an evolutionary explanation for this ability to perceive color. Any highly evolved system such as the eye exhibits differences across species. These differences result from different needs in the different environments to which animals must adapt and survive. Ladd-Franklin first suggests, and then demonstrates with evidence collected in the laboratory, that color vision has evolved in three stages. The ability to perceive light and dark evolved first, because it is the most necessary for survival. Next appeared blue–yellow sensitivity. The last cells to appear in evolution were those sensitive to red–green wavelengths. The most recently evolved cells are the most fragile, and this explains why color-blindness is more common to red–green wavelengths than to blue–yellow wavelengths (Ladd-Franklin, 1929).

The significance of these discoveries for psychology is that Ladd-Franklin demonstrates a clear connection between physiology and the contents of consciousness. Humans do not see a red apple or a blue flower because of some immaterial psyche. Humans perceive color because seeing some color aided in survival and adaptation.

Psychological Characteristics

Physiological psychologists suggest that sensory systems furnish consciousness with the basic mental elements of perception, and learning transforms sensory experiences into complex thoughts. In addition to a physiological basis for the functioning of sensory systems, therefore, there must also be a physiological basis for the process of learning. Thorndike (1898) suggests that mental associations are the result of connections between neurons in the brain. Although there are technological limitations to understanding brain functions, a number of theories about relationships between the physiological and the psychological are proposed at this time.

William James, for example, proposes a physiological theory of the origin and reason for the existence of emotions. He proposes that mental states, like fear, anger, or sadness, do not cause physiological changes but they are instead a result of physiological changes. For example, he suggests, imagine that you are walking in the woods one day and you come upon a bear on the trail ahead. Folk psychology says you would first become frightened and then turn and run. But, based on the work of Danish physiologist Carl G. Lange (1834–1900), James proposes that we first begin running, and it is the awareness of our pounding heart and rapid respiration that causes us to feel fearful. Thus, the psychological state of emotion is really only the awareness of a physiological state. This idea is called the **James–Lange motor theory of mind**.

✓ Stop and think.

Try to describe the feeling of a strong emotional state you have experienced without referring to any bodily changes.

At about the same time, Margaret Washburn also proposes a motor theory of psychological states in her book *Movement and Mental Imagery: Outline of a Motor Theory of Consciousness* (1916). In this work, she explains consciousness as the consequence of stimulation that sets off two or more competing motor responses. All of this activity takes place at the level of neurons, thus providing a physiological explanation for mental images.

Physiological states may give rise to mental images, but how could the psychological process of learning be described as the result of physiological functioning? Thorndike's hypothesis that learning is a process of forming connections between neurons is difficult to examine empirically, given the technology available in this era.

Eventually, the question falls to another young American psychologist, John B. Watson (1878–1958). Early in his career, Watson studies comparative psychology using a variety of species. In his work with white rats, he develops a kinesthetic theory of maze learning. He suggests that the rat does not learn to run the maze by thinking about and remembering correct and incorrect turns but that it is the rat's muscular, or kinesthetic, system that "learns" to run the maze.

Several other theorists propose other ideas about the physiological basis of learning. German physician and former student of Wundt's, Hugo Münsterberg (1863–1916), is hired to take over the psychology laboratory at Harvard when William James returns to his interests in philosophy. Münsterberg suggests that discovering that physiological systems adequately explain psychological characteristics like emotions and learning is an indication that even the "will" may have a physiological basis. If the brain and central nervous system shape behaviors by associating sensations with effective responses, what is the will doing? Maybe the will is only a concept used when the physiological processes that produce behavior are not fully understood. Münsterberg explains that the human sense that choices are freely made may be really nothing more than an awareness that the body is getting ready to act. Awareness of the body getting ready to behave makes humans feel as though they have willed that action.

Echoing many of his contemporaries, American philosopher and educator John Dewey (1859–1952) argues that our sense of self, our sense of having will, even consciousness itself, are nothing more than the reflex functioning of the brain. Furthermore, the brain is an evolved organ like any other and both it and its functions exist for the purpose of allowing the human organism to adapt to changing environments.

These and other physiological explanations for psychological states give rise to serious skepticism about the very existence of a mind that is independent of the body. More accurately, there is such skepticism when it comes to the question of animal mind. After all, as comparative psychologists have been careful to point out, animal mind must be inferred from animal behavior because no direct testimony of mind can be gathered from animals. If animal mind must be inferred from behavior, there is always the chance that the inference is incorrect and that, beyond a complex relay station for neural impulses, animal mind does not exist at all.

Instincts and Habits

✓ **Stop and think.**
If instincts explain much of animal behavior, how much do they explain of human behavior?

The term **instinct** is used to refer to a set of species-specific behaviors that do not appear to be a consequence of learning. Instincts are presumed to arise from the pressures of natural selection during evolution. Instincts are proposed to account for much of both nonhuman and human behavior. According to early 20th-century philosophers, instincts explain many aspects of human behavior. The argument about the existence of human instincts raises several interesting questions, not the least of which are questions about nominalism (Beach, 1955; see also Diamond, 1974).

✓ **Stop and think.**
If you explain that a certain behavior is the result of an instinct, have you explained the behavior?

Additionally, the argument in support of human instincts assumes that these instincts exist as a result of biological evolution, so that whatever is instinctual is not subject to either free will or learning. Several theorists propose solutions to the dilemma of how to accept the existence of instinctual pressures and still maintain a belief in free will and learning. Some suggest that instincts account for reflexes among very young humans, such as sucking and grasping, but learning takes over from these early instinctual responses. The learned responses are labeled habits.

Habits are conceived of as strongly ingrained patterns of behavior that allow the individual to respond without thinking. Borrowing largely from British philosopher Alexander Bain and many others, William James speculates that habits are formed as a result of repeated experience that is recorded in neurons. Thus, neural pathways are actually built by experience. Habits are formed because each time those pathways are activated, they become more and more easily activated. Furthermore, once acquired, habits are extremely resistant to change because they are part of how the brain has become structured.

✓ Stop and think.

If learning is a consequence of neuronal pathways being built, and this learning is resistant to later change, what does this imply about what you should or could do if you have acquired a habit you would prefer not to have acquired?

According to James, the way to change habits is to avoid activating the brain pathways to be eliminated and actively exercise the pathways to be created and strengthened. Thus, James recommends that to change habits you must behave as though you already are the person you wish to be (James, 1892/1985).

The Behaviorists' Manifesto

In a series of lectures at Columbia University in 1912–1913, John Watson, who is a professor of psychology at Johns Hopkins University, delivers what has come to be called the behaviorists' manifesto, *Psychology as the Behaviorist Views It*. In these lectures, Watson proposes at least three major revisions to the traditional study of psychology. First, he questions assumptions about the existence of a nonphysical consciousness or any other nonmaterial mental event. Next, he proposes that psychologists' goal should be to predict and control behavior, not to understand the structure, contents, and functioning of consciousness and mental life. "Psychology as the behaviorist views it is a purely experimental branch of natural science. Its theoretical goal is the prediction and control of behavior" (Watson, 1913, p. 158).

Finally, Watson proposes that only publicly observable evidence, meaning behavior, be allowed in the study of psychology. He criticizes introspection as a subjective, unobservable, and mostly unmeasurable method of study. Watson rejects both the study of mental elements and associations and also the study of the functions of consciousness and other mental events. Both structuralism and functionalism suffer, in Watson's view, from vague and indefinable terms. Furthermore, the assumptions of both will remain forever subject to debate and confusion. The scope of natural science should not extend beyond the publicly observable, and both the goals (understanding consciousness) and the methods (introspection) of structuralism and functionalism violate that scope. Watson argues that if psychology is to be a natural science and provide real explanations, it must be the study of what is publicly observable, meaning behavior. Thus, the only dependent variable for psychologists, the only variable that can be measured, is behavior: "I believe we can write a psychology . . . and . . . never use the terms consciousness, mental states, mind, content, introspectively verifiable, imagery, and the like. . . . It can be done in terms of stimulus and response, in terms of habit formation, habit integrations and the like" (Watson, 1913, pp. 166–167).

At the time that Watson delivers this address, most of his contemporaries in psychology regard the observation of behavior as an alternative to introspection or a supplemental method for studying mental life and do not regard his proposal as anything radically new in the field (Samelson, 1981). They see their carefully designed and measured laboratory methods of standardized introspection as just as scientific and objective as any observation could be and more direct evidence of mental life than any description of behavior. Thus, in their view, objective and positivistic methods are not new to psychology in 1913.

For these reasons, Watson's manifesto makes few waves when it is issued. However, on careful reading, some of his ideas are unusual. For example, at the time behavior is thought of as a clue to underlying mental processes. Mental events are assumed to exist, and they are qualitatively different from physical events. Even animals and human infants are assumed to have consciousness. Because it is impossible to ask them to introspect, researchers using animals and human infants as subjects are forced to observe behavior instead, but even here, behavior is observed for the purpose of illuminating underlying mental processes. The goal for psychologists is an abstract one, to understand mental life, presumed to exist, but directly observable only through introspection. For most psychologists, behavior is an indirect clue to consciousness. For Watson, the very existence of consciousness is in some doubt.

A second way in which Watson's ideas are different has to do with applications. Watson's goal, to predict and control behavior, is concrete, with many immediate applications to solving real-world problems. The idea that psychologists should find ways to solve problems is not new, but most of Watson's contemporaries are satisfied with seeking understanding through basic research and are not as concerned with practical applications:

> In the main, my desire in all such work is to gain accurate knowledge of adjustments and the stimuli calling them forth. My final reason for this is to learn general and particular methods by which I may control behavior. . . . If psychology would follow the plan I suggest, the educator, the physician, the jurist and the business man could utilize our data in a practical way, as soon as we are able, experimentally, to obtain them. (Watson, 1913, p. 168)

Watson furthers the movement toward finding practical applications for psychology. The rumblings of a Western world moving inexorably toward a terrible great war, World War I, also provide reasons for psychology to be useful.

PSYCHOLOGICAL TESTING

Histories of testing for psychological characteristics in the West usually begin with the work measuring sensory acuity done by Francis Galton and Paul Broca's studies of skull capacity. By the end of the 19th century, it is understood that intellectual capacity is not related to brain size, and many even question its relationship to sensory acuity. Instead, some now argue that intellectual capacity may be equated with, or is at least related to, the learned ability to reason about and solve practical and abstract problems. Ways to test individual differences in acquired knowledge and reasoning ability are being devised. By the early decades of the 20th century, there is much interest in testing for intellectual capacity.

✓ **Stop and think.**
What is intelligence? How could it be measured?

Research on testing for intellectual capacity is carried out primarily on two fronts, one in the United States and one in France. Galton's assumption that intellectual capacity is related to sensory abilities is pursued by James McKeen Cattell (1860–1944), an American who earns his doctorate from Wundt at Leipzig. A professor of psychology at the University of Pennsylvania and later at Columbia University, Cattell uses measures of sensory acuity and reaction time to test for individual differences in intellectual capacity from about 1888 until about 1901.

In France, researcher Alfred Binet (1857–1911) begins his study of intellectual capacity by measuring skulls, but he soon rejects this as an unreliable measure. Then, as a devoted father, Binet becomes interested in the development of intellectual capacity by carefully observing his two daughters, Madeleine and Alice. He investigates their intellectual growth by devising simple tasks, some of them very similar to those later developed by a later Swiss researcher, Jean Piaget (Cunningham, 1997). Binet concludes that intellectual capacity consists of the learned ability to reason. Working first with his colleague Victor Henri (1872–1940) and then later with Theodore Simon (1873–1961), Binet develops tests of the ability to reason. At the request of the French minister of public education, Binet and Simon devise a way to evaluate the intellectual capacities of school students. The purpose of such testing is to identify those students who are in need of special help in developing their intellectual capacity. Binet and Simon assume that intellectual capacity is reflected in basic processes of reasoning and the ability to solve problems encountered in everyday life. The processes of reasoning assumed to underlie intelligence are memory, imagery, imagination, attention, comprehension, suggestibility, aesthetic judgment, moral judgment, force of will, and judgment of visual space (Cunningham, 1997).

The test devised by Binet and Simon consists of many different tasks using these skills and is administered to individual students by trained examiners. The test measures children's abilities in relationship to their age and results in an average score on the many tasks, useful for identifying students who are in need of some additional training in using their reasoning skills. Binet firmly believes that all students can improve their reasoning ability and advocates training all students to increase their desire to learn, their ability to pay attention, and their intellectual self-discipline. He calls this training "mental orthopedics" and even includes physical exercises in the program.

The test Binet devises has two serious problems. First, it takes a great deal of time to administer and requires highly trained people to give the tests and evaluate the results. This makes the test not very useful for assessing large numbers of students. Second, as Charles Spearman (1863–1945) argues, if the skills demonstrated on the tasks all reflect a single underlying variable, like intellectual capacity, then scores on all the various tasks should be statistically related to one another, but they are not (Spearman, 1904). For example, in 1899 American psychologist Stella Sharp publishes findings showing no correlation among the various skills measured on the test of intellectual capacity developed by Binet and Henri. This is evidence that there is no single factor underlying all of these skills. Thus, the assumption that intellectual capacity is reflected in these several basic processes of reasoning remains in doubt (Sharp, 1899).

In North America, Cattell's tests of sensory acuity and reaction time suffer a similar fate. These measures are not related to one another, do not predict success in college, taken to be a real-life measure of intelligence, and in fact are not correlated with any other measure (Sokal, 1980).

✓ **Stop and think.**
Is intelligence a single characteristic or the sum of several?

Despite these problems, the interest in measuring differences in intellectual capacity continues. The idea that intelligence results from the set of the skills measured by Binet and Simon proves a popular one. They continue to revise their scale to make it easier to administer, they collect data to provide age comparisons, and they make the test useful for measuring differences in intellectual capacity, even among normally achieving students. Once age norms are established, individuals' scores on the test represent their intellectual age, which can then be compared with their chronological age to determine if the individual scores above, below, or on a par with age-mates. At the time of Binet's death in 1911, the Binet–Simon scale of intellectual age has become a relatively quick and easy-to-administer measure, has been translated into English, and is used in several countries in Europe and North America.

After Binet's death, his measurements of intellectual capacity are taken over by others. German psychologist William Stern (1871–1938), for example, argues successfully that children's measures of intellectual age should be divided by their chronological age, resulting in their intelligence quotient (IQ). When the intellectual age is exactly equivalent to the chronological age, the IQ is 100.

In the United States, Henry Goddard (1866–1957), the director of a psychological laboratory at a school for mentally retarded youngsters, translates the Binet–Simon scale into English and begins to use this English version with his students. He also tests students at nearby public schools and makes the shocking discovery that a significant number of those students test below normal in intelligence. Shortly after this, Goddard's English translation of the Binet–Simon scale comes to the attention of Lewis Terman (1877–1956) at Stanford University, who revises it to provide more reliable results with children in the United States. First published in 1912, Terman's version of the scale is revised in 1916, 1937, and again in 1960 (Minton, 1988). *Still used today, Terman's scale is called the Stanford–Binet.*

Terman, Goddard, and Cattell are among many in this era who believe, like Galton, that intelligence is an inherited characteristic. In 1912, Goddard publishes the results of his research, *The Kallikak Family, a Study in the Heredity of Feeble-Mindedness*, supporting the popular belief that intelligence is inherited. When combined with Herbert Spencer's earlier argument that societies degenerate if the wrong kinds of people are allowed to have children, Goddard's work becomes a powerful argument for the 20th-century movement to control reproduction called **eugenics**.

Immigrant Testing

The widespread belief that lower intelligence leads to criminal behavior adds fuel to the fire to control the reproduction of anyone deemed to be below average in intelligence or undesirable for other reasons. Ultimately, this leads to an invitation for Goddard to administer intelligence tests to thousands of immigrants entering the United States from Europe. Beginning in 1912, he and his associates give the English version of the Binet–Simon test to immigrants as they disembark from their journey in crowded ships across the Atlantic. Many, if not most, of these immigrants do not speak English, have never gone to school, and have not even held a pencil before. Not surprisingly under the circumstances, up to half of these immigrants test in the range of intelligence Goddard calls "morons." Thousands of immigrants are deported back to their countries of origin solely on the basis of these tests (Shapiro, 1991).

Army Testing During the Great War

Paper-and-pencil testing for individual differences in intellectual capacity begins in schools and institutions for the purpose of evaluating children's needs for remedial education. But the real growth in testing for intellectual capacity occurs at the entry of the United States into the Great War, later called World War I, in 1917. In an attempt to establish their new science as both a practical field and a respectable science, psychologists volunteer to help with the war effort:

> As mobilization for World War I approached, Yerkes got one of those "big ideas" that propel the history of science: could psychologists possibly persuade the army to test all of its recruits? If so, the philosopher's stone of psychology might be constructed: the copious, useful, and uniform body of numbers that would fuel a transition from dubious art to respected science. (Gould, 1996, p. 223)

Thus, Robert Yerkes (1876–1956), a comparative psychologist at Harvard University and the president of the American Psychological Association, sees a chance to finally establish psychology as a useful science. In 1917, the United States Army asks him to test recruits to help identify those with mental deficiencies and those who have sufficient intelligence to profit from officer training. Less than 2 years later, the Army testing program is terminated, but during this time, more than 1.75 million recruits and civilians are tested. Although the results are mostly ignored by Army officers, the data collected have a significant impact on the history of psychology after the war.

The Great War

In the late spring of 1914, war breaks out in Europe after the assassination of the Archduke and Archduchess of Austria–Hungary by a Serbian loyalist. The war quickly engulfs most of continental Europe, from France to Turkey and Russia. Shortly after, Britain is also drawn into the conflict. The war drags on for more than 4 years, with the United States entering the conflict in April 1917. Although more than 5 million men and women in the United States are in some form of military service by war's end, it is Europe that suffers the most devastating human and economic losses. By November 1918, when the Armistice is finally signed, monarchies all across Europe have collapsed. Whole industries and transportation systems have been destroyed, and huge areas of farmland and forest have been left uninhabitable by chemical weapons and unexploded armaments. More than $337 billion has been lost, causing countries across Europe to incur crippling debts. More than 31 million soldiers have been killed or wounded, and even today no one knows how many civilian lives are lost in this Great War.

The consequences of the war on intellectual life are even harder to measure. The brutality of the carnage shatters faith in the superiority of European culture, although people in the United States emerge with an increased sense of the power and prestige of their nation. German universities and laboratories no longer draw as many students from other countries, and there is increasing respect for doctoral degrees granted from universities in North America. After stepping in to fill the civilian roles in business and industry vacated by men recruited into the military, women enjoy an increase in status, opportunity, and earning power. It is shortly after the end of this war that women are given the right to vote in most Western countries.

Army Testing After the War

In the decade after the Great War, the massive data on intellectual capacity collected during army testing have a significant impact on the history of psychology and on society in general in the United States. As the data are compiled and published, the findings are shocking. The data reveal that the average intellectual age of those tested in the Army is just 13 years. Furthermore, the average intellectual age of European immigrants to the United States is even lower than that. More recent immigrants, especially those from southern and eastern Europe, have even lower averages. The lowest averages of all are found among those citizens of the United States of African descent, particularly those who live in states in the South.

As disturbing as these data are, there is little effort made at the time to validate these results, to consider whether these scores represent actual ability, or to consider the conditions under which the tests were administered. Instead, because most people believe that intellectual capacity is determined by inheritance, these results only serve to empower the growing eugenics movement.

The second decade of the 20th century sees the introduction of sophisticated statistics to determine the validity and reliability of psychological tests. In spite of this, when problems are found with the Army intelligence tests or with the conditions under which they are given, the proponents of the tests ignore these problems. For example, significant correlations are found among African Americans between place of residence and score on the test such that those who live in the North, where they have had access to more and better education, score better than those who live in the South, where they are mostly uneducated. This is a correlational finding; thus, as any undergraduate knows, great caution should be taken in assuming the direction of cause and effect. Nevertheless, one could easily infer from this finding that living conditions and years of education play an important role in influencing test scores. And there are plenty of data available to test this hypothesis, even in the 1920s. Instead, psychologists argue that those who are more intelligent have moved to the North and sought out education, whereas the less intelligent have stayed in the South laboring in the fields (Gould, 1996).

Beliefs that intelligence is inherited have more pernicious results when it comes to the findings about immigrants. The fear is already widespread in the United States that immigrants from Europe, particularly those with darker skins from southern Europe, those speaking strange-sounding languages from eastern Europe, and those of Jewish descent, will weaken the "pure" White American stock. Many believe that these immigrants have already had an impact on lowering average intelligence. Allowing more of them into the United States will lead inevitably to the further decay and degeneration of American intellectual and moral fiber. The test results increase pressures to sterilize and segregate undesirables. In 1924, the Immigrant Restriction law is passed, establishing quotas limiting immigration from certain European countries to no more than 2% of 1890 levels (Snyderman, & Herrnstein, 1983).

Eugenics

In the early decades of the 20th century in the United States, support for eugenics finds many educated adherents. James Cattell, for example, argues in support of providing incentives for intelligent people to marry other intelligent people and even offers $1,000 to each of his children if they will marry the child of a college professor. Goddard, Terman, and many others argue in favor of the sterilization or segregation of the feeble-minded to prevent them from having children. This movement gains steadily in popularity. By 1928, there are 376 courses in eugenics being offered in colleges across the United States, and 28 states have passed laws allowing for the surgical sterilization of the feeble-minded, mentally ill, and criminally insane (Proctor, 1991).

At this time, it is widely believed that lack of intelligence is the chief cause of criminal, antisocial, and immoral behavior. Terman writes extensively on the social consequences of allowing the feeble-minded to reproduce: "Not all criminals are feeble-minded, but all feeble-minded persons are at least potential criminals. That every feeble-minded woman is a potential prostitute would hardly be disputed by anyone" (Terman, 1916, p. 11).

Fed by beliefs such as these, between 1907 and 1945, more than 73,000 people in the United States are sterilized (Proctor, 1991), many for no reason other than having been caught drinking alcohol, violating curfew, or engaging in some other minor misbehavior during adolescence. Some are sterilized simply for belonging to families looked down on by neighbors. Voices in support of the practice of euthanasia on these same populations are also growing louder in the United States.

School Testing

Although the testing program during World War I proves less than useful to the Army, intelligence testing in other settings increases in popularity during the years after the war. It is in this period between wars that psychology expands from being strictly an academic discipline pursued in laboratories on university campuses to also being a profession practiced in schools, businesses, and industrial settings. The testing programs instituted in these places are based on assumptions that intelligence is inherited and that scores on the tests reveal innate ability that can only be slightly altered by environmental factors.

By 1900 in the United States, compulsory education laws are enacted in every state, and public schools are established to ensure that every citizen is taught basic skills. A new political movement emerges, the Progressive Party, which encourages the application of scientific findings to improve society and advocates widespread testing for intelligence in public schools. By 1921, 2 million school children in the United States are being tested for intelligence annually (Snyderman & Rothman, 1988), and students are "tracked" into high-, average-, and low-achieving classrooms based on the results of these tests. The purpose of tracking is to ensure that those with high innate ability are given the best education possible so as to maximize their potential as leaders. Because other students have less innate ability, educational advantages would only be wasted on them. Those in the lowest tracks will be provided only with vocational training, as this is the level of education from which they will profit most. The Scholastic Aptitude Test (SAT) is introduced in 1926 as a tool to aid in college admissions decisions, although it does not gain widespread acceptance until after World War II.

Industrial Applications

Testing for the purpose of making employment decisions has been practiced for much longer than just the past century. The Chinese have been using civil service tests for government employment for more than 2,000 years. In the West, Münsterberg and other psychologists practicing industrial psychology have used tests since the 19th century. With the advent of intelligence testing for innate ability, the tools are now available to identify the right applicant to fit each job. With employees assigned to jobs for which they are innately suited, American industry has the power to maximize productivity and become the economic giant that it is destined to become.

Unfortunately for employers, it soon becomes evident that testing for placement is not working. Employees placed into positions based on their test scores do not reliably perform any better than those assigned to positions based on the judgments of supervisors. Other studies, explored in the next chapter, establish that motivational and social factors are as important to productivity as intelligence. Employment testing becomes very popular in the United States, but not until after World War II, when more valid and reliable tests are available.

BEHAVIORISM AFTER THE GREAT WAR

Behaviorists assert that, because consciousness must be inferred from observations of behavior, it is inappropriate as an object of study in the natural sciences. Furthermore, nothing can be understood by studying mind that cannot be understood just as well by studying behavior. Therefore, mind does not matter.

Later in John Watson's career, as behaviorism becomes more accepted and the physiological origins of psychological characteristics are better understood, Watson and other behaviorists deny the very existence of consciousness as anything other than physiological functioning. Thus, for the behaviorists, the ancient mind–body problem vanishes. No longer must philosopher/scientists struggle to find where and how the material body communicates with the immaterial mind. There is no immaterial mind, only body. There is no immaterial aspect of the human. There is only matter, just as is true for all other animals. Consciousness is nothing more than an awareness of what the body is doing and has no place in science. Behavior is the mechanical functioning of a mechanical body. All that remains to understand is how this very complex machine, the human, works.

Stimulus–Response Theory

Recall that behaviorism requires that the variable to be measured be publicly observable. The research method in all forms of behaviorism is the observation, measurement, and description of behavior. Behaviorists assume only one psychological process, and that is learning. If humans begin life as blank slates and behavior originates in the association of stimuli with responses, then it is important to understand the process of how and why those associations are formed. Like many other psychologists and philosophers, Watson assumes that learned associations cause behavior.

This view stands in stark contrast to that of hereditarians, who argue that innate limits on intelligence determine each individual's destiny. Watson's assertion that, given the right conditions, he can raise any healthy infant to fulfill any role in society (Watson, 1930, p. 104) is much more in keeping with traditional values in the United States. In the United States the belief is common that, with enough effort "any boy can grow up to be President."

✓ **Stop and think.**
Why assume that learning causes behavior? What is the evidence? How could this hypothesis be tested?

It is at this point that Watson's speculations diverge from the structuralists, the functionalists, and even from most of his contemporary behaviorists. Watson argues that the independent variable, that which causes behavior, should be as observable as the dependent or outcome variable. He has read some of the work of the Russian physiologists Pavlov and Bekhterev reviewed in the following section and eventually settles on the **conditioned reflex** as the cause of behavior. In other words, in Watson's view, behavior is not caused by mental events like desire, will, motivation, or consciously thought-out plans. An organism begins by emitting a reflex action in response to environmental stimulation. The reflex action may then be associated with a satisfactory outcome or not and thus may be more or less likely to be repeated in the future. It is always an environmental stimulus (S) that becomes associated (-) with an observable response (R). For this reason, Watson's form of behaviorism is called S-R theory.

Russian Physiological Associationism

During the late 19th century and the early years of the 20th century, Russian physicians Ivan Pavlov and Vladimir Bekhterev are conducting experiments on human and animal physiology. Like their older colleague Sechenov, Pavlov and Bekhterev share the materialist assumption that all mental experience is reducible to the functioning of matter. Consciousness is only the awareness of sensory experience and physiological reflexive responses (Joravsky, 1989).

For example, it is as Pavlov is carrying on his research into the reflexes of the digestive system that he almost accidentally makes the discoveries that have led to such renown in the West. Initially, he is seeking only to understand the functional relationships between a sensory experience, like the taste of food, and a physiological reflex, in this case, salivation. Instead of asking human subjects to introspect, or report on their sensory experiences, as the Germans have been doing, Pavlov elects to examine what he views as a more objective measure, the amount of salivation and gastric fluids produced when a hungry animal is presented with food. This is a more invasive procedure, requiring the surgical implantation of tubes and shunts into his canine subjects, but Pavlov views this as a more direct and defensible measure of the physiological reflexes. His goal is to know more about how the amount and quality of stimulation affects the reflexive response.

After a time, researchers in Pavlov's laboratory notice that the food-deprived dogs begin to salivate as soon as they hear the lab workers coming into the laboratory and when they see the dishes in which the food powder is stored. Salivation when food powder is put into the mouth is viewed as a direct physiological reflexive response to the food. But salivation in response to the sound of the lab workers or the sight of the food dishes requires another level of explanation. How could a sound or a sight trigger the physiological response of salivation? To Pavlov, this seems very similar to the "action at a distance" problem of magnets or gravity faced by the physicists of an earlier era. What is the mechanism that allows an auditory or visual sensation to trigger a response that was previously only seen to the sensory stimulation of taste?

At first, Pavlov calls this mechanism a "psychical" reflex, argues that it is the psychical reflex that sets off the physiological reflex, and then sets about attempting to understand the functional relationship between the two types of reflexes. However, as he soon realizes, calling salivation to an auditory or visual stimulus a psychical reflex is only a form of nominalism, that is, giving the phenomenon a name and doing nothing to explain it. Thus, Pavlov begins to think in terms of the excitation and inhibition of cortical responses. By this time, it is known that neurons in the nervous system and brain respond to physical stimuli by electrical firing, so that when food powder is placed in the mouth, sensory neurons fire, sending that information to the brain. This information is then sent by electrical signals to the muscles and physiological systems governing the production of salivation and gastric fluids. When visual and auditory stimuli occur at the same time as taste stimuli, neurons in all those parts of the brain are excited. With enough pairings of the sound of the lab workers approaching, the sight of the food dishes, and the presentation of the food powder, this spread of electrical activation eventually causes these auditory and visual stimuli to result in salivation. To distinguish salivation to auditory or visual stimulation from the unconditioned physiological response of salivation to the taste of food, Pavlov calls the former the "conditional response." Salivation to an auditory or visual stimulus is conditional on the previous pairing of those sights and sounds with the presence of food.

Vladimir Bekhterev, the Russian physiologist who establishes the first Russian experimental psychology laboratory, is working at about the same time as Pavlov. Bekhterev's work also focuses on relationships between physical events and psychological characteristics, and, well ahead of his colleagues in the United States, he emphasizes observable behavior as the object of study in psychology. Bekhterev differs from Pavlov by asserting that the study of associations between environmental stimuli and motor reflexes is more directly relevant to human behavior than Pavlov's study of gastric secretions. Bekhterev should also be noted for his establishment in 1908 of an institute for the graduate study of psychology that allows unrestricted access to both women and Jews, the first of its kind in the world.

Personality

As Pavlov works with many different breeds of dogs, he notices that some breeds are more excitable and nervous, whereas others are calmer and quieter. His increased understanding of cortical functioning leads him to speculate that these personality differences are grounded in differing levels of cortical excitation and inhibition. Thus, Pavlov suggests, the basis of personality or temperament is a result of innate differences in physiological responses to the environment. Some individuals are more likely to respond to even very low levels of environmental stimulation, whereas very high levels of stimulation are required to elicit a response in others. Most individuals fall somewhere between the two extremes in responsiveness.

Later in his career, Pavlov becomes interested in the clinical applications of his research. He speculates that some individuals are more prone to succumbing to neuroses than others. Continuing his experiments with dogs, he produces what he calls "experimental neuroses" by presenting the dogs with ambiguous stimuli. For example, a dog might be trained to respond to a picture of a circle, but to inhibit any response to a square. After the dog is trained, a picture of a square with very rounded corners is presented, making it hard for the dog to know whether to respond or inhibit a response. Under these circumstances, many dogs exhibit nervousness and anxiety, similar to the characteristics labeled neuroses in humans. This work leads Pavlov and many others to hope for a scientific explanation of personality based on measurable physiological differences. Pavlov also argues that eventually scientific theories of interpersonal relationships will be grounded in the individual differences found in physiological responses to environmental stimulation.

The Conditioned Reflex

Although neither Pavlov's nor Bekhterev's writings are widely available in English until 1927–1928 (Samelson, 1981), this is some of what Watson reads as he is developing his ideas about behaviorism. For Watson, Pavlov's conditional response is the piece he has been looking for to establish the purely physiological basis of behavior, the piece that eventually allows him to speculate that consciousness is nothing more than an awareness of the body's reflex responses to external stimulation. Watson argues that Pavlov's conditional response is the physiological explanation for the philosophers' concept of association. According to Watson, learning is the basis of all behavior, but it is not some mysterious conscious effort of a metaphysical will. Learning is based on the spread of cortical activation in response to sensory stimulation.

John Watson firmly believes that the process of association, what he calls the conditioned reflex, explains nearly all of behavior. In the case of emotions, for example, he speculates that only fear, rage, and love are innate emotions. The full range of adult emotions can be explained by conditioned reflex. Furthermore, from previous work with infants, Watson concludes that there are only two environmental stimuli that innately cause the experience of fear. Specifically, human infants are innately fearful of sudden loud noises and of a sudden loss of physical support. All other fears are learned by association with these two innate triggers of fear. To establish the experimental evidence to support his speculations, Watson and his graduate assistant, Rosalie Rayner, attempt to condition an infant, known since as "Little Albert," to be afraid of a variety of stimuli to which he initially shows no fear.

The Story of Little Albert

Although Albert is a normal infant, he has been reared almost from birth in the Harriet Lane Home for Invalid Children, where his mother is employed as a wet nurse. He is described by Watson and Rayner as being, on the whole, stolid and unemotional, and they decide that they can do Albert relatively little harm by their attempts to condition him to be afraid of additional stimuli.

First, they must establish whether or not Albert has already been conditioned to be fearful of other stimuli. When Albert is about 9 months old, the researchers confront him suddenly, and presumably for the first time, with a white rat, a rabbit, a dog, a monkey, masks with and without hair, cotton wool, burning newspapers, and other objects. According to their descriptions, Albert's most common response is to attempt to reach out to touch and handle these objects. At no time does he show fear of any of the stimuli.

Albert is also tested to see if he exhibits the expected innate fears. The researchers try dropping Albert a short distance and jerking a blanket on which he is lying, but Albert shows no fear. Watson speculates that this innate fear may be effective only in younger children, may be experienced only by less placid infants, or may be already lost due to previous conditioning. Albert is also tested to see if he exhibits fear of a sudden loud noise. Directly behind his head, a steel bar is struck with a hammer. For the first time Albert shows a fearful response. He startles to the sound, then, after the second strike of the hammer on the steel bar, his lips begin to pucker and tremble, and on the third stimulation, he begins to cry.

Watson and Rayner express some reluctance to cause Albert experimentally to develop a new fear, but they eventually conclude that he will develop other fears sooner or later anyway. What might be learned about how fear responses can be conditioned overrides their concern about the consequences for Albert. At about 11 months of age Albert is returned to the laboratory, and it is determined again that he shows no fearful responses to any of the neutral stimuli. Thus, they begin attempting to condition a new fear in him.

A white rat is taken suddenly from a basket and presented to Albert. He reaches for the rat and just as his hand touches the animal the steel bar is struck immediately behind his head. Albert startles and falls forward, but does not cry. Again the rat is presented, and again, just as he touches the rat, the bar is struck. Albert again falls forward and whimpers.

No further tests are made for 1 full week. Then, Albert is brought to the laboratory and presented with the rat again, this time with no sound. He looks at the rat but does not attempt to touch it. When the rat is brought nearer, Albert begins tentative reaching movements, but when the rat noses his hand, Albert pulls it away. A second trial is then conducted, jointly presenting the rat and the sound. At the sound, Albert again falls over but does not cry. A third and then a fourth trial result in the same response. On the fifth trial, the rat is presented without any sound. Albert whimpers and withdraws his body from the rat. Only after the sixth trial, presenting the rat and striking the steel bar together, does Albert whimper, and on the seventh trial he begins to cry. At the eighth trial, the rat is presented alone. Albert begins to cry immediately, turns, and crawls away. Watson and Rayner conclude that they have successfully conditioned Albert to be afraid of a previously neutral stimulus.

Five days later, the researchers test to see if the fear will transfer to other objects. They present Albert with a rabbit, a dog, a fur seal coat, cotton wrapped in paper, Watson's hair, the hair of other observers, and a Santa Claus mask. Between each of these trials, they give Albert his blocks to play with. Albert expresses mild fearfulness of almost all of the stimuli, but readily calms down when given the blocks. Watson and Rayner conclude that Albert's conditioned fear of the rat has transferred to these other objects.

Five days after this, at 11 months and 20 days, Albert is again brought to the laboratory. He is presented with the rat, rabbit, and dog again. Sometimes, the steel bar is struck at the time the animal is presented and sometimes not. Albert's response is again to withdraw, sometimes to attempt to crawl away, but rarely to cry.

Albert is moved to a different room and again presented with the rat, rabbit, and dog. The steel bar is struck again just as the rat is presented. Albert's responses to all three animals are again mildly fearful, although he calms immediately when presented with the blocks. Curiously, no description is given of the response of the rat, rabbit, or dog to the sudden loud sound of the steel bar at the time they are placed in front of Albert, although on one occasion, the dog does bark loudly, startling everyone in the room.

Watson and Rayner wish to determine the effect of the passage of time on the fear they believe they have conditioned in Albert. So exactly 1 month later, just before Albert's mother leaves her employment and takes Albert out of the hospital, they test him again. Albert still shows mildly negative responses to being forced to touch the Santa Claus mask, fur coat, rat, rabbit, and dog. Watson and Rayner conclude that conditioned fears persist, although with a certain loss of intensity across time. They further speculate that these conditioned fears modify personality throughout life. (Watson & Rayner, 1920)

Even though they know well in advance that Albert will be leaving the hospital, and they have some interest in the process of the "detachment" or removal of conditioned responses, Watson and Rayner make no effort to decondition Albert's experimentally induced fears. This may be for the best, given their proposal for how to remove these fears. If fear of the rat can be conditioned by pairing its presentation with an innately fear-causing stimulus (a loud sound), they suggest that fear of the rat might best be removed by pairing the rat with an innately love-causing stimulus. For a behaviorist like Watson, the emotion of love is caused by physical stimulation. He thus suggests pairing the presentation of the rat with simultaneous stimulation of Albert's erogenous zones, beginning with the lips, then the nipples, and finally the sex organs (Watson & Rayner, 1920).

Although they do not attempt to decondition Albert, Watson and Rayner do make a presumably tongue-in-cheek guess as to what his Freudian psychoanalyst might say some 20 years hence when Albert presents himself to be cured of his lifelong fear of furry objects. They also suggest that Freud's assertion that sex (what Watson and Rayner call love) is the primal emotion is not supported by this study of conditioned fear. Fear, they say, is just as primal an emotion as love in influencing personality.

Shortly after the Little Albert study is concluded, Watson and Rayner become embroiled in a personal scandal when their illicit romantic affair is discovered and Watson's wife divorces him. Watson is fired from his faculty position at Johns Hopkins University, never holds another academic position, and his research with infants comes to an end. Later researchers repeatedly attempt to replicate his findings on conditioned fears, but are largely unsuccessful. Thus, one study with one infant serves as Watson's only experimental support for his assertion that conditioned reflexes form the basis of human behavior.

Despite this, behaviorism in its various forms comes to dominate experimental psychology during the first half of the 20th century in the United States. This dominance is sometimes explained as a consequence of the strength of John Watson's personality and the inferences he draws for many years from the study of Little Albert. Others attribute the popularity of behaviorism to its reliance on observable evidence and rejection of metaphysical assumptions.

Until the 1960s, most experimental psychologists in the United States share the assumptions of behaviorism. These include assumptions that humans begin life as blank slates, that behavior is a consequence of learned associations, that *learning* can be defined as the gradual appearance of a predicted response to a specific stimulus, and that behavior, not consciousness, is what psychologists should explain. Furthermore, they adopt positivism as their shared method of research. Both the stimulus and the response must be publicly observable.

WEIRD SCIENCE

Throughout history, science and magic are easily confused, and technological achievements can seem like magic, from long distance communication to human flight. These advances in technology accelerate in the 20th century.

Physical Science and Science Fiction

At the same time that mechanistic ideas and positivistic methods are taking over psychology, the other sciences are having second thoughts about both. Physics, for example, has moved beyond positivistic methods by early in the 20th century. In 1905, Albert Einstein publishes his special theory of relativity. In developing this theory, Einstein relies not so much on observations and measurements as he does on logical deduction. In his special theory of relativity, Einstein asserts that time and distance are not absolutes but appear to vary depending on the speed of the observer. Thus, time slows down the faster one moves through space. In fact, this theory suggests, if one could move fast enough, time would move backwards.

Subsequent observations have proven Einstein's theories of relativity to be more accurate throughout most of the universe than were Newton's notions of absolute time and space, but the idea that time and space are relative sounds like pure comic-book science fiction to many nonscientists. Thus, the literary genre of science fiction is born from scientific and technological changes occurring during the last few decades of the 19th century (Fayter, 1997). Stories like H. G. Wells' *The Invisible Man*, published in 1895, or Charlotte Perkins Gilman's *Herland*, published in 1915, explore the blurry boundaries between science and fiction.

Psychic Research

The distinctions between science and pseudoscience are likely to be confused in the study of consciousness as well (Leahey, & Leahey, 1983). In 1882, the Society for Psychical Research is founded in England for the purpose of investigating phenomena that may be beyond the scope of nature, but somehow still within the reach of the by now well-respected methods of science. These phenomena include claims of telepathic communication and clairvoyance, as well as the Spiritualists' interests in hauntings and communication with the dead. In 1884, William James helps found a similar organization in the United States, the American Society for Psychical Research. Popular interest in telepathy and clairvoyance far exceeds popular interest in experimental psychology. Most people are clearly "more interested in whether people could communicate with the dead, and ESP," than they are with "the 'range of perception' and the 'timing of thought' " (Coon, 1992).

William James is fascinated with the possibility of telepathy. In 1902, he writes in *The Varieties of Religious Experience* about elements in the universe that humans cannot grasp through either sensory or rational powers, but that can be glimpsed through the window of mystical experience. Because, for James, the authority of experience is absolute, he is reluctant to dismiss entirely accounts of mystical experience. Although mystical experiences represent reality for the individual who has the experience, James recognizes the existence of hallucinations and delusions. Thus, some experiences represent a reality that is not external to the individual. James also has doubts about the possibility of communication with the dead. After attending a number of seances, he expresses concern that the spirits of those who had passed over have nothing of much interest to report about their afterlife. Instead, they only communicate such trivial facts as that the still-living wife has moved the place of their photograph. Despite this, James does believe that if communication with the dead could be achieved, it would be found to be explicable in natural terms and would thus yield to scientific investigation (James, 1902).

William James is not alone in hoping that the methods of science will reveal that there is more in the universe than nature and that humans are more than well-developed apes, as Thomas Huxley once referred to them. One leading 19th-century researcher in psychical phenomena is Fredric Myers (1843–1901), who argues that within each individual, there is a "subliminal self" that is powered by psychical energy. It is this subliminal self, Myers believes, that allows for communication with the dead. Psychologists study claims of communication with the dead and the possibility of telepathy through the early decades of the 20th century. By midcentury however, the complete lack of publicly observable evidence for any of these phenomena has caused most psychologists to lose interest. Parapsychology, as the field comes to be known, is a largely discredited and somewhat embarrassing stepchild of psychology in the last half of the century.

⏰ The Times

By 1900, unregulated business and industrial expansion in the United States is coming to an end. In response to public outrage, President Theodore Roosevelt pushes for the enforcement of antitrust legislation and succeeds in breaking up business monopolies, culminating in the dissolution of Standard Oil in 1911. Labor unions gain power and are able to improve working conditions, shorten working hours, and significantly increase wages for their members.

In the decade after the end of the Great War, the economy expands rapidly as the growing middle class pours money into the stock market. Stock prices soar, unrelated to the actual value of the investments. A very small number of families amass huge fortunes. They build homes modeled after European palaces, import millions of dollars worth of European art and ancient artifacts from around the world, and generally do their best to imitate the now mostly vanished European aristocracy.

The power of electricity is harnessed for human use in the 19th century and by the early 20th century is a common feature of everyday life in the West. The electric light bulb, for example, transforms night into day and changes the daily rhythm of life for nearly everyone. From 1920 to 1930, the number of automobiles on roads in North America triples from 8 million to 23 million, spawning whole new industries in road construction, gasoline and service stations, and tourism. Urban populations continue to grow, while the percentage of people living on farms and in rural areas declines. The middle classes enjoy a prosperity that brings them radios and a vastly expanded selection of radio programming, telephones to maintain contact with ever more widely scattered family members, and electric "labor-saving" devices, such as washing machines. On the newly invented "weekends," even working people can afford to seek urban entertainment, such as professional sporting events, and worship sports heroes like Babe Ruth and boxer Jack Dempsey. They can go to the new motion picture shows called "movies" and admire glamorous film stars like Mary Pickford and Douglas Fairbanks, Sr.

In January 1920, Prohibition is passed in the United States, outlawing the sale of liquor. Illegal "speakeasies" spring up in urban centers, catering to what are referred to as the "Flaming Youth." Young people thrill to the increasingly fast pace of life, speeding around in automobiles, drinking bootleg liquor, dancing the Charleston, and listening to jazz. Also in 1920, conservative Warren G. Harding is elected to the presidency by promising to return the country to "normalcy," pursue an isolationist foreign policy, reduce government regulation of business, and decrease the power of organized labor. Throughout the United States, the Ku Klux Klan grows stronger and blames modern problems on a variety of scapegoats, from Bolsheviks to Jews to Roman Catholics.

In late October 1929, the entire economic house of cards collapses with the crash of stock markets in the United States and around the world. The popular culture that emerges during the Great Depression is a sharp contrast to the optimistic, but now disappeared, Roaring Twenties.

9

Paradigms Proliferate: Is There an Unconscious Mind?

In this chapter the various domains of psychology that begin to emerge in the West during the first half of the 20th century are explored. The chapter begins in Germany with Gestalt psychology. Its proponents are then followed across the Atlantic. In North America, the various practical applications found for psychology are examined, including early industrial psychology, clinical applications, child study, and social psychology. Psychoanalytic theory is also covered, especially as it affects psychology and popular culture.

GESTALT PSYCHOLOGY

During the early decades of the 20th century, psychology in Germany is prospering. Brentano's "act" psychology provides a precedent for psychologists who doubt that consciousness can be fully explained by a set of basic elements of mind associated together through a set of laws. This new way of viewing the contents of consciousness is named "Gestalt" psychology. Gestalt ideas are influenced by arguments that consciousness is directed toward achieving goals, by the increasing focus in physics on fields of force, by anomalies in research, and by common experience. Gestalt psychologists argue that the contents of consciousness cannot be adequately explained by cataloging a set of basic elements and laws of association. Instead, they argue, holistically perceived sensory information is given form by fields of force in the brain. These fields of force create perceptions that are not only more than the sum of the individual sensory elements, but also are often completely different than the sum of the parts.

The need for a Gestalt explanation for the contents of consciousness is made apparent as a result of several experimental anomalies for which structuralists have no explanation. Two examples will serve as illustrations.

The Phi Phenomenon

In 1910, German psychologist Max Wertheimer (1880–1943) asks a provocative question that throws doubt on the entire structuralist paradigm. Wertheimer notices that if two lights placed close together are lighted, first one and then the other, they will be perceived as two lights, just as an elementalist psychology would predict. And if the two lights are shown at exactly the same moment, they are usually perceived as one light. But if the two lights are shown successively with a very brief interval between them, the **phi phenomenon** occurs: They are perceived as one light moving across space.

✓ **Stop and think.**
Why would motion be perceived when there really are two separate lights?

Wilhelm Wundt has an explanation for why motion is perceived when there are really two separate lights. He suggests that when the two lights are flashed with a brief interval between them, the eyes travel quickly from one light to the next. It is eye movement, the same movement that the eyes make when an object really is moving across the visual field, that causes the perception of two lights as one light moving.

✓ **Stop and think.**
How could you test Wundt's explanation?

Wertheimer finds a way to test Wundt's explanation for the illusion of movement by using two pairs of lights instead of one pair. For each pair, one light is flashed just slightly before the other, but in one pair, the right light is flashed first and the left one second, and in the other pair, the left light is flashed first and the right one second. Using this design, motion is still perceived. Because the eyes cannot move in both directions at the same time, the illusion of movement that is perceived cannot be a result of eye movements (Wertheimer, 1912/1968). It must be a phenomenon of perception. It is a phenomenon that is familiar today in the form of motion pictures which, although made up of a series of still pictures, are perceived as moving images.

The phi phenomenon is important for the science of psychology for several reasons. It is an anomaly that cannot be explained by an elementalist account of perception. More importantly, perceiving movement where there really is none means that perception does not represent reality perfectly. Perceptions are thus not reducible to elements of sensory information.

✓ **Stop and think.**

What does it mean for science, and for the science of psychology, to suggest that perceptions, although originating in reality, are not perfect representations of reality?

Max Wertheimer continues to be fascinated with thinking throughout his life. He and Albert Einstein become good friends, and the last major substantive chapter of Wertheimer's posthumous book, *Productive Thinking* (1945/1959), based on extensive interviews of Einstein by Wertheimer, deals with the thought processes Einstein used to come up with the theory of relativity (M. Wertheimer, personal communication, March 31, 2005).

Animal Insight

The second set of experimental anomalies that illustrate a weakness in the elementalist paradigm are the findings on animal insight made by German scientist Wolfgang Köhler (1887–1967). Köhler's work challenges Edward Thorndike's conclusion that animals can only solve problems through trial and error. Köhler observes that animals in the real world appear to be solving problems using a variety of techniques. He therefore sets similar kinds of problems for the apes he studies at the Anthropoid Research Station in the Canary Islands off the West Coast of Africa. His hypothesis is that being able to see the whole problem is key to being able to use alternative problem-solving strategies. Animals—even humans—use trial and error when only a small part of the problem can be seen, but having a wider perspective of the problem may influence the strategies used to solve the problem. In one of Köhler's studies, a banana is placed outside of a wire enclosure. The ape inside, Sultan, is provided with two bamboo sticks, neither of which is long enough to reach the banana. Sultan attempts to reach the banana with first one stick and then the other, but fails. Then, apparently having lost interest in the banana, he sits and idly manipulates the sticks. After a short period of this, he discovers that the two sticks can be joined by pushing the thinner stick into an opening in the end of the thicker stick, creating a much longer tool. Almost before he has them fully together, Sultan is racing toward the railing where he reaches through and retrieves the banana with his new invention. Köhler calls this behavior "insight."

Insight is differentiated from trial and error, first because it is not incremental learning. Insight occurs suddenly in a kind of "aha" flash of understanding. Insight is also differentiated from trial and error because it does not require reward. Although putting the sticks together enables Sultan to reach the banana, he solves the problem before he actually retrieves the reward. Finally, as Köhler points out, solutions reached through insight are generalizable to similar problems encountered later, because these solutions are not dependent on a series of trials and errors (Köhler, 1917/1925).

✓ **Stop and think.**
How would you test whether animals learn by just "getting the idea," the way Gestalt psychologists would predict or whether they learn to respond to specific stimuli through trial and error?

An Experimental Test of Gestalt Theory

Köhler tries an experimental study to test whether insightful learning or trial and error best explains how animals learn. He designs a study that allows him to test whether learning is a response to a specific stimulus or to the relations among stimuli.

First, he trains two hens to peck grain only from the darker of two papers (one dark and one light) glued side by side on a wooden board outside their cage. As a control, he trains two other hens to do just the opposite. Grain is scattered in equal amounts on both papers. Whenever a hen in the first pair pecks at the grain on the dark paper she is allowed to eat, but the grain on the light paper is glued down. After from 400 to 600 trials, in which the positions of the papers are frequently switched to prevent any association of the stimulus with the right or left side, the experimental hens at last learn to select the dark stimulus and to avoid the light stimulus most of the time.

Next, Köhler changes the papers. He keeps the dark paper on the board, but substitutes an even darker paper for the light one. The question is whether the hens will continue to peck at the specific paper from which they have been laboriously trained to eat or whether they will respond to the brightness relationship and select the new darker paper from which they have never eaten grain before.

✓ **Stop and think.**
Which do you think they will do?

Köhler's results are conclusive. The hens select the darkest paper in about 70% of the trials. What this means is that the hens have not learned to respond to a specific stimulus and eat only from paper of a certain degree of darkness. Instead, they have learned to respond to the relationship between stimuli, that is, they have learned a rule: to eat only from the darkest paper. Köhler finds the same pattern of results with the control hens. He also tries similar experiments with chimpanzees and even with a 3-year-old child, with similar results (adapted from Garrett, 1951, pp. 70-71).

✓ **Stop and think.**
What does this finding mean for the assumptions of behaviorism?

Gestalt psychologists, along with others, suggest that animals demonstrate trial-and-error problem solving and learning when experimenters present them with a problem that can only be solved through trial and error. In other words, by placing them in puzzle boxes, Thorndike has required the cats to accidentally solve the problem through random behavior. To then conclude that animals can only solve problems and learn through trial and error is fallacious reasoning based on insufficient evidence. Köhler's chickens provide evidence that animals are capable of more sophisticated problem-solving strategies.

Gestalt psychologists use a fundamentally different approach to understanding the contents of consciousness than do elemenentalists and structuralists and are able to explain real-world observations for which others have no explanation. Gestalt approaches to consciousness owe much to developments in the science of physics at the turn of the century, as is acknowledged by Köhler. The ideas of Gestalt psychology are first made available in English in the writings of Kurt Koffka (1886–1941), who becomes the spokesperson for Gestalt psychology in North America. Because Koffka's first paper in English focuses on Gestalt theories of perception (Koffka, 1922), the influence of Gestalt ideas on North American psychologists early in the 20th century is limited primarily to these theories of perception.

Gestalt Principles of Perception

The principles of perception developed in the Gestalt school are grounded in the belief that, as is true in the physical universe, the mental universe of the brain is a dynamic arena of self-organizing force fields. All sensory stimuli entering consciousness are organized by mental forces into meaningful wholes. In the same way that a set of iron filings will be organized in a characteristic pattern around the pole of the magnet, sensory stimuli will be organized into patterns in consciousness.

The law of Prägnanz explains Gestalt principles of perception. This law states that the mind organizes perceptions into as complete and as meaningful wholes as conditions will allow. It is the law of Prägnanz that explains why the human mind perceives patterns, even in very jumbled stimuli, such as perceiving a face from the shadows thrown by craters on the surface of the moon. Human minds are drawn toward simple meaningful patterns that form complete wholes.

Gestalt Notions of Consciousness

Gestalt psychologists also propose some ideas about how consciousness functions that diverge from the elementalist tradition. Most of these ideas are based on the same behavioral evidence used by past philosophers of nature, but Gestalt psychologists test these ideas experimentally. German psychologist Kurt Lewin (1890–1947) suggests that humans are motivated by fields of force in the mind. According to Lewin, at any given time, consciousness is influenced not just by elements of past experience, but also by dynamic forces, both internal and external.

For example, one of Lewin's students, Bluma Zeigarnik (1890–1990), who goes on to have an illustrious career as a clinical psychologist in the Soviet Union, is remembered in the West for her experiments concerning the role of tension in motivating learning and problem solving. She hypothesizes that the need to solve a problem creates tension in consciousness that is only released once the problem is solved. It is this tension that motivates the organism to seek a solution. The idea that this tension is only relieved when the problem is solved or the task is completed is referred to as the "Zeigarnik effect." Later psychologists of consciousness conclude that the release of this tension alone can serve as reinforcement that cements learning.

Just prior to his death, Lewin also begins a research program exploring the implications of Gestalt principles for interactions among people in small groups. In Lewin's view, the behavior of individuals in any given group is shaped by the complex interactions of the fields of force brought to the group by the individuals. Additionally, various aspects of the structural organization of the group, such as the leadership style exercised in the group, also influence the behavior of the individual members.

By the mid-1930s, all of the Gestalt psychologists discussed earlier have left Europe for the United States. They leave because of the increasing persecution of Jews in Germany during this time and the social and academic disruption caused by the rise to power of the Nazi party. Even Köhler, who is not Jewish, leaves because of the increasingly chilly atmosphere at the universities and in German society in general toward free thought and speech. Unfortunately for these psychologists, the academic community in the United States is only marginally more welcoming. These German, mostly Jewish, Gestalt psychologists find positions only at private liberal arts colleges or in private research institutions, neither of which have graduate programs.

A variety of reasons are offered for the fact that Gestalt ideas have little influence on psychology early in the 20th century in North America, including the lack of graduate students to train at the institutions where Gestalt psychologists are employed. Additionally, behaviorism is entering its heyday in the United States, becoming a paradigm that then dominates psychology for many decades. Gestalt theories stand in opposition to the more accepted behaviorist ideas, and Gestaltists' experimental findings often present anomalies to this more dominant paradigm. It is not until the 1940s that Gestalt ideas begin to influence social psychology and the 1960s before Gestalt theories begin to influence clinical and cognitive psychology.

APPLICATION VERSUS PURE SCIENCE

Early 20th-century psychologists are not just concerned with the structure and contents of conscious mind. In the West, many psychologists in this era are more concerned with solving practical problems. One major battle defining the intellectual questions of psychology early in the 20th century is the debate between academic and applied psychologists. Academics argue that psychology should uphold its future as a pure science by focusing on basic research. In contrast, applied psychologists argue that psychology can also make major contributions to solving real-world problems.

The conflict is exemplified by Titchener's organization of The Experimentalists in 1904. In forming this group, he hopes to distinguish those conducting basic experimental research into the structures of mind from the "functionalists." Those who argue in support of psychology as a pure science are concerned that the "premature" application of psychological findings will result in failures that will cause the brand-new science of psychology to lose the respect of the other sciences. They are also embarrassed by programs in psychical research, by William James' broad application of psychology to religious and spiritualistic questions, and by what they see as the movement of psychology away from pure science, toward becoming just a technique for solving problems. Having only recently extricated themselves from 19th-century philosophy, academics are afraid that the new psychology will disappear into 20th-century technology. In fact, Titchener refers to John Watson's behaviorism as a technology, not a science (O'Donnell, 2002), and in Germany, applied psychology is referred to as "psychotechnics" (van Drunen, 1997).

By the 1920s, academic experimental psychologists, who are nearly all male and are mostly employed in university faculty positions, are concerned with preserving what they view as their higher status over those engaged in the applied aspects of the field. Although women are now admitted to graduate study in psychology, and although compared with the other sciences women constitute a larger proportion in this field (Furumoto, 1987; Koppes, 1997), they are significantly less likely to be employed in academic positions than are men. Instead, the women are found in applied settings, where women constitute the majority (Capshew & Laszlo, 1986; Koppes, 1997).

Those favoring an applied approach to psychology argue that the other sciences are providing solutions to important problems. Even the purest science, physics, is solving problems of aerodynamics and allowing humans successfully to take flight in aeroplanes. There appears to be no end to the applications that practical chemistry is finding. Why should psychology not also participate in helping to solve problems, especially when there are so many in need of solution?

Five decades ago the psychologists began to devote themselves to the most minute description of the mental experiences and to explain the mental life in a way which was modeled after the pattern of exact natural sciences. Their aim was no longer to speculate about the soul, but to find the psychological elements and the constant laws which control their connections. Psychology became experimental and physiological. For more than thirty years the psychologists have also had their workshops. Laboratories for experimental psychology have grown up in all civilized countries, and the new method has been applied to one group of mental traits after another. And yet we stand before the surprising fact that all the manifold results of the new science have remained book knowledge, detached from any practical interests. Only in the last ten years do we find systematic efforts to apply the experimental results of psychology to the needs of society. (Münsterberg, 1913, pp. 4–5)

INDUSTRIAL PSYCHOLOGY

Nowhere is the distinction between scientific research and applied technology more blurred at the turn of the century than in the field of industrial psychology. In 1917, the *Journal of Applied Psychology* begins publication, reporting the results of research in this field. The editors hope that the application of scientifically derived knowledge will result in "increasing human efficiency and human happiness by the more direct method of decreasing the number of cases where a square peg is condemned to a life of fruitless endeavor to fit itself comfortably into a round hole" (Hall, Baird, & Geissler, 1917). This movement is facilitated by the Progressive Party's encouragement to use scientific advances to improve everyone's quality of life. At the same time, business owners are also hoping that the application of psychological knowledge will lead to increased profits for their new and growing manufacturing industries.

Psychologists' Advice for Increasing the Supply

Management

Psychologist May Smith places the beginning of industrial psychology in the 16th century with a book by Spanish natural philosopher Juan Huarte (ca. 1530–ca. 1592; Smith, 1944). Huarte was concerned with vocational guidance and selection.

More recent historians give credit for founding modern industrial psychology to German experimental psychologist Hugo Münsterberg. In 1913, Münsterberg publishes *Psychology and Industrial Efficiency*, in which he discusses psychology and the scientific selection of workers, the proper design of work environments to maximize productivity, and the use of psychology in promoting sales. The ideas expressed in this book are based on his experimental study of the working conditions in several industries, including electric railway and telephone service.

The assumption is that psychological principles might be of value in helping management to make decisions that might increase profits. One of the earliest applications of psychological testing to business is in the selection of salesmen. Some people seem to be able to sell just about anything, are able easily to persuade others, and can make successful careers in sales, whereas many other people have none of these skills.

✓ **Stop and think.**
Among a group of applicants, what would be the best way to identify those who will be successful in sales?

Business leaders believe that there must be some reasonably easy way to identify those who will make good salesmen, and late in the 19th century, they find a shortcut in physiognomy. **Physiognomy** is the belief that it is possible to identify people's character, to test the limits of their intellect, and to foreordain the career that they are suited for by observing their facial appearance. Physiognomy enjoys a brief but widespread popularity, primarily in the United States, at about the same time that phrenology is popular. Like phrenology, physiognomy is a pseudoscience that has all the trappings of a science without any of the evidence to support its contentions.

Needless to say, both phrenology and physiognomy fail to identify successful salespeople. Thus, the establishment of the Bureau of Salesmanship Research at the Carnegie Institute of Technology in 1916 is a welcome addition to the effort (Katzell & Austin, 1992). Funded by 27 national organizations, the establishment of this institute represents an early example of the kind of cooperation between academia and industry that comes to have increasing influence over research universities in the later part of the 20th century.

Work Efficiency

Management is also concerned with worker morale. Although labor is cheap in this era, training new employees is expensive. Keeping trained workers happy and on the job, preferably without paying them more, is an important goal. The major concern of owners of manufacturing plants is to increase profits by increasing productivity and lowering production costs.

Frederick Taylor, who is not a psychologist but a former manufacturing employee and might best be described as an early sort of management consultant, argues that there is a "best way" to perform every job. He suggests that "the best management is a true science, resting upon clearly defined laws, rules, and principles as a foundation" (Taylor, 1911, p. 7). If there is one best way to perform each job and if jobs can be broken down into their component parts, Taylor argues, then it should be possible to identify the most efficient way, both in time and energy, to perform each job. Thus, the assembly line is introduced to industrial production.

After the introduction of assembly lines, engineer, industrial psychologist, and management consultant Lillian Gilbreth (1878–1972) advocates for what are referred to as **"time and motion"** studies. In these studies, the time it takes to perform each segment of a job and each movement required is carefully measured, and all unnecessary effort is systematically eliminated. The results of these time and motion studies are responsible for the creation of assembly lines and the subsequent mass production of consumer goods from textiles to automobiles. In some instances, production is increased fourfold by the establishment of assembly lines, substantially increasing profits for the owners of the manufacturing plants. Initially, when workers are still being paid "by the piece," their income also goes up as productivity increases, but within a short time, the owners begin paying workers an hourly wage instead, thus reaping greater profits for themselves.

Gilbreth's distinguished career in industrial management is made all the more remarkable by her personal accomplishments. She publishes her dissertation *The Psychology of Management* in 1914 (Gilbreth, 1914/1973) and earns a doctorate in psychology in 1915, the same year that she gives birth to her seventh child (Koppes, 1997). The Gilbreths eventually have 12 children, and the principles of scientific management she advocates in industrial settings are also used in the Gilbreth home (Kelly & Kelly, 1990).

One set of classic studies in industrial psychology conducted during the 1930s is commonly referred to as the Hawthorne studies because they are carried out at the Western Electric assembly plant in Hawthorne, Illinois. In cooperation with management at the plant, psychologist and professor of industrial research Elton Mayo (1880–1950) and his colleagues from the Graduate School of Business Administration at Harvard University conduct a series of experiments. Their goal is to identify optimal working conditions in the assembly rooms. Systematically, the researchers vary conditions such as the level of lighting and the lengths of the breaks the women workers are allowed to take. Curiously, productivity increases no matter what change is made in the working conditions.

✓ **Stop and think.**
Why do you think productivity increases?

A variety of explanations are offered for this finding. Perhaps the workers are flattered at the attention they are receiving from researchers at prestigious Harvard University. Maybe the workers are trying to help the researchers be successful or maybe they are responding to the mere presence of the researchers. The increase in productivity is transient, and productivity returns to normal levels after periods ranging from a few days to 2 years. Thus, the psychologists conclude that the workers are responding to novelty, so that any change in the workplace will increase productivity. This is referred to as the "**Hawthorne effect**" (Mayo, 1933).

Today, researchers know that at least some of the increase in productivity reported in the Hawthorne studies can be attributed to the replacement by management of two less efficient workers with more efficient workers midstudy (Gillespie, 1988). Also, the reputed improvements in productivity have recently been found not to be statistically reliable (M. Wertheimer, personal communication, November 8, 2004). Despite these problems, it is widely believed that these studies have a significant impact on understanding the importance of psychological factors in the workplace (see Bramel & Friend, 1981). Most agree that, prior to these studies, industrial managers generally regard workers as human capital, part of the machinery needed to produce goods. Managers' efforts focus on finding the right piece of machinery, meaning the right person to do the job, and the one best way to assemble the product. After the Hawthorne studies, there is recognition that there are a variety of psychological factors that must be taken into consideration before optimal production can be achieved. For example, the influence and social dynamics of employee work groups is recognized. The importance of employee attitudes is more likely to be considered, along with the interpersonal relationships between employees and supervisors. In short, managers are reminded of the need to treat workers as people, rather than part of the machinery (Baritz, 1960).

The increase in productivity that results in part from the efforts of early industrial psychologists yields an increase in the supply of consumer goods and a satiation of demand, sometimes even requiring the lowering of prices. Industrial managers discover that they can produce more goods than can be sold.

Increasing the Demand: Advertising

As a consequence of the increased supply of products, psychologists discover that they also have a role to play in increasing consumer demand. By applying psychological principles to the new field of advertising, psychologists attempt to increase demand, both for products and for their own services. In the 19th century and before, advertising consisted mostly of informing potential consumers about the qualities of the products available, but by the early 20th century, the idea emerges that there are powers of persuasion that can be brought to bear to convince people to buy things they never even knew they needed or wanted.

In the 20th century, psychologists find that hypnotic-like states can be exploited to tap the power of unconscious influences, and suggestion can be used as a means to influence people. Early in the century, suggestion is used in medicine to influence states of mind and improve health. As advertising develops, the power of suggestion is exploited to create demand and convince consumers that they need the products that the increasingly large manufacturing sector can produce. Early advertising psychologist Walter Dill Scott (1869–1955) suggests that, through clever means of suggestion, people can be persuaded that their purchases are rational when in fact they have only been manipulated by advertising:

> In the same way we think that we are performing a deliberate act when we purchase an advertised commodity, while in fact we may never have deliberated on the subject at all. The idea is suggested by the advertisement, and the impulsiveness of human nature enforces the suggested idea, hence the desired result follows in a way unknown to the purchaser. (Scott, 1913 p. 83)

In the 1920s, large advertising firms, employing many psychologists, are established to persuade consumers to purchase products. For example, after losing his professorship at Johns Hopkins University, the behaviorist John Watson is employed in 1921 by the J. Walter Thompson advertising agency to use learning techniques to influence consumer buying habits. Within 3 years, he is made a vice president of the firm and is considered a leader in the field of advertising. Although employed in the lower-status field of applied psychology, by 1930, Watson is making $70,000 a year, more than 10 times what his academic salary had been at Johns Hopkins (Hergenhahn, 2005).

CLINICAL APPLICATIONS

Mental Hygiene

By early in the 20th century, the serious disturbance in thoughts and behavior referred to in earlier times as madness is mostly attributed to organic causes. The psychological effects of morphine addiction, alcoholism, and syphilis are documented and well established. There is even a new branch of medical science, psychiatry, which is charged with developing and administering treatments for psychoses and neuroses. Unfortunately, there are no effective treatments. Still, for organic problems, there must be organic solutions, and in these early days of psychiatry, desperate interventions are tried. It is during this period that the mass sterilization of psychiatric patients occurs, mostly in the United States. This "treatment" is based on the assumption that future generations may be protected from insanity by preventing the insane from reproducing. Rudimentary forms of brain surgery are also practiced. If the mind is ill, and the brain is the location of the mind, then it seems logical that mental illness can be treated by brain surgery. Hundreds of psychiatric patients have all or part of their prefrontal lobes removed in attempts to control their psychotic illnesses. This very radical form of treatment is practiced significantly more often on women than on men (Braslow, 1997).

In 1896, psychologist Lightner Witmer (1867–1956) founds a clinical training program at the University of Pennsylvania, mostly for the treatment and care of mentally defective children (McReynolds, 1987). Witmer is trained as a research scientist in Wundt's laboratory in Leipzig and continues throughout his career to advocate a good background in experimental research for all psychologists, even for those wishing to apply their psychological training to providing treatment for the mentally ill. In 1907, Witmer names the field of treatment "**clinical psychology**."

Psychoanalysis

At about the same time on the other side of the Atlantic, Viennese neurologist Sigmund Freud (1856–1939) presents his explanation for mild mental illnesses and proposes the treatment called **psychoanalysis**. The practice of psychoanalysis thus begins as a method to treat neuroses, primarily hysteria. Throughout the 20th century, psychoanalytic theories of personality continue to have a powerful influence on psychology, as well as on popular culture.

Hysteria

Just before the turn of the century, the respected German neurologist and researcher Josef Breuer (1842–1925) and his younger colleague Sigmund Freud conduct their studies on hysteria. As explained earlier, hysteria is the term used to describe a wide variety of behaviors and complaints. In the late 19th century, the cause of hysteria is a matter for speculation, but some believe it to be employed, usually by otherwise powerless women, as a devious method to gain attention. Others believe there must be physical causes, but many, like Breuer and Freud, suggest instead that hysteria results from disordered psychological functioning.

Suggestion and Hypnosis

At this point in medical history, there are no agreed on techniques for the treatment of hysteria, although successes are claimed for suggestion. This technique requires the therapist to talk in a positive and supportive manner to the patient and suggest recovery from the symptoms. Various people, including Charcot, are using suggestion performed during hypnosis and reporting some successful findings with hysterical patients.

In his *Principles of Psychology*, published in 1890, William James argues that through hypnosis the physician might be able to reach a secondary personage, or nonconscious level of mind. After a good talking to, this secondary personage might be persuaded to release control of the affected part of the hysteric and allow the primary personality to regain normal control. French physician Hippolyte Bernheim demonstrates that if a highly suggestible person believes the physician's suggestion that symptoms will improve, they often do. He also shows that suggestions made to a patient during hypnosis can influence behavior after the therapeutic session, even if the patient has no conscious memory of the suggestions made while under hypnosis. Furthermore, memories of the suggestion can be brought to conscious awareness if the patient is strongly encouraged to remember them. As a part of his medical training, Sigmund Freud attends some of Bernheim's lectures on hypnosis.

The Talking Cure

Back in Vienna, Breuer is using hypnosis to help one of his patients, a brilliant and insightful young woman, Bertha Pappenheim (described as Anna O. in the literature). During his sessions with her, Breuer attempts to relieve Ms. Pappenheim of her symptoms through posthypnotic suggestion, but these efforts prove unsuccessful. Breuer and Pappenheim do discover, however, that, after a session in which Ms. Pappenheim is allowed simply to talk about her various symptoms while under hypnosis, her memories of the first time the symptoms appeared, and her feelings at the time, the symptoms disappear. Much to their surprise, just talking about the memories and the feelings associated with them while hypnotized seems to cure the symptoms. Pappenheim calls this "the talking cure."

✓ **Stop and think.**

Can you develop a theory of hysteria that explains the effectiveness of the talking cure? In other words, if talking about problems while under hypnosis results in a relief from symptoms, what do you think might be causing the symptoms?

There is controversy about the effectiveness of the talking cure. Pappenheim herself eventually gives it little credit, and she continues to receive other forms of care after her experience with Breuer. *Recent scholarship and newly recovered medical records suggest that many of Pappenheim's symptoms should be attributed to drug dependence and her later relief from those symptoms to the recovery from that dependence (Ramos, 2003).* Nevertheless, Pappenheim's successes as she goes on to have a distinguished career in the field of social work, as an author, and in feminist activism are sometimes held up as evidence of the efficacy of the talking cure. Breuer tells his colleague, Freud, about the apparent cure that he has stumbled on for hysteria. In 1895, 13 years after Pappenheim's treatment has ended, Breuer and Freud publish their research attributing hysteria to disturbing memories trapped somewhere in mind that are manifesting in physical symptoms. The cure they propose is to bring the intense feelings associated with certain memories to conscious awareness. This allows for a "cathartic" release and a subsequent relief from neurotic symptoms (Freud & Breuer, 1895/1966).

The Structures of Mind

Philosophers and psychologists have long been concerned with the nature or structure of mind or consciousness. Many have noted that even everyday experience leads to a belief that there must be aspects of mind that are, at least at times, not available to conscious awareness. Thus, there must be at least two minds, a conscious mind and an unconscious mind. To these two structures of mind Freud eventually adds a third, which he calls preconscious mind. These three minds are defined on the basis of the activities occurring in each. Conscious mind contains everything in current awareness. Preconscious mind contains that which can be thought about, but which is not being thought about in the moment. The existence of the preconscious mind is made necessary by the functions Freud assigns to unconscious mind. Unconscious mind is where all thoughts and ideas originate, and the contents of unconscious mind must, by definition, always remain unavailable to conscious awareness. According to Freud's theory, the thoughts and ideas originating in unconscious mind are what motivate humans. Freud's theory of unconscious motivation reflects the ideas of many others at this time, that the reason behavior is sometimes so inexplicable is that it is often motivated by thoughts and ideas that originate in an aspect of mind that is unavailable to conscious awareness.

✓ **Stop and think.**
If Freud is correct, that certain thoughts are unavailable to conscious mind, what might be different about those thoughts?

Revealing the Secrets of the Unconscious

According to Freud's theory, the thoughts, memories, and feelings that are causing hysterical symptoms must be so upsetting that they are unacceptable to conscious mind. Conscious mind must actively try to defend itself against the intrusion of these unacceptable thoughts into consciousness. To relieve hysterical symptoms, Freud must bring these thoughts into consciousness, even while the patient's unconscious mind is actively trying to prevent the thoughts from entering consciousness. Freud must find a way to circumvent the patient's own defenses. Hypnosis seems to be one way, but not all patients can be hypnotized. Beyond that, given its questionable roots in Mesmerism and its very unscientific flavor, hypnotism seems mired in spiritualism. Freud begins to experiment with other techniques for getting around patients' defenses.

One technique he finds effective he calls **free association**. Here, the patient is placed in a quiet and restful setting with all distractions removed. The patient is asked to report out loud whatever thoughts pass through conscious mind without trying to screen or make sense of them. By listening carefully, Freud believes he may be able to identify hidden thoughts or symbols of memories and feelings buried in unconscious mind. Another technique Freud uses is **dream analysis**. His hypothesis is that the threshold between conscious and unconscious mind weakens during sleep, and the secrets of the unconscious sometimes slip into dreams. Often, however, these thoughts during sleep are so disturbing that they would awaken the sleeper (which they sometimes do during nightmares, for example). To preserve sleep, the unacceptable thoughts are usually disguised as symbols in a dream. For example, a dream in which you find yourself wandering through a half-constructed house might really represent your concerns about what sort of a person you are becoming, or, if you are a man, concerns about your ability to achieve and maintain an erection, according to Freudian interpretations.

As Freud listens to his patients, and as they bring into conscious awareness previously unremembered thoughts, many of them do experience some relief from their symptoms. For Freud, this is strong evidence that he is on the right track about the origins of hysteria. Unfortunately, he also finds that even when the symptoms initially disappear they often return. He concludes that the thoughts being unearthed only reflect even earlier and even more disturbing memories. As he delves deeper and deeper into his patients' thoughts, he begins to hear about disturbing sexual thoughts or minor sexual experiences during puberty. Unconvinced that these minor events could cause serious hysteria, he delves deeper into their memories. Eventually, in all 18 of the cases he is treating, he uncovers memories of terrifying sexual abuse and rape, usually violent and brutal, experienced at 2, 3, and 4 years of age. Equally shocking is the fact that, in most of these cases, it is the patient's own biological relative, a brother or a father, who is remembered as the perpetrator of this abuse. Memories of these experiences are so troubling, even (literally) paralyzing to these young adults, that patients are only able to recall them after many sessions of sensitive and careful analysis.

The Abuse Hypothesis

Freud concludes that his patients are experiencing symptoms of a serious mental illness that can be directly attributed to having been sexually abused when they were only toddlers. In April 1896, Freud presents his findings at the meetings of the *Society for Psychiatry and Neurology* in Vienna, his first major address to this group. His audience is made up of his colleagues, fellow physicians, neurologists, and researchers (Freud, 1896/1984).

Freud's initial presentation is not well received. Freud himself describes the reaction to his paper as "icy," and reports that the noted sex researcher and chair of the Department of Psychiatry at the University of Vienna, Dr. Richard von Krafft-Ebing, comments, "It sounds like a scientific fairy tale" (Freud, 1917). Nine years later, in 1905, Freud retracts the hypothesis of early sexual abuse as the cause of hysteria. He replaces it with the Oedipal theory of neurosis, which is more readily accepted.

A variety of explanations have been offered for why Freud abandons the hypothesis that neuroses may have origins in early sexual trauma and abuse. No explanation is accepted by all, and even a careful analysis of Freud's personal papers does not yield a final answer to the question. It has been suggested that Freud never really gives up the belief that the sexual abuse of children is common and that this abuse is the real explanation for adult neuroses. Some say that because the abuse hypothesis is unacceptable to most, Freud adopts the Oedipal story out of a desire to be accepted back into the professional circles that have ostracized him (Masson, 1984). This assertion is, however, quite controversial (Gleaves & Hernandez, 1999).

The Story of Oedipus Rex

In the 5th century BCE the Greek playwright, Sophocles, produces a stage version of the story of Oedipus. The prophesy at Oedipus' birth is that he will someday kill his father, King Laius, and marry his mother, Queen Jocasta. After being adopted as an infant into another family, a series of convoluted twists in the plot, and without realizing consciously what he is doing, Oedipus does eventually kill Laius and wed Jocasta. He then becomes Oedipus Rex, the King.

Sigmund Freud is an aficionado of archeology and ancient history, particularly Egyptian, Greek, and Roman mythology. When he realizes that he must give up the abuse hypothesis but still account for the thoughts about early sexual abuse that his patients are having, Freud adopts the story of Oedipus Rex. He concludes that the disturbing thoughts of incest that his patients are having are not real memories of real events but are incestuous wishes and desires. Instead of having been childhood victims of sexual abuse, it is the patients' own childhood desires to sexually possess the parent of the opposite sex and eliminate the same-sex parent that are appearing in hypnotic trances, free association, and their dreams. It is the patients' attempts to repress these memories of sexual desire and hostility that are causing the neurotic symptoms.

Freud hears these stories of childhood sexual experiences from his neurotic patients but, after much thinking about it, he also recovers a memory from his own early childhood about his mother. In addition, he realizes that at least minor forms of neuroses are widespread in the population of Vienna. If neurotic symptoms are common, and even normal people like himself can recall memories of a very early interest in sexual activity with his mother, he concludes that sexual desire for the opposite-sex parent must be a normal experience for every child.

Freud asserts that from birth every child is motivated by strong sexual desires. Children seek pleasure from their erogenous zones, which, in normal development, change from age to age as children progress through what Freud calls psychosexual stages. At first, in the oral stage, sexual desires are gratified by sucking on objects. Next, during the anal stage, sexual desires are gratified by learning to control the functions of the bowel. By age 5 or 6, these sexual desires become focused in the desire for genital sex with the opposite-sexed parent. The boy child wishes to have sexual intercourse with his mother and sees in his father a frightening rival, one who may even be the agent of the boy's own castration. In normal development, it becomes clear to the boy that the father is too formidable a foe and that the boy will never realize his desire to sexually possess his mother. The boy must then learn to identify with the father, to want to be as much like the father as possible, and to regard women as inferior because of their castrated and powerless state. By identifying with his father, the boy will escape the father's wrath and may someday possess a woman of his own. Freud is never as clear about the story for young girls and women. He thinks even very young girls would be unlikely to want to identify with women who they see as castrated and therefore powerless. In Freud's version of psychoanalytic theory, learning to resolve the conflicts associated with sexual desire for the opposite-sex parent is the major developmental task for every young child. Failure to resolve these conflicts results in neurotic symptoms that emerge later in life.

✓ Stop and think.

Imagine that this story seems implausible to you, that you personally have no memory of wanting to have sexual intercourse with your parent, and in fact you cannot even imagine that you ever felt that way. Why is that not evidence that the theory is incorrect, at least in your case?

Although these early sexual desires are a normal part of development for every child, almost no one has any memory of these feelings. Freud's explanation for this is that the memories of these feelings are hidden in unconscious mind. Even with his neurotic patients, Freud finds that he must delve deeper and deeper into earlier and earlier memories. Psychoanalysis must proceed session after session, week after week, constantly encouraging patients to recall more and more disturbing experiences and helping them to analyze the hidden sexual meanings of free associations and dream symbols. Only after many sessions are patients finally able to produce some memory of early sexual desire. It is not surprising that most people have no conscious memory of these feelings because the theory predicts that. Even many of Freud's own patients remain resistant to the idea.

Instincts and Personality

Psychoanalysis begins as a treatment for hysteria, but as psychoanalytic theory is developed over the course of Freud's life, it becomes a theory about how even normal personality is formed. Freud is a medical doctor and is convinced throughout his lifetime that the theoretical constructs of personality he proposes will eventually be found to have a basis in physiology. He also accepts the principles of evolution by natural selection, so he looks to nature for an explanation for why infants have sexual motivations. Adults' interest in sex can be explained on the basis of the instinct to reproduce. On what similar instinct might an infant's interest in sex be based? According to Freud, the first instinct is the desire to seek pleasurable and gratifying states of being. This he identifies as Eros, the instinct to achieve physical pleasure. The fact that infants receive nutritional sustenance by sucking is secondary to the oral gratification achieved by the act of sucking. All humans are born with a variety of impulses that promote survival, including the impulses to eat and to have sex. Freud locates the origins of these impulses in the unconscious mind and calls this set of impulses the "**id**." The id is the first major component of personality and is a set of unregulated impulsive energies, incapable on its own of realistically achieving its ends. Thus, Freud postulates there must also be regulatory functions that both keep the impulses of the id under control and help the id to achieve its goals. These regulatory psychological functions might include the ability to delay gratification, skills at problem solving, or being able to remember a set of behaviors. Freud calls this set of regulatory functions the "**ego**." The ego is developed as realistic and successful strategies for controlling the impulses of the id and achieving its goals are learned. Because most people are not consciously aware of them, Freud concludes that most functions of the id and the ego must be performed in the unconscious mind.

Much later, in 1923, Freud adds the "**superego**" as another set of functions conducted in unconscious mind. The superego is a set of moral values and attitudes learned from parents and the surrounding culture, including attitudes about the self. Poor self-esteem, for example, derives from having adopted the attitude of a parent who disapproved of or felt ashamed of the child, according to Freud's theory.

Also according to psychoanalytic theory, personality is shaped by the dynamic ways in which the boundaries are negotiated between the id, the ego, and the superego. For example, a strong ego has a variety of mechanisms or defenses available to prevent itself from being overwhelmed by the id. One of these is what Freud calls "**sublimation**." The id's inappropriate but procreative sexual impulses may be sublimated by the ego into other forms of creative activity such as writing a novel, designing a building, or becoming a respected leader. According to Freud, sublimation provides the foundation of culture and civilization.

As long as these ego defense mechanisms are working, the personality continues to function as it should. Neuroses appear when the defense system breaks down, and the id threatens to overwhelm the ego. At that point, the person develops neurotic symptoms. Therapy involves a controlled release of unacceptable thoughts from unconsciousness in the presence of a competent analyst.

Secessions From Freud

Even early in the psychoanalytic movement, other theorists, many of whom worked with Freud earlier in their careers, develop revisions to the theory. The theories of personality development and the ideas about the origins of neuroses developed by these later thinkers are consistent in only one regard: They deny that it is the resolution of early childhood desires for sexual intercourse with adults that is the major developmental task. These alternative theories are sometimes referred to as **psychodynamic** theories, because they posit that it is dynamic interactions between psychological factors internal to the child and the external rearing environment, particularly the parents, that sets the stage for personality development. The psychodynamic theorists who follow Freud include Alfred Adler, Carl Jung, Karen Horney, and Margaret Mahler. All of them agree that the origins of neuroses lie in psychological conflict and its resolution, but they disagree about what might be the basis of that conflict (Hoffman, 1994; Horney, 1945).

Although these later theorists call themselves psychoanalytic theorists, Freud insists that they are not practicing true psychoanalysis. He calls their revisions of his theory "secessions," and he has one explanation for why these people refuse to recognize the sexual basis of personality. He charges that, like many of his patients, these theorists suffer from their own unconscious mechanisms of resistance. Freud is disappointed, but not surprised, at the popularity of these secessions because unconscious resistance is widespread, and most people are both unable and unwilling to recognize their own sexual thoughts and memories. But Freud regards this resistance to the sexual basis of personality as the best evidence of the truth of his theory (Freud, 1917).

Relations Between Psychoanalysis and Psychology

From the first, psychoanalytic theory proves problematic for the new science of psychology. By Freud's own admission, his work is "not in the reviewed professional literature of the day" (Freud, 1917, p. 15). Although this might be interpreted to mean that his peers are unwilling to examine his evidence, it is hard to imagine how they could, because his evidence consists only of the memories he is able to evince through long hours of private analysis with individual patients. Even through the 1930s, there is little or no coverage of psychoanalysis in psychology textbooks (Hornstein, 1992).

For most experimental psychologists, psychoanalysis is just one of many "mind cures" popular in this era, none of which are based on scientific evidence. Early on, it is regarded as mildly amusing and an innocent diversion for the easily titillated and gullible. As psychoanalysis becomes more widely known, psychologists become more alarmed. The distinction they draw between psychology and psychoanalysis is lost in popular culture. It is a source of frustration to psychologists that everywhere outside of psychology psychoanalysis is confused with psychology—as remains true even in the present day (Morawski & Hornstein, 1991). During the last half of the 20th century, Freud's picture appears no fewer than three times on the cover of *Time* magazine, which declares him one of the 20th-century's greatest minds (Fancher, 2000).

Experimental Tests of Psychoanalytic Theory

Is it possible to validate psychoanalytic theory using the scientific method in experimental tests? If Freud could be asked this question today he would insist, as he did when the theory was developed, that he already had all of the empirical support for psychoanalysis that will ever be needed. His evidence is gathered from the many psychoanalytic sessions where, after much work, memories of infant sexual desire do eventually emerge (Freud, 1917).

A key element of experimental science is that it seeks to predict, on the basis of theory and hypotheses, what will happen next. It is exactly this element that is missing from psychoanalysis and from most of the tests of the theory. Psychoanalytic theory draws conclusions about what must have been so in the past to explain current conditions (postdictions), but predictions often fail. For example, no evidence can be found that children who have certain kinds of experiences early in life will, later in life, exhibit certain types of neurotic symptoms (Eysenck & Wilson, 1973).

It is true that many psychoanalytic terms are vague or hard to define operationally. Despite that, it is also true that hundreds of studies of many major psychoanalytic constructs are published. The majority of these studies are conducted in the 1930s through the 1960s. The results of these studies are somewhat ambiguous, with a few claiming to find support for Freud's theory, but not most. In general, researchers looking for support for psychoanalytic theory tend to find support, and those looking to refute the theory find evidence to refute it (see Eysenck & Wilson, 1973).

American Psychology, Behaviorism, and Psychoanalysis

Although the practice of psychoanalysis in clinical settings spreads rapidly around the developed world, it is in North America that the theory receives the warmest reception. As the popularity of psychoanalytic ideas spreads, they begin to be co-opted into the language of behaviorism. Thus, Freud's impulses of the id become, in behaviorists' terms, the reflexes, which are gradually shaped by learning into effective behaviors, or what Freud calls ego (Horowitz, 1994).

Psychoanalytic Influences on Clinical Psychology

Psychoanalysis begins as a method of treatment and, in that capacity, makes many inroads into clinical psychology. This is reflected even today among the current membership of the American Psychological Association (APA), the organization founded in 1892 by G. Stanley Hall and others as a forum for furthering the science of psychology. Today, APA membership is made up primarily of clinical and counseling psychologists. Even as early as the 1930s, many of these psychologists identify psychoanalytic theory as a preferred approach to treatment: "Today there is hardly a corner of abnormal psychology into which psychoanalytic interpretations have not penetrated. No symptom is too trivial, no disorder too formidable for the zeal, the industry, and the all but incredible ingenuity of those who try to fit the Freudian key into every lock" (Heidbreder, 1933, p. 396).

Many attempts are also made to test the efficacy of psychoanalytic clinical treatments, also finding mixed results. The techniques employed by psychoanalysts are variable, and a large percentage of people recover spontaneously from neuroses, making evaluation of the effectiveness of any one treatment difficult. Again, those researchers who support psychoanalytic theory generally find that psychoanalytic therapies are slightly more effective than no therapy, but no more effective than other approaches (Fisher & Greenberg, 1985; Fisher & Greenberg, 1996). And those researchers who do not support the theory find that the patients of psychoanalytic therapists show an even lower recovery rate than neurotics who receive no treatment at all (Eysenck & Wilson, 1973). These researchers go on to conclude, "For all intents and purposes, psychoanalysis has been shown to have little if any effect on neurotic or psychotic disorders" (Eysenck & Wilson, 1973, p. 374).

Although for the first few decades Freud's theories do not have much impact, they do eventually capture the imagination of the public. In the popular culture of the West during the 1920s and 1930s, the Oedipal story, and especially Freud's focus on sex, generate a good deal of excitement. Identifying and remarking on behaviors like "Freudian slips," making jokes about women who smoke cigars, and allusions to hidden thoughts and desires, become standard party conversation in this era, much as they continue to be today. The public loves Freud's narrative of the dynamics of unconscious mind, and many of his ideas do seem to explain much about social discourse. Freud himself regards his dream interpretation as the most significant part of his work (Mitchell & Black, 1995), and that also remains a favorite in popular culture.

By the end of Freud's life, his theory of personality remains, as it was when he first proposed it, a narrative or a story. Several psychologists refer to it not as anything resembling a science but, instead, as a literary form, much like a novel. *The literary nature of psychoanalytic theory doubtless explains why today it has a major impact in literary criticism and popular culture or in some forms of clinical practice, but no more influence in the science of psychology than it ever had.*

Freud's Cultural Context

Throughout his career, Freud's professional and personal ambitions are thwarted by anti-Semitism. Although he does not engage in religious practice and is often critical of organized religion (Freud & Pfister, 1918/1963), he is repeatedly denied research opportunities and academic positions because he is of Jewish descent. Late in his life, he is forced to leave Vienna for England as the Nazi party rises to power in Austria.

✓ **Stop and think.**
How might these frustrations have influenced Freud's thinking about psychology?

After experiencing the brutality of World War I in Europe, Freud expands his theory to include a human instinct for aggression or destruction (Freud, 1920/1950). Both the aggressive instinct and the sexual or procreative instinct serve the ends of self-preservation. For example, the instinct to procreate may be served by using aggression to acquire the desired partner. These instincts may also oppose one another in that the destructive instinct may trigger actions that drive potential partners away (Freud, 1932/1964).

In one of his last works, *Civilization and Its Discontents* (1930/1961), Freud considers the role played by civilization in helping individuals mediate between constructive and destructive instincts and the antagonism between the instincts that impel us toward individual freedom of expression and the restrictions imposed by living with others in a civilized society.

CHILD STUDY AND DEVELOPMENTAL PSYCHOLOGY

At the turn of the century, the study of the mental and physical development of children is important in mainstream psychology. There are several questions that form the core of early child study. These include the debate concerning the relative importance of biological or evolutionary bases of psychological characteristics referred to as "nature" and environmental influences referred to as "nurture," and how each of these may be manipulated to optimize outcome. An objective measure of "will," "persistency," "determination," and "spunk" is shown in Fig. 9.1. The child is instructed to raise his heels 1/4 inch off of the platform. When the heels touch the platform, a buzzer sounds. Questions about how many and which aspects of development can be described in universal terms and which show significant individual differences also become more important. This leads to questions about the progress of intellectual development, both normal and abnormal.

FIG. 9.1.   A measure of "spunk" (Popplestone & McPherson, 1994,
p. 69). Photo courtesy of the Archives of the History of American
Psychology. J. E. Wallace Wallin papers.

Questions about the universal features of development are reflected in theories
such as those proposed by Canadian psychologist J. Mark Baldwin (1861–1934)
in his book *Mental Development in the Child and the Race* (Baldwin, 1895). Baldwin proposes a stage theory of intellectual development, suggesting that children

pass through three qualitatively different ways of logical thinking as they grow up. Questions about the universality of developmental issues also fuel interest in studying child development and child-rearing practices across cultures. Anthropological studies such as those conducted by Franz Boas (1858–1942) among native Americans in the Pacific Northwest provide evidence in support of behaviorists' theories that cross-cultural differences found in psychological characteristics are primarily the result of environmental factors.

Also early in the century, a variety of social causes and movements play important roles in changing the direction of the study of psychological development in children (Cahan, 1997). As ever larger numbers of immigrant families enter the United States, there are movements to provide quality early education to all young children and to provide day nursery care for the children of mothers who must work outside the home. Reforms are sought in the treatment of orphans and in other aspects of child welfare based on solid scientific evidence. The child labor movement, in particular, draws attention to children and their physical and psychological needs (Cahan, 1997). In 1912, the Children's Bureau is founded as a federal agency to provide advocacy for children. The Children's Bureau bases its policy recommendations on facts known about children through the application of scientific study. The child study movement continues to grow in power and prestige through the 1930s.

In spite of this, the applied child study movement has a "long and entangled history of relations between reformers, advocates, and developmental psychologists" (Cahan, 1997). Again, experimental psychologists are in conflict about how much to associate themselves, and their high-status academic experimental work, with those who seek to apply science to the resolution of problems.

By the 1920s, behaviorism and the movement in psychology away from descriptive study and toward experimental study are coming to influence the field of child development. Behaviorism's assumption of learning as the primary, if not the only, influence on psychological characteristics dictates studies that explore the processes of learning, both in humans and animals. Even after Watson loses his academic position at Johns Hopkins, he continues to be interested in the psychological development of children and publishes several government pamphlets and one book in which he provides advice for parents on how to raise infants and children.

Behaviorist assumptions about learning are presumed to hold true across all species. Thus, although there are differences in biologically based capacities to learn across species, or even between individuals in the same species, the principles of learning are the same in all species. Differences between individuals in psychological characteristics like personality are presumed to be primarily the result of individual differences in experience. For behaviorists, the goal is not to describe and explain psychological characteristics but to predict and control observable behavior.

No one today knows enough to raise a child. The world would be considerably better off if we were to stop having children for twenty years (except those reared for experimental purposes) and were then to start again with enough facts to do the job with some degree of skill and accuracy. Parenthood, instead of being an instinctive art, is a science, the details of which must be worked out by patient laboratory methods. (Watson, 1928, p. 16 [italics in original])

Psychoanalytic theory also makes contributions to the study of child development. Psychoanalytic theory acknowledges the importance of biologically based patterns of behavior at the very earliest stages of development, but it focuses primarily on learned bases of behavior in the first few years of life. Even the processes theorized to be occurring in an unconscious mind are derived from interactions between early biologically based patterns and experiences with the caregiving environment.

SOCIAL PSYCHOLOGY/SOCIOLOGY

If the definition of social psychology requires that the positivistic methods of science be brought to bear on questions about how psychological characteristics interact with the social environment, then the beginnings of the field are usually traced to the late 19th or early 20th century (Jones, 1998). It is not until then that the need for the controls of science on speculation about the social environment, and the power of these methods to provide useful information, begins to be recognized by psychologists (Morawski, 2000).

Just at the turn of the century, for example, functionalist principles inspire an interest in the influence of social relationships on athletic performance. French scholar Philippe Tissié (1852–1935) publishes two studies on the physiological and psychological aspects of competitive bicycle racing (Bäumler, 1997). At about the same time, Italian physiologist Angelo Mosso (1846–1910) publishes the results of his studies on the physical and psychological functioning of mountain climbers. Among his observations is the "competition effect," a condition of enhanced performance which appears only when the climbers are training in groups, as opposed to individually (Bäumler, 1997).

One experimental study, often cited as the beginning of the field of sports psychology, is published about this time by Norman Triplett (1861–1934) at Indiana University. Triplett tests the competition effect by constructing an apparatus that allows two participants to observe one another while competing to roll up ropes. Triplett finds that the act of observing the performance of another person leads to increased performance by most people (Triplett, 1897). The question of interest for Triplett, and other early social psychologists, concerns "what change in an individual's normal solitary performance occurs when other people are present" (Allport, 1954, p. 46).

In the ensuing several decades, strong cultural and social forces shape the progress of social psychology. During the 1920s and 1930s, the questions asked by social psychologists reflect major social, political, and economic developments in the world at large. Research interest in work-related and social attitudes continues to increase during the 1930s.

⏱ The Times

The collapse of Western economies in 1929 signals the beginning of world-wide economic depression. In North America, this period, which lasts more than 10 years, is referred to as The Great Depression. At its height in 1933, more than 25% of the workforce is unemployed, millions of farmers are losing their land, and thousands of middle-class people in the United States lose their homes and life savings in bank failures. Extreme poverty is widespread. Millions are forced by hunger to visit soup kitchens and wait in bread lines, and many others die of malnutrition and disease. Shanty-towns, where entire families live in anything they can find, from rusting car bodies to flimsy packing boxes, spring up all over the United States. These towns are called "Hoovervilles" after wealthy President Herbert Hoover does little to help the economy recover. Some Hoovervilles are as large as 10 miles wide and 10 miles long. In the 1930s, overgrazing and a prolonged drought across the Great Plains states creates a giant dust bowl, wiping out entire communities of farmers and ranchers and further tightening food supplies.

Some people can still afford to go to movies, and for a few pennies misery can be escaped for a couple of hours. Moviegoers are charmed by little Shirley Temple or by handsome Ronald Reagan on the big screen. The 1936 Summer Olympics go on as planned, held in Berlin, where African American Jesse Owens stuns the world with his achievements in track and field events. On the "Left Bank" of the Seine in Paris, philosophers like Jean-Paul Sartre sip coffee and discuss existential philosophies with artists like Pablo Picasso, writers like Gertrude Stein, and other American expatriates, even as France crumbles around them.

In Europe, life is grim. In addition to widespread poverty, international war looms again. In 1933, the Germans, who have never really recovered from the devastation of the Great War, elect Adolf Hitler to lead them. Germany rebuilds its military and, in 1939, invades first Czechoslovakia, then Poland. In April 1940, German armies march into Denmark and Nor-way, and by June they have conquered France.

An official government policy of anti-Semitism is adopted in Germany, stripping Jews of their citizenship, seizing their property, incarcerating them in concentration camps, and eventually murdering over 6 million, along with at least 4 million mentally ill or physically disabled people, gypsies, gays and lesbians, and political dissidents. Scapegoating Jews for the economic depression is not limited to Germany. Massacres of Jews in Russia occur during this time as well. The United States is not immune to the evils of anti-Semitism, fueled by attacks against Jews in the popular media led by public figures like Henry Ford, founder of the Ford Motor Company (Dinnerstein, 1994). At colleges and universities across the United States, the sons and daughters of Jewish immigrants excel academically. By the mid-1920s, this leads to official quotas limiting the number of Jewish students admitted to many universities. The fear is that if college admissions are based on merit alone, the Jewish students will be very nearly the only ones admitted. Faculty positions at universities in the United States are similarly routinely denied to Jewish scholars during this period (Dinnerstein, 1994).

10

Age of Theory: Why Are There So Many Different Psychological Theories?

The purpose of this chapter is to explore the landscape of Western psychological theories from about the 1930s until the mid-1950s. This period marks the peak of psychologists' conviction that learning answers all of psychology's questions. Thus, it is characterized by theories and research about when, why, and how learning occurs, schedules of reinforcement, and if and how learning is extinguished. Nearly all domains of psychology are influenced by learning theories. In the second half of the chapter, personality, social, developmental, and clinical psychology are viewed through the lenses of the prevailing paradigms of this era, behaviorism and psychoanalytic theory.

PSYCHOLOGY AND THE SCIENTIFIC METHOD

North American psychologists in the 1930s resolutely embrace the method of logical positivism as a means to conduct their science, even as the physicists who first advocated it are moving away from the method. Positivism requires that all of the terms included in a body of research refer to observable aspects of nature. The number of hours since the rat last ate is an example of an observational term. The introduction of logic enlarges the scope of positivism by allowing the

267

inclusion of theoretical terms, as long as those terms are defined in publicly observable ways. For example, hunger is an internal and not publicly observable state that is theorized to exist in organisms that have not eaten for some time. Positivism would reject the concept of hunger as an explanatory variable because it is both theoretical and subjective. **Logical positivism**, however, accepts the theoretical term hunger as long as it is defined as, for example, "number of hours since the rat last ate." That definition turns the theoretical and subjective term hunger into a publicly observable variable and thus makes "number of hours since the rat last ate" into an operational definition for the concept hunger. The adoption of logical positivism opens up many more aspects of behavior to scientific exploration.

As is true in all branches of science, measurement remains of paramount importance in psychology. It is the requirement that the variables of interest be both publicly observable and measurable that distinguishes the science of psychology from other ways of exploring thoughts, feelings, and behaviors.

Developments in Statistics and Measurement

During the first half of the 20th century, statisticians and mathematicians develop a variety of new statistical methods that enable psychologists to analyze data, revealing much about the nature of relationships among variables. One particular challenge for psychologists is that often their variables cannot meaningfully be said to fall along a measuring scale that begins at zero.

✓ **Stop and think.**
Can you measure a variable for which there is no zero point, such as a personality trait like sociability? How would you measure such a variable?

Intelligence is a good example of a psychological characteristic for which a zero point is meaningless. Psychologists measure intelligence by comparing the performance of one person to the performance of others. Using this method, any psychological characteristic can be measured. Thus, scores on tests of psychological characteristics represent an individual's score in relationship to the scores of others.

Another approach to the problem of measuring a psychological variable that has no zero point is a technique called factor analysis, developed early in the century by Charles Spearman (1863–1945). Factor analysis allows a complex set of correlations to be mathematically reduced to a small number of dimensions or factors (Hornstein, 1988; Spearman, 1904). To perform a factor analysis, the researcher must first develop a large set of survey items or tasks believed to be related to the variable in question. In Spearman's case, that variable is intelligence. Correlations are then calculated among the scores of a large number of subjects on all of the items. In any such analysis, sets of items will always emerge as correlated with one another. If researchers can make logical sense of the sets of correlated scores that emerge, they may then theorize that an underlying factor exists that unites those items that are correlated. As an example, on the basis of his factor analytic studies, Spearman concludes that there is a higher-level factor explaining scores on all items on his test of intelligence. He calls this factor "g" for general intelligence. In other words, he concludes that there is really just one kind of intelligence, so that individuals who are high in "g" will do well on almost any kind of a task that requires intelligence.

With the development of these statistical techniques, even hard-to-define variables like intelligence are transformed from subjective, or what Galileo called secondary, qualities into objective, or primary, qualities, and psychology becomes a true science. Once intelligence tests are developed, questions about the definition of the word intelligence or about the function of intelligence are increasingly ignored in favor of pursuing more and more sophisticated ways of measuring intelligence. This focus on statistical technique over definition becomes an enduring issue in the field of psychological measurement. For example, in the 1940s, critics complain that social psychologists too often focus on "segmental bits of behavior" simply because those are easier to measure. In doing so, they are accused of ignoring the study of large-scale social movements, contributions to understanding made by those in other disciplines, and the meaning of social behavior (Cottrell & Gallagher, 1941). Similar transitions to measuring variables rather than defining variables occur in a variety of other domains of psychology as well.

Charles Spearman is also credited with the addition of the "error term" to psychological measurement in his investigations of intelligence. Including this error term makes it clear that intelligence is now defined only as a score on a test.

One of the most significant developments in testing in the early decades of the 20th century is the appearance of large group testing and comparisons of sets of scores from one group with sets of scores from other groups on the same test. With group testing, the more individuals that contribute a score to the group, the lower the error variance. Whole new sets of statistics are needed to determine how many scores are needed from each group, to understand the results of these group tests, and to draw meaningful comparisons between groups.

Early in the 20th century, psychologists are using measures of central tendency, fitting curves to normal probability distributions, and calculating measures of correlations, including multiple correlations (Kelley, 1923). By midcentury, psychologists have added such sophisticated statistical techniques as a variety of analyses of variance including F and t tests, numerous additional measures of correlations including regression equations, and methods to test the reliability and validity of tests and test items (Garrett, 1947; Goodenough, 1949). These are all tools that are needed to understand the results of group measures of psychological variables.

Weber, Fechner, and other psychophysicists measure the ability to discriminate among changes in a physical stimulus. Even nonhuman animals may be taught to make discriminatory responses, helping scientists to understand more about the range of perceptual abilities in animals. As Pavlov demonstrates, teaching a dog to respond differently to a circle than a square allows for the determination of just how much a square has to be changed before the dog will perceive it as a circle. Discriminations can also be made with human subjects by having them assign numbers to a set of stimuli. This technique works as well in measuring attitudes and opinions as it does in measuring sensory perceptions.

In 1932, Rensis Likert (1903–1981) publishes a doctoral dissertation in which he refines earlier techniques for the measurement of attitudes. Instead of comparing an individual's response on an item to the responses of others, Likert's technique asks subjects to indicate the extent of their agreement with the item (Likert, 1932). This eliminates the need for a comparison group and works well enough that "Likert scales" are still a popular method for measuring attitudes and opinions today.

LEARNING THEORIES

✓ Stop and think.

If humans start out as blank slates, and everything is learned, can you design a research study to answers questions about human behaviors?

The assumptions that all organisms begin as virtual blank slates and that learning explains everything have important consequences for experimental psychology early in this century. One may infer, for example, that there is continuity across all species such that what is understood about learning in one species may be applied across all species. According to this **law of phylogenetic continuity**, species differ only in the number and complexity of learned associations that can be made. Thus, it makes no difference what organism is studied; the findings about learning will apply across all species.

Similarly, it should also make no difference whether the learning is occurring in a complex real-world environment or in a more easily controlled laboratory setting. The principles of learning will remain the same across all environments. This belief in the continuity of the principles of learning is partly what accounts for the whole-sale adoption of the Norway white rat as the almost exclusive representative of all phyla and the laboratory as the domain of experimental psychologists for many decades. Rats are relatively inexpensive to keep, are easy to care for, and breed readily in captivity. By 1949, more than half of all studies published in journals of comparative psychology are conducted on white rats, and more than half of the experimental studies published are reports on conditioning and learning (Beach, 1950). Psychologists disagree about how completely the questions of psychology may be answered using only operational terms or how much of the human experience might be reducible to mere statistics. But there is general agreement in this era that experimental psychology using rats and conducted in laboratories can at last be defined as a true natural science with many of the explanatory and predictive powers of the other sciences.

> ✓ **Stop and think.**
> If learning explains everything, then what is mind?

Learning Theorists' Goals

The goal for mid-20th-century experimental psychologists, immersed as they are in the behaviorist paradigm, goes far beyond the simple description of psychological phenomena. If learning explains thoughts, feelings, and behaviors, then a complete understanding of learning should be sufficient to predict these phenomena. If people do what they do because of what they have learned, then knowing what they have learned should, at least theoretically, allow for a prediction about what they might do in the future. So if psychologists understand what kind of learning leads to which thoughts, feelings, and behaviors, they should be able to control psychological phenomena by controlling learning.

Questions About Learning

If learning explains thoughts, feelings, behaviors, motivations, and relationships, what are the important questions to ask about learning? In their laboratory work, experimental psychologists uncover a number of characteristics of, and influences on, learning. Sets of theories are developed to explain why and when learning occurs, what it is that is learned, and whether learning can be unlearned, or extinguished. These are the questions about reinforcement and extinction that are explored in experimental psychology in the 1920s through the 1940s. Recall, for example, how the "radical" behaviorist John Watson (Calkins, 1921; Jastrow, 1927; Wheeler, 1923), explores how fear of a previously neutral stimulus could be learned and reinforced by pairing with an innately fear causing stimulus. In 1924, Mary Cover Jones (1896–1987) publishes her studies with a baby named Peter demonstrating how conditioned fears may be extinguished in the laboratory using the same principles of learning (Jones, 1924).

Much of the experimental work that is done from the mid-1930s until well into the 1950s within the behaviorist paradigm begins to diverge in important ways from Watson's radical behaviorism. Many experimental psychologists of this period are referred to as neobehaviorists. **Neobehaviorists** share the basic underlying assumptions of behaviorism: that individual organisms begin life as virtual blank slates and that learning shapes thoughts, feelings, and behaviors. Neobehaviorists also believe that useful information about learning can be gleaned from carefully controlled studies with animals in laboratories, that well constructed operational definitions and precise measurements will yield truth, and that the prediction and control of behavior are the rewards to be gained from this research. Neobehaviorists, like radical behaviorists, thus admit only a very narrow scope of explanation for psychological characteristics. Their questions are mostly ones about the nature of reinforcement and about extinguishing the connections between stimuli and responses. Neobehaviorists are distinguished from behaviorists by being more open to explanatory variables that might not be publicly observable.

✓ Stop and think.

Is reinforcement necessary for learning to occur, or is mere contiguity sufficient?

Three general ways to answer these questions about learning predominate during the heyday of behaviorism. The first set of answers is physiological and is exemplified by the work of neurophysiologist Karl S. Lashley (1890–1958) at Harvard University and the Yerkes Laboratories of Primate Biology. The second set of answers is mechanical and mathematical, and posits that learning occurs in response to the need to reduce motivating drives within the organism. This set of answers is represented by the theories developed by psychologist Clark L. Hull (1884–1952) of Yale University. The third set of answers is closely related to Gestalt theories of self-organizing perceptions and is illustrated by the ideas expressed by psychologist Edward C. Tolman (1886–1959) at the University of California at Berkeley.

Learning Theorists' Answers

Physiological Answers

According to Pavlov's theories, what is traditionally referred to as a psychological characteristic may be reduced to reflex mechanisms in the brain. Conditioning consists of a connection formed between centers of the brain. Extinction refers to the dying back of such a connection. Radiation is a situation in which a stimulus similar to the conditioned stimulus causes a response and refers to the excitation of nearby centers of the brain. Inhibition refers to the suppression of excitation between centers. This Russian tradition of reflexology thus seeks to explain all behavior in these neurophysiological terms. Radical behaviorist John Watson finds this physiological explanation for learning convincing, and he popularizes these ideas in Western psychology.

Karl Lashley begins with the assumption that the connection between stimulus and response is an actual physiological connection formed in the brain of the organism. Thus, a stimulus–response connection is very much like the connection on an old-fashioned telephone switchboard. When something is learned, the connection is plugged in; when learning is extinguished, the connection is broken. Thus, Lashley reasons, surgically cutting connections in an organism's brain should result in the loss of learning. He trains rats to run mazes in the laboratory and then surgically destroys various parts and amounts of the animals' cortexes. After the rats have physically recovered from the surgeries, he returns them to the maze to see if the learning has indeed been broken along with the physiological connections.

✓ **Stop and think.**
Learning should have extinguished along with the destroyed brain matter, right?

Lashley's results are surprising. He finds that fairly large amounts of the cortex must be destroyed before there is any loss in the rate, efficiency, or accuracy of maze learning. This does not support the theory of the cortex as a set of neural switches. Lashley calls his finding the "**principle of mass action**," meaning that, for complex learning like that required in running a maze, the cortex operates as a unified whole rather than as a set of discrete switches. Instead of finding neurophysiological support for the behaviorists, Lashley's evidence is more supportive of Gestalt theories of a holistically functioning brain.

Second, Lashley's experimental findings demonstrate that within a functional area of the brain, such as within the visual cortex, an undamaged part of that area will take over if part of the area is destroyed. Lashley calls this "**equipotentiality**," meaning that, within a given functional area of the cortex, all cells have an equal potential to perform that function. Lashley's findings thus raise more questions than they answer about the nature of the physiological connections between stimuli and responses (Lashley, 1923a, 1923b).

Perhaps because of Lashley's results, fewer psychologists pursue research into the mechanisms of sensation and perception in the early decades of the 20th century. Throughout this era, the Harvard psychologist S. Smith Stevens (1906–1973) preserves the study of relationships between the physical properties of stimuli and the perception of those stimuli. It is not until late in the century that research into sensation and perception regains its importance in Western psychology.

✓ **Stop and think.**
What is extinction? Is it the dying back of a stimulus–response connection? Or is it, as psychologist Edwin Guthrie suggests, the overlaying of a previous stimulus–response connection by a newer one?

Mathematical/Mechanistic Answers

Other neobehaviorists take the position that, although an environmental stimulus may be necessary, it is not necessarily sufficient to cause a response. These theorists suggest that the stimulus together with a whole set of other variables, including many internal to the organism, come between the stimulus and the response. These variables might include an organism's intention, purpose, or motivation in making a response. They might also include mental events not available to public observation.

One set of theories of behavior that uses variables intervening between stimulus and response is illustrated by the work of Clark Hull and his students. Hull's mathematical/mechanistic behaviorism views the organism as though it is a machine executing responses as a function of the strength of various stimuli. Thus, a given response may be predicted from the intensity of the environmental stimulus, the strength of a previously acquired habit, and the degree of an unsatisfied internal drive, such as hunger. Each of those variables may be assigned a weight, allowing for the mathematical calculation of the likelihood that a response will be made.

This approach to behaviorism operationally defines all of the theoretical terms and provides more flexibility in explanations for behavior than does the strictly stimulus–response explanation offered by Watsonian behaviorism. For example, mathematical/mechanistic behaviorism offers an explanation for very complex behaviors and for sets of responses. Stimuli and responses can be associated together, creating chains that explain complex sets of behaviors. In this way, experimental anomalies, research findings that appear to violate the assumptions of the behaviorist paradigm, may be explained. For example, studies in which rats are found to consistently run only part of the maze or where they repeatedly turn down blind alleys present apparent anomalies to the behaviorist. But if running to the goal box is described as a "goal response," then running partway to the goal box could be described as a "fractional goal response." A rat that turns down a blind alley before reaching the goal box might be said to be anticipating the goal box and thus exhibiting an "anticipatory goal response" (Hull, 1943). Using the term "fractional anticipatory goal response," Hull is able to explain a variety of behaviors exhibited by rats in experimental situations that are not predicted by stimulus–response theories of learning without giving up the assumptions of behaviorism.

✓ Stop and think.

What can serve as a reinforcer? Does it need to be publicly observable? Or can learning be reinforced by something intangible?

Purposive Answers

Edward Tolman and his students offer a third set of answers to questions about what learning is and what it is that is learned. They suggest that the behavior of organisms is not caused just by environmental stimuli, but it also looks as though it is intended to achieve some purpose. In making this suggestion, they are sometimes accused of reintroducing subjective and mentalistic terms into what is struggling to be a purely objective psychology. "Purposive" behaviorists, as Tolman calls them, defend their theories by insisting that their data are as publicly observable and objective as any and their theoretical terms equally as operational. The purposive behaviorists suggest that what is ultimately to be understood is the molecular level of behavior, the smallest discrete unit of behavior. However, before that level may be understood, they argue, one must first examine the molar level, or whole purposive acts. What is learned to accomplish molar behavior is a complex set of bits of knowledge about the environment and the learner's relationship to it (Gleitman, 1991). These sets of pieces of knowledge become available to the learner as fields of information that can be accessed and used, even when there are small changes in the environment or in the learner's internal motivation. In other words, behavior is a consequence of both publicly observable environmental stimuli and internal variables representing these previously acquired sets of knowledge that intervene between stimulus and response.

As Tolman points out, at any given time, there are myriad environmental stimuli available to a learner, but only a few are selected for and acted on. That process of selection must somehow be explained, and it can only be explained on the basis of internal variables. As evidence in support of these theories, Tolman offers a series of research findings from the laboratories of purposive behaviorists that he applies to issues of learning in both rats and humans (Tolman, 1948). For example, in traversing a previously encountered maze, rats give clear evidence of having formed a "mental" representation of how the maze goes, so that if one pathway is blocked, they can find alternative routes to the goal. Tolman calls this mental representation of the maze a "**cognitive map**." He refers to the following anecdote from Lashley's lab, in which the rats appear to have formed not just a cognitive map of the maze, but also of the entire room.

> ... the case of a couple of his rats who, after having learned an alley maze, pushed back the cover near the starting box, climbed out, and ran directly across the top to the goal-box where they climbed down in again and ate.
>
> (Tolman, 1948, p. 203)

The more conservative learning theorists have their doubts about purposive theories of cognitive processes in learning. The behaviorist Edwin Guthrie (1886–1959), for example, accuses Tolman of "leaving the rat buried in thought" at each choice point in a maze (Guthrie, 1952, p. 143).

Tolman is not dissuaded from his purposive ideas and goes on to offer explanations for a variety of psychopathological behaviors in humans and for some phenomena from social psychology. He suggests, for example, that racial prejudice might be exhibited by people who have formed only narrow cognitive maps about groups other than their own or that under conditions of high stress humans all tend to use only a small part of the information they actually possess (Tolman, 1948).

One of the most intriguing sets of findings from the laboratories of the purposive behaviorists concerns the evidence they uncover for the existence of **latent learning**, defined as learning that occurs in the absence of reinforcement. Latent learning is only demonstrated when conditions favoring its appearance occur. For example, if nonhungry rats are put into a maze, they wander around with little direction. Later, when they are food-deprived, these rats show clear evidence of having learned the layout of the maze by heading for the goal box. Latent learning violates Thorndike's law of effect and is one among several of the anomalies that behaviorism has difficulty explaining.

Comparative Psychology and Learning

During the 1920s to 1940s, comparative psychologists share the assumption that learning shapes psychological characteristics. For example, during this era, comparative psychologists consider questions about how a species having a close genetic relationship to humans, like the chimpanzee, might respond if exposed from earliest infancy to the same environmental experiences as a human infant. To test this question, Luella and Winthrop Kellogg and their 10-month-old son Donald adopt a $7^{1}/_{2}$-month-old female chimpanzee, Gua, into their home. For 9 months, Gua and Donald are exposed to the same experiences, and Gua is treated as much like a human infant as the Kelloggs are able. She is even dressed like a human infant, as can be seen in Fig. 10.1. At the end of the study, the Kelloggs conclude that Gua learns a wide variety of behaviors during her experience that she would not otherwise exhibit. Some of these behaviors Gua learns even more successfully than does Donald, such as being able to eat using a spoon, but much of her behavioral repertoire is still strongly influenced by apparently innate chimpanzee typical behavior (Kellogg & Kellogg, 1933/1967).

During these decades, the agenda of comparative psychology is focused on the study of animals for the purpose of more fully understanding and improving the human condition. This is clearly the agenda for one of the most influential comparative psychologists, Robert Yerkes (1876–1956). Yerkes promotes the study of primates, almost exclusively chimpanzees, and in 1930, establishes a research facility for the study of his captive animals. Although no single research question dominates the studies conducted at this facility, the hope is that the body of information gathered about chimpanzees will be "of service to humanity through the discovery of more rational ways of living" (Dewsbury, 1996, p. 100).

Learning Theory and the Psyche

✓ **Stop and think.**
If our choices can all be explained as a result of the mechanics of learning, what is free will?

FIG. 10.1. Gua and Donald (Kellogg & Kellogg, 1933/1967, Frontispiece).

Mind

If mind is only a collection of learned associations or an awareness of what the body is doing, where is the inner-directing self? Where is the captain of the ship? Is the "ghost in the machine" really only just a ghost, a metaphysical apparition, as the radical behaviorists suggest? Do the causes of behavior lie only in the mechanical functioning of the laws of nature? Radical behaviorists have no qualms about eliminating consciousness and free will from the discussion. In their view, imagining that there is a freely choosing self is only wishful thinking borne out of an unwillingness to recognize humans' own true natures as evolved organisms. Eventually, the radical behaviorists deny the very existence of mind as anything other than perceptions and learned associations.

✓ **Stop and think.**
If mind really is a set of learned associations, could a machine that can make associations be said to have a mind?

Artificial Intelligence

Is there evidence that humans are anything more than just very complex organic machines? This question has haunted philosophers at least since the time of Descartes. Since the 17th century, mathematicians, philosophers, and psychologists have attempted to answer this question by designing machines that "think" like humans. If a mechanical mind could be created that could engage a human in a conversation indistinguishable from one with another human, what would that mean about the possibility that humans might be merely biological machines? If a form of artificial intelligence could be created that would be indistinguishable from human intelligence, would we be justified in saying that that machine could think?

In 1642, French mathematician Blaise Pascal (1623–1662) invented a mechanical calculator. By the 19th century, mathematical philosophers were working out how machines might be built that could perform a variety of analytical operations. Their designs hinged on the possibility that not just arithmetic calculations but even problems in logic might be represented as a series of "if/then" operations. Unfortunately, it proved impossible to construct the machines they envisioned using the cog wheels and steam power technology of their times. It was not until 1888 that a punch-card system for data entry was developed.

Joseph Jacquard developed a punch-card system in 1801 for the purpose of automating the manufacture of complex patterns in fabric. Jacquard later joined the cards to form an endless loop that represented the program for repeating patterns. Based on Jacquard's system, Herman Hollerith developed a counting machine that revolutionized the compilation of large and complex data sets later in the century. It took over 7 years to compile the 1880 census in the United States, but using Hollerith's punch-card system, the 1890 United States census data were compiled in only 6 weeks (Russo, 2003).

In 1937, British mathematician Alan M. Turing (1912–1954) describes a hypothetical computing machine that would do much more than compile data. A few years later, during World War II, an electromechanical rotor machine is invented by an obscure British postal worker. This machine is used by the British military to decode secret messages sent by the German "Enigma Machine" and helps the Allies to win the war in Europe. At war's end, work continues to create a form of mechanical intelligence based on this electromechanical model. These efforts are so successful that, by 1951, the Universal Automatic Computer (UNIVAC), a machine so large that it fills an entire room at the U.S. Bureau of the Census, can be used to call the election of President Dwight D. Eisenhower just 45 minutes after the polls have closed.

Psychologists working in the field of artificial intelligence ask questions about the possibility of creating machines that will demonstrate powers of reasoning, have visual or auditory awareness of the world, and be able to learn from previous experience. If a machine could do those things, would it be different from human intelligence in any important way? In 1950, Alan Turing proposes and funds a contest to find a form of artificial intelligence that can conduct a conversation indistinguishable from one that might occur between two people (Turing, 1950). Each year, more and more sophisticated and successful computer programs are entered in the Turing Test, so that today, more than one computer program exists that can reliably pass the Turing Test. Developments in artificial intelligence continue to have a major impact on Western culture and psychology in the decades that follow.

SOCIAL AND PERSONALITY THEORY

A serious argument may be made that all of psychology is social psychology, because it is very nearly meaningless to talk about psychological characteristics without reference to interactions with others. Russian psychologist Lev Vygotsky (1896–1934), for example, argues that consciousness itself originates in the processes of social interaction that humans are a part of from the moment of birth, and thus consciousness cannot be understood without reference to the social environment (Vygotsky, 1930/1978).

✓ **Stop and think.**
Can you define a psychology that does not refer in any way to the actual, imagined, or implied presence of others? What would be studied in such a psychology?

Theories about social interactions that comprise social psychology are inextricably interwoven with theories about the origins and nature of personality that comprise personality psychology. That these two domains have been bound up with one another from the beginning and remain closely connected even in the present day, is illustrated by the title of the most prestigious journal in this field, The Journal of Personality and Social Psychology, *established in 1965.*

Methods in Social Research

Social psychology is distinguished from other disciplines that observe social interactions by positivistic methods of research. Like other psychologists, social psychologists come to their conclusions by operationally defining, in advance, a specific set of variables to be measured and by recording their measurements in a publicly verifiable way. There are many aspects of human social behavior that, on the basis of personal anecdotes or experience, seem like they must just be a certain way, but that the careful measurements of social psychologists find not to be the case. For an example of this, see the box titled "Attitudes and Behaviors."

Social Theorists' Questions

As in all fields of science, social psychologists are on a quest to find a few laws in nature. Can a few universal principles be found to explain human social interactions? A variety of candidates are offered in the theories of social psychologists.

Most personality psychologists' theories about motivation postulate causes that lie primarily within the individual. Freud's idea of an unconscious motivation directed to serve the pleasure principle, for example, is an idea about a motivational mechanism that operates from within the individual. The learning theorists' contention that reinforcements are important in shaping behavior is another example. Both of these mechanisms are theorized to operate similarly in any environment, social or otherwise.

Social psychologists however, are more likely to focus on variables that arise from or are related to interactions with others. Even terms referring to internal personality variables derive most of their meaning from social interactions. For example, introversion/extraversion is one dimension of personality theorized by social psychologists to motivate much of human social behavior. In other words, the degree to which an individual needs or wants the company and attention of others shapes many of their behaviors.

Group Mind

Social philosophers have also long been interested in the influence of others on individuals' thoughts and feelings. Introduced in the previous chapter, Kurt Lewin asks questions about group dynamics, both in and out of workplace settings, and the effects of different leadership styles on group dynamics. Earlier, Wilhelm Wundt argued that there really must be two psychologies: one physiological and internal to the individual, and one social and built up out of interactions with others. In the early decades of the 20th century, social theorists ask about the existence and definition of a "group mind." There is no question that the culture in which people grow up influences many of their beliefs. Does that mean that there exists a cultural group mind that is made up of, but more than, the sum of the individual minds of its members? Wundt, for example, suggested that the existence of a shared and dynamic language is sufficient evidence to prove the existence of group mind. Cultural anthropologist Emile Durkheim (1858–1917) nominated religion as evidence of the existence of group mind (Allport, 1954). If there is a group mind, where does it come from, and how can it be influenced? More interesting still from the standpoint of the psychologist, what is the nature of the relationship between the group mind and individual minds? How much influence can one person, maybe a very charismatic leader like Adolph Hitler, have on the group mind? How easily influenced is the individual by the group mind?

Questions such as these are explored not just by social psychologists, but by cultural anthropologists as well. It seems clear to many that the only way really to answer these questions, indeed the only way to find the universal principles that govern human social behavior, is by conducting comparative research studies across a variety of cultures. Beginning in the 1930s and 1940s, cultural anthropologists, like Franz Boas, Ruth Benedict, and Margaret Mead, publish a steady stream of ethnographic descriptive research. These studies are conducted in cultures around the world, focusing on questions about how much of human thoughts, feelings, and behaviors can be attributed to universal laws of nature and how much is shaped by the surrounding culture.

Attitudes

At the same time that industrial psychologists become interested in workers' attitudes toward their jobs in the early decades of the 20th century, social psychologists also become interested in the impact of attitudes on behavior. As measurement techniques such as Likert scales become refined, the measurement of attitudes in a variety of domains begins. Always interested in more than just overt behavior, social psychologists in the 1930s ask questions about how opinions and attitudes might influence social behaviors.

Attitudes and Behaviors

A common assumption is that it is relatively easy to predict how a person might behave toward someone of a different racial or ethnic group if that person's attitude toward people in the different group is known. Psychologist Richard LaPiere tests the truth of this assumption in his study of the relationship between attitudes and behaviors.

Prejudicial attitudes toward those of different racial and ethnic groups are common and commonly accepted in the United States in the early decades of the 20th century. Among those toward whom such prejudice is directed are people of Asian descent. In 1930 and 1931, LaPiere travels throughout the United States with a young Chinese couple, staying at hotels and dining at restaurants across the country. In all of their travels, only once do they encounter someone who refuses them service on the basis of their ethnicity. Thus, widespread social attitudes of prejudice do not translate into discriminatory behavior in this study.

Approximately 6 months after their trip, LaPiere mails questionnaires to the same establishments asking if they would serve Chinese guests. Nearly all (90%) of the responses state that those establishments would not serve Chinese guests, even though nearly all of them had done just that 6 months earlier. This seems to be clear evidence that attitudes are *not* necessarily linked directly to behaviors. Questions like this continue to be explored by social psychologists in the decades that follow. (adapted from LaPiere, 1934)

In the 1930s, as the West gears up for and enters a second major war, social psychologists are also concerned about how being a part of a group might facilitate individual behavior that would never occur in the absence of the group influence. They want to know how the perceived prestige of a leader might inspire loyalty and group action. And they are interested in the impact of group pressures to conform and in what happens to individuals who express opinions that deviate from the norm in their group (Schacter, 1951; Sherif, 1947; Thomas, 1933). For example, social psychologist Solomon Asch is interested in how impressions of others' personalities are formed (Asch, 1946). His research launches the still-popular field of impression formation research in social psychology.

As a reminder that prevailing social values influence even the objective practice of science, the degree to which social psychologists' questions and the answers they find are influenced by the values of the surrounding social environment should be noted. A good example of this, and one that should help to identify the same forces at work in North American research agendas, is the work of Russian psychologist Vladimir Bekhterev. As the historian of social psychology, Gordon Allport, reports, shortly after the Bolshevik revolution created the socialist Soviet Union in 1917, Bechterev and his colleagues turn their attention to questions about the relative efficacy of collective or group judgments versus private or individual judgments. They find that collective thinking is often superior to private thinking. The relative merits of competition versus cooperation are also investigated by Russian psychologists, who find that cooperation is, in general, superior to competition (adapted from Allport, 1954). At the same time, researchers in the United States find that competitive thinking is superior (Lewin, Lippitt, & White, 1939).

Even today, social psychology remains especially sensitive to the agendas set by prevailing values in the surrounding culture. As the landscape of social psychology continues to be explored in the next chapter, other examples of how social, political, and economic events influence the questions and answers in this field are discussed.

DEVELOPMENTAL THEORY

During the middle of the 20th century, child study becomes developmental psychology. Developmental psychologists ask questions about changes across time in a variety of physical, intellectual, and socioemotional domains. During the 1930s and 1940s in the West, most developmental interest is focused on documenting the normal experiences of children. The term "normal children" is defined very narrowly in this era as Caucasian middle-class European or North American children, usually boys. In general, it is necessary to look to the work of cultural anthropologists to find developmental research being conducted in other populations.

Physical Development and Psychology

Previous to this era, the work of physiologists has generally supported assumptions that neural connections are formed in response to experience in the environment. The problem with this view is that it does not square with the evidence that appears in the 1930s and 1940s. In a variety of species, studies of embryology find that neurological development occurs as a function of the passage of time, not in response to experience. In fact, there is even an overgrowth of neural cells during early development, which are then pared down in response to environmental influences, very nearly the opposite of earlier ideas. In nonhuman animal studies, researchers find that it is the maturation of neural systems that allows for the emergence of certain motor skills, not motor skills that cause neural development (Coghill, 1933). This perspective is called "**maturationism**," because of the conviction that it is maturation occurring during the passage of time that drives development in all areas, including psychological characteristics. Intellectual and personality development and even the development of social skills result from the maturation of the nervous system as the young organism gets older. Mental functions, in other words, grow along with the nervous system and are subject to the same principles of natural selection that have shaped the body during evolution.

Contemporary with both behaviorism and psychoanalytic theory, maturationism stands in stark contrast to these learning theories. Developmental researchers like Arnold Gesell (1880–1961) and Myrtle McGraw (1899–1988) argue that normative behavioral patterns emerge naturally and in a regular sequence, as the organism gets older. Thus, development is a consequence of physiological maturation, particularly neurological growth, and is relatively impervious to learning. From the view of the maturationist, the role of families and the surrounding environment is to provide an optimal environment so as to allow children to maximize their own innate potential (Gesell, 1954).

After years of painstaking observations of children from the earliest moments of life, Gesell details hundreds of stages of developing physical, intellectual, and socioemotional skills. From Gesell's work, for example, come the basic "motor milestones" of the first few months of life listed in every developmental psychology textbook. Which is it that drives development, experience or maturation? In 1935, Myrtle McGraw, research psychologist at the Normal Child Development Clinic at Columbia Medical Center, publishes her longitudinal test of this question, the study of Johnny and Jimmy.

The Study of Johnny and Jimmy

McGraw's primary subjects in this study are twins (zygosity undetermined), Johnny and Jimmy. The boys begin their participation in research at the moment of their births, which are filmed, and thereafter behavioral data are carefully collected. At 20 days of age, the boys begin to spend 7 hours a day, 5 days a week in the laboratory. From these very early days of life, one of the twins, Johnny, who at birth appears to be physically less well developed than Jimmy, is given constant exercise and training in a wide variety of physical skills. Jimmy, on the other hand, spends most of his first 2 years in the laboratory in his crib, allowed to play with only two toys at a time. Both boys go home to their large family on evenings and weekends. Month after month for 22 months, Johnny is provided with practice and training, whereas Jimmy is restricted to his crib. It seems inevitable that Johnny will be advanced by all this practice. In the end, however, although Johnny is somewhat more deliberative about his actions and Jimmy slightly more fearful, their physical development is comparable.

Johnny is also given training in language comprehension and eventually shows a slight advancement when Jimmy is first tested. In general, however, McGraw and her colleagues find little evidence in this study that practice or experience will accelerate the appearance in a normal child of either physical or cognitive skills and only meager evidence for critical periods when a skill must be acquired. On tests of intelligence (the use of which is highly questionable in infancy), for example, at 2 years of age, both boys achieve almost the same score. McGraw concludes that, parents can relax, enjoy their children, and not to try to push their development ahead of the normal maturational stage. (adapted from McGraw, 1935)

Another consequence of the view that the development of psychological characteristics is an aspect of physical maturation and that both are subject to the principles of natural selection is the conclusion that individual differences in psychological characteristics like intelligence or personality may be partly biologically based. Thus, personality differences may be influenced by differences in the physical constitution of each person. This idea encounters serious resistance in an era when the practice of eugenics is falling into disrepute and when behaviorism is preaching the power of learning to shape personality. The idea that some aspects of personality may be influenced by individual differences in physiology does not resurface for several decades, despite strong supporting evidence.

Intellectual Development

Identifying the motor milestones of infancy divides growth into "stages" of development. That is, if at one age it is normal for a child to exhibit certain characteristic ways of moving around, like crawling, but at another age an entirely different way of moving, like walking, is exhibited, it is natural to describe these as different stages of physical development. The same may be said of intellectual development. This idea is brought to fruition in Swiss psychologist Jean Piaget's (1896–1980) stage theory of the development of rational thought.

Influenced by Binet (Siegler, 1994), Piaget's ideas are published in English in the late 1920s and remain influential in educational psychology even today. Among his contributions to developmental psychology are his research methods, which are strictly empirical. Piaget carefully observes and describes his young subjects. He also creates and presents the subjects with a variety of problems to be solved, conducts extensive interviews, and engages the children in question-and-answer sessions (Piaget, 1926).

Piaget provides accurate descriptions of young children's behaviors as they solve problems. His descriptions reveal different patterns of behavior and responses during problem solving for different ages of children. Thus, he concludes, rational thought progresses through several stages or ways of organizing information. These stages represent universal features of the development of rational thought. They emerge as children mature and engage in interactions with objects and other people in age-characteristic ways.

Another, and perhaps more enduring, impact of Piaget's work is his conviction that these maturationally linked psychological characteristics cause the child to be an active seeker of knowledge and organizer of information. Unlike the behaviorist, who views the child as a blank slate mechanically forming associations and being conditioned by experience, Piaget's theories see the child as "a little scientist," actively seeking out and interpreting experience.

The Russian social psychologist Vygotsky challenges these notions of stages of intellectual development by pointing out an interesting finding in intelligence testing. Typically, a child may achieve one score on a test of intellectual development if working alone, but if tested with an adult present who asks questions and interacts with the child, the child's score may be pushed to a higher level. Vygotsky calls this the child's "zone of proximal development" and demonstrates that even something as internal to the individual as intellectual capacity is not necessarily limited to definable stages and not strictly internal, but is also constructed from interactions with others (Wertsch & Tulviste, 1994).

The Development of Personality

Developmental theories are also closely tied with personality theories and are influenced in the 1930s and 1940s by both behaviorism and psychoanalytic ideas. Developmental psychologists adopt the research methods of the behaviorists, and many developmental psychologists also adopt behaviorists' assumption that the environment is the major, if not the only, influence on personality and psychological characteristics. By the late 1940s, many developmental psychologists assume that each infant begins life as nearly a blank slate and that personality is molded by the environment. Experiences within the family are assumed to be the most important influences on personality development.

> Give me a dozen healthy infants, well-formed, and my own specified world to bring them up in and I'll guarantee to take any one at random and train him to become any type of specialist I might select—doctor, lawyer, artist, merchant-chief and, yes, even beggar-man and thief, regardless of his talents, penchants, tendencies, abilities, vocations and the race of his ancestors. (Watson 1930, p. 104)

This emphasis on conditioning explains, in large part, the behaviorists' interest in early infancy. Presumably by carefully observing infants and experimentally manipulating their environment, one may actually see the effects of learning and experience on development. Even the appearance of personality characteristics, such as fearfulness or persistence, are viewed as the result of conditioning experiences (McGraw, 1935). According to the behaviorist, developmental progression is linear and cumulative, and does not occur in stages. Although the radical behaviorist John Watson contributes little research on development, he has a major impact on the field by providing rather dogmatic advice on child-rearing (Horowitz, 1994), disseminated mostly in the popular media. His advice strongly encourages parents actively to strive to shape their children's personalities through reinforcement.

Freudian psychoanalytic theory also influences developmental psychologists. This theory posits that the way in which a mother responds to her infant's needs is of prime importance in shaping the infant's eventual personality and characteristic ways of responding to the environment and other people. This primary relationship that the infant has with the mother serves as a prototype for all subsequent relationships. The responsibility for ensuring an optimal outcome falls squarely and completely on the shoulders of the mother. Her child's personality is seen as a direct outcome of her skill as a mother.

According to the psychoanalyst, normal development proceeds through a series of stages, each characterized by psychosexual conflict centered on a particular part of the body. The child's task, with the support of the mother, is to resolve each set of conflicts in a constructive way that allows for continued self-preservation. By successfully mastering these conflicts, the child builds a functioning and healthy ego and avoids a future tormented by neuroses. Later psychodynamic theories maintain the focus on conflict and its resolution as the engines of development, but suggest that the conflicts are more about issues like interpersonal relationships (Horney, 1945; Klein, 1932), overcoming inferiority (Adler, 1929), establishing trust (Erikson, 1950), or separation and individuation (Mahler, Pine, & Bergman, 1994).

Both behaviorist and psychoanalytic theories of personality acknowledge that there are individual differences in personality. However, these theories explain individual differences on the basis of past experience and learning, not as a result of physiological or innate characteristics. Thus, learning plays a central role in behaviorist, psychoanalytic, and psychodynamic theories about the development of personality.

CLINICAL PSYCHOLOGY

Before World War II, the term clinical psychology refers to all of the professional applications of psychology, including testing applications in business, industry, and education, as well as the diagnosis and treatment of both psychoses and neuroses. It is not until the 1950s that the term is applied mainly to the diagnosis and treatment of mental illness.

Personnel Testing

Personnel and employment tests continue to be refined in business settings during the middle decades of the 20th century. By the time the United States enters World War II, psychologists are ready to take up the task again of testing recruits and officers. By this time, psychologists have also earned the respect of business, military, and political leaders, and the results of their tests are taken more seriously. By the end of the war, when thousands of soldiers return to take up roles in the civilian economy, virtually no company of any size would consider hiring or placing a new employee without first administering some sort of psychological test (Napoli, 1981).

Educational Testing

The development and use of tests in educational settings proliferates during the 1920s and 1930s. As early as the mid-1920s, millions of school children are tested each year to justify placement in aptitude-related educational tracks (Hornstein, 1988). The SAT is used extensively in college admissions decisions. Periodically revised after its introduction in 1926, the SAT remains under serious criticism for ethnic, gender, and class bias.

Intelligence Testing

Psychologists are increasingly interested in the ways that individuals differ on these tests and the reasons for those differences. A pioneer in the field of testing and development, Leta Hollingworth (1886–1939), develops techniques for identifying and educating intellectually "gifted" children. Her careful research also helps illuminate some of the "adjustment" problems faced by many children during adolescence and some of the social factors that lead to those problems. For example, Hollingworth's interest in social factors influencing intellectual functioning is illustrated by her dissertation research, published in 1914, investigating the then-popular opinion that women experience **"functional periodicity,"** a kind of monthly psychological impairment associated with the menstrual cycle. She concludes that there are no differences on motor, sensory, or intellectual tasks at different times of the month, even though there are widespread beliefs that monthly impairments exists (Hollingworth, 1914). This work is one of the earliest studies in a field that will later be called the psychology of women.

✓ **Stop and think.**
What happens to really intelligent children when they grow up?

In the early decades of the 20th century, it is also widely believed that, although very intelligent children may "ripen" early at academic subjects, their lives go downhill from there. They suffer from more physical illnesses, exhibit a variety of abnormalities such as near-sightedness, are more likely to fall victim to mental illness, and by early adulthood, have begun to "rot." Their adult lives are unproductive and characterized by disappointing personal relationships.

In 1921, Lewis Terman and his colleagues at Stanford University begin a study to determine the truth of these common beliefs. Also motivating Terman in this study is his conviction that to be successful, a society needs the leadership that only the highly intelligent can provide. Thus, it is in society's best interests to identify the intellectually gifted and to nurture their well-rounded development. Intended at first only to examine the characteristics of intelligent children across a 10-year period, the study eventually expands into one of the most extensive longitudinal studies of development ever undertaken. This research follows most of the 1,470 subjects for nearly 60 years.

From the first round of data collection to the last, the evidence supports Terman's hypotheses. As children and adolescents, the gifted show high academic achievement and well-rounded personalities, and are popular with their peers. Curiously, the gifted girls do not maintain their early intellectual promise, a fact that Terman attributes to an "earlier cessation of mental growth" (Minton, 1988). As adults, the gifted show higher levels of achievement in their careers than those of average intelligence, healthy physical and mental well-being, and average or above-average happiness in their personal relationships, including in marriage. At midlife, many of the men have gained respect and public recognition in their chosen careers and report happy and satisfying marriages and family relationships. The gifted women in the study, unfortunately, are not able to report the same level of career success or recognition, a fact that even Terman must admit may be due to external factors, such as expectations of gender-role conformity and discrimination in employment (Burks, Jensen, & Terman, 1930).

The results of Terman's study demonstrate that the widely accepted belief in gifted children's "early ripe, early rot" is false. Thus, this longitudinal study is an example of how the methods of careful scientific research have the power to demonstrate that even what is widely believed is not always true.

Diagnostic Testing

In the 1930s, a variety of tests are used to diagnose all forms of mental illness, both neurotic and psychotic. Projective tests, such as the Rorschach Inkblot Test developed by Swiss psychologist Hermann Rorschach in 1921 and the Thematic Aperception Test created by Christiana D. Morgan and Henry A. Murray in 1935, are used to get patients to reveal unconscious thoughts that they might not consciously tell the psychiatrist (Morgan & Murray, 1935). In general, projective tests present the subject with an ambiguous stimulus, such as an inkblot, and the subject is asked to interpret the stimulus. The subject's mental health is then evaluated on the basis of the interpretation given. Projective tests are developed for the purpose of revealing hidden and unconscious thoughts that, in this era, are often presumed to be causing mental illness and distress.

Psychotic Mental Illness

By midcentury, it is generally agreed that psychotic forms of mental illness should be treated with medical interventions in the same way that physical illness is treated. It is assumed that the disordered thoughts, feelings, and behaviors diagnosed as mental illness have physiological causes. Throughout the history of the modern era, those entrusted with the care of the psychotic have had to decide whether they should provide only custodial care or whether they could offer any actual curative therapies. They have also been confronted with the task of controlling the disruptive behaviors often associated with many forms of psychosis. In the early days of institutional care for the mentally ill, both physical restraint and discipline, are used liberally but very little is attempted in the way of treatment. It is not until late in the 19th century that treatments for mental illness are tried.

Early in the 20th century, psychiatrists and neurologists devise a variety of new physical techniques used both to discipline patients' behaviors and to provide physical treatments. For example, sexual sterilization is adopted as a form of psychosurgery. Sterilization is most often performed on female mental patients to prevent the complications associated with pregnancy and parenthood, but for males, it is argued that sterilization is actually psychologically therapeutic. The belief is that sterilization will allow the reabsorption of essential male fluids into the body, thus strengthening the male psyche (Braslow, 1997).

✓ **Stop and think.**
If you thought mental illness was caused by disorders of the brain, what would you suggest as a treatment?

Although physical restraints are still used as disciplinary devices, from the 1920s to the 1950s, barbiturates are available and widely used to sedate disruptive patients. A variety of hydrotherapies, such as continuous cold baths, are also used through this period. Beginning in the late 1930s, insulin injections are used to induce insulin shock in patients exhibiting disruptive behaviors. Patients are placed into comatose states with insulin, and some are left in this condition for up to 60 days. All of these procedures are assumed to have some curative power and are thus used both as therapies and as discipline for agitated or stubborn behavior.

In the late 1930s, electroshock is introduced in North America to replace the expensive and time-consuming insulin shock procedure. Causing patients to have epileptic seizures by sending electrical charges through their brains is reported in many studies to lessen the behaviors associated with mental illness and make formerly disruptive patients into docile institutional residents. By 1949, 60% of psychotic mental patients in the United States are being subjected to electroshock therapy, and the practice continues well into the 1950s (Braslow, 1997). Also by the late 1940s, the newest form of psychosurgery, the frontal lobotomy, is available to treat mental patients. In 1949, Portuguese neurologist Egas Moniz is awarded the Nobel Prize in physiology and medicine for his work in developing the lobotomy as a treatment for mental illness. As is true for nearly all of the most invasive procedures, many more women than men are subjected to the lobotomy in spite of the fact that more men are admitted to mental institutions (Braslow, 1997).

The popularity of these radical forms of treatment wanes dramatically in the decades that follow, so that by the 1960s when psychiatrists have recourse to psychoactive medications, lobotomy and electroshock are rarely practiced and regarded as somewhat barbaric. Late in the twentieth century, when some of the drawbacks of medication are better known, more targeted forms of electroshock begin to show a resurgence in popularity.

Neurotic Mental Illness

The aftermath of World War II is commonly regarded as the beginning of modern Western clinical practice for the treatment of neuroses. Many young men returning from military service present themselves at veterans' clinics and hospitals with complaints of mild to moderate depression, insomnia, problems controlling anger, alcoholism, and other conditions related to stress. There is, thus, growing pressure for the application of psychological knowledge. The suddenly increased demand for the services of clinical psychologists results in a significant increase in enrollments in university and hospital training programs. This increased demand is also largely responsible for the greater number of practicing psychologists than scientific and academic psychologists that is apparent in the present-day membership of the APA.

During the 1930s, psychoanalytic and psychodynamic theories blossom into an international movement, and by the end of the war, the term psychotherapy largely refers to some form of analytic treatment. Veterans suffering from a general inability to adjust to civilian life, for example, are asked to talk about their relationships with their fathers and encouraged to work through their unresolved Oedipal issues. Women, upset and depressed at suddenly finding themselves unemployed when their jobs are taken by returning servicemen, are prescribed tranquilizers and encouraged to resolve their penis envy by having babies rather than wanting to work at men's (higher-paying) jobs. The treatment of neurotic symptoms is taken seriously, but there is little evidence that the treatments available are of much help. Fortunately for all, neurotic symptoms are typically short-lived and often subject to spontaneous recovery.

Finally, it is during this era that ethnographic studies done by cultural anthropologists, particularly the work of Ruth Benedict, raise questions for psychologists about the dependence of definitions of psychological abnormality on cultural values. A diagnosis of neurosis, in other words, is largely dependent on the social expectations of the surrounding culture. For example, in a culture such as that in North America, where extraversion is expected, extreme shyness might be seen as neurotic, but in a culture more accepting of introversion, such as in China, that same degree of shyness might be seen as much more normative. As Benedict (1934) points out, culture is one factor influencing the placement of the normative score. Because psychological characteristics are measured by comparing individual scores to normative scores, any factor that changes normative scores will influence the diagnosis of neurosis.

⏱ The Times

In 1932, Democrat Franklin Roosevelt is elected President of the United States, promising to institute a "New Deal" to alleviate the Depression. The New Deal is a package of financial policies, bank deposit insurance programs, public works projects for the unemployed, and other types of government assistance. The late 1930s sees the enactment of laws governing minimum wages and child labor, and the passage of the Social Security Act. These measures provide a small degree of economic security for some, although many people are left out of this safety net. Roosevelt enjoys widespread popularity and is reelected for a total of four terms in office, but the nation does not really begin full-scale economic recovery until after it enters World War II in 1941.

At that time, a collective spirit of nationalism sweeps the country. Ten million soldiers are drafted in the United States, and millions of citizens go to work in the plants manufacturing military supplies. Business, government, and the military cooperate to pump up the atmosphere of war fever. But there are those who dissent. Nearly 500,000 of those drafted either refuse to fight and are imprisoned or simply do not show up for service. Labor strikes proliferate, as business profits soar while workers' wages are frozen as part of the war effort. In 1940, the Smith Act is passed to control dissenters, making it a crime to advocate the overthrow of the government by force. This act of Congress gives the government broad powers to identify, arrest, and try anyone alleged to belong to any organization that advocates the overthrow of the government and leads to a growing atmosphere of fear. Racism against citizens of Japanese descent leads to the arrest and detention in camps of Japanese American families in the United States for up to 3 years. Their homes, businesses, and bank accounts are also seized by the U.S. government.

It is in this climate that the United States and Britain justify and begin the "heaviest bombardment of civilians ever undertaken in any war" in Germany and Japan (Zinn, 1998), climaxing in the firestorm that kills over 100,000 civilians and destroys the city of Dresden, Germany, in April 1945. The United States then becomes the only nation ever to use atomic weapons against humans by dropping a single bomb on the Japanese city of Hiroshima on August 6, 1945, leaving 100,000 people dead and thousands more poisoned with radiation. This is followed 3 days later with another atomic bomb over the city of Nagasaki, killing 50,000 people.

Wartime manufacturing weakens the power of the labor unions and concentrates wealth into the hands of fewer and more powerful companies. By the end of the war in 1945, British imperial power throughout most of the world has collapsed, and the United States has moved in to take its place. Business interests in the United States dominate oil in the Middle East, and foreign markets around the world are opened for goods manufactured in the United States.

In addition to dramatic increases in the number of people seeking help for mental illness, research agendas in social and developmental psychology are also affected by the events of the war, leading to the increasing importance of these fields during the latter half of the century.

11

When Motivation Is the Question: Why Do We Do What We Do?

In the mid-1950s continuing through about 1975, psychology is not a single unified landscape. Instead, it is more like a large rambling house with many rooms, as psychologists pursue many interests. Behaviorists take up questions about learning and motivation: Physiological psychologists study the role of the brain in leaning, Hull's hypothetico-deductive theory of motivation is widely accepted, and Skinner's radical behaviorism explores the contingencies of reinforcement. Comparative, developmental, social, and clinical psychologists also explore questions about motivation within their domains. A mechanistic model of thinking called information processing appears and grows in importance at the same time that humanistic/existential forms of psychology become popular.

EXPERIMENTAL PSYCHOLOGY

During this period, experimental psychologists spend most of their time elaborating on the theories of learning developed before World War II, and providing experimental evidence in support of their ideas. For the most part, white rats are used as models to understand the processes of learning in many settings such as the radial arm maze seen in Fig. 11.1.

FIG. 11.1. Training the laboratory rat (photo courtesy of Heather Butler).

Learning and Motivation

By the early 1950s, learning theorists have settled on "the science of behavior"
as their definition of psychology. By science they mean the attempt to "bring
order to the world of observable events" (Kimble, 1953, p. 156). What makes
an event observable is not just the scientists' sensory experience, but also their
"report of such experiences" (p. 156). By behavior, they do not mean whole sets
of activities, but a "limited portion of behavior called responses" (p. 156). The
definition of responses is some further "abstracted characteristic like the speed or
the magnitude of the response" (p. 156).

A primary assumption of this paradigm is that responses are "related to events
in the person's past and present environment" (Kimble, 1953, p. 157). These events
are the stimuli. For example, the response "the efficiency of a learned reaction"
depends on "the number and spacing of practice trials," "the amount of reward," and
other environmental stimuli (p. 157). Note that these stimuli are just as quantifiable
as are the responses. The task for experimental psychologists is to identify the
relationships that exist between responses and stimuli: "What psychologists are
after is a set of laws of the general type: $R = f(S)$, where R is some aspect of
a response, S is a stimulus event and f represents the functional relationship"
(Kimble, 1953, p. 157).

Theories of learning take the form of hypotheses about variables intervening between S and R. Some suggest that it is physiological processes that
intervene between S and R. Others argue that a variety of mechanical-like psychological processes serve as intervening variables. Still others insist that the
intervening variables are more like whole thought processes. There are some behaviorists, however, who suggest that not only are there no intervening variables,

but theorizing itself leads us away from a true understanding of the laws of conditioning.

Physiological Learning

Physiological psychologists make the assumption that stimuli produce physiological changes in the organism, and it is these physiological changes that explain the response. Recall that in the previous chapter, Karl Lashley hypothesizes that it is the functioning of the cortex that explains behavior. He concludes that in cases of complex learning the cortex must operate in a unified way, through mass action. He also concludes that, within a given functional area of the cortex, all cells exhibit equipotentiality in performing that function. Having come to these conclusions, Lashley expresses the opinion that attempting to explicate further the exact mechanisms by which the nervous system accomplishes its tasks is "futile" (Lashley, 1930, p. 1). It remains to Lashley's student Donald O. Hebb (1904–1985) to explore the implications of Lashley's research. One quarter of a century after Lashley's search for the physiological mechanisms of learning is abandoned, Hebb revives the search in his book, *The Organization of Behavior* (1949), based on his work with animals. Hebb argues that the mass action and equipotentiality of the cortex can be explained by "**cell assemblies**." A cell assembly is a set of cells connected to one another into neural circuits. Events or images are represented in the cortex by activity in these cell assemblies. Cell assemblies are formed in the cortex when sensory stimulation sets up a pattern of reverberating neural activity: "When an axon of cell A is near enough to excite cell B and repeatedly or persistently takes place in firing it, some growth process or metabolic change takes place in one or both cells such that A's efficiency, as one of the cells firing B, is increased" (Hebb, 1949, p. 62).

Furthermore, clusters of cell assemblies are linked together into "**phase sequences**" that form the bases of thoughts and ideas. Phase sequences are fired when one or more associated cell assemblies are activated, and the firing of a phase sequence leads to a whole series of ideas. It is the activation of cell assemblies triggering the firing of whole phase sequences that causes thoughts to seem like what William James called a flowing stream of consciousness. After cell assemblies are formed, the activation of cell assemblies and phase sequences may be triggered either by external sensory stimulation or by internal processes, such as associated thoughts and ideas.

The next goal is to identify the growth processes or metabolic changes that cause the formation of cell assemblies and phase sequences. The functioning of the cortex as it causes thoughts, feelings, and behaviors must also be explained. Roger Sperry (1913–1994), for example, explores the nature of cortical connections by cutting the bundle of nerve fibers that connect the right and left hemispheres of the brain (Sperry, 1964). Later in his career, Hebb provides fascinating data on the effects of rich versus deprived sensory environments on the density and complexity of neural circuitry in developing cortexes (in rats).

Mathematical/Mechanistic Learning

Clark Hull's theory that what intervenes between stimulus and response are variables that can be assigned mathematical values is pursued by his students, including Kenneth Spence (1907–1967). Hull is convinced that learning can be explained better by reinforcement than by motivation, and by the early 1950s, his theory is the most widely cited in the field of learning and motivation (Glickman, 1996). Hull calls his theory a **hypothetico-deductive** system because he recommends beginning with a set of hypotheses and then deducing an expected response from these hypotheses.

Hull argues that the potential that the response will occur (reaction potential) can be predicted if the organism's biological need (drive) and the number of previous times the drive has been satisfied by that response (habit strength) is known. Each of these variables can be assigned a mathematical value, so that the reaction potential is some function of the number of hours of food deprivation times the number of previous trials in which that hungry rat pressed the lever and was fed. The importance of drive in this model is illustrated by a study in which rats will turn toward a goal box with food in it when they are food-deprived but, in the same maze, will turn the opposite direction toward water when thirsty.

The concept of drive as a motivator of behavior was formally introduced into psychological theory by Robert Woodworth (1869–1962) in his "dynamic psychology" in 1918. By 1950, motivation is a variable of primary significance in animal learning laboratories, social psychology, psychoanalytic theories, group dynamics, and developmental theories.

Spence and other learning theorists answer questions about motivation using rats in laboratories. It is possible to test a dizzying number and variety of hypotheses about motivation with rats in mazes, puzzle boxes, and operant conditioning chambers. For example, support for various psychoanalytic concepts, like repression, is sought in rat models, although little evidence is found. Animal models of intrapersonal conflict are tested by presenting barriers and noxious stimuli between the motivated rat and the goal box. Ambivalence is examined by presenting the rat with two equally attractive but mutually exclusive goals.

The definition of motivation changes as it becomes clear that animals are motivated by more than just biological needs for food and water. In 1939, for example, O. Hobart Mowrer shows that a reduction of fear serves as a motivator. Daniel Berlyne (1966) finds that rats can be motivated solely by curiosity. Harry Harlow (1905–1981) and his colleagues propose a "manipulation drive" after finding that monkeys are motivated to take latches apart for no reason beyond the satisfaction of solving the problem (Harlow, Harlow, & Meyers, 1950).

What unites this research is the conviction that no matter how motivation is defined, whatever reduces drive (or motivation) reinforces habit strength and thus increases the likelihood of that response when motivation is again present. Reinforcement depends on the reduction of motivation. This makes a fuller understanding of reinforcement an obvious next step for learning theorists.

The Contingencies of Reinforcement

Several years before, in 1938, B. F. Skinner (1904–1990) publishes *The Behavior of Organisms*, in which he argues for the primacy of reinforcement in understanding behavior, but it is not until the early 1950s that the book has much influence over popular learning theory. Skinner's point in this book is that it really does not matter if a stimulus triggers the firing of sets of cell assemblies, or if an organism seeks to reduce drive, or even if the organism has developed a cognitive map of the situation. What matters is understanding the conditions under which reinforcement will occur. If the conditions under which reinforcement will occur can be identified, what Skinner calls the "**contingencies of reinforcement**," the response can be predicted. Because behavior is correlated with reinforcement, if the reinforcer can be controlled, the behavior can be controlled. Skinner defines a **reinforcer** as anything that increases the probability of a response.

Skinner's major concern is with behaviors that are emitted by the organism and then reinforced. He calls these behaviors **operants** because the organism is operating on the environment. Skinner feels that operant behaviors are far more common, and thus more important to understand, than simple associations between stimuli. Besides, describing operant behavior does not require one to identify the exact stimulus that caused the response, so these studies should be easier to conduct.

The thousands of studies prompted by Skinner's system of psychology are conducted in **operant conditioning chambers**, small boxes equipped with only a device for recording responses, such as a lever, and a food dish or other place to deliver the reinforcer. It is in these operant chambers that studies on the effects of various schedules of reinforcement are conducted. Skinner argues that he is not studying learning because what happens in the operant chamber is not learning, but only the gradual "shaping" of behaviors the organism already knows how to perform. Thus, Skinner rejects Thorndike's theory that practice alone improves performance, arguing instead that performance improves only as closer and closer approximations of the desired behavior are reinforced.

✓ **Stop and think.**
Reread carefully "The Story of Little Albert." Is that a study of classical conditioning, as Watson said, or of operant conditioning?

Skinner also rejects the label "theorist" because he claims that he does not engage in theory making. All he does is describe organisms' responses under varying contingencies of reinforcement. Unlike other behaviorists, Skinner denies the existence of theoretical "fictions" like Thorndike's satisfying consequences, Hull's drive reduction, or Tolman's cognitive maps and expectancies. None of those internal variables are necessary to predict the rate of response (Skinner, 1938). Because in this view the organism brings nothing important to the situation, Skinner is accused of studying the "empty organism."

His interest is focused mainly on the effects of positive reinforcement, because he believes that this is the most effective way to shape desired behaviors. Even extinguishing undesirable behaviors may be accomplished most effectively by positively reinforcing alternative behaviors. He finds that punishment will cause undesirable behaviors to be suppressed, but not extinguished, because they very often return after punishment is removed.

Operant conditioning finds many real-world applications, including behavior modification techniques, found to be especially useful in the reduction of phobic responses. Token economies, in which desired behaviors are reinforced with tokens exchangeable for merchandise or other treats, are useful in controlling behaviors in classrooms and group-home settings. Skinner's opponents refer to his work as merely "a technology for modifying behavior" rather than a contribution to psychological theory.

Skinner popularizes the principles of operant conditioning with his novel *Walden Two* (1948), and with his later work *Beyond Freedom and Dignity* (1971). *Walden Two* is the fictional story of a Utopian community founded on principles of positive reinforcement and has become something of a cult classic among college students in the years since its publication. *Beyond Freedom and Dignity* is Skinner's very controversial argument in support of applying operant conditioning to contemporary society.

Learning and Loss of Motivation

Among the issues addressed by psychologists in this era are questions about when and why motivation is lost. To understand motivation, it is also necessary to understand the lack of motivation.

✓ **Stop and think.**
Explain why organisms sometimes do not move away from a noxious stimulus, even when they can.

In the mid-1960s, psychologists Martin Seligman and Steven Maier wonder why organisms who find themselves in the middle of an uncomfortable situation sometimes appear not to be motivated to move. Seligman and Maier begin a series of experiments to test these questions. They put a dog into a small cage, flash warning lights, and then electrify the floor of the cage, delivering a painful shock to the dog. No matter what the dog does, it cannot escape. Later, the same dog is put into a similar cage, but the new cage has a nonelectrified section where the dog will not be shocked. Again, the warning lights are flashed, but even though the dog could escape merely by running into the safe section of the cage, it sits and receives the shock. Seligman and Maier call this response **learned helplessness** (Seligman & Maier, 1967). The dog has learned that it can do nothing to help itself so that later, when escape is possible, it is helpless to respond.

Psychologist Carolyn Rovee-Collier tests similar questions with human infants but without electrical shocks. She ties one end of a ribbon to the bootie of an infant's sleeper and the other end to a mobile over the crib. Infants quickly learn that they can make the mobile move by kicking their feet, and most infants respond with a significant increase in kicking behavior and excited interest in the mobiles. For other infants in other cribs, there are no ribbons. The mobiles are moved, but not in response to the infants' efforts. These infants do not engage in as much kicking behavior and are less interested in the mobiles. Up to 2 weeks later, when the infants are returned to the laboratory, the infants who previously learned that they could control the mobiles again began to kick, but the infants who learned that they had no control lie quietly in their cribs, even after they are outfitted with ribbons to control the mobiles (Rovee-Collier & Fagen, 1981).

✓ **Stop and think.**
What do the findings in the research described previously imply about when and why motivation is lost?

INFORMATION PROCESSING

Recall that Tolman hypothesized that animals engage in purposive behaviors in learning situations. In other words, the behavior of rats in the maze looks as though it is directed toward achieving some goal. The idea that rats are behaving with intent violates the assumptions of the radical behaviorist paradigm. Then, in 1948, mathematician Norbert Wiener publishes *Cybernetics*, a treatise in which he explains the mechanism by which any machine may be built so that it looks as though the machine is behaving purposively. This mechanism is the feedback loop and is familiar in the form of thermostats on heaters. The thermostat causes the heater to turn on and off, making it look as though the heater intends to maintain temperature at a given level.

The Gestalt notion that the mind actively categorizes information is another concept that violates the behaviorist assumption that the mind passively makes mechanistic-like associations. After World War II, researchers working on telephone technologies develop mechanical means of transforming communications into bits of information that can be transmitted electronically and then turned back into communication at the receiving end. Based on emerging computer technologies, these communication machines take in and process bits of information and produce meaningful output. Some begin to argue that the brain is a similar information-processing device.

Research programs are launched in efforts to understand the mechanisms by which the brain processes information. These include mechanisms for the short-term retention of information, for placing some information into longer-term storage, and for formulating and executing responses to information. In 1956, for example, psychologist George A. Miller (1920–) presents his finding that the average human short-term memory mechanism is capable of processing seven plus or minus two pieces of information at one time (Miller, 1956). If the pieces of information can be organized into meaningful "chunks," short-term memory can still handle seven chunks of superordinate information. So although a shopping list of 10 items would be hard to hold in short-term memory, a list of 4 categories, such as dairy, fruit, bread, and meat, with only 2 or 3 items in each, would be easily remembered.

By the late 1960s, human information processing is becoming an area of active interest in psychology. In 1967, Ulric Neisser (1928–) publishes *Cognitive Psychology*, in which he defines cognitive psychology as the study of "all the processes by which ... sensory input is transformed, reduced, elaborated, stored, recovered, and used" (Neisser, 1967, p. 4). In 1969, the first cognitive psychology journal begins publication.

There are three major organizing principles that define the scope of cognitive psychology as it continues to develop through the remainder of this century. The first of these takes its cue from Piaget's notions of the mind as sets of **schemata** representing information encountered in the environment. The brain is viewed as a mechanism that actively organizes information using hierarchical structures to create schemata and place information into them. The second principle uses the metaphor of the brain as a complex computer. Even the jargon of computer technologies becomes the language of the psychologist, so that, for example, stimulus becomes input and response becomes output. Psychologists studying human cognition find themselves aligned with other disciplines, including computer science, mathematics, engineering, and neurophysiology. Together, these are referred to as cognitive science. Finally, the third major organizing principle for cognitive psychologists is the adoption of strict positivistic methods of observation and measurement so that research in cognitive psychology is laboratory based. By 1975, psychology is clearly heading in the direction of cognitive science.

COMPARATIVE PSYCHOLOGY

By about 1950, there are two separate fields in the study of animal behavior: ethology and animal psychology (Dewsbury, 1978).

Ethology

Those engaged in ethological study are typically European and usually trained as zoologists. Their methods of study concentrate on the description of sets of behaviors in natural habitats. They observe a wide variety of animal species from paramecia, insects, and birds, to all kinds of mammals. The questions that concern ethologists have to do first with evolution, or trying to understand the effects of natural selection on shaping behaviors. Second, ethologists seek to understand the function that behavior plays in the ability of organisms to adapt to the environment and to changes in the environment. During this era, ethologists look for instincts, or what they call **"fixed action patterns"** of behavior, in each species that explain why each species behaves as it does in its environment.

Animal Psychology

Animal psychologists, on the other hand, are typically found in North America and have usually received their education in the field of psychology. In fact, they are the same scientists found in experimental psychology laboratories. They accept Edward Thorndike's assertion that the principles of learning are the same across all species and in all situations (Thorndike, 1911). This allows them to conduct their studies in carefully controlled settings in laboratories. Animal psychologists expect to find a set of general laws or principles of learning that apply across all species in all settings. Thus, they look first for the immediate cause of behavior, meaning the stimulus that caused the response. Second, they look for how experiences across the life-span of the individual organism have shaped behaviors.

Interactions

The study of both ethology and animal psychology as separate disciplines peaks in the early 1950s, and most interactions between them are quite contentious (Dewsbury, 1978). Scientists within each discipline believe they are focusing on the questions that will eventually provide the most complete answers as to why behaviors occur. As research continues, however, anomalies appear that throw doubt on each of these paradigms.

Ethological studies find that fixed action patterns, or instincts, are often inadequate to explain the behaviors being observed. Instead, organisms are seen changing behaviors in response to changes in the environment. The environment thus provides something like feedback to the organism, which results in a change in behavior that allows for adaptation. An assumption that behavior occurs as a result of fixed action patterns leaves no room for the ongoing changes in behavior in response to a dynamic environment called learning.

Animal psychologists also find that they often cannot identify the stimulus that caused the behavior or that a single stimulus alone is often not adequate to explain the behavior. For example, psychologists attempting to operantly condition some animals have only partial success and see some animals engaging in behavior patterns that are never reinforced. Often, these behaviors seem specific to the species of animal being observed. Psychologists and animal trainers, Marian and Keller Breland, for example, report that their trained raccoons, after being conditioned to put coins into a piggy bank, begin rubbing the coins together before putting them into the bank in species-typical washing behavior. The Brelands are both students of B. F. Skinner and are trained in the radical behaviorist tradition, but they conclude that explanations for behavior that rely on learning alone do not adequately take into account the organism's "instinctive patterns, evolutionary history, and ecological niche" (Breland & Breland, 1961, p. 684). The animal, it seems, is not an "empty organism" after all.

✓ Stop and think.

If you give rats flavored water to drink and later they get sick, how soon after drinking the water do the rats have to get sick for them to learn not to drink that water?

Equally disturbing to animal psychologists, and equally ignored at the time, are the findings of aversion learning by psychologist John Garcia. Garcia and Koelling (1966) find that if rats receive a warning signal while drinking water and are immediately given a foot shock, they will avoid the water again when the warning signal is presented. This finding is consistent with those of many other behaviorists. But Garcia and his colleagues also find that if rats drink flavored water and are then exposed to radiation, causing them to become nauseated about one half hour later, they will refuse, in the future, to drink the flavored water. Furthermore, rats learn not to drink the flavored water again in only one trial. Animal psychologists have previously reported that rats need immediate contiguity between stimulus and response before an association will be formed and that several trials are necessary before learning will occur. Thus, Garcia's finding that rats learn flavored water will make them sick one half hour later, and learning this in only one trial, are ignored by his senior colleagues. Journals in Garcia's field even refuse to publish his findings (P. Worden, personal communication, April 25, 2003).

As if this is not enough to get Garcia into trouble among established psychologists, he includes two other conditions in his study. One group of rats is made sick one half hour after drinking unflavored water. Another group receives the foot shock while drinking flavored water (without the warning light). Garcia reports that neither of these groups learns to avoid the water.

✓ Stop and think.

How do you explain why rats learn to avoid flavored, but not unflavored, water after they get sick? How do you explain why rats avoid unflavored water paired with a warning signal after receiving a foot shock, but do not avoid flavored water after receiving a foot shock?

Garcia and his colleagues argue that they have found evidence for two separate learning systems in the rat, one for learning about events in the external world, such as happens in operant conditioning chambers, and one for learning about internal events, such as illness and taste. Garcia suggests that although laboratory rats studied by the behaviorists may be able to get by with only the first learning system, rats living in the real world need both systems to live as rats (Garcia & Koelling, 1966).

✓ **Stop and think.**

If rats need these two learning systems, what and how many learning systems might humans need?

Both animal psychologists and ethologists come under criticism for their methods. Ethologists are charged with too often anthropomorphizing the animal behavior they observe and with a general lack of control and experimental rigor in their research. Animal psychologists are criticized for their very narrow focus on learning in rats in sterile laboratories. The importance and usefulness in understanding complex animal behavior from the results of their studies of very isolated behaviors are criticized.

Integration and Synthesis

By the mid-1970s, these two fields have begun to merge and, with input from a variety of disciplines, a new set of questions is put forward. These questions are first about proximal causes of behavior, such as stimuli in the immediate environment and the developmental history of the organism under study. Second, they are about more distal causes of behavior, such as the organism's evolutionary history and the function that the observed behavior plays in helping the organism adapt to its environment. These questions thus set the agenda for comparative psychology through the end of this century (Dewsbury, 1978).

DEVELOPMENTAL PSYCHOLOGY

By the 1950s, developmental concerns are focused on the origins and consequences of individual differences and changes across time. Furthermore, interest has shifted from an emphasis on physical maturation to an emphasis on social and emotional development. Piaget's theories about how knowledge is organized and new information is assimilated into existing knowledge structures has increasing importance in developmental studies. The major areas of study in developmental psychology from about 1950 to about 1975 regard questions about attachment, theories of social learning, and ideas about how individual differences in temperament might influence the development of personality.

Attachment and Loss

World War II leaves thousands of orphans throughout Europe, especially in England, where children were often sent to live in foundling homes in the countryside during the aerial bombardment of London. What impact does being left parentless have on the development of an infant's personality? Given that most normal infants become attached to their caregivers, what is the function of this attachment? These are the questions that attachment theorists, most notably Canadian psychologist Mary Salter Ainsworth (1913–1999) and Englishman John Bowlby (1907–1990), tackle in the early years after the war.

From psychoanalytic theory, these researchers adopt the idea that an infant's attachment to its caregiver forms as a result of the dynamics of infant–caregiver interactions. Optimal outcome is predicted by a sensitive caregiver, one who responds appropriately to the infant's bids for attention. The sensitive caregiver's responses in times of need soothe the infant, organize the infant's emotional state, and teach the infant important self-management skills (Bowlby, 1969).

According to Ainsworth, when an infant has formed a secure attachment to its caregiver and the attachment figure is available, the infant is more likely to actively explore the environment. Exploration maximizes opportunities for learning and finding resources. Thus, the infant who forms a secure attachment is more likely to survive and prosper, so attachment has been selected for in evolution. Attachment is also interpreted through Hull's drive reduction model of learning, in which the drive to maintain an optimal level of alert attention and to avoid disorganizing emotional states may be satisfied by contact with an attachment figure.

Ainsworth's detailed in-home observational studies reveal significant differences in maternal sensitivity and responsiveness to infant bids for attention. Months later, in her innovative "strange situation" laboratory assessment, infants of more responsive mothers do indeed demonstrate more secure attachments to their mothers (Ainsworth, 1983).

Social Learning Theory

Social learning theorists are concerned with the influence of the social environment on shaping behavior and personality. Their questions derive initially from a combination of traditional Hullian learning theory, in which behaviors are viewed as directed toward the reduction of primary drives, and psychoanalytic interests in the dynamics of parent–child interactions. For example, learning theorists argue that attachment to a caregiver is only a secondary or acquired drive that results from the reduction of primary drives. In other words, the child becomes attached to the caregiver because the caregiver provides food and thus becomes associated with the satisfaction of the primary drive of hunger.

However, social learning theorists do not believe that stimulus–response learning theory, either Hullian or Skinnerian, adequately explains how children come to internalize the values, attitudes, and behaviors of their cultures. These theorists are especially concerned with how children learn acceptable expressions of aggression, appropriate sex-role behaviors, and the ability to regulate their own behavior. There is little evidence, they contend, that behaviors in these domains are either subject to the pressures of drive reduction or shaped in successive approximations. Instead, watching accepted models is a significantly more efficient way to learn these social behaviors. The acquisition of language, for example, is better explained by observational learning and imitation than by successive approximations.

Social learning theorists of this era, like Pauline Sears (1908–1993) and Robert Sears (1908–1989), initially focus on the parents as the most potent models for observational learning. Research reveals that children are more likely to imitate the behavior of models they like and respect (Sears, Pintler, & Sears, 1946). As a result, variables, such as parental warmth, discipline style, and permissiveness, become important in the agendas of these researchers. Later, Albert Bandura (1925–) and his colleagues discover that television is another social influence and is at least as powerful a model as are parents. Children are as likely, if not more likely, to imitate and learn from behavior they see on television as they are to learn from parents (Grusec, 1994).

In 1973, social learning theorist Diana Baumrind publishes the results of her studies comparing parenting styles and child outcome measures among nursery school children. She finds significant relationships between warm versus cold and permissive versus strict parenting styles and children's independence, sociability, and self-control (Baumrind, 1973). According to this research, parents and parenting styles appear to have a major influence on the development of children's personalities. Social learning theory plays an important role in increasing interest in theories about social cognition and the growth of cognitive psychology.

✓ **Stop and think.**
If child outcome can be predicted from parenting style, wouldn't all children from the same family turn out more or less the same? Do they?

However, like all learning theories, social learning theory begins to decline in influence toward the end of the 1970s. This is partly because the importance of observational learning is widely acknowledged by this time. *No study conducted today would purport to explain childhood outcome variables without taking into account the models to which the children have been exposed.* The decline in interest in learning theories must also be attributed to the increasing recognition of the importance of variables internal to the child and the part played by the child in the dynamic relationship between parent and child.

The Dangers of Too Little Mother Love:
The Story of Harry Harlow's Infant Monkeys

Trained as a traditional behaviorist, the psychologist Harry Harlow wonders about a psychological science that does not ask questions about love. When he attends graduate school, love is not a variable studied by psychologists and, in fact, the word itself is suspect. Organisms may "seek proximity," an observable behavior; but feelings, like love, are best left to the poets.

According to the behaviorists, whatever attachment a young organism, including a young human, may feel for its caregiver is simply a secondary consequence of drive reduction. The caregiver provides food, reducing the hunger drive, and thus becomes associated with the satisfaction of hunger. According to psychoanalysts, attachment to the one who feeds is secondary to the oral gratification provided by the act of sucking. But, Harlow asks, might the feeling of love be a primary motivator? How would one test that question?

After several years of working with infant monkeys and many hours of conversation among psychologists, graduate students, and others who work with the monkeys, Harlow's research team devises a way to test their hypothesis that a young monkey's attachment to its mother is not based either on food or oral satisfaction. They fashion surrogate monkey mother bodies from wire and terry cloth that allow them to manipulate the variables in question (Blum, 2002). Their findings surprise scientists, but not mothers. According to Harlow's findings, infant monkeys have a primary need for "contact comfort" and they will form an attachment to a terry cloth surrogate mother that provides this soft contact, even when food is provided by the wire monkey mother. Much like Ainsworth's securely attached human infants, monkey infants who have the soft surrogate are more likely to explore their environments and will return to the soft surrogate for contact when frightened or stressed.

Infant monkeys who are fed and well cared for but never allowed to have contact with a comforting soft surface present a very different and very sad picture. Huddled miserably on the wire floor of the cage, they shiver uncontrollably when frightened. They lose weight, are not responsive to gentle attention, and they sometimes die (Harlow, 1958).

The research from Harlow's laboratory, along with that of Bowlby, Ainsworth, and others, revolutionizes the care of children in institutions. Based primarily on Watson's assertion that cuddling and physical contact would lead to emotionally dependent children, policy in most institutions has been to minimize contact with infants and children. Even when a child must be admitted to hospital, parents are encouraged cheerfully but quickly to say goodbye, then leave the child alone, visiting only occasionally. As evidence about the emotional harm caused by these methods mounts, however, policies are changed. There are dangers of too little mother love.

In 1946, Dr. Benjamin Spock publishes *Baby and Child Care*, in which he argues that parents, not psychologists, are the experts when it comes to caring for children. Parents should thus trust themselves. They should cuddle with their children if they wish, feed babies when they seem to be hungry instead of when the clock says it is time, and reason with children, explaining rules instead of simply demanding obedience. The book is a runaway best seller for decades to follow.

✓ **Stop and think.**

Is it ethical to deprive a healthy infant monkey of contact with its mother, leave it isolated in a wire cage, or allow it to have no contact with others, just to see how the infant reacts? Is that ethical if knowledge is gained, or if it helps humans? Under what conditions would such a study be ethical?

Temperament

By the 1960s, some psychologists are beginning to question the assumption that learning is entirely responsible for shaping personality. Parents know that, even from the beginning, babies play active roles in shaping both their environments and the relationships that develop with their caregivers. In 1963, psychologists Alexander Thomas (1914–2003) and Stella Chess (1914–) and their colleagues publish the findings of a multiyear study of infant temperament. **Temperament** is defined as "biologically determined innate characteristics" of personality (Thomas, Chess, Birch, Hertzig, & Korn, 1963). These researchers find individual differences in the temperaments of infants who show significant interactive relationships with environmental variables. For example, some infants cry more readily than others and are difficult to soothe. If these irritable infants are paired with easily irritated parents (which they are very likely to be, because infant characteristics are influenced by genetic inheritance), the outcome is not likely to be good. Temperament research is the modern exploration of the influence of interactions between biological and environmental variables on personality.

SOCIAL PSYCHOLOGY

Throughout its history, social psychology is closely tied to a number of other disciplines. For example, in 1935, psychologist Muzafer Sherif (1906–1988) provides a demonstration of the influence of the social environment on perception. If research participants are put into a room that is totally dark except for one small light and asked to focus on the light, they perceive the light to be moving around, even though it is actually stationary. This effect is caused by small movements in the neck and eye muscles, the "autokinetic effect" (Sherif, 1935). But if participants are put into the same room with several confederates of the researcher, and if the confederates report that they see the light moving in a particular direction, the research participants will report that they perceive the light moving in that same direction. Perception is shaped by what the participants think others are perceiving (Sherif, 1935).

✓ **Stop and think.**
What implications do the findings regarding perception have for understanding how opinions are influenced by the presence of others?

The Zeitgeist

Social psychology's research themes are more closely tied to the social and political zeitgeist than are those in other disciplines (Jones, 1998). This is exemplified by the founding in 1936 of the Society for the Psychological Study of Social Issues. During the 1950s and 1960s, social research focuses on understanding how the German people and their military could have been persuaded to participate in Hitler's plan for world domination. Research is conducted on sthe characteristics, leadership styles, and power of "authoritarian" personalities. Social psychologists examine **social facilitation effects**, in which people can be persuaded to engage in behaviors with others that they would never engage in when alone. And the limits of individuals' resistance to authority are tested in Stanley Milgram's famous study of obedience (Milgram, 1963). Milgram's finding that ordinary people will deliver painful, even deadly, electrical shocks to an innocent person if told to do so by an authority is profoundly disturbing to many.

When the United States is rocked by Senator Joseph McCarthy's House Un-American Activities Committee's hearings implicating the loyalty of thousand of citizens, the fear of communism grips the country. This culminates in 1953 in the execution of Julius and Ethel Rosenberg, a young couple alleged, on very flimsy evidence, to be spies. Social psychologists turn their research toward questions of conformity. They try to understand how suspicion and paranoia can be propagated across an entire nation and to explain the power of the social group to enforce conformity by rejecting people who express opinions that are different.

In 1964, 28-year-old Kitty Genovese is attacked by a knife-wielding assailant while walking toward her apartment in New York City. According to newspaper reports, she screams for help, and several neighbors look out their windows, but no one comes to her aid or even calls the police. Mortally wounded, Genovese crawls into the lobby of a nearby building and dies. Later, social psychologists conduct numerous studies to try to understand why and when bystanders will intervene to help a person in need. They also focus attention on questions related to urban alienation and the psychological effects of living in crowded, impersonal environments.

During the Cold War, when disarmament is a concern, social psychologists become interested in how people judge risk, how much they are willing to risk in order to win, and how they negotiate satisfactory solutions to disagreements with others. In 1961, Muzafer and Carolyn Sherif and their colleagues publish the results of the "Robber's Cave" study. This study demonstrates how easy it is to create factional competitive groups within an initially similar population and tests how far an "in-group" will go to destroy an "out-group." The studies also show that competition between warring groups can be decreased by the introduction of a common goal (Sherif, Harvey, White, Hood, & Sherif, 1961).

The business climate of the 1960s and 1970s draws social psychologists' interests to individual differences in achievement motivation. The civil rights movement and racial strife prompt questions about police brutality. In 1971, Philip Zimbardo conducts his prison simulation study, demonstrating how assigned power can negatively influence interactions between former peers. The Surgeon General's 1964 report that smoking causes cancer means smokers must either quit or find a way to convince themselves that continuing to smoke makes sense. Throughout the 1970s, Leon Festinger's research into **cognitive dissonance** dominates much of social psychological research. He and his colleagues are concerned with how the dilemma is resolved when behaviors are not consonant with beliefs (Festinger, 1957).

Social Statistics and Research Designs

Research in social psychology often measures more variables and uses more subjects than a typical operant chamber conditioning study with rats. Analyses of variance are required to examine the data in studies measuring multiple variables. These complex statistics help to interpret the main and interaction effects found in social psychology's multifactorial designs (Harris, 1985). Developments in statistics proceed in a reciprocal relationship with the creation of complex research designs.

By the mid-1960s, social psychologists are also discovering that productive research into many of their questions requires manipulating or deceiving subjects. The 1962 study of the determinants of emotional states by Stanley Schachter and

Jerome Singer is a good example of this research. Emotions are often assumed to be more or less automatic and also to represent important internal truths. Thus, decisions based on intense emotions are bound to be correct. For example, individuals who get nervous and jumpy every time they think about going to a party may decide on the basis of those feelings not to go to the party. Going to the party must not be "right." The Schachter and Singer study challenges the truth of that common assumption. In this study, subjects are brought into the laboratory and, after being deceived into believing that they are participating in a study on the effects of vitamin injections on vision, are injected with a mild dose of epinephrine. Epinephrine is a naturally occurring hormone that typically results in mild heart palpitations, tremors, sometimes flushing of the face, and accelerated breathing. After waiting a brief period for the effects of the epinephrine to be felt, research confederates enter the room and exhibit either joyful or angry emotions. Despite the fact that all subjects experience the same symptoms of physiological arousal caused by the epinephrine, their emotional states turn out to be highly dependent on whether they are exposed to a joyful or an angry confederate. In the absence of any other explanation for their physiological arousal, subjects assume their heart palpitations, flushed face, and accelerated breathing are the result of internal feelings of joy or anger. By deceiving these subjects and giving them an injection, Schachter and Singer manipulate their subjects' emotional states, but they also discover something important and interesting about how emotions can be influenced by thoughts and physiological states. The finding that there is a cognitive component to the experience of emotion poses a serious challenge to common assumptions about the origin of emotions (Schachter & Singer, 1962).

Ethics in Research

Schachter and Singer could not have conducted this research without deceiving the subjects. Is what they learn important enough to justify deceiving the subjects and injecting them with a psychoactive substance? By this time, medical review boards have been established to approve the ethics and justifiability of research designs in medicine, where invasive procedures are often used. Their criterion for approval of a proposed study is to weigh the importance of what might be learned against the level of potential harm caused to the subjects. In 1925, the APA adopted the American Medical Association regulations on the use of animals in experiments. Since 1953, the APA has also included in its statement of members' ethical responsibilities a section detailing experimenters' responsibilities to human research subjects. These responsibilities include the removal of experimentally induced distress.

In the early 1960s, the ethics of studies like Schachter's and Singer's, and especially Milgram's 1963 study of obedience, are criticized (see Baumrind, 1964). Festinger's studies, in which subjects are deliberately put into dissonant cognitive states, are among many where subjects are promised rewards they never receive,

threatened with physically uncomfortable procedures, or caused to make disturbing decisions, all in the interest of furthering research interests. APA guidelines
encourage researchers to remove the distress induced by studies such as these.

✓ **Stop and think.**
Is it really possible fully to remove the effects of this distress? If subjects
are deceived during the study, will they believe the researcher later when
told that it was all a deception? What will their attitudes toward researchers,
or science in general, be in the future?

In the early 1970s, APA guidelines regarding the use of deception in psychological research are updated. The new principles, published in 1973, consider all deception and passive withholding of information ethically questionable. Researchers
are required to explain to subjects what will happen during their participation
and allow them to withdraw if they wish. After collecting data, the researchers
must explain the true purpose of the research to the subjects and must remove all
misconceptions.

✓ **Stop and think.**
Is it ethical to induce high levels of anxiety in students by requiring them
to write difficult course examinations? Is long-term damage to their self-
esteem caused by assigning grades and comparing their performance to that
of other students? Stanley Milgram asks these questions when confronted
with ethical questions about his experiments on obedience (Blass, 1996).

Kurt Lewin argues that part of the mission of a social psychologist is to go into
the world outside the laboratory for the purpose of causing social change and building a better world. The research programs engaged in by the social psychologists
in the decades after World War II are directed at illuminating aspects of human
social interactions and the influence of the social environment on individuals.

Psychologists Change the World

When the United States Supreme Court prepares to write its historic 1954
Brown v. the Board of Education decision against school segregation,
developmental psychologists Mamie and Kenneth Clark are in a unique
position to provide the research evidence that the Court uses in support
of its decision. The Clarks have carefully documented the negative effects
of racial segregation on the identities and self-esteem of African American
children. Educated themselves in segregated institutions and among the

tiny cadre of African Americans admitted to graduate study in all-White universities, both Clarks receive their doctorates from Columbia University. Mamie Clark writes, "My husband was the first black graduate student to earn a Ph.D. in the psychology department [at Columbia] (in 1940) and in 1943 I was the second and last" (Clark, 1983, p. 270).

Collecting data in both northern and southern states and in urban and rural locations, the Clarks find that African American children become aware of their racial identity at about 3 years of age and simultaneously acquire a negative self-image. The Clarks attribute this decline in self-image to "negative attitudes" toward Americans of African descent in the surrounding White culture (Clark & Clark, 1947, p. 175). They view school desegregation as a first and necessary corrective step, as does the Supreme Court. For the remainder of their professional lives, the Clarks devote themselves to efforts to "securing the self-esteem of children of color" (Lal, 2002, p. 20) and provide services to improve the lives of all minority children in the United States. Kenneth Clark also writes extensively on the effects of racism on both minority and White children. In increasingly pessimistic terms through the 1960s and 1970s, he writes on the status of race relations in the United States (Keppel, 2002; see also Jackson, 2000; Scott, 1997).

THE HUMANISTIC/EXISTENTIAL MOVEMENT

During the 1960s and 1970s, approaches to personality theory and clinical psychology based on humanistic and existential philosophies appear. The organizing principles of the humanistic/existential movement stand in sharp contrast to behaviorism and psychoanalysis. At the time of the emergence of the humanistic movement in the 1950s, however, the contrast is not so evident. For example, the basic tenets of humanistic psychology echo many earlier themes. William James' interest in the role of experience in understanding psychology, the importance of the self, and his holistic view of consciousness are all precursors to humanistic ideas. Franz Brentano's emphasis on the phenomena of consciousness in shaping experience and meaning is reflected in Soren Kierkegaard's 19th-century existential philosophy and even later in the philosophy of existentialist Martin Heidegger (1889–1976). Heidegger's psychological speculations focus on understanding how individuals bring meaning to their lives. Most people, he says, tend to plod through life behaving as they are expected to behave and thus living **"inauthentic lives."** Anxiety keeps them from choosing an "authentic life," one more in keeping with their own inner values (Heidegger, 1927). All of these themes are reflected in the humanistic movement. Finally, the psychoanalyst Carl Jung (1875–1961) uses the concept of self as a major organizing principle of his theory and refers to the development of the self as a primary goal in life (Jung, 1933). These ideas become central concepts in the humanistic movement.

Reasons for Humanistic Theory

The reasons for the appearance of the humanistic movement in the middle of the 20th century in North America usually include disenchantment with the narrowness of behaviorism and with the focus in psychoanalytic theory on "crippled" psyches. Because the humanistic movement is viewed as an alternative to these two major forces in the field, it is referred to as "third force" psychology. In its original formulations, the humanistic movement is concerned not with replacing behaviorism or psychoanalysis but with expanding the scope of what should be considered in the search for the answers to psychology's questions.

Basic Tenets

The beliefs of those who adopt a humanistic approach fall into these categories:

1. Psychology should seek to understand life experiences that are unique to humans. The human is an experiencing person, not a rat, not even merely a behaving organism.
2. An individual's subjective reality, the way that individual thinks reality really is, is of prime importance in understanding motivations. For example, most people experience themselves as having free will. Therefore, their subjective reality includes the experience of free will.
3. Whole meaningful problems faced by real humans should be the focus of study. Psychologists should develop and be willing to use a wide variety of methods to study these problems and not limit their studies because of adherence to a preferred method.
4. The scope of humanistic study must include seeking to understand human dignity, helping all individuals achieve their full potential, and the search for meaning in life.

Humanistic Psychology as Personality Theory

The man who names humanistic psychology in 1954, Abraham Maslow (1908–1970), is trained as a behaviorist and completes his doctorate in Harry Harlow's primate lab at the University of Wisconsin. The theory of personality that Maslow offers in his 1954 book, *Motivation and Personality*, bears many similarities to a Hullian drive-reduction theory of motivation. Maslow views the human experience as holistic, dynamic, and purposive. His theory of motivation and personality development takes the shape of a hierarchy. Maslow speculates that individuals are motivated to meet their needs in a set of ascending categories.

Maslow's Hierarchy of Needs
Self-actualization
Need to feel competent and esteemed by others
Social needs
Physical safety
Physiological needs

Physiological needs, such as the need for sleep, water, and food, must be met first before the individual can think about anything else. Once these needs are met, the need for physical safety from pain or injury, the elements, or any other danger becomes the organizer of behavior. After safety needs are minimally met, social needs, such as the need for love, to belong, and to share one's life with others takes precedence. Maslow speculates that unfulfilled needs for love and affection constitute the most common reason for psychological problems. This is the level where most people remain. If all of the prior needs have been adequately met, then the need to feel competent, to feel useful, and to be able to respect oneself, as well as the need to feel respected and esteemed by others, becomes the primary focus. People working at this level seek a sense of self-worth and recognition by others of their accomplishments.

Finally, for the rare individual who has met all of these needs, the major organizing principle of life becomes the need to self-actualize. Self-actualization is the process whereby individuals seek to realize their full potential. This is different for each individual. Scientists, such as the Gestalt psychologist Max Wertheimer and the cultural anthropologist Ruth Benedict, make significant and meaningful contributions to science. Humanitarians like Albert Schweitzer or Jane Addams achieve success in the field of providing service to those in need. Poets like Ralph Waldo Emerson or Walt Whitman write superior poetry. Maslow is able to identify only a few people who he believes are working on self-actualization. They are people who perceive reality accurately but still maintain a healthy sense of nondeprecating humor. They accept themselves and others but maintain social ties with only a few. Their outlook retains a sense of wonder and excitement. They seek to know themselves, maintain a strong sense of being inner-directed, and reject meaningless social conventions. They conduct their lives as though to fulfill a destiny or mission without regard to the constraints imposed by the external world.

Maslow rejects the behaviorists' goal of predicting and controlling behavior. Instead, the goals for humanistic psychologists strongly reflect Western cultural values of independence and self-determination. They wish to practice a psychology that will release individuals from external controls over their lives and make individuals freer, more creative, and more motivated by inner values. Maslow's ideas are appealing to many but, as the next chapter reveals, they do not hold up well under scientific scrutiny.

Humanistic Psychology as Therapy

As a form of psychotherapy, the humanistic approach is one of the first serious challenges to Freudian psychoanalysis. Humanistic therapists are not concerned with uncovering unconscious motivations, identifying unresolved conflicts, getting patients to conform to social expectations, or to engage in a process of adjustment. Humanistic therapists like psychologist Carl Rogers (1902–1987) argue that therapies that label patients with a diagnosis or that try to fix them will only prevent patients from taking responsibility for their own growth.

Instead, humanistic approaches to therapy begin by respecting individuals, now referred to as "clients," and their subjective reality. The root of clients' problems can only be found in their own subjective reality. Humanistic therapists maintain an optimistic view of human nature, believing that individuals are not motivated mainly by selfishness but are growth-oriented and seek to exercise their own power to help themselves. As Rogers argues, if an open, honest, and caring relationship can be established between client and therapist, and if the therapist can maintain an atmosphere of unconditional positive regard toward the client and the client's subjective reality, then the client will achieve more healthy functioning. Humanistic counseling techniques are focused on helping healthy individuals achieve more of their potential.

Carl Rogers is widely respected in both therapeutic and scientific circles, in part because of his efforts to bring scientific methods to the therapeutic setting. One example is his series of studies on the effectiveness of therapy. According to Rogers, individuals who present themselves for therapy feel a discrepancy between the self they feel they should be, the "ideal" self, and the self that they really are, the "real" self. Rogers and his colleague Rosalind Dymond use a "Q-sort" technique in which clients sort a stack of about 100 cards, each bearing a single self-descriptive statement. The client must first sort the cards to form a representation of the attributes of the ideal self. Then they sort the cards into a representation of the real self. Theoretically, as therapy proceeds, the discrepancy between these two views of self decreases. The decrease in this discrepancy thus may be used as a measure of the progress and effectiveness of therapy (Rogers & Dymond, 1954).

✓ **Stop and think.**
When reading over the description of the Q-sort technique, did you assume that the goal of both client and therapist is to help the client become more like the ideal self?

The goal of therapy, according to Rogers, is not to become the ideal self. In fact, the ideal self represents all of the external world's demands about how we should be. The goal of therapy is to eliminate these external pressures and to come to know fully and accept a real self that is inner-valued and whose choices and actions reflect internal values and beliefs.

The Fate of the Humanistic Movement

The humanistic movement has influenced mostly applied psychology, especially counseling techniques, in educational settings, and child-rearing advice. Even in these areas, there is no one approach that can exclusively be labeled humanistic. Many of the terms used by humanistic therapists have high face validity and popular appeal. Who would not want to be the recipient of unconditional positive regard? Who wants to lead an inauthentic life? The problem is that there is no clear definition or agreement as to the meaning of those terms. Without agreed on definitions, coherent theories, or testable hypotheses, the humanistic movement remains more a philosophy than a psychological science.

Perhaps for this reason, or maybe because the optimistic zeitgeist of the mid-1960s dissolves by the end of the decade, the humanistic movement lost what little influence it had over academic mainstream psychology. However, humanistic predictions that marital bliss is achievable, that it is possible to raise happy children, and that personal and professional dreams may be fulfilled by applying the innate potential for growth and self-actualization continue to have a major impact on popular culture and the self-help movement. These promises have also left many people disillusioned and disappointed. If the goal of the humanistic movement is to release individuals from external controls over their lives and to make individuals freer, more creative, and more motivated by inner values, then its promise is still waiting to be fulfilled.

CLINICAL PSYCHOLOGY

Like all wars, World War II takes a terrible psychological toll on the victors as well as the vanquished, on combatants and civilians alike. Returning Allied soldiers present themselves at hospitals for psychological care in record numbers, and that is just the beginning. The ink is barely dry on Japan's surrender before the Cold War and continuing threats of the further use of atomic and nuclear weapons instills the fear of imminent destruction in everyone's mind. It is ironic that the citizens of the only country ever to have used atomic weapons against humans, the United States, are the very ones who should suffer this fear so intensely.

By 1960, competition for enrollment in clinical psychology graduate programs is fierce, and most students are pursuing the degree because they hope to become psychotherapists (Reisman, 1991). Clinical training programs are rushed into place at many universities across North America to help fill the demand for psychotherapists. Clinicians are trained, but there is no agreement on what causes mental illness, what constitutes effective therapy, or how to determine when a cure has been achieved.

Defining Personality

Tests for Intellectual Functioning

Intelligence testing continues unabated throughout this era. Factor analytic studies of intelligence tests continue to reveal a variety of factors, and the idea becomes more popular that there must be different kinds of intelligence. This forms the basis for educational tracking, so that secondary and even primary students across North America are assigned into academic or vocational tracks based on the results of these tests. Some psychologists, like Anne Anastasi (1908–2001), continue to argue that intelligence scores result from an interaction of both genetic and environmental influences (Anastasi, 1958), but educators apparently assume that the intelligence die has already been cast by the time students enter school.

The influence of physiological factors on intelligence and school performance is also beginning to be recognized. Down syndrome, for example, is found to be the result of a metabolic abnormality. Certain types of "learning disabilities" or "dyslexia" are associated with brain dysfunction.

Diagnostic Tests for Mental Illness

The Minnesota Multiphasic Personality Inventory (MMPI) is a test of personality functioning developed using factor analytic techniques. The MMPI asks for responses to a large set of potential self-descriptors and compares an individual's responses to those of previously identified normal and pathological norming groups. Projective tests also continue to be popular for understanding personality and revealing pathologies in mental functioning. Tests like the Rorschasch inkblots and the Thematic Apperception Test are still widely used to elicit responses that might reveal unconscious thoughts.

✓ **Stop and think.**
What would a mentally healthy person say about an inkblot? In other words, how is "normal" defined by projective personality tests?

A variety of problems with these projective tests becomes apparent, not the least of which is that it is never clear what distinguishes the response of a normal person from that of a mentally ill person. Not only are the results not useful for diagnosing categories of mental illness, but the tests have no predictive validity either. The results of these tests do not predict who will benefit from therapy

(Zax & Klein, 1960) or even what sort of therapy to provide. Carl Rogers claims that the tests hinder therapy by putting the emphasis on the therapist knowing clients, when it is really the clients who should be knowing themselves. Later studies reveal that untrained novices or even a computer program (Kleinmuntz, 1967) are as able as fully trained clinical psychologists to interpret the results of these tests.

Causes of Mental Illness

By the mid-20th century, the disordered thinking that Kraepelin called dementia praecox has been renamed schizophrenia and remains among the most puzzling of the major mental illnesses. Psychologists generally assume that schizophrenia is the result of disturbed relationships in early childhood. Repeated childhood traumas that are being repressed, confusing and contradictory communication patterns, and other failures of the parent–child relationship are identified as probable causes. Infantile autism is also blamed on distant, punishing, and emotionally cold parents. The autistic child is typically delayed in verbal development, makes little eye contact, and engages in repetitive movement that may be self-damaging. Even parents who profess genuinely to love their children can cause these reactions, according to clinicians in the 1960s, because infants are capable of sensing the parents' hidden ambivalence. Children are victims of an irrational environment, where they are told they are loved but yet know that they are not (Bettelheim, 1967). Depression in all its forms and a wide variety of anxiety-related neuroses are also attributed to environmental influences.

As early as the mid-1950s, there are known to be physiological markers for some mental illness, including evidence for genetic-relatedness in schizophrenia. The zeitgeist, however, so strongly supports the learning model that any physical correlates of mental illness uncovered during this era are interpreted as effects that were caused by earlier failures in parenting and the learning environment.

Therapy

The Medical Model

As always, there are two tasks facing those who must deal with the mentally ill. First, the frequently disruptive behavior of the mentally ill must be controlled, and they must be prevented from harming themselves or others. Only after that is achieved will there be any hope of approaching the second task, that of finding a cure. The medical response to controlling behavior is to find a medical solution. At the beginning of the 1950s, electroshock and insulin-shock are still widely used in hospitals to control behavior. Some patients undergo "inhalation therapies" of carbon monoxide or ether. Lobotomies and other psychosurgeries are also conducted, but outcome studies show discouraging results, and the use of these techniques declines during this period.

In 1952, a root extract, **reserpine**, is found to calm institutionalized psychotic patients and make them more cooperative. In 1954, another drug, **chlorpromazine**, is found to reduce the disturbing hallucinations of schizophrenia. These drugs are relatively inexpensive and easy to administer. Almost overnight, hospital wards are transformed, as formerly difficult patients become quiet and manageable. The movement begins to stabilize patients on medications and release them to the care of their families or community mental health facilities. One after another, large public mental hospitals are closed and their patients sent away.

There is no claim that reserpine or chlorpromazine cures mental illness, only that symptoms are reduced. There are some serious side effects to the medications, and once released from the hospital, many patients refuse to continue to take the medications. Families and communities are ill-equipped to deal with the problems associated with this population, and before long, the homeless mentally ill become common sights on the streets of large cities across the United States. It is not until years later that studies reveal serious long-term and permanent consequences of taking these drugs.

It is not just psychotic patients who are taking psychoactive medications. In 1961, diazepam, under the trade name Valium, a powerful tranquilizer, appears on the market and quickly becomes the drug of choice for the treatment of depression and anxiety. Infamously, Miltown, another tranquilizer, commonly known as "mother's little helper," is prescribed to millions of housewives having trouble finding satisfaction and fulfillment in their roles as mothers and homemakers in the 1950s and 1960s. These drugs also have serious side effects and are found to be highly addictive. The psychoactive effects of many drugs are explored and one, lysergic acid diethylamide (LSD), is found that mimics some forms of psychoses. Initially, this drug is used in experiments to explore the neurological effects of psychosis in unsuccessful efforts to try to find a cure. Later, of course, LSD becomes a "street drug."

Children are not immune to drug prescription for the treatment of minor behavior problems (Reisman, 1991). The stimulant Ritalin begins to be given to children in the 1960s, when teachers or parents complain of children's high activity levels. Ritalin is still widely prescribed to children today, and its use remains very controversial.

The Psychological Model

In addition to drug treatment, a confusing plethora of psychotherapeutic techniques appears during this period. If failures in learning and early relationships have resulted in mental illness, then it stands to reason that a therapy that can correct those early psychological disappointments might alleviate mental illness. Psychodynamic therapies in which patients are regressed to childhood and Rogerian humanistic techniques are joined by many other treatments. Albert Ellis (1913–) uses a rational-emotive approach, encouraging patients to challenge the illogical assumptions that are making them miserable. George Kelly (1905–1967) advocates a fixed-role strategy, in which the therapist helps the patient identify and adopt a role to play for several weeks, both in and out of therapy, that will facilitate personality change (Kelly, 1955). Fritz Perls (1893–1970) leads a therapy movement, encouraging group participants to get in touch with their deepest feelings. Perls calls this Gestalt therapy, but it is not related to the Gestalt theories of perception and thinking discussed earlier.

These therapy movements spread across North America and move far from the traditional therapeutic settings. Kurt Lewin's work on group dynamics gives rise to "**t-groups,**" or training groups, where coworkers meet over several hours to share their real feelings about issues in the workplace and come to better understand both themselves and others in the group. A variety of "encounter group" strategies gain popularity. Often leaderless, groups of individuals are encouraged to break down the social barriers between them by expressing both positive and negative feelings freely. To facilitate the free release of feelings, participants are sometimes asked to stay awake and involved in the process for 24 to 48 hours at a time. Abraham Maslow interprets this interest in group encounters as a symptom of unfulfilled needs for affiliation. **Transactional analysis** (TA) theory suggests that interpersonal interactions are like games that people play, in which the roles of Parent, Child, or Adult are acted out. These are all part of an important social transformation that popularizes psychology and encourages the general public to think of themselves as experts in psychology. Everywhere people are urged to explore their "true" feelings, both conscious and unconscious. To "get in touch" with the unconscious, psychologist Timothy Leary advocates the use of drugs like LSD. By making people temporarily psychotic, he argues, these drugs can reveal hidden levels of the mind.

In the late 1960s, after decades of conforming to social conventions, most Americans over the age of 30 are wary of the message to "tune in, turn on, and drop out" but many of their children adopt it wholeheartedly. And in some way rather hard to describe, this message is interpreted by the popular culture as being rooted in psychology. Enrollments in undergraduate programs in psychology skyrocket.

The Effectiveness of Therapy

With all of these choices in therapy, questions about the effectiveness of therapy or the relative effectiveness of one type over another are inevitable. Numerous studies are conducted to make these comparisons. Nearly all of these studies, if conducted carefully, find that none of these therapies are very effective (Zax & Klein, 1960). For example, in 1952, Hans Eysenck publishes his survey blasting the effectiveness of psychotherapy. Although highly controversial, his study finds that neurotics receiving no treatment report more improvement in their symptoms than do neurotics after a course of therapy (Eysenck, 1952). Other studies find that humanistic therapies, which are significantly less expensive than psychoanalysis, are about as effective as talking to an empathic friend. Although individual anecdotal reports of the positive effects of almost any therapy are not hard to find, controlled scientific studies documenting effective psychotherapies are rare. These disappointing results influence insurance coverage for mental health care, but do not cause any decrease in the public's demand for services.

One conclusion that can be drawn by the end of this era is that advances in clinical psychology do not increase understanding or solve the problems of mental illness. Instead, these advances allow for a greater appreciation of the complexity of mental illnesses, along with causes and potential cures (Reisman, 1991).

Learning and the Myth of Mental Illness

In 1960, psychiatrist Thomas Szasz makes the argument that what is referred to as mental illness is either not mental or else it is not an illness. If it is an illness, then it is a physical illness, meaning an illness of the body. In that case, medical doctors should treat the illness using drug treatments, just as they do with other physical illnesses. If the problem really is mental, then it is not an illness but only a problem with learning. Some people have overwhelming problems in their lives. They need to be taught better strategies for coping with the problems they face. Everyone is occasionally confronted with more and bigger problems than they know how to deal with, so everyone could benefit from learning more effective coping strategies. According to Szasz, the concept of mental illness is a myth. Therapy is not about curing but is about teaching (Szasz, 1960). Although many agree that Szasz's argument has merit, he finds few advocates among psychotherapists.

⏱ The Times

The end of World War II marks the beginning of a long period of anticommunist fervor in the United States. In 1947, President Truman issues an executive order authorizing searches for the "infiltration of disloyal persons." Eventually, almost 7 million citizens in the United States are investigated, thousands lose jobs and livelihoods, detention camps have been reactivated (although not occupied), and two U.S. citizens are executed.

The manufacturing sector of the U.S. economy enjoys substantial growth, fed in large part by an increase in military spending and fueled by the atmosphere of fear. In 1950, military spending consumes about 30% of the federal budget, but by 1960, at a time when the country is at peace, this has increased to at least 50% of the budget. By 1962, the United States has more than enough nuclear weapons to destroy every major city in the world and more than all other countries in the world combined. This huge arsenal does not lead to a feeling of safety. Instead, American children are taught to "duck and cover" under their school desks for protection from enemy attack.

Not everyone enjoys the benefits of the booming economy. Throughout the 1920s, 1930s and 1940s, incidents of lynching against Americans of African descent increase. At the end of the war, many African Americans are forced to leave good jobs in defense plants to make room for returning White men. By the early 1950s, African Americans' outrage moves them to take action. In 1955, in Montgomery, Alabama, housekeeper Rosa Parks is arrested for sitting on a seat (at the front of the bus) that she paid for, and young Black Americans begin a nonviolent boycott of the Montgomery bus system. In 1960, they quietly take chairs reserved for White people in public restaurants and refuse to leave when they are not served. In 1964, White and Black college students board public buses and ride together through the South. They are arrested, beaten, and sometimes murdered for their offense. Federal civil rights laws are passed in 1957, 1960, 1964, 1965, and 1968, but very little changes. Unemployment for Blacks continues to be far worse than it is for Whites. By the summer of 1965, anger in urban ghettoes explodes into riots, repeated again in 1966 and 1967. In April 1968, Martin Luther King, Jr., is assassinated. By the following summer, many young Black males have been drafted and sent to the growing war in Vietnam. Both urban violence and this very active phase of the civil rights movement fade.

In 1963, Betty Friedan publishes *The Feminine Mystique.* A warning shot across the bow of complacent suburban society, the book is passed around neighborhoods from housewife to housewife. The revolutionary message of the book is that Freud was wrong, that not every normal adult woman feels completely fulfilled by cooking and cleaning for men and giving birth to and caring for children. Throughout the 1970s, the message spreads.

In California, small groups of migrant farm-workers try the same techniques of boycotts and nonviolent demonstrations used by Blacks in the South. Largely ignored by most labor unions, these workers achieve some success when laws regulating working and living conditions in the farm labor industry are passed, but their struggle continues, even today.

In June 1969, a small group of gay men and lesbians in New York City refuse to be persecuted by law enforcement any longer. Called the Stonewall riot, this marks the beginning of the gay rights movement. After decades of being beaten and arrested for offenses such as not wearing enough gender-appropriate clothing, gays and lesbians begin to fight back.

By late 1964, the United States is fully committed to waging war in the country of Vietnam.

From 1964 to 1972, the wealthiest and most powerful nation in the history of the world made a maximum military effort, with everything short of atomic bombs, to defeat a nationalist revolutionary movement in a tiny, peasant country—and failed. (Zinn, 1998, p. 213)

More than 50,000 young Americans die in the jungles of Vietnam, and several hundred thousand Southeast Asians are killed. Many more, Americans and Vietnamese, soldiers and civilians, are physically wounded and emotionally scarred, and no one is ever quite certain why. At home, millions are involved in what seem like largely futile efforts to stop the bloodshed. In May 1970, four unarmed students are shot and killed on the campus of Kent State University in Ohio for nonviolently protesting the war. Despite the fact that his political operatives are caught burglarizing Democratic headquarters, Richard Nixon is reelected president in 1972. Voter turnout among young White Americans declines to unprecedented levels.

12

The Mind Returns:
What Questions Are
Psychologists
Exploring Now?

If psychology at midcentury is a big house with many rooms, then at the end of the 20th century, the doors between the rooms are mostly opened to one another, and there are even conversations going on in the hallways between the rooms. What's more, psychologists are also chatting with the next-door neighbors, biologists; across the back fences with sociologists, anthropologists, and political scientists; and even with the engineers and computer scientists across the street. The purpose of this chapter is to explore current issues in cognitive, comparative, social, developmental, industrial/organizational, and clinical psychology. Recent developments in statistics are covered, and emerging domains, such as positive psychology, the psychology of women, and the psychology of religion, are also discussed. Throughout, we try to peer ahead to the future and think about where psychology may be headed.

FROM LEARNING TO COGNITION

As discussed previously, research reveals a number of anomalies that violate the assumptions of the behaviorist paradigm. These anomalies help to explain the shift in the last half of the century away from radical behaviorism. Animal behaviorists Keller and Marian Breland argue, for example, that three assumptions of the behaviorist paradigm are violated by their work in training animals. First, it is clearly not true "that the animal comes to the laboratory as a virtual tabula rasa" (Breland

& Breland, 1961, p. 684), or blank slate. Instead, important differences between individuals, even within the same species, are apparent. The reasons behind these individual differences are explored by the work of behavior geneticists, discussed later in the chapter. Second, the Brelands argue, it is also not true "that species differences are insignificant" (p. 684). Different species are motivated by, and react in different and species-specific ways to, similar environmental stimuli. Comparative psychologists explore these differences, and that work is also discussed later in the chapter. Finally, the Brelands conclude, it is not true "that all responses are about equally conditionable to all stimuli" (p. 684). The evidence gathered in their animal studies violates this assumption. Early information-processing models based on learning theory also leave many questions unanswered about mental states and strategies employed in learning and problem solving. In the view of linguists, behaviorism and learning theories also fail to explain the acquisition and use of language (Chomsky, 1972). The rise of cognitive psychology reflects, in part, the failure of learning theory to explain these anomalies.

Cognitive Science

Information-processing theory is compatible with most forms of behaviorism (Miller, 2003). Although it is true that information-processing theory posits the existence of unobservable mental events, the activities of the mind are limited to the input of discrete units of information, the sorting, storage, and retrieval of that information, and the output of observable behaviors. On the other hand, cognitive psychology toward the end of the century is seen by many as profoundly incompatible with the behaviorist paradigm.

The topics studied by cognitive psychologists are the same mental processes studied throughout most of the history of psychology, prior to the era of behaviorism. These include memory, learning, reasoning, problem solving, creativity, language, and other mental processes reflecting abstract thought. The gatekeeper into all of these mental processes is perception, so mechanisms of attention and perception are an important part of cognitive psychology.

If cognitive psychology in the 1980s can be said to operate as a paradigm, the assumptions of the paradigm include first, an assumption that there are organizing mental structures that allow humans to perceive and process information. A second assumption is that the individual plays an active role in the organization of information. Finally, cognitive psychologists share the empirical research methods of behaviorists, mostly rejecting theoretical speculation. Although the topics of interest for cognitive psychologists are unobservable mental events, their methods are objective and require observation and measurement. Cognitive psychology is interdisciplinary, readily forming links with the other social sciences, philosophy, linguistics, physics, engineering, and computer science. These interdisciplinary links are sometimes referred to together as **cognitive science**.

In the 1980s, cognitive psychologists generally fall into one of two camps. Many continue to pursue questions about abstract higher level mental processes, such as learning, memory, and motivation. Only now, instead of trying to identify the S-R units, they look for mental mechanisms that process incoming information and produce responses. Some of these cognitive psychologists work with other cognitive scientists to develop machine models of learning, pattern recognition, and other forms of artificial intelligence. Other psychologists, the neuroscientists, follow the Lashley and Hebb tradition and try to understand neurophysiology and neural activity.

Artificial Intelligence

Artificial intelligence (AI), the creation of mechanical models of thought, is an engineering branch of computer science focused on answering some of psychology's questions. During the last 30 years of the 20th-century, researchers in AI have worked primarily in two areas. Some of them develop machine models of human thinking, learning, and perceiving. The belief that machines can be built that will think the way humans think is referred to as **strong AI**. The goal for those who believe in strong AI is to build thinking machines for the purpose of understanding these processes in human mind. Others have been trying to develop machines that can perform some activities as well as or better than a human can. The belief that machines can be built that will perform some activity as well as a human but that machines will not ever "think" the way humans think is referred to as **weak AI**.

✓ **Stop and think.**
Can a computer be programmed to carry on a conversation with you that could not be distinguished from one you would have with another human, and would that be evidence that human mind is only a sophisticated program?

To build any machine, the task it will be required to accomplish must be representable as a series of operations. In the case of AI, the operations of the model must be computable, meaning that its operations must be written as a series of mathematical statements.

✓ **Stop and think.**
Can human thought be reduced to a series of mathematical statements? If so, can all of human thought be reduced in that way? If only some of human thought can be reduced to mathematical statements, what is it that cannot be reduced?

Thus, those working in AI must determine whether it is possible to represent human thought as a series of mathematical statements, and if so, whether there are limits to what can be represented in that way. Information-processing computational models of thinking and learning use the idea of a single computer, operating in a linear manner, to simulate how humans might process discrete units of information. Although this idea is interesting, it is not a very satisfactory explanation for complex human thought. Later theorists suggest a model using whole banks of computers operating parallel to one another. In addition, these computers interact with one another, so that the processing of information is distributed across computers. This complex model of information-processing is referred to as **parallel distributed processing**, or **connectionism.** Banks of computers operating in this parallel and distributed manner resemble nothing so much as mechanical schematics of physiological neural networks. For a time, it is thought that this connectionist computer modeling is the key to understanding learning in humans. By the end of the 20th century, however, many cognitive scientists have given up this idea.

The Chinese Room

In 1982, John Searle proposes an experiment to support his argument that just because a computer program could produce output that resembles what a human could produce, that does not mean that the computer is thinking. Imagine, suggests Searle, that you are locked in a room with boxes full of cards with Chinese symbols printed on them and a book of rules in English about when to choose which symbol. The rules say things like "the squiggle-squiggle sign is to be followed by the squoggle-squoggle sign." Someone outside the room passes a card under the door that shows the squiggle-squiggle sign. Your task is to look through the book for the appropriate rule and then pass back out the squoggle-squoggle sign in response. Suppose that, unknown to you, the signs are actually questions in Chinese, and if you follow the rules in the book, the signs you pass back are the answers to the questions. If you become very skilled at following the rules and knowing which sign to pass out in response to the ones you are given, you might even be able to respond as quickly as a native Chinese speaker. Those outside the room might think you actually understand Chinese, but you are really only following rules.

Searle's point is that you are only manipulating symbols without attaching any meaning to them. Furthermore, this is exactly what a computer does. A human, according to Searle, attaches meaning to symbols. He concludes that this thought experiment proves that human mind is more than a sophisticated computer program. As he says, "This simple observation will enable us to refute the thesis of mind as program" (Searle, 1982, p. 4).

What cognitive scientists discover is that inventions of the human mind, like games, or other rule-bound activities, are relatively easy to compute, but human mental operations, many of which may be largely unconscious, are difficult, if not impossible, to compute (M. Atkins, personal communication, April 3, 2003). This is the distinction that Gordon Ryle (1949) made between "knowing how" and "knowing that." Knowing *how* to win a game of chess is computable, but knowing *that* the chess pieces represent battling feudal armies is not.

It seems that the tasks that are easiest for human minds are the most difficult for computers. Many human mental functions do not operate in law-like ways as the associationists have long assumed. Thus, some suggest that the Master Program with which the human mind is programmed will never be written (Dennett, 1989), and there will never be a unified theory that explains all of human cognition (Papert, 1989). Isaac Newton thought God was a mathematician, and thus everything about humans would function according to mathematical laws. Biologists now understand that evolutionary pressures act more like an inventor who makes tiny changes in function until the thing functions well enough. The pressures to evolve stop when the organism works well enough to survive and reproduce. Thus, there is no reason to believe that all mental activity is governed by mathematical laws that are similar to the rules of chess.

Although there now appear to be limits to what is computable, the study of AI is making important strides in mimicking human activities. Machines are in use today that recognize and respond to human language. Devices for the blind, for example, can turn speech into written form, and other machines can turn the written word into spoken language. The limits of what can and cannot be computed are not yet known.

Neuroscience

Neuroscientists' goal is to explain thoughts, feelings, and behaviors in terms of neurological activity. Mental activity, even very abstract activity, such as imagination, is presumed to originate in the physiological functioning of the brain. Neuroscientists are concerned with how the various structures and systems of the brain work, including the roles played by whole brain structures and circuitry to individual neurons and even molecules. For neuroscientists, behavior is of no interest in and of itself, but is only a clue to what may be going on in the brain. Even the self "is not the infamous homunculus, a little person inside our brain perceiving and thinking about the images the brain forms. It is, rather, a perpetually re-created neurobiological state" (Damasio, 1994, p. 99).

Advances in measurement technology, including brain imaging, have had a profound impact on this field in the past 30 years. Today, neuroscientists are able to visualize the metabolic activity in a living brain at the very moment that information is being processed. Some of their discoveries can be made sense of in terms of whole brain systems, such as the finding that criminals incarcerated for committing murder are significantly more likely than nonhomicidal controls to show a measurable lack of functioning in the prefrontal cortex (Ishikawa & Raine, 2002; Raine, Meloy, Bihrle, LaCasse, & Buchsbaum, 1998). Other results are more difficult to interpret, including the finding that even the firing of a single neuron must be understood as the consequence of complex electrical and chemical events. These events include the firing rate and pattern of that cell, the specific chemicals released, the receptive capacity of the next cell, and the short- and long-term internal biochemical changes in both cells. Neuroscientists are only beginning to appreciate these levels of complexity in brain activity (K. Trujillo, personal communication, April 14, 2003).

Cognitive Neuroscience

By late in the century, a synthesis of cognitive psychology and neuroscience is emerging. Its proponents are the psychologists who believe that perception, language, memory, and cognition "cannot exist apart from the functioning brain" (Sperry, 1993). Cognitive neuroscientists use data from brain-imaging technologies to support hypothetical models of cognition. So, for example, a cognitive neuroscientist might hypothesize that the brain uses two different systems for recognizing natural and manmade objects. A research subject is placed into a brain-imaging device, presented with examples of both types of objects, and must make a decision about them. The researcher looks for different patterns of brain activation associated with each type of object and, if these are seen, concludes that the hypothesis has been supported (Joseph, 2001). So the evidence of neuroscience is used to support models of how cognition happens.

Among the most significant discoveries being made are the many ways that unconscious mental processes shape perceptions, understandings, and behavior (Bargh & Chartrand, 1999; Wilson, 2002). These unconscious mental processes, for example, cause perceptions to be erroneous in systematic ways. The **availability heuristic**, for example, identified by Tversky and Kahneman (1973), is the human tendency to base estimates of probability on information that is familiar, vivid, or recent, instead of on what is most relevant. People are more likely to believe that they may die in a terrorist attack shortly after such an attack has been in the news than they are many months after the attack. Sigmund Freud speculated about many of these unconscious mental processes in psychoanalytic theory, but it is not until late in the 20th century that cognitive neuroscientists are able to provide the observational data to support the existence of such processes.

A cognitive model of visual object recognition is shown in Fig. 12.1. A schematic like this, showing how the process functions in a normal brain, can be used to construct tests of cognitive function. Thus, this model can help to determine exactly where in the brain the damage has occurred in the event of neurological

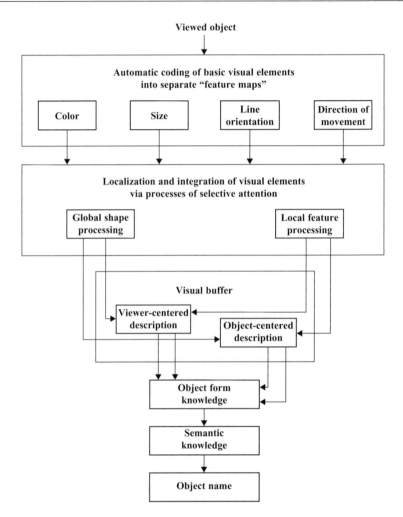

FIG. 12.1. A schematic hierarchical model of visual object recognition (photo reprinted with permission from "Cognitive Neuropsychology," by P. W. Halligan and J. C. Marshall. In R. Fuller, P. N. Walsh, & P. McGinley (Eds.), *A Century of Psychology, Progress, Paradigms and Prospects for the New Millennium* (p. 274). London: Routledge).

injury or insult. This model also helps to illustrate how much of visually recognizing and naming an object is carried out by unconscious mental processes.

✓ **Stop and think.**
If thoughts are the results of neural activity, is free will only an illusion?

Suggesting that decisions and choices are the result of complex brain activity implies that free will is only an illusion, or "the mind's best trick" (Wegner, 2003). Philosophers have been suggesting for centuries that the conviction that humans consciously and freely choose their actions might only be the consequence of assuming a causal relationship between thoughts about an action and the subsequent performance of the action. At the end of the 20th century, cognitive neuroscientists are collecting evidence that thinking about an action is not the cause of that action, and thus, that the experience of free will is only a mental illusion (Wegner & Wheatly, 1999).

COMPARATIVE PSYCHOLOGY

Why should it be the case, as the Brelands find, that different species respond in such different ways, even in very similar environments? The behaviorists thought that, given the same contingencies of reinforcement, differences between species would not matter, but it turns out they do. Why? The general answer that the comparative psychologists come up with is that different species have evolved to fill different ecological niches and so the contingencies of reinforcement are rarely the same for different species.

Sociobiology

In 1975, the entomologist E. O. Wilson publishes *Sociobiology*, his analysis of the biological bases of social behavior as shaped by the pressures of natural selection among insects and animals. In this book, Wilson explores the adaptive significance of social behaviors. **Adaptive significance** refers to the influence that a given characteristic may have had on survival in the environment in which the organism evolved into its present form. Sociobiologists argue that social behaviors exhibited today have their roots in characteristics that had adaptive significance during evolution. So, for example, cooperative social behaviors exist today in some insects and animals because, during evolution, cooperation enhanced survival. Sociobiologists believe that both physical forms and social behaviors are shaped by the pressures of natural selection.

✓ **Stop and think.**
What might be the adaptive significance of happiness or joy?

From its beginning, sociobiology has been controversial in psychology. Psychologists are initially resistant to extending sociobiological theories to human behavior. In the 1970s, sociobiologists fall victim to the same complaints of anthropomorphizing that plagued earlier animal psychologists. Many are fearful that sociobiological explanations equate human behavior with, for example, the behavior of insects. It is not until the end of the century that some psychologists are willing to acknowledge that, because humans are also an evolved species, explanations for human social behavior that take evolutionary pressures and adaptive significance into consideration might be informative. To distinguish this line of inquiry from the biologists' sociobiology, psychologists call their new field evolutionary psychology.

Evolutionary Psychology

Evolutionary psychology represents continuing efforts to understand the ways that behavior is influenced by characteristics that appeared as the result of the pressures of natural selection during evolution. All animals, including humans, show evidence of these adaptive characteristics. Evolutionary psychologists attempt to overcome the objections that derailed sociobiology by recognizing the powerful impact that learning has as it interacts with biologically based traits and by acknowledging that not every characteristic can be explained on the basis of adaptive significance. As comparative psychologist Frans de Waal says, some traits are simply part of "a package, and only the whole leads to survival and reproduction, not only a single trait" (as cited in Azar, 2001, p. 18). The principles of evolutionary psychology are influencing all of the domains of psychology, from cognition to clinical psychology.

A good example of this influence is seen in Fig. 12.1. Each of the various functions shown in the process of visual recognition is a product of the long process of shaping by natural selection. Each distinctive mental operation has evolved as an adaptation to solve specific survival problems (Halligan & Marshall, 1997). Viewed as the complete mental operation of object recognition and naming, the event can seem daunting in its complexity, as though it can only be the product of a planful creator. Reduced to its component processes, the event seems more comprehensible.

Animal Language Learning

Questions about the nature of language, how it is acquired, and whether or not other species use language remain fascinating for psychologists. A great debate rages between behaviorists, who believe that all behavior is learned, including language, and those who believe that the capacity to acquire and use language is a uniquely human trait. Several attempts are made to teach apes to use a human-like language to test the behaviorist assumption.

Earlier on this journey, the Kellogg family compared the early development of a common chimpanzee with the development of their own son. By the end of the experiment, the chimp showed signs of language comprehension for almost 100 English words, but never learned to say a single word. In the 1950s, another family adopts a newborn chimpanzee and tries for 7 years to teach her to speak English. Although this effort fails, at least one observer records that the chimp apparently teaches her human companions to use a chimp vocalization to communicate danger (Hayes & Hayes, 1951; Thorne, 1997).

Hypothesizing that earlier efforts have failed because the vocal apparatus of chimpanzees is different from that of humans, subsequent researchers use a variety of other methods to teach language to apes. Language is the use of symbols to represent and communicate shared understood meanings. Thus, there are attempts to teach apes to use hand gestures as a kind of sign language (Gardner & Gardner, 1969), to manipulate small chips with pictures of objects or words on them (Premack, 1976), and even to type signs on a specially designed computer keyboard (Rumbaugh, 1977). These efforts produce results that can more easily be explained on the basis of operant conditioning. That is, some of the apes can use a few of the symbols if their use has been carefully shaped through reinforcement, leading to the conjecture that most of what the apes do is the result of operant conditioning (Gibbons, 1991). Later, work that specifically avoids the use of operant reinforcement ultimately proves almost as disappointing (Savage-Rumbaugh, 1988; Wallman, 1992).

Today, comparative psychologist Irene Pepperberg is teaching African Grey parrots to speak English words and respond to spoken requests in ways that indicate they understand the meaning of the words they are hearing and using. In their natural environments, parrots are highly vocally communicative social animals. They also possess the vocal apparatus needed to make human-like sounds. Pepperberg's work raises intriguing possibilities and questions about cognition, communication, and language use among nonhuman animals (Pepperberg, 1999, 2002).

SOCIAL PSYCHOLOGY

Research programs in social psychology continue to be influenced by current social problems, and the results of this research continue to be interpreted through the lens of prevailing paradigms. By the 1970s, this lens is increasingly a cognitive one. In social psychology, attribution theory dominates research in the 1970s, influenced by ideas originating in information processing. **Attribution theory** is the notion that how we explain events in the world to ourselves has a great deal to do with what we believe and how we interact with others.

Social psychologists are receptive to the idea that unconscious mental processes influence conscious perceptions. Social psychologists have long known that it is the perceived world, not the objective world, that shapes thoughts, feelings, and behaviors (Jones, 1998). By 1980, psychologist Robert Zajonc states, "cognition pervades social psychology" (p. 181).

Social Cognition

Along with others, social psychologists recognize that unconscious processes influence conscious interpretations and even influence what is perceived. In other words, unconscious expectations cause errors in perception.

Unconscious Processes Shape Perceptions

Psychologist Jean Mandler tells the following story about how expectations and unconscious processes shaped perceptions in her classroom:

Some time in the 1970s, I decided to cease using masculine pronouns in my lectures when I wanted to talk about people in general. Changing wording is easy enough to do when writing, but much more difficult when lecturing, because one is thinking about what to say rather than about the vehicle itself. Nevertheless, I tried to use plural pronouns some of the time, and when talking about an individual in an example, to say "he" half of the time and "she" the other half of the time. Toward the end of the course, I happened to mention that this was what I had done. Immediately I heard a murmur around the classroom. I stopped and asked what was the matter. Someone raised his hand and said, "What do you mean you gave 'he' and 'she' equal time? You never said 'he' once during the entire course." We discussed this a bit, and then I asked for a head count. How many students thought I had always said "she"? The answer was unanimous. Every student in the class thought I had used "she" 100% of the time. I protested, of course; after all, I had worked hard to equalize my usage of the two pronouns. Then I remembered I had taped my lectures. So I recruited a couple of students to take two lectures at random and to count the number of times I had used each of the terms. The resulting count shocked us all. I had said "she" only 20% of the time. I was chagrined at how badly I had accomplished my mission, but the students were equally upset at having estimated 20% to be 100% and 80% to be zero (an effect of the magnitude we would always like to find in the lab). What had happened, of course, was that the students weren't paying attention to the language I was using—they were attending to its content. They probably couldn't have reproduced exactly any phrase I had used. They were totally used to hearing "he" to refer to an individual. But in those days, one simply did not use "she" to stand for a generic person, and each usage stuck vividly in their minds. When I asked them to make a conscious judgment of my uses of "he," they examined their explicit memory (the only memory accessible to them), and there they found a great many "she's" and no "he's." (adapted from Mandler, 2004)

As this story illustrates, errors in perception caused by unconscious processes do not occur randomly, but are systematic. And that, social psychologists discover, is part of what accounts for the formation and maintenance of stereotypes. Expectations about how certain people will look and behave are based on which group they have been categorized into based on initial perceptions. Thus, when people in these groups look or behave in unexpected ways, those behaviors are less noticed and less remembered in the cognitive phenomena referred to as selective attention and selective recall.

Thus, like other psychologists, social psychologists are finding "increasing signs that, in many important respects, we are out of touch with many determinants of our behavior" (Jones, 1998, p. 43). The mechanisms of attention and memory that shape social behaviors, relationships, and interactions with others operate largely outside of conscious awareness.

The ways in which people think about and organize information about their social world and the unconscious processes that influence those thoughts is called **social cognition**. Social cognition dominates social psychology today. Unconscious perceptions about body language, for example, influence how we respond to others (de Roten, Darwish, Stern, Fivaz-Depeursinge, & Corboz-Wanery, 1999; Flack, Laird, & Cavallaro, 1999). Perceptions of gender result in whole sets of unconscious expectations for behavior (Spence, Deaux, & Helmreich, 1985). To get a sense of how powerful gender expectations are, for example, recall the experience of encountering someone whose gender is difficult to determine.

Cultural Influences on Social Behavior

At the end of the 20th century, social psychologists are concerned with how much the findings from middle-class, educated, European, and North American populations can be generalized across classes and across cultures. Are there really universal psychological laws about social life, or is there so much variability across cultures that the search for universal laws should be abandoned? A good example of this is the phenomenon called the **fundamental attribution error**. This attribution error is the tendency to explain personal successes in terms of personal characteristics and dispositions (I got a good grade because I'm smart, and I know how to study effectively), but failures in terms of the situation (I got a poor grade because the professor asked picky questions). People making the fundamental attribution error exhibit the reverse pattern when making attributions about other people's successes and failures. Other people succeed because of the situation (the exam was easy), and they fail because of personal characteristics (they are stupid or undisciplined). The fundamental attribution error has been found in many different research studies and has been assumed to be a universal principle of human social life.

That assumption is challenged by cross-cultural studies. These studies reveal that it may only be European and North American cultural groups that exhibit this error in attribution. Among these groups, the individual is viewed as independent of others, possessing a relatively fixed personality, and able to choose behaviors freely. In many, in fact most, other cultures, the individual is viewed as interdependent with others, and any analysis of behavior requires the consideration of the social roles played by that individual and the obligations of those roles. Personality in these other cultures is viewed as dynamic and emerging from the role and situation in the moment. Research participants in these cultures do not commit the fundamental attribution error. Thus, social psychologists are now finding that this error is not a universal principle of social life at all, but is highly dependent on the culture in which the data are collected (Fiske, Kitayama, Markus & Nisbett, 1998). Clearly, the future search for universal principles governing social life will need to take cultural factors into consideration.

DEVELOPMENTAL PSYCHOLOGY

Since about 1975, the study of developmental psychology has undergone transformations as well, and many of these have brought the field closer to other domains of psychology than ever before. For example, developmental psychobiologists explore links between physical and psychological processes during development in human and nonhuman animals. Cognitive developmentalists search for the appearance and development of cognitive mechanisms of attention, information processing, and problem solving. Psychologists interested in emotion and motivation seek to understand how young children come to be able to regulate their own emotional experience and expression and the processes that allow them to function effectively in a social world.

Infant Skills

The 1970s and 1980s see an expansion in research with very young infants, and data are even collected within hours of birth. Study after study reveals that infants arrive with an impressive array of skills and characteristics, enabling them to adapt quickly and effectively to the extrauterine environment and to form essential social connections with their caregivers (Brazleton, Nugent, & Lester, 1987). Far from being blank slates, human newborns have remarkably well-formed temperaments and, as is true in many other species, are actively ready to engage their environment. Because these characteristics and abilities are present at birth, they most likely are a result of the pressures of natural selection. The realization that even young infants play active roles in establishing relationships and creating the environments in which they learn (Scarr, 1992) raises questions about how much of any given outcome measure, from intelligence to personality, results from natural attributes and how much is learned.

> **✓ Stop and think.**
> How much of who a person turns out to be is a result of natural endowments, and how much is learned from the environment?

Behavior Genetics

Like evolutionary psychology, the field of behavioral genetics bridges both biology and psychology. The difference between the two areas is that evolutionary psychology is primarily focused on species-typical behaviors that appear today as a result of the pressures of natural selection during evolution, and behavioral geneticists are interested in behavioral variability among individuals that results from genetic influences. During the height of the rat-learning era, distinct lineages of rats are bred, based on their ability to run mazes. The breeding of "maze-bright" and "maze-dull" rats, the earlier eugenics movement, the longitudinal studies of gifted youngsters, and the large study of temperament conducted by Alexander Thomas and Stella Chess all contribute to the conviction that genetic variability accounts for some individual differences in personality and behavior.

Behavioral geneticists explore these questions using comparisons of adopted infants with their biological and adoptive parents and of pairs of identical and fraternal twins. When the degree of genetic relatedness between two individuals is known, as it is with these groups, a numeric estimate can be made about how much of the variance found between individuals on observable measures is due to genetic influences. This numeric estimate is called **heritability**. Estimates of heritability can range from 1.0 for a trait that is almost completely due to genes, like fingerprints, to .0 for a trait over which genes have almost no influence, like the language the individual speaks.

Many studies of heritability conducted during the 1980s find that somewhere between 20% and 60% of the variance found between individuals on any given psychological characteristic can be attributed to genes. For example, the heritability measure for intelligence is about .70, meaning that about 70% of the variance between individuals on intelligence scores can be attributed to genetic influences. Many psychological traits long assumed to be learned are found to be influenced by genes. In one of the more dramatic examples, McGue and Lykken (1991) find that the likelihood that an individual's marriage will end in divorce is heritable. Because of repeated findings that "genetic factors play a substantial role in the origins of individual differences with respect to all psychological traits"

(Rutter, 2002, p. 2), behavior genetics becomes an important area of developmental study by the end of the century.

The Role of Nurture

By the end of the century, environmental influences on development are beginning to be viewed more realistically. No longer is maternal deprivation seen as a sentence to future psychopathology. Even parental disciplinary styles are no longer seen as crucial in shaping child personality (Maccoby & Martin, 1983). This does not mean that the social environment does not influence development. Persistent and continuing negative social interactions do have long-term consequences for psychological functioning (Seligman, 1993). These negative social interactions may occur within the family, but they may also occur among peers, at school, or even in the wider social community. Children do not completely create the social environment in which they grow up, and environments sometimes have profound effects on individual psychological functioning. Research continues today into the influences on development of the social ecologies in which individuals exist.

✓ **Stop and think.**

How would you test the question of whether the development of personality is more strongly influenced by nature or by nurture?

The Story of John/Joan

There is perhaps no more dramatic story of the test of nature versus nurture than the story of John/Joan. In this case, the outcome measure of the test is gender identity, the degree to which a person feels like a culturally stereotypic male or female. Is gender identity a set of learned characteristics, or is it the consequence of physiological factors, such as chromosomal make-up, hormones, or genital structures? In the 1960s, a horrific medical accident gives one psychologist an opportunity to test this question.

The story begins in August 1965, when John and his identical twin brother are born. Both boys are healthy and developmentally normal through the first several months of infancy. At 8 months of age, the boys are brought to the hospital to be circumcised because their foreskins are closing, making urination difficult. Although his brother's operation concludes normally, John's penis is completely destroyed by the electrocautery needle used to perform the surgery. A psychiatrist consulted on the case concludes that as a result of the loss of his penis, John "will be unable to consummate marriage or have normal heterosexual relations; he will have to recognize that he is incomplete, physically defective, and that he must live apart" (Colapinto, 2000, p. 16). John's parents are devastated.

Several months later, the parents contact sex researcher Dr. John Money after hearing about his pioneering work at Johns Hopkins University with transsexuals. Transsexuals are people whose gender identity does not match their physical sex. Money believes that gender identity is not a result of physical sex, but is learned. After examining both boys, Money convinces the parents that John can be successfully taught to assume a female gender identity using an intensive program of social, mental, and hormonal conditioning. For Money, this sad case presents a nearly perfect opportunity to test scientifically the roles of nature and nurture in the formation of gender identity. This case makes it possible to begin his study with an infant, and the identical twin brother provides a genetically matched control who will be raised as a normal male.

When John is 22 months old, the study begins. The little boy undergoes surgical genital reconstruction to make his physical appearance resemble a female, and John becomes Joan. The parents are instructed never to talk about the change, not to tell Joan about the operation, and never to waver in their decision to treat Joan as a girl. This they try valiantly to do for the next 12 years.

In the professional literature, Money reports the experiment as an unqualified success. These results have far-reaching consequences. As many as one in every 2,000 babies is born with ambiguous genitals. For purely psychosocial reasons, these infants are raised as one sex or the other, and the results of Money's John/Joan experiment encourage both doctors and parents that an arbitrary assignment of gender will work with these children or any child. Today, genital surgery is often performed on infants with ambiguous genitals, and they are assigned a gender.

Told from Joan's point of view, this is an entirely different story. From the age of 2 until midadolescence, John tries and fails to form a female gender identity. He is the victim of ceaseless teasing and is an outcast among his peers. By age 15, Joan has reassumed a male identity, and at 16, he voluntarily undergoes genital reconstructive surgery and becomes a man (adapted from Colapinto, 2000). On May 4, 2004, the man known as John/Joan commits suicide.

One might conclude that gender identity is based in biology, but there are many transsexuals with the anatomy of one sex and the gender identity of the other. These people are usually raised in congruence with their anatomy and treated throughout childhood as the gender matching their anatomy. Still, their gender identity differs from their anatomy.

Questions about the relative influence of biological and environmental factors remain among the most fascinating and controversial in the field

of developmental psychology. This story also exposes one of the most
disturbing scandals in recent psychological research and one that has not
yet been resolved.

The Nature of the Interaction

By the early 1990s, it is clear that both nature and nurture contribute to development. The real question is not how much is nature and how much nurture, but
how interaction between innate attributes and the learning environment influence
development. Questions about which comes first are not very meaningful, because
both nature and nurture are present from the first moment of life. And, as Rutter
(2002) argues, "Empirical research findings suggest that genetic vulnerabilities
operate, in part, through their role in bringing about an increased susceptibility to
environmental hazards" (p. 10).

A good example of the influence of genes on developing social relationships can
be found in Dymphna van den Boom's exhaustive study of neonatal temperament
and infant attachment. Temperament is innate whereas, according to Bowlby and
Ainsworth, attachment is a learned behavior. Van den Boom finds that, although
infant attachment at 12 months can indeed be predicted by earlier measures of maternal responsiveness, that same maternal responsiveness during the first 6 months
can be predicted from neonatal measures of infant irritability (van den Boom,
1989). In other words, at birth, some infants are innately less likely to cry and
easier to soothe than others, and mothers are more responsive to these infants than
they are to infants who are innately irritable and harder to soothe.

> ✓ **Stop and think.**
> Are infants securely attached because their mothers are responsive, or are
> mothers responsive because their infants are easier to care for? Which
> comes first?

Future Directions

Longitudinal studies are those that follow participants across long periods of time,
for example, through childhood, adolescence, and even into adulthood. After many
decades of longitudinal study, it becomes clear that stage theories of development
related to specific age groups are inadequate. Development in all domains, from
cognition to emotion, continues throughout life. The social and historical contexts
in which humans live undergo dramatic changes across the course of a single
lifetime, and these changes influence developmental pathways in both subtle and
obvious ways. By the end of the century, it is clear that emerging concepts of

human development should be ones that can be applied to processes and dynamics across the entire life-span (Elder, 1998).

STATISTICAL AND METHODOLOGICAL CHANGES

Both developmental and social psychology are plagued by the wish to uncover causal factors while often constrained by the impossibility of experimentally manipulating variables. Often, only correlational research is possible when more powerful causal tests would be more informative. What might be learned if a developmental scientist could raise a group of children from birth in a specified environment? What if one could assign infants to parents who use a specified parenting style to see if parenting style really makes a difference? What would be learned if a social scientist could manipulate the socioeconomic level of participants in a study and vary that with ethnic identity to examine the influence of these variables on attitudes? Studies in which variables can be systematically manipulated provide the strongest evidence of cause and effect, but in the developmental and social realm, these studies are usually unethical, impossible, or both.

Psychologists turn instead to new statistical techniques called causal models. In causal modeling, the researcher hypothesizes a causal set of variables and then tests to see if the data are consistent with this model. Using correlational data, researchers hope to identify the relative amount of variation in an outcome measure that can be attributed to each variable in the model. Variance in an outcome measure of child personality, for example, might be influenced by several variables, including temperament at birth, sex, birth order, number and sex of siblings, parenting style, and characteristics of the neighborhood of rearing. A causal model assigns a value to each of these variables that represents the amount of variance in the outcome measure that is accounted for by that variable.

These statistical models, as well as a variety of other methodological developments, result in large part from advances in computer technology. Faster and more powerful computers allow for more complex statistical analyses and make possible more in-depth analyses of the responses to items in survey research. For example, computers can be used more readily to identify when participants are using some strategy to respond to the survey, rather than responding to the issues addressed in the items themselves. Computers can present and measure reaction times to sensory stimuli in a variety of modalities. The data collected by the computer can then be transferred directly into statistical software for analysis, thus reducing human error. Even clinical psychologists are using computers for tasks that were never imagined a generation ago, such as doing intake interviews, psychological assessments, and even diagnosing depression. The limits of computer use in psychology are yet to be discovered.

CLINICAL PSYCHOLOGY

At the end of the 20th century, explanations for both psychoses and neuroses are shifting away from environmental causes and toward physiological factors. Schizophrenia, for example, is now believed to be primarily a brain disease that may have origins in prenatal exposure to certain viruses (Megginson, 1996; Venables, 1996). Various forms of depression are also strongly influenced by physiological predispositions. For many people, the symptoms of depression are dramatically relieved by the use of serotonin blockers and other drugs that influence brain chemistry.

The diagnosis of mental illness remains an inexact art. Clinicians still must depend on their own assessments of presenting symptoms for diagnosing and categorizing mental illness, much as they have since the 19th century. At least one clinical historian refers to the present-day state of the diagnosis of mental illness as "organized confusion" (Reisman, 1991).

Treatments

Confusion in the diagnosis of mental illness does not preclude the practice of a wide variety of treatments or the development of new treatments. Among these are many psychoactive medications that appear in the last quarter of the 20th century. Targeted at various neurochemical systems that regulate neural activity, these medications are successfully used to treat mood disorders, activity levels, hallucinations, and disturbing behavioral symptoms. Many who use these medications experience dramatic relief from years of psychological discomfort and even report feeling that their entire personality has changed (Kramer, 1993). This raises intriguing questions about what personality really is and where it comes from.

Psychologists also practice many forms of psychotherapy. By 2004, some states permit appropriately trained psychologists to prescribed medications. However, many psychologists continue to use "talk" psychotherapies.

Object Relations

Psychoanalytic and psychodynamic approaches to therapy are concerned with interpersonal relationships in the client's life or how the client relates to others. This approach requires many sessions over at least several months. This allows the therapist to learn the client's social history and patterns of interactions with others, making it possible for the therapist to offer suggestions for improving interpersonal relationships. A recent transition in the practice of object relations therapy is the use of the current interactions between client and therapist as a model to facilitate change in the client's interpersonal relationships (Liff, 1992).

Behavior Therapy

Behavior therapies appear to be effective at helping the client to change a particular behavior, such as recovering from a fear of flying or to stop smoking. These therapies are based on operant conditioning techniques, including the gradual desensitization to noxious stimuli. The legacy of B. F. Skinner's form of radical behaviorism is seen in these behavior modification therapies.

Cognitive Therapies

Several psychotherapeutic approaches that encourage individuals to restructure their thinking become popular during the 1970s and remain so today. Both Albert Ellis, who develops Rational Emotive Therapy (RET), and Aaron Beck, the founder of cognitive therapy, report that they create these new approaches because they find psychoanalytic methods to be less than satisfying in their effectiveness with clients (Arnkoff & Glass, 1992). A therapist practicing RET confronts clients with the irrational beliefs that are making them miserable. A cognitive therapist usually takes a less confrontive approach, but still challenges clients with their unrealistic thoughts and beliefs. Therapists using these approaches assume that helping individuals to change their thoughts will result in a change in feelings and behaviors as well. The movement in psychology toward considering the importance of cognition in motivating feelings and behaviors is seen in this relatively new approach to therapy.

Eclectic Therapy

Many therapists take an eclectic approach in their practices, meaning that they use whatever technique they think will be most useful in any given session. Thus, they may begin with a humanistic, open, and accepting session, then later introduce some cognitive interventions, getting clients to recognize irrational thoughts. These therapists may even recommend the addition of some psychoactive medications to relieve immediate symptoms while psychotherapy proceeds.

The Efficacy of Therapy

Studies conducted by practitioners of any given form of therapy still tend to find in favor of the effectiveness of that form of therapy. Studies conducted by opponents to a particular therapy, or to psychotherapy in general, tend to find against the effectiveness of therapy. Some studies have found that professionally trained psychotherapists provide no more effective therapy than do untrained paraprofessionals (Berman & Norton, 1985). This leaves both consumers and the insurance companies that pay for these services at a loss, and the controversy continues to rage (see Perez, 1999; Schneider, 1999).

Some newer forms of cognitive therapy are proving to be effective, even for clients suffering from long-standing problems with depression. These therapies are also effective in as few as five or six sessions (O'Hanlon & Weiner-Davis, 1989). This is having a profound impact on the practice of psychotherapy. For example, for clients who have insurance coverage for mental health care, insurance company rules largely dictate the care allowed. Because some cognitive therapies are effective in such a short time, it is now common to permit only five or six sessions of psychotherapy annually. For psychotherapists, this means that they must constantly be generating new clients.

The Future of Clinical Psychology

Clinical psychology is taking a number of new directions. For example, in 1980, a new division called health psychology joins the APA. Health psychologists are interested in the psychological characteristics associated with both maintaining physical health and preventing illness. They find medical models of illness that focus exclusively on physiological factors to be too deterministic and believe that these do not adequately explain the complexity of even physical illness (Belloch, 1997). Behavioral variables, such as lifestyle choices, explain more of the variance in physical health than do biological factors, such as genes (M. Wertheimer, personal communication, November 8, 2004). Other movements are also influencing clinical psychology.

Multiculturalism

Clinical psychologists are increasingly interested in cultural influences on both mental illness and psychotherapy. Individuals from different cultural groups are differentially likely to suffer from some forms of mental illness. And, if they want to be effective with their clients, therapists must be aware of how the ethnic, religious, and socioeconomic backgrounds of both client and therapist affect the therapeutic setting. The influences of gender, age, and sexual orientation must also be considered in clinical practice (Pickren, 2004).

A Pluralism of Problems and Solutions

The practice of psychotherapy is moving into new arenas, and psychologists must be prepared for these changes. In this century, disaster relief is becoming almost as important a role for psychotherapists as it is for firefighters. Therapies are needed that include all family members and that consider the communities in which they interact. As more is learned about which therapies are most effective for specific problems, therapists need to become skilled in the practice of a variety of approaches. Also, as economic pressures increase, and as more is learned about how therapy works, individuals will be encouraged to engage in more self-help, facilitating the growth of coping skills and enhancing life experiences for themselves

(Norcross & Freedheim, 1992). This new form of self-help will be clinically val-idated and distinctly different from current "popular" psychology and recovery movements that pathologize and disempower individuals and encourage them to follow charismatic leaders (Kaminer, 1992).

POSITIVE PSYCHOLOGY

A recent outgrowth of clinical psychology is the emerging field of positive psy-chology. Psychologists working in this area are concerned with the ways in which individuals can enhance the good in their lives; enjoy mutually supportive, sat-isfying, and lasting friendships and love relationships; find meaning and fulfill-ment in work experiences; and live a socially "good life." Positive psychologists are concerned with human virtues like generosity, compassion, cooperation, re-sponsibility, creativity, and wisdom. They study the experiences that make people feel good and the personality traits that are associated with reports of feeling happy.

This interest in positive psychology may seem like a recent event, but it has actually been a part of this field for a very long time. Recall that Aristotle was concerned with the nature of friendship and that William James provided advice for how to be the person you wish to become. Psychoanalytic emphases on the dark demands of the id, conflicts in unconsciousness, and the death instinct have overshadowed positive approaches since early in the 20th century. John Watson studied how to induce fear and discouraged parents from showing affection to their children. And, for many decades after the close of World War II, the emphasis in clinical psychology has been on healing sick and disturbed minds.

Credit for reintroducing questions about how to achieve and maintain a positive life is usually given to the same Martin Seligman who researched questions about learned helplessness. By early in the 21st century, Seligman and his colleagues in positive psychology are interested in how some people are able to maintain an optimistic outlook despite all odds and the degree to which those skills can be learned. Seligman argues that depression can be avoided by changing how we explain disappointments to ourselves. People who explain a recent failure as the result of factors external to themselves over which they have no control, like blaming a poor exam score on picky questions or a mean professor, will have negative feelings and are prone toward depression. Similarly, pessimists, who explain failures as the result of permanent personal characteristics, such as being stupid, are also prone toward depression. But optimists, who explain failures as a result of temporary conditions that are mostly under their control and who believe that even negative personal characteristics are changeable, have mostly positive feelings and are significantly less likely to succumb to depression (Seligman, 1993). There are many questions that remain to be explored about the experience of happiness and how to enhance positive life experiences.

> ✓ **Stop and think.**
> Is happiness a means or an end?

PSYCHOLOGY OF WOMEN

Earlier, the entry of women into psychology resulted in research specifically aimed at understanding the psychology of women; Hollingworth's dissertation refuting the myth of decreased functioning during menstruation is a good example. Much of this research examined variables internal to individual women, such as poor self-esteem, to explain psychological issues related to women. But other early studies took into consideration the sociopolitical context in seeking to understand why women think, feel and behave the way they characteristically do. Helen Bradford Thompson concluded in her 1903 dissertation, for example, that social influences accounted for the sex differences she found (Milar, 2000). Other women psychologists pointed out the effect of social forces on the research itself: "There is perhaps no field aspiring to be scientific where flagrant personal bias, logic martyred in the cause of supporting a prejudice, unfounded assertions, and even sentimental rot and drivel, have run riot to such an extent as here" (Woolley, 1910, p. 340).

By the 1970s, when another wave of feminism inspires more research into the psychology of women, the focus has moved to trying to document discrimination against women and to understanding the psychological consequences of discrimination in women's professional, social, and personal environments. Many studies provide clear evidence of pervasive discrimination against women, both subtle and overt. Among these are a series of "eye of the beholder" studies, documenting that people of both sexes judge the same work or the same behavior differently, and usually less positively, if they believe the work or behavior was done by a woman rather than a man (Goldberg, 1968; Paludi & Strayer, 1985).

At the turn of the century, there are at least two very divergent views and research agendas focused on the psychology of women. One sees sex differences as the essential question. These differences are presumed to arise from the biological categories of male and female, so that gender differences are really sex differences. In this view, research involves observing and describing the emergence of these differences and measuring the nature and size of the differences at various stages of life. The life experiences of individuals are seen as a natural consequence of their biological sex. The ultimate question underlying this view is one about whether equality between the sexes can ever be achieved, and if it is possible, how it might happen.

The second view sees gender as a social construction against which individuals are measured. In other words, the social context has defined a masculine model and a feminine model. As individuals move through life, expectations for what characteristics they will exhibit are defined by these models independently of individuals' actual characteristics. In this view, differences between males and females arise from differences in culturally assigned power. The essential questions here have to do with the same dynamics between powerful and nonpowerful groups that apply in any situation where there is a significant power difference. The life experiences of individuals are a consequence of the cultural role that they have been assigned. In this view, power is achieved by recognizing the role one has been assigned and rejecting it when it does not fit. The ultimate question underlying this view is about how to recognize the role one has been assigned, rejecting the power difference, and claiming one's own power, thus leading to social change (Unger, 1997).

Social cognition research illuminates some of the unconscious cognitive mechanisms that influence thoughts, feelings, and behaviors about gender, power, and the self. For example, psychologists have found that, although many younger women report that they have never experienced sex discrimination, experimental studies find that "women use selective awareness to deny personal discrimination" (Crosby, 1984). The role played by unconscious mechanisms in influencing the dynamics between men and women continues to be a rich area of exploration.

PSYCHOLOGY OF RELIGION

Another area of interest in psychology that is reemerging at the beginning of the 21st century is the psychology of religion. This is the scientific study of how people think about religion, what it means to them, various types of religious behavior, and how religious beliefs influence other aspects of people's lives (Hester, 1998). Religious beliefs are among the most powerful forces for both good and evil operating in our social environment. The psychology of religion is one of the oldest topics in the field, but one of many that were not studied during the height of behaviorism. Given that differences in religious beliefs are currently among the most important geopolitical issues, the study of the psychology of religion is today taking on increasing importance.

INDUSTRIAL/ORGANIZATIONAL PSYCHOLOGY

The same developments that influence the rest of psychology also find expression in industrial psychology. After World War II, attention was focused on motivation in the workplace, applications for operant conditioning techniques, and how the processing of information influenced job performance. Today, organizational psychology has much more influence in the field. Organizational psychologists ask questions about whole work systems as opposed to individuals' work lives. For example, the earlier work of Lewin and social psychologists on leadership styles was followed by interest in the functioning and effectiveness of teams in the workplace. Organizational psychologists study the ways in which achievable goals and objectives are determined and reached in work teams and processes of strategic planning.

The transition from a manufacturing-based to a service-based economy in the United States, the positive climate for business during the 1950s and 1960s, and various socioeconomic movements result in near-full employment among working- and middle-class White males during these years. Full employment allows employees more flexibility in job selection. Influenced by humanistic psychology's emphasis on self-actualization, employees become concerned about job satisfaction and self-fulfillment. Industrial/organizational (I/O) psychologists are called on to help employers develop employment situations that provide employees with satisfying careers that have the potential to meet a wide variety of employees' personal and professional needs.

Issues of fairness in hiring, compensation, and promotion also become important as concerns in the wider world turn first to racial and ethnic discrimination, and later, to discrimination based on sex, age, disability, and sexual orientation. I/O psychologists are charged with designing systems that minimize the influence of prejudice against these now-protected groups in the workplace.

At the end of the century, sociopolitical forces continue to influence the emerging questions in I/O psychology. An increasing convergence of work and nonwork domains raises issues related to the merging of these aspects of people's lives. The personal and psychological consequences of telecommuting, for example, raise concerns as advances in technology make possible many alternatives to the traditional work model. Sexual harassment and drug testing create problems for employers and employees alike. The continued lack of affordable and quality day care for both children and aging parents creates problems for many families, especially as economic conditions and expectations of higher standards of living push all able-bodied adults in the family into the workplace. Economic slowdowns and "downsizing" create the need for I/O psychologists to help employees adapt to career changes later in life. The aging of the "baby boomers" creates a large segment of employees moving into retirement and raises questions about how to negotiate that transition successfully. In the 21st century, I/O psychology is a vibrant and dynamic field with many fascinating avenues yet to explore.

Organized Psychology

In 1892, the APA was founded at a meeting of fewer than a dozen psychologists held at the home of G. Stanley Hall. The purpose of this new organization was "to promote psychology as a science." It was decided that there would be a new president elected each year, and the president would be chosen on the basis of having made a significant contribution to the science of psychology. Hall was elected as the first president. In 1905, Mary Calkins was elected as the 14th president, the first woman to be so honored.

From the very beginning, there were tensions between psychologists with different interests and goals for this new endeavor. A variety of different organizations have been founded in the years since 1892, representing these divergent views. Over the years, the most divisive tensions have arisen between those who view psychology as a purely scientific discipline and those who view the field as an applied and helping profession. In 1918, the first division within the APA was formed to address the interests of those calling themselves clinical psychologists.

By 1944, a major reorganization of the APA was needed to reflect the changes occurring in psychology. The goals of the organization were changed to "advance psychology as a science, as a profession, and as a means of promoting human welfare." Eighteen relatively independent divisions were formed, each with its own mission and president and each reflecting some aspect of the goals. This reorganization was undertaken to preserve the unity of the APA in the face of continuing and growing tensions between those who advocated psychology as a science and the increasing number of members who practiced psychology as an applied discipline.

At the end of the 20th century, membership in APA continues to reflect the changes in the field of psychology, increasing dramatically from 7,250 members in 1950 to 159,000 members today. The ratio of scientists to practitioners also changes during these years. In 1940, 70% of APA members are scientists, but by 1994, 70% of APA members are health care providers (Wiggins, 1994). In 1988, scientific psychologists become so disenchanted with the preponderance of practitioners in APA that they form their own organization, the American Psychological Society (APS). By the year 2000, nearly 16,000 scientific psychologists belong to APS.

PSYCHOLOGY FOR TOMORROW

At the dawn of the new century, there are new questions for psychology to explore. New technologies provide new ways to examine the operations of the mind. In addition to wondering about relationships between human animals and nonhuman animals, scientists also wonder about relationships between human minds and artificial minds and about how humans relate to machines in general. Whole new research programs in "human factors" are opening up to try to understand interactions between humans and machines.

The search for the few laws that govern psychological life must increasingly take into consideration the generalizability of those laws to a global population. Those exploring social psychology ask more questions about the psychological impact of living in a crowded, diverse, and overpopulated world. As the world becomes more crowded, issues of interdependence among nations and among individuals take on importance. Psychologists are challenged to find a culturally universal psychology.

The Western assumption that humans are motivated by self-interest, greed, or fear are being called into question. Returning to center stage are questions about motivation based on the desire to be thought of well; the role of generosity, compassion, and cooperation in our social lives; and our wish to live in virtue.

⊕ The Times

At the end of the 20th century, the term "the West" no longer accurately identifies a unified geopolitical region. Instead, the distinction is drawn between the developed world, which includes Japan, Australia, and Israel in addition to North America and Western Europe, and the developing world, which includes Central and South America as well as Africa, most of Asia, most of Eastern Europe, and the Middle East.

The social environment in the developed world at the beginning of the 21st century might best be characterized by the twin themes of connection and consumption. In the same way that the different domains of psychology increasingly overlap with one another and psychology is strengthening its connections with other disciplines, the rest of the world also seems to be becoming more closely connected. Millions of people in the developed world have access to the Internet, and information flows freely among individuals and across national boundaries. Millions carry mobile phones, connecting with friends and family at any time or place. The advent of cable television in the 1970s allows for the proliferation of news and entertainment outlets, and cross-national broadcasts are available to those who seek them out. Crises also cross national boundaries, such as global warming and the rapid spread of deadly diseases. Responses can also be mounted globally through the United Nations and, as information is spread through the Internet, through the unified actions of millions of concerned individuals.

At the same time, world population continues to grow exponentially and natural resources continue to be depleted. Demand for material goods, personal services, and information skyrockets in the developed world. By the end of the 20th century in the United States, there is one automobile for every person in the country, and consumer debt has increased to an average of $10,000 per person (Brobeck, 1997). At the same time, the developing world provides cheap labor and natural resources.

The power of profit-making business also grows and becomes global. Corporate power is consolidated through the formation of multinational corporations, the World Trade Organization, the International Monetary Fund, and the World Bank. Corporate powers use computers to connect with consumers by collecting huge databases on buying habits and personal lives. And, although there may be many more news outlets, they are controlled by fewer and larger profit-making corporations.

This era is also characterized by disturbing disconnections. Students, who used to study between classes, may now chat with friends on their mobile phones while ignoring potential new friends sitting right next to them. Since the advent of television, local communities have seen participation decline in community activities. Suburbs spread for miles, dotted with identical mini-markets and malls, but without a sense of connection to the community. Families can live for years in the same house and never know their neighbors. One in every three marriages ends in divorce, and even in two-parent families, both parents are likely to be working and spending many hours a week commuting. The whole family sitting down to dinner together has become a charming anachronism from some earlier era.

Glossary

Adaptive significance refers to the influence that a given characteristic may have had on survival during evolution.

Androcentric means male-centered.

Animism is the belief that humans share the world with extraordinary, extracorporeal, and invisible beings.

Anomaly is a piece of research evidence that violates one or more of the assumptions of the paradigm.

Anthropomorphize is to attribute human characteristics to nonhuman animals.

Archival research is done by collecting data from the historical record.

Associationism is the belief that knowledge about the world is acquired by associating new information with previously experienced objects and events.

Assumptions are beliefs that are not questioned or tested.

Astrology is the foretelling of the future by the position of planets and stars during Babylonian times.

Attribution theory is the notion that how we explain events in the world to ourselves has a great deal to do with what we believe and how we interact with others.

Availability heuristic identified by Tversky and Kahneman refers to the human tendency to base estimates of probability on information that is familiar, vivid, recent, instead of on what is most relevant.

Bell–Magendie law is the name given to the discovery that there are sensory nerves that carry impulses from the sensory organs to the brain, and motor nerves that carry impulses from the brain to the muscles of the motor system.

Blind in scientific usage means that the research participant does not know what variables are being studied or the hypothesis being tested.

Cell assembly is a set of cells connected to one another into neural circuits. Events or images are represented in the cortex by activity in these cell assemblies.

Chlorpromazine is a drug used to reduce hallucinations in schizophrenia.

Circular arguments use the premises as evidence of the validity of the conclusions.

Clinical psychology as named by Witmer is the domain of psychology related to treatment. Early 20th-century uses refer mostly to institutional testing.

Cognitive dissonance as named by Festinger refers to the cognitive state that results when behaviors are not consonant with beliefs.

Cognitive map as named by Tolman refers to a mental representation of the surrounding environment.

Cognitive science refers to links formed among psychology, philosophy, linguistics, physics, engineering, and computer science.

Comparative psychology is the study of psychological characteristics among animals, both human and nonhuman.

Conditioned reflex in John Watson's view is the result of a reflex action being repeatedly paired with a satisfactory outcome, thus making the action more likely to be repeated in the future.

Confirmation bias is the tendency to pay attention only to evidence that supports an already accepted belief and ignore evidence that refutes that belief.

Connectionism refers to the belief that banks of computers operating both parallel and in interaction with one another will simulate the action of physiological neural networks.

Contingencies of reinforcement named by Skinner are the conditions under which reinforcement will occur.

Corporeal has to do with the physical body.

Correlation occurs when two or more variables tend to change together in a way not expected by chance.

Cosmogenic refers to the beginning of the universe.

Determinism in philosophy is the belief that all events are caused by matter acting on matter, and, in psychology, it is the belief that behavior is caused (by matter), not freely willed.

Dionysian faith practiced secret religious rites and promised benefits in an afterlife to believers.

Dizygotic refers to a twin originating from a different fertilized egg cell than its twin.

Double-blind in scientific usage means that both the researchers who collect the data and the participants are unaware of the variables being studied or the hypothesis being tested.

Dream analysis is a technique used in the practice of psychoanalysis to help the analyst identify patients' repressed thoughts.

Ego as named by Freud is a set of regulatory functions that both keep the impulses of the id under control and help the id to achieve its goals. Ego is the second major component of personality.

Elementalist psychology is based on the assumption that conscious mind is made up of basic mental elements associated together.

Empiricism is the philosophy that experience should form the foundation for belief.

Epistemology is the study of knowledge and how knowledge is acquired.

Equipotentiality as named by Lashley means that within a given functional area of the cortex all cells have an equal potential to perform that function.

Eucharist is the ritualized and figurative sacrifice and eating of the body and blood of Christ.

Eugenics was a 20th-century movement to control human reproduction so that only people with desirable characteristics would be allowed to have children and people with undesirable characteristics would be eliminated.

Experimental science is the systematic observation and measurement of nature.

Face validity occurs when an answer appears or seems as though it must be true.

Faculty is a mental power or ability.

Fixed action patterns as named by ethologists refer to patterns of behavior, sometimes called instincts, and are used to explain why each species behaves as it does in its environment.

Folk psychology is a set of assumptions derived from superstitions, the desire to remain affiliated with others, trust, everyday reason, and unstructured observations.

Free association is a technique used in the practice of psychoanalysis to help the analyst identify patients' repressed thoughts.

Free will is the idea that behavior varies as a function of individuals' choices uninfluenced by any cause.

Functional periodicity was thought to be a kind of monthly psychological impairment associated with the menstrual cycle.

Functionalism is the 20th-century domain of psychology that seeks to understand the functions served by consciousness.

Fundamental attribution error refers to the Western tendency to explain personal successes in terms of personal characteristics and dispositions, but personal failures in terms of the situation and the reverse pattern when making attributions about other people's successes and failures.

Geocentric means the Earth is at the center.

Hawthorne effect refers to any change in the workplace that appears to increase productivity.

Hedonism is the philosophy that happiness lies in seeking pleasure and avoiding pain.

Heliocentric refers to the idea that the sun is at the center of the solar system.

Heritability refers to the numeric estimate that can be made about how much of the variance found between individuals on observable measures is explained by genetic influences.

Heterodoxy is the wrong ways to think and believe.

Hindsight bias is the tendency to believe, after learning an outcome, that one would have foreseen exactly that outcome.

Historical refers to a time when written records were kept.

Holism, or dynamic psychology, is the perspective that a real understanding of psychological characteristics must take into consideration the whole organism or person in interaction with a whole environment.

Hominids are erect, bipedal, primate mammals, including ancestral forms of humans.

Homunculus is a fully formed human in miniature believed to reside in the sperm cell until implantation in the uterus, where it would grow to full size.

Humanism was a 16th-century philosophical movement that focused on human powers of reason as opposed to supernatural powers.

Hypothesis is a guess about a relationship between variables.

Hypothetico-deductive system named by Hull begins with a set of hypotheses from which an expected response is deduced.

Hysteria is a purported neurosis mainly afflicting women and characterized by paralysis in various parts of the body, the loss of sensation or disturbances in sight or hearing, severe headaches, palpitations of the heart, abdominal pain, or a stubborn cough.

Id as named by Freud is a set of unregulated impulsive energies, incapable on its own of realistically achieving its ends and is the first major component of personality.

Inauthentic lives as named by 20th-century humanistic psychologists result when people choose to behave as they are expected to behave rather than being guided by their own inner values.

Insanity is the term used beginning in the 16th century to describe those whose thoughts, feelings, and behaviors are significantly different from those of most other people.

Instinct refers to species-specific behaviors that are not a consequence of learning.

Intuition is an awareness that seems to arise from within, so that individuals feel they have direct and immediate knowledge.

James–Lange motor theory of mind makes the argument that the psychological state of emotion is really only the awareness of a physiological state.

Latent learning is defined as learning that occurs in the absence of reinforcement and is only exhibited when needed to achieve an end.

Law of phylogenetic continuity states that there is continuity across all species such that what is understood about learning in one species may be applied across all species. According to this law, species differ only in the number and complexity of learned associations that can be made.

Learned helplessness as named by Seligman and Maier, refers to the tendency of an organism to passively accept punishment, even when escape is possible, as a consequence of an earlier learning experience in which escape was not possible.

Learning can be defined as the gradual appearance of a predicted response to a specific stimulus, and the behavior, not consciousness, is what psychologist should explain.

Logical positivism is a form of positivism that accepts an unobservable theoretical term as long as it is defined as a publicly observable operation.

Materialism is the philosophy that everything is made of matter.

Maturationism is the theory that it is maturation occurring over the passage of time that drives development in all areas, including psychological characteristics.

Melancholia is another name for depression.

Mind–body problem is the question about how and where a nonmaterial aspect of the human interacts with the material aspect.

Misogyny is the hatred of women.

Monozygotic refers to a twin originating from the same fertilized egg cell as its twin.

Motivational bias is a tendency to answer questions in a particular way because of a desire or wish to answer them in that way.

Naturalism is the belief that nature is governed by a set of laws and that those laws also apply to humans and human behavior.

Nature versus nurture is the question of the relative importance of inherited characteristics and environmental effects on development.

Neobehaviorists share the basic underlying assumptions of behaviorism but are distinguished from behaviorists by accepting the methods of logical positivism.

New psychology is the 20th-century term used to distinguish the empirical approach to the study of mental functions in North America from an older moral psychology.

Nihilism is the tearing down of all belief systems and the view that existence has no meaning.

Nominalism is the belief that universal words such as "justice" are just names given to sets of instances.

Noumena from Kant's philosophy are the actual objects of reality.

Null hypothesis is the hypothesis that there are no differences between research groups.

Objective inference occurs when one infers in another only those mental powers that may be verified by public observation and measurement.

Ockham's razor refers to the argument that one should accept the explanation that requires the fewest assumptions.

Oligarchy is a form of government in which a few select wealthy individuals hold power.

Ontology is the study of what is real and the nature of reality.

Operant as named by Skinner is a behavior in which the organism is operating on the environment.

Operant conditioning chamber is a small box equipped with a device for recording responses, such as a lever, and a place to deliver a reinforcer.

Opinio is the Latin term for probable knowledge, or opinion.

Orthodoxy is the right way to think and believe.

Pantheism is the belief that God is present everywhere and at all times because everything is God.

Parallel distributed processing refers to the belief that banks of computers operating both parallel and in interaction with one another will simulate the action of physiological neural networks.

Parsimony is the assertion that explanations that use the fewest assumptions are the most likely to be true.

Personal equation is a factor used by astronomers to attempt to eliminate individual differences in reaction time from astronomical observations. Each observer has his or her own factor of adjustment or personal equation.

Phase sequences are clusters of cell assemblies linked together that form the bases of thoughts and ideas.

Phenomena from Kant's philosophy are those aspects of reality that are known through sensory experience.

Phi phenomenon is the perception of movement that occurs when separate stimuli are displayed in rapid sequence.

Philosophy is the love of knowledge, typically sought through reason and logic.

Phrenology, literally science of the mind, is the later name given to cranioscopy, which is the measurement of the shape and size of the skull in a living person.

Physiognomy is the study of character, intellect, and future success by observation of facial appearance.

Placebo effect refers to a neutral treatment that has an effect because the patient believes that it will.

Positivism is the belief that only those aspects of the universe that can be publicly observed can be known for certain.

Premises are assertions that are presumed to be true.

Principle of mass action as named by Lashley means that, for complex learning, the cortex operates as a unified whole rather than as a set of discrete switches.

Projective inference occurs when one's own mental experiences are projected onto another.

Pseudoscience is a field that uses the language of science but is not supported by evidence based on the scientific method.

Psychoanalysis begins as a method to treat neuroses, primarily hysteria. Psychoanalytic theory postulates that childhood sexuality in interaction with the surrounding environment sets the stage for personality development.

Psychodynamic theories are alternatives to psychoanalytic theories because they posit that it is dynamic interactions between psychological factors internal to the child and the external rearing environment, particularly the parents, that set the stage for personality development, rather than childhood sexuality.

Rationalism is the philosophy that reason and logical argument should form the foundation for belief.

Realism is the belief that universal words, such as "justice," represent something real.

Recapitulation is the 19th-century theory that, during prenatal development, the human goes through each successive stage of evolution experienced as the human species evolved.

Reductio ad absurdum is logic that reduces the argument to a level where it no longer makes any sense.

Reinforcer as named by Skinner is anything that increases the probability of a response.

Reserpine is a root extract used to calm institutionalized psychotic patients and make them more cooperative.

Rhetoric is the skillful use of words to outline an argument.

Romanticism is the philosophy that intense emotion is the most important motivator of behavior and what brings meaning to human experience. Emotion cannot be known through orthodox religious practice or logic and is not made of matter.

Schemata refers to Piaget's notion of the mind as sets of pieces of related information encountered in the environment.

Scholastics were Christian clerics who attempted to interpret the writings of Classical Greek philosophers to support Roman Christian orthodoxy.

Scientia is the Latin term for certain knowledge.

Secular powers are those related to the worldly and not associated with the Church or spiritual.

Selective attention is the tendency to attend to only part of the available evidence.

Selective recall is the tendency to remember evidence that supports a preexisting belief and to forget evidence that refutes the belief.

Skepticism is questioning accepted wisdom.

Social cognition refers to the ways in which people think about and organize information about their social world and the unconscious processes that influence those thoughts.

Social facilitation effects as named by social psychologists refer to the fact that people can be persuaded to engage in behaviors with others that they would never engage in when alone.

Spencer–Bain principle states that when a behavior is followed by a pleasant or successful outcome, the behavior will tend to be repeated, but when behavior is followed by an unpleasant or unsuccessful outcome it will tend not to be repeated.

Strong AI refers to the belief that machines can be built that will think the way humans think.

Structuralism is the 20th-century domain of psychology that seeks to identify and measure the basic mental elements and their attributes and to understand how those elements combine to produce complex conscious thought.

Sublimation as named by Freud is an unconscious defense mechanism used to protect the ego from being overwhelmed by the impulses of the id.

Superego as named by Freud is a set of moral values and attitudes learned from parents and the surrounding culture, including attitudes about the self.

Superstitious belief is formed when a particular response is falsely believed to be associated with a reward.

Survey research is done by asking participants to supply the data by responding to researcher's questions.

Tabula rasa is Latin for a blank slate.

Teleology is the idea that there is design or purpose in nature.

Temperament is defined as biologically based characteristic ways of responding to the environment that shape personality.

T-groups, named by humanistic or training groups, are groups in which coworkers meet over several hours to share their real feelings about issues in the workplace and come to better understand both themselves and others in the group.

Theories are plausible but hypothetical abstract ideas that are tested through observation.

Time and motion studies measure the time and motion it takes to perform each segment of a job and then eliminate all unnecessary effort.

Transactional analysis is a theory that interpersonal interactions are like games that people play between themselves.

Transformism is the idea that life forms currently found on Earth were not created in their present form by God, but emerged from primordial matter as a result of the laws of nature and evolved slowly into those that are present today.

Transmigration of the soul is the movement of the soul from one body to another.

Utilitarianism is a doctrine that the goodness of an action is determined by its usefulness: the greatest happiness for the largest number.

Valid in science means being supported by objective truth.

Vitalism is the discredited belief that living matter possesses a special type of energy or life-force.

Weak AI refers to the belief that machines can be built that will perform some activity as well as a human can, but that machines will not ever think the way humans think.

Worldview is a culturally specific perspective regarding the nature of reality.

Young–Helmholtz theory of color vision states that color vision is a result of three types of receptors on the back of the eye, each chemically responsive to different wavelengths of light.

Zeitgeist is a German word meaning the spirit of the times.

References

Adler, A. (1929). *The science of living*. Garden City, NY: Garden City Publishing.

Ainsworth, M. D. S. (1983). Mary D. Salter Ainsworth. In A. N. O'Connell & N. F. Russo (Eds.), *Models of achievement. Reflections of eminent women in psychology* (pp. 201–219). New York: Columbia University Press.

Alexander, F. G., & Selesnick, S. T. (1966). *The history of psychiatry: An evaluation of psychiatric thought from prehistoric times to the present*. New York: Harper & Row.

Allport, G. W. (1954). The historical background of modern social psychology. In G. Lindzey (Ed.), *The handbook of social psychology* (Vol. I, pp. 3–56). Cambridge, MA: Addison-Wesley.

Anastasi, A. (1958). Heredity, environment, and the question "how?" *Psychological Review, 65*, 197–208.

Aristotle. (1961). *De anima* (D. Ross, Trans.). Oxford, England: Clarendon Press. (Original work written ca. 330 BCE)

Arnkoff, D. B., & Glass, C. R. (1992). Cognitive therapy and psychotherapy in integration. In D. K. Freedheim (Ed.), *History of psychotherapy. A century of change* (pp. 657–694). Washington, DC: American Psychological Association.

Asch, S. E. (1946). Forming impressions of personality. *Journal of Abnormal and Social Psychology, 41*, 258–290.

Augustine. (1947). *Faith, hope, and charity* (L. A. Arand, Trans.). Westminster, MD: The Newman Bookshop. (Original work written ca. 420 CE)

Axtell, J. L. (1968). *The educational writings of John Locke*. London: Cambridge University Press.

Azar, B. (2001, December). Darwin 101. A primatologist urges psychologists to embrace Darwin, but with more sophistication. *Monitor on Psychology*, p. 18.

Bacon, F. (1859). *The works* (B. Montague, Ed. & Trans.). Philadelphia: Parry & Macmillan. (Original work published ca. 1605)

Bain, A. (1885). *The senses and the intellect*. New York: D. Appleton and Company.

Baldwin, J. M. (1895). *Mental development in the child and the race*. New York: Macmillan.

Bargh, J. A., & Chartrand, T. L. (1999). The unbearable automaticity of being. *American Psychologist, 54*, 462–479.

Baritz, L. (1960). *The servants of power. A history of the use of social science in American industry*. Middleton, CT: Wesleyan University Press.

Bark, W. C. (1958). *Origins of the medieval world*. Stanford, CA: Stanford University Press.

Barnes, J. (Ed.). (1984). *The complete works of Aristotle*. Princeton, NJ: Princeton University Press. (Original work written ca. 330 BCE)

Baumgartner, E., & Baumgartner, W. (1997). Brentano: Psychology from an empirical standpoint. In W. G. Bringmann, H. E. Lück, R. Miller, & C. E. Early (Eds.), *A pictorial history of psychology* (pp. 61–65). Chicago: Quintessence.

Bäumler, G. (1997). Sports psychology. In W. G. Bringmann, H. E. Lück, R. Miller, & C. E. Early (Eds.), *A pictorial history of psychology* (pp. 485–489). Chicago: Quintessence.

Baumrind, D. (1964). Some thoughts on ethics of research: After reading Milgram's "behavioral study of obedience." *American Psychologist, 19*, 421–423.

Baumrind, D. (1973). The development of instrumental competence through socialization. In A. D. Pick (Ed.), *The Minnesota symposia on child psychology* (Vol. 7, pp. 3–46). Minneapolis: University of Minnesota Press.

Beach, F. A. (1950). The snark was a boojum. *American Psychologist, 5*, 115–124.

Beach, F. A. (1955). The descent of instinct. *Psychological Review, 62*, 401–410.

Beard, G. M., & Rockwell, A. D. (1871). *A practical treatise on the medical and surgical uses of electricity.* New York: William Wood and Company.

Belloch, A. (1997). One hundred years of clinical psychology. In R. Fuller, P. N. Walsh, & P. McGinley (Eds.), *A century of psychology. Progress, paradigms and prospects for the new millenium* (pp. 85–106). London: Routledge.

Benedict, R. (1934). *Patterns of culture.* Boston: Houghton Mifflin.

Bergmann, M. S. (1992). *In the shadow of Moloch. The sacrifice of children and its impact on Western religions.* New York: Columbia University Press.

Berkeley, G. (1920). *A treatise concerning the principles of human knowledge.* Chicago: Open Court Publishing. (Original work published in 1710)

Berlyne, D. E. (1966). Curiosity and exploration. *Science, 153*, 25–33.

Berman, J. S., & Norton, N. C. (1985). Does professional training make a therapist more effective? *Psychological Bulletin, 98*, 401–407.

Bettelheim, B. (1967). *The empty fortress.* New York: Free Press.

Bevan, E. (1913). *Stoics and Skeptics.* Oxford, England: Oxford University Press.

Blass, T. (1996). Stanley Milgram: A life of inventiveness and controversy. In G. A. Kimble, C. A. Boneau, & M. Wertheimer (Eds.), *Portraits of pioneers in psychology* (Vol. 2, pp. 315–331). Mahwah, NJ: Lawrence Erlbaum Associates.

Blum, D. (2002). *Love at Goon Park.* Cambridge, MA: Perseus.

Boakes, R. (1984). *From Darwin to behaviorism: Psychology and the minds of animals.* New York: Cambridge University Press.

Boring, E. G. (1957). *A history of experimental psychology* (2nd ed.). New York: Appleton-Century-Crofts. (Original work published in 1929)

Bowlby, J. (1969). *Attachment and loss: Vol. 1. Attachment.* New York: Basic Books.

Bramel, D., & Friend, R. (1981). Hawthorne, the myth of the docile worker, and class bias in psychology. *American Psychologist, 36*, 867–878.

Braslow, J. (1997). *Mental ills and bodily cures. Psychiatric treatment in the first half of the twentieth century.* Berkeley: University of California Press.

Brauns, H. (1997). Ernst Heinrich Weber. In W. G. Bringmann, H. E. Lück, R. Miller, & C. E. Early, (Eds.), *A pictorial history of psychology* (pp. 97–100). Chicago: Quintessence.

Brazleton, T. B., Nugent, J. K., & Lester, B. M. (1987). Neonatal behavioral assessment scale. In J. D. Osofsky (Ed.), *Handbook of infant development* (2nd ed., pp. 92–120). New York: Wiley.

Breland, K., & Breland, M. (1961). The misbehavior of organisms. *American Psychologist, 16*, 681–684.

Bremmer, J. (1983). *The early Greek concept of the soul.* Princeton, NJ: Princeton University Press.

Brentano, F. (1981) *Sensory and noetic consciousness. Psychology from an empirical standpoint III* (L. McAlister, Ed., & M. Schättle & L. L. McAlister, Trans.). New York: Routledge & Kegan Paul. (Original work published in 1874)

Bridenthal, R., Koonz, C., & Stuard, S. (1987). *Becoming visible: Women in European history.* Boston: Houghton Mifflin.

Bringmann, W. G., Voss, U., & Ungerer, G. A. (1997). Wundt's laboratories. In W. G. Bringmann, H. E. Lück, R. Miller, & C. E. Early (Eds.), *A pictorial history of psychology* (pp. 126–132). Chicago: Quintessence.

Brobeck, S. (1997, February). The consumer impacts of expanding credit card debt. Consumer Federation of America.

Brozek, J. (1972). Russian contributions on brain and behavior. In J. Brozek and D. I. Slobin (Eds.), *Psychology in the U.S.S.R.: An historical perspective* (pp. 18–21). White Plains, NY: International Arts and Sciences Press.

Burke, J. (1985). *The day the universe changed*. Boston: Little, Brown.

Burke, R. B. (1962). *The Opus Majus of Roger Bacon* (R. B. Burke, Trans.). New York: Russell & Russell. (Original work published ca. 1267)

Burks, B. S., Jensen, D. W., & Terman, L. M. (1930). *Genetic studies of genius, Vol. 3, The promise of youth: Follow-up studies of a thousand gifted children*. Stanford, CA: Stanford University Press.

Burrows, G. M. (1976). *Commentaries on the causes, forms, symptoms, and treatment, moral and medical, of insanity*. New York: Arno Press. (Original work published in 1828)

Butterfield, L. H. (Ed.). (1951). *The letters of Benjamin Rush* (Vol. 2). Princeton, NJ: Princeton University Press. (Original works written ca. 1810)

Cahan, E. D. (1997, Fall). On the uses of history for developmental psychologists, or, on the social necessity of history. *Newsletter of the Society for Research in Child Development, 40*, pp. 2, 6, 8.

Calkins, M. (1961). Mary Whiton Calkins. In C. Murchison (Ed.), *A history of psychology in autobiography* (pp. 31–62). New York: Russell & Russell.

Calkins, M. W. (1921). The truly psychological behaviorism. *Psychological Bulletin, 28*, 1–18.

Campbell, R. H., & Skinner, A. S. (Eds.). (1982). *The origins and nature of the Scottish Enlightenment*. Edinburgh: John Donald.

Cantor, N. F. (2001, April 27). Studying the Black Death. *The Chronicle of Higher Education*, pp. B7–10.

Capshew, J. H., & Laszlo, A. C. (1986). "We would not take no for an answer": Women psychologists and gender politics during World War II. *Journal of Social Issues, 42*, 157–180.

Chiarugi, V. (1987). *On insanity and its classification* (G. Mora, Trans.). Canton, MA: Science History Publications. (Original work published in 1793)

Chomsky, N. (1972). *Language and mind* (enlarged ed.). New York: Harcourt Brace Jovanovich.

Clark, C. W. (1997). The witchcraze in 17th century Europe. In W. G. Bringmann, H. E. Lück, R. Miller, & C. E. Early (Eds.), *A pictorial history of psychology* (pp. 23–29). Chicago: Quintessence.

Clark, K. B., & Clark, M. P. (1947). Racial identification and preference in Negro children. In T. N. Newcomb & E. L. Hartley (Eds.), *Readings in social psychology* (pp. 169–178). New York: Henry Holt.

Clark, M. P. (1983). Mamie Phipps Clark. In A. N. O'Connell & N. F. Russo (Eds.), *Models of achievement. Reflections of eminent women in psychology* (pp. 267–277). New York: Columbia University Press.

Clarke, D. (1995). Experience and other reasons given for belief and disbelief in paranormal and religious phenomena. *Journal of the Society for Psychical Research, 60*, 371–384.

Clemens, D. T. (1998). "The want most keenly felt": University YWCA the early years. *Chronicle of the University of California, 1*, p. 20.

Coghill, G. E. (1933). Neuro-embryonic study of behavior: Principles, perspective and aim. *Science, 78*, 131–138.

Cohen, I. B. (1985). *Revolution in science*. Cambridge, MA: Harvard University Press.

Colapinto, J. (2000). *As nature made him—the boy who was raised as a girl*. New York: HarperCollins.

Comte, A. (1974). *The positive philosophy* (H. Martineau, Trans.). New York: AMS Press. (Original work published in 1855)

Conan Doyle, A. (1900). *A scandal in Bohemia*. New York: Rand McNally.

Conan Doyle, A. (1930). *The edge of the unknown*. New York: Berkley.

Coon, D. J. (1992). Testing the limits of sense and science: American experimental psychologists combat spiritualism, 1880–1920. *American Psychologist, 47*, 143–151.

Coon, D. J. (2002). Testing the limits of sense and science: American experimental psychologists combat spiritualism, 1880–1920. In W. E. Pickren & D. A. Dewsbury (Eds.), *Evolving perspectives on the history of psychology* (pp. 121–139). Washington, DC: American Psychological Association.

Cooney, M. P. (1996). *Celebrating women in mathematics and science*. Reston, VA: National Council of Teachers of Mathematics.

Cottrell, L. S., & Gallagher, R. (1941). *Developments in social psychology, 1930–1940*. New York: Beacon House.

Cowles, M. (1989). *Statistics in psychology. An historical perspective*. Hillsdale, NJ: Lawrence Erlbaum Associates.

Crosby, F. (1984). The denial of personal discrimination. *American Behavioral Scientist, 27*, 371–386.

Cunningham, J. L. (1997). Alfred Binet and the quest for testing higher mental functioning. In W. G. Bringmann, H. E. Lück, R. Miller, & C. E. Early (Eds.), *A pictorial history of psychology* (pp. 309–314). Chicago: Quintessence.

Damasio, A. R. (1994). *Descartes' error. Emotion, reason, and the human brain*. New York: Putnam.

Dampier, W. C. (1948). *A history of science and its relations with philosophy and religion*. Cambridge, England: Cambridge University Press.

Danziger, K. (1979). The positivist repudiation of Wundt. *Journal of the History of the Behavioral Sciences, 15*, 205–230.

Darwin, C. (1859). *On the origin of species by means of natural selection*. London: Murray.

Darwin, C. (1896, 1916). *The expression of the emotions in man and animals*. New York: D. Appleton and Company. (Original work published in 1872)

Daston, L. J. (1982). The theory of will versus the science of mind. In W. R. Woodward & M. G. Ash (Eds.), *The problematic science. Psychology in nineteenth-century thought* (pp. 88–115). New York: Praeger.

Davidson, H. A. (1992). *Alfarabi, Avicenna, and Averroes, on intellect*. New York: Oxford University Press.

Dawes, R. M., & Mulford, M. (1996). The false consensus effect and overconfidence: Flaws in judgment or flaws in how we study judgment? *Organizational Behavior and Human Decision Processes, 65*, 201–211.

de Roten, Y., Darwish, J., Stern, D. J., Fivaz-Depeursinge, E., & Corboz-Wanery, A. (1999). Nonverbal communication and alliance in therapy: The body formation coding system. *Journal of Clinical Psychology, 55*, 425–438.

Deater-Dekard, K., Dodge, K. A., Bates, J. E., & Pettit, G. S. (1996). Physical discipline among African American and European American mothers: Links to children's externalizing behaviors. *Developmental Psychology, 32*, 1065–1072.

Demand, N. (1994). *Birth, death, and motherhood in classical Greece*. Baltimore, MD: Johns Hopkins University Press.

Dennett, D. C. (1989). When philosophers encounter artificial intelligence. In S. R. Graubard (Ed.), *The artificial intelligence debate. False starts, real foundations* (pp. 283–295). Cambridge, MA: MIT Press.

Descartes, R. (1986). *Meditations on first philosophy. With selections from the objections and replies* (J. Cottingham, Trans.). New York: Cambridge University Press. (Original work published in 1641)

Dewsbury, D. A. (1978). *Comparative animal behavior*. New York: McGraw-Hill.

Dewsbury, D. A. (1992). Triumph and tribulation in the history of American comparative psychology. *Journal of Comparative Psychology, 106*, 3–19.

Dewsbury, D. A. (1996). Robert M. Yerkes. In G. A. Kimble, C. A. Boneau, & M. Wertheimer (Eds.), *Portraits of pioneers in psychology* (Vol. 2, pp. 87–105). Mahwah, NJ: Lawrence Erlbaum Associates.

Diamond, S. (1974). Four hundred years of instinct controversy. *Behavior Genetics, 4*, 237–252.

Dickens, C. (1987). *Hard times*. T. Eagleton (Ed.). New York: Methun. (Original work published in 1854)

Digby, A. (1985). *Madness, morality and medicine. A study of the York Retreat, 1796–1914*. Cambridge: Cambridge University Press.

Dinnerstein, L. (1994). *Antisemitism in America*. New York: Oxford University Press.

Diogenes L. (1972). *Lives of eminent philosophers* (R. D. Hicks, Trans.). Cambridge, MA: Harvard University Press. (Original work published ca. 500 CE)

Dover, K. J. (1978). *Greek homosexuality*. Cambridge, MA: Harvard University Press.

Edelstein, L. (1967). The Hippocratic oath: Text, translations and interpretation. In O. Temkin & C. Temkin (Eds.), *Ancient medicine, selected papers of Ludwig Edelstein* (pp. 3–63). Baltimore, MD: Johns Hopkins University Press.

Ehrenberg, V. (1968). *From Solon to Socrates. Greek history and civilization during the 6th and 5th centuries BC*. London: Methuen.

Elder, G. H. (1998). The life course as developmental theory. *Child Development, 69*, 1–12.

Epictetus. (1948). *The enchiridion* (T. W. Higginson, Trans.). Indianapolis, IN: The Bobbs-Merrill Company. (Original work published ca. 138 CE)

Erikson, E. H. (1950). *Childhood and society*. New York: Norton.

Eysenck, H. J. (1952). The effects of psychotherapy: An evaluation. *Journal of Consulting Psychology, 16*, 319–324.

Eysenck, H. J., & Wilson, G. D. (1973). *The experimental study of Freudian theories*. London: Methuen.

Fakhry, M. (1983). *A history of Islamic philosophy* (2nd ed.). New York: Columbia University Press.

Fancher, R. E. (1996). *Pioneers of psychology*. New York: W. W. Norton.

Fancher, R. E. (2000). Snapshots of Freud in America, 1899–1999. *American Psychologist, 55*, 1025–1028.

Fayter, P. (1997). Strange new worlds of space and time: Late Victorian science and science fiction. In B. Lightman (Ed.), *Victorian science in context* (pp. 256–280). Chicago: University of Chicago Press.

Festinger, L. (1957). *A theory of cognitive dissonance*. Evanston, IL: Row, Peterson.

Fink, R. (2003). *On the origins of music*. Saskatoon, CA: Greenwich.

Fischhoff, B., Slovic, P., & Lichtenstein, S. (1977). Knowing with certainty: The appropriateness of extreme confidence. *Journal of Experimental Psychology: Human Perception and Performance, 3*, 552–564.

Fisher, S., & Greenberg, R. P. (1985). *The scientific credibility of Freud's theories and therapy*. New York: Columbia University Press.

Fisher, S., & Greenberg, R. P. (1996). *Freud scientifically reappraised. Testing the theories and therapy*. New York: Wiley.

Fiske, A. P., Kitayama, S., Markus, H. R., & Nisbett, R. E. (1998). The cultural matrix of social psychology. In D. T. Gilbert, S. T. Fiske, & G. Lindzey (Eds.), *Handbook of social psychology* (Vol. 2, pp. 915–981). Boston: McGraw-Hill.

Flack, W. F., Jr., Laird, J. D., & Cavallaro, L. A. (1999). Separate and combined effects of facial expressions and bodily postures on emotional feelings. *European Journal of Social Psychology, 29*, 203–217.

Frame, D. M. (1965). *Montaigne. A biography*. New York: Harcourt, Brace & World.

Fredriksen, P. (1988). *From Jesus to Christ: The origins of the New Testament images of Jesus*. New Haven, CT: Yale University Press.

Freeman, K. (1956). Ancilla to the pre-Socratic philosophers. A complete translation of the fragments in Diels, *Fragmente der Vorsokratiker*. Cambridge, MA: Harvard University Press.

Freud, S. (1917). *The history of the psychoanalytic movement* (A. A. Brill, Trans.). New York: Nervous and Mental Disease Publishing.

Freud, S. (1950). *Beyond the pleasure principle* (J. Strachey, Trans.) London: Hogarth Press. (Original work published in 1920)

Freud, S. (1961). *Civilization and its discontents* (J. Strachey, Ed. & Trans.). New York: Norton. (Original work published in 1930)

Freud, S. (1964). New introductory lectures on psychoanalysis. In J. Strachey (Ed.), *The standard edition of the complete psychological works of Sigmund Freud* (Vol. 22, pp. 3–182). London: Hogarth Press. (Original work published in 1932)

Freud, S. (1984). The aetiology of hysteria (J. Strachey, Trans.). Address read before the Society for Psychiatry and Neurology, Vienna, April 21, 1896. In J. M. Masson (Ed.), *The assault on truth. Freud's suppression of the seduction theory.* Toronto, Canada: Collins Publishers. (Original work read in 1896)

Freud, S., & Breuer, J. (1966). Fräulein Anna O. (Breuer). In J. Strachey (Ed. and Trans.), *Studies on hysteria* (pp. 55–82). New York: Avon Books. (Original work published in 1895)

Freud, S., & Pfister, O. (1963). Letter of 9 October 1918. In E. L. Freud & H. Meng (Eds.), *Psychoanalysis and faith: The letters of Sigmund Freud and Oskar Pfister* (p. 64). New York: Basic Books.

Friedan, B. (1983). *The feminine mystique.* New York: Norton. (Original work published in 1963)

Frolov, Y. P. (1937). *Pavlov and his school. A theory of conditioned reflexes.* London: Kegan Paul, Trench, Trubner & Co.

Fuchs, A. H., & Milar, K. S. (2003). Psychology as a science. In I. B. Weiner (Ed.), *Handbook of Psychology: Vol. 1. History of Psychology* (pp. 1–26). New York: Wiley.

Furumoto, L. (1987). On the margins: Women and the professionalization of psychology in the United States, 1890–1940. In M. G. Ash & W. R. Woodward (Eds.), *Psychology in twentieth-century thought and society* (pp. 93–113). Cambridge, England: Cambridge University Press.

Furumoto, L. (1988). Shared knowledge: The Experimentalists, 1904-1929. In J. G. Morawski (Ed.) *The rise of experimentation in American psychology* (pp. 94-113). New Haven, CT: Yale University Press.

Galileo. (1957). Il Saggiatore (S. Drake, Trans.). In *Discoveries and opinions of Galileo* (p. 274). Garden City, NY: Doubleday Anchor Books. (Original work published in 1623)

Galton, F. (1869). *Hereditary genius: An inquiry into its laws and consequences.* London: Macmillan.

Galton, F. (1874). *English men of science: Their nature and nurture.* London: Macmillan.

Garcia, J., & Koelling, R. A. (1966). Relation of cue to consequence in avoidance learning. *Psychonomic Science, 4,* 123–124.

Gardner, R. A., & Gardner, B. T. (1969). Teaching sign language to a chimpanzee. *Science, 165,* 664–672.

Garrett, H. E. (1947). *Statistics in psychology and education.* New York: Longmans Green.

Garrett, H. E. (1951). *Great experiments in psychology.* New York: Appleton-Century-Crofts.

Gaukroger, S. (1995). *Descartes. An intellectual biography.* Oxford, England: Oxford University Press.

Gesell, A. (1954). The ontogenesis of infant behavior. In L. Carmichael (Ed.), *Manual of child psychology* (pp. 335–373). New York: Wiley.

Gibbons, A. (1991). Déjà vu all over again: Chimp-language wars. *Science, 251,* 1561–1562.

Gilbreth, L. M. (1973). *The psychology of management.* Easton, PA: Hive Publishing. (Original work published in 1914)

Gillespie, R. (1988). The Hawthorne experiments and the politics of experimentation. In J. G. Morawski (Ed.), *The rise of experimentation in American psychology* (pp. 114–137). New Haven, CT: Yale University Press.

Gilman, C. P. (1980). Herland. In A. J. Lane (Ed.), *The Charlotte Perkins Gilman Reader* (pp. 189–199). New York: Pantheon. (Original work published in 1915)

Gilovich, T. (1991). *How we know what isn't so: The fallibility of human reason in everyday life.* New York: Free Press.

Ginzburg, C. (1985). *Night battles. Witchcraft and agrarian cults in the sixteenth and seventeenth centuries* (J. Tedeschi & A. Tedeschi, Trans.). Baltimore: Johns Hopkins University Press. (First published as *I benandant* in 1983)

Gislebertus. (ca. 1100). *Weighing the souls of the damned.* Retrieved November 1, 2001, from http://www.icehouse.net/john_benham/Fr-Sl-4.htm.

Gleaves, D. H., & Hernandez, E. (1999). Recent formulations of Freud's development and abandonment of seduction theory: Historical/scientific clarification or a continued assault on truth? *History of Psychology, 2*, 324–354.

Gleitman, H. (1991). Edward Chace Tolman: A life of scientific and social purpose. In G. A. Kimble, M. Wertheimer, & C. White (Eds.), *Portraits of pioneers in psychology* (pp. 227–241). Hillsdale, NJ: Lawrence Erlbaum Associates.

Glickman, S. E. (1996). Donald Olding Hebb: Returning the nervous system to psychology. In G. A. Kimble, C. A. Boneau, & M. Wertheimer (Eds.), *Portraits of pioneers in psychology* (Vol. 2, pp. 227–244). Mahwah, NJ: Lawrence Erlbaum Associates.

Goddard, H. H. (1912). *The Kallikak family, a study in the heredity of feeble-mindedness.* New York: Macmillan.

Goldberg, P. A. (1968). Are women prejudiced against women? *Transaction, 5*, 28–30.

Goldstein, J. (1987). *Console and classify: The French psychiatric profession in the nineteenth century.* Cambridge: Cambridge University Press.

Golomb, J. (1989). *Nietzsche's enticing psychology of power.* Ames: Iowa State University Press.

Goodenough, F. L. (1949). *Mental testing. Its history, principles, and applications.* New York: Rinehart & Company.

Goodman, L. E. (1992). *Avicenna.* New York: Routledge.

Gould, S. J. (1996). *The mismeasure of man.* New York: W. W. Norton.

Grant, M. (1973). *Gods and mortals in classical mythology.* Springfield, MA: G. & C. Merriam.

Graunt, J. (1975). *Natural and political observations mentioned in a following index and made upon the bills of mortality.* New York: Arno Press. (Original published in 1662)

Grimal, P. (1965). *Larousse world mythology* (P. Beardsworth, Trans.). New York: Putnam. (Original work published 1963)

Grob, G. N. (1994). *The mad among us: A history of the care of America's mentally ill.* New York: Free Press.

Gross, C. G. (1998). *Brain vision memory Tales in the history of neuroscience.* Cambridge, MA: MIT Press.

Grusec, J. E. (1994). Social learning theory and developmental psychology: The legacies of Robert R. Sears and Albert Bandura. In R. D. Parke, P. A. Ornstein, J. J. Rieser, & C. Zahn-Waxler (Eds.), *A century of developmental psychology* (pp. 473–497). Washington, DC: American Psychological Association.

Guthrie, E. R. (1952). *The psychology of learning* (Rev. ed.). New York: Harper.

Hacking, I. (1975). *The emergence of probability.* Cambridge, England: Cambridge University Press.

Hall, G. S. (1885). The new psychology. *Andover Review, 3*, 120–135, 239–248.

Hall, G. S. (1907). *Adolescence. Its psychology and its relations to physiology, anthropology, sociology, sex, crime, religion, and education* (Vol. 2). New York: D. Appleton.

Hall, G. S., Baird, J. W., & Geissler, L. R. (1917). Foreword. *Journal of Applied Psychology, 1*, 5–7.

Halligan, P. W., & Marshall, J. C. (1997). Cognitive neuropsychology. The good, the bad, and the bizarre. In R. Fuller, P. N. Walsh, & P. McGinley (Eds.), *A century of psychology Progress, paradigms and prospects for the new millennium* (pp. 271–295). London: Routledge.

Harlow, H. F. (1958). The nature of love. *American Psychologist, 13*, 673–685.

Harlow, H. F., Harlow, M. K., & Meyers, D. R. (1950). Learning motivated by a manipulation drive. *Journal of Experimental Psychology, 40*, 228–234.

Harris, R. J. (1985). Multivariate statistics. When will experimental psychology catch up? In S. Koch & D. E. Leary (Eds.), *A century of psychology as a science* (pp. 678–697). New York: McGrawHill.

Hayes, K. J., & Hayes, C. (1951). The intellectual development of a home-raised chimpanzee. *Proceedings of the American Philosophical Society, 95*, 105–109.

Hebb, D. O. (1949). *The organization of behavior.* New York: Wiley.

Heidbreder, E. (1933). *Seven psychologies.* Englewood Cliffs, NJ: Prentice-Hall.

Heidegger, M. (1927). *Being and time.* Halle, Germany: Niemeyer.

Helmholtz, H. (1961). A treatise on physiological optics. In T. Shipley (Ed.), *Classics in psychology* (pp. 79–127). New York: Philosophical Library. (Original work written in 1856–1866)

Herbert, G. B. (1989). *Thomas Hobbes. The unity of scientific and moral wisdom.* Vancouver, Canada: University of British Columbia Press.

Hergenhahn, B. R. (2005). *An introduction to the history of psychology.* Belmont, CA: Thomson Wadsworth.

Hester, M. P. (1998). The status of psychology of religion: An interview with Raymond F. Paloutzian. *Teaching of Psychology, 25,* 303–306.

Hobbes, T. (1958). *Leviathan.* New York: The Liberal Arts Press. (Original work published in 1651)

Hoffman, E. (1994). *The drive for self. Alfred Adler and the founding of individual psychology.* Reading, MA: Addison-Wesley Publishing Company.

Hollingworth, L. S. (1914). *Functional periodicity.* Contributions to Education, No. 69. New York: Columbia University Press.

Horney, K. (1945). *Our inner conflicts. A constructive theory of neurosis.* New York: Norton.

Hornstein, G. A. (1988). Quantifying psychological phenomena: Debates, dilemmas, and implications. In J. G. Morawski (Ed.), *The rise of experimentation in American psychology* (pp. 1–34). New Haven, CT: Yale University Press.

Hornstein, G. A. (1992). The return of the repressed: Psychology's problematic relations with psychoanalysis, 1909–1960. *American Psychologist, 47,* 254–263.

Horowitz, F. D. (1994). John B. Watson's legacy: Learning and environment. In R. D. Parke, P. A. Ornstein, J. J. Rieser, & C. Zahn-Waxler (Eds.), *A century of developmental psychology* (pp. 233–250). Washington, DC: American Psychological Association.

Howells, J. G. (1975). *World history of psychiatry.* New York: Brunner/Mazel.

Hull, C. L. (1943). *Principles of behavior.* New York: Appleton-Century-Crofts.

Hume, D. (1878). *A treatise on human nature, being an attempt to introduce the experimental method of reasoning into moral subjects and dialogues concerning natural religion* (T. H. Green & T. H. Grose, Eds.). London: Longmans Green and Company. (Original work published in 1739–1740)

Ishikawa, S. S., & Raine, A. (2002). Psychophysical correlates of antisocial behavior: A central control hypothesis. In J. Glicksohn (Ed.), *The neurobiology of criminal behavior. Neurobiological foundation of aberrant behaviors* (pp. 187–229). Dordrecht, Netherlands: Kluwer Academic.

Ivry, A. L. (1974). *Al-Kindi's metaphysics.* Albany: State University of New York Press.

Jackson, J. P., Jr. (2000). The triumph of the segregationists? A historiographical inquiry into psychology and the *Brown* litigation. *History of Psychology, 3,* 239–261.

Jackson, S. W. (1999). *Care of the psyche. A history of psychological healing.* New Haven, CT: Yale University Press.

James, W. (1890). *The principles of psychology* (Vols. 1–2). New York: Henry Holt.

James, W. (1902). *The varieties of religious experience.* New York: Longmans, Green.

James, W. (1948). *Essays in pragmatism* (A. Castell, Ed.). New York: Hafner Publishing. (Original work published in 1907)

James, W. (1956). *The will to believe and other essays in popular philosophy.* New York: Dover Publications. (Original work published in 1896)

James, W. (1985). *Psychology: The briefer course* (G. Allport, Ed.). Notre Dame, IN: University of Notre Dame Press. (Original work published in 1892)

Jastrow, J. (1927). The reconstruction of psychology. *Psychological Review, 34,* 169–195.

Jones, E. E. (1998). Major developments in five decades of social psychology. In D. T. Gilbert, S. T. Fiske, & G. Lindzey (Eds.), *Handbook of social psychology* (pp. 3–57). Boston: McGraw Hill.

Jones, M. C. (1924). A laboratory study of fear: The case of Peter. *Pedagogical Seminary, 31,* 308–315.

Joravsky, D. (1989). *Russian psychology. A critical history.* Cambridge, MA: Basil Blackwell.

Joseph, J. E. (2001). Functional neuroimaging studies of category specificity in object recognition: A critical review and meta-analysis. *Cognitive, Affective & Behavioral Neuroscience, 1,* 119–136.

Jung, C. G. (1933). *Modern man in search of a soul.* New York: Harcourt Brace Jovanovich.

Kagan, J. (1998). *Three seductive ideas.* Cambridge, MA: Harvard University Press.

Kaminer, W. (1992). *I'm dysfunctional, you're dysfunctional. The recovery movement and other self-help fashions.* Reading, MA: Addison-Wesley.

Kant, I. (1927). *Critique of pure reason* (F. M. Müller, Trans.). New York: Macmillan. (Original work published in 1781)

Kantor, J. R. (1963–1969). *The scientific evolution of psychology.* Chicago: The Principia Press.

Katzell, R. A., & Austin, J. T. (1992). From then to now. The development of industrial-organizational psychology in the United States. *Journal of Applied Psychology, 77,* 803–835.

Kearney, M. (1984). *World view.* Novato, CA: Chandler & Sharp.

Kelley, T. L. (1923). *Statistical method.* New York: Macmillan.

Kellogg, W. N., & Kellogg, L. A. (1967). *The ape and the child: A study of environmental influence upon early behavior.* New York: Hafner. (Original work published in 1933)

Kelly, G. A. (1955). *The psychology of personal constructs: A theory of personality* (Vols. 1–2). New York: Norton.

Kelly, R. M., & Kelly, V. P. (1990). Lillian Moller Gilbreth. In A. N. O'Connell & N. F. Russo (Eds.), *Women in psychology: A bio-bibliographic sourcebook* (pp. 117–124). New York: Greenwood Press.

Kemp, S. (1996). *Cognitive psychology in the Middle Ages.* Westport, CT: Greenwood Press.

Keppel, B. (2002). Kenneth B. Clark in the patterns of American culture. *American Psychologist, 57,* 29–37.

Keuls, E. C. (1985). *The reign of the phallus. Sexual politics in ancient Athens.* Berkeley: University of California Press.

Kimble, G. A. (1953). Psychology as a science. *Scientific Monthly, 77,* 156–160.

Kirsch, I. (1985). Response expectancies as a determinant of experience and behavior. *American Psychologist, 40,* 1189–1202.

Klein, M. (1932). *The psycho-analysis of children.* New York: Norton.

Kleinmuntz, B. (1967). Sign and seer: Another example. *Journal of Abnormal Psychology, 72,* 163–165.

Knoff, W. F. (1970). A history of the concept of neurosis, with a memoir of William Cullen. *American Journal of Psychiatry, 127,* 120–124.

Knox, B. (1993). *The oldest dead white European males and other reflections on the classics.* New York: Norton.

Koenigsberger, L. (1965). *Hermann von Helmholtz* (F. A. Welby, Trans.). New York: Dover. (Original work published in 1906)

Koffka, K. (1922). Perception: An introduction to Gestalt-Theorie. *Psychological Bulletin, 19,* 531–585.

Köhler, W. (1925). *The mentality of apes.* London: Routledge and Kegan Paul. (Original work published in 1917)

Koppes, L. L. (1997). American female pioneers of industrial and organizational psychology during the early years. *Journal of Applied Psychology, 82,* 500–515.

Kraepelin, E. (1971). *Dementia praecox and paraphrenia* (R. M. Barclay & G. M. Robertson, Trans.). Huntington, NY: Robert E. Krieger Publishing. (Original work published in 1911)

Kramer, P. D. (1993). *Listening to prozac. A psychiatrist explores antidepressant drugs and the remaking of the self.* New York: Penguin.

Kuhn, T. (1970). *The structure of scientific revolutions.* Chicago: University of Chicago Press.

La Mettrie, J. O. de. (1912). *L'homme machine* [Man a machine] (M. W. Calkins, Trans.). La Salle, IL: Open Court. (Original work published in 1748)

Ladd-Franklin, C. (1929). *Colour and colour theory.* New York: Harcourt Brace

Lal, S. (2002). Giving children security. Mamie Phipps Clark and the racialization of child psychology. *American Psychologist, 57,* 20–28.

Lane, H. (1976). *The wild boy of Aveyron.* Cambridge, MA: Harvard University Press.

LaPiere, R. T. (1934). Attitudes and actions. *Social Forces, 13,* 230–237.

Larson, C. A., & Sullivan, J. J. (1965). Watson's relation to Titchener. *Journal of the History of the Behavioral Sciences, 1*, 538–554.

Lashley, K. (1930). Basic neural mechanisms in behavior. *Psychological Review, 37*, 1–24.

Lashley, K. S. (1923a). The behavioristic interpretation of consciousness I. *The Psychological Review, 30*, 237–272.

Lashley, K. S. (1923b). The behavioristic interpretation of consciousness II. *The Psychological Review, 30*, 329–353.

Leahey, T. (1981). The mistaken mirror: On Wundt and Titchener's psychologies. *Journal of the History of the Behavioral Sciences, 17*, 273–282.

Leahey, T. H. & Leahey, G. E. (1983). *Psychology's occult doubles. Psychology and the problem of pseudoscience.* Chicago: Nelson-Hall.

Leary, D. (1978). The philosophical development of the conception of psychology in Germany, 1780–1850. *Journal of the History of the Behavioral Sciences, 14*, 113–121.

Leary, D. E. (1992). William James and the art of human understanding. *American Psychologist, 47*, 152–160.

Lerman, H. (1996). *Pigeonholing women's misery. A history and critical analysis of the psychodiagnosis of women in the twentieth century.* New York: Basic Books, Harper Collins.

Lerner, G. (1986). *The creation of patriarchy.* New York: Oxford University Press.

Lewin, K., Lippitt, R., & White, R. K. (1939). Patterns of aggressive behavior in experimentally created "social climates." *Journal of Social Psychology, 10*, 271–299.

Liff, Z. A. (1992). Psychoanalysis and dynamic techniques. In D. K. Freedheim (Ed.), *History of psychotherapy. A century of change* (pp. 571–586). Washington, DC: American Psychological Association.

Likert, R. (1932). A technique for the measurement of attitudes. *Archives of Psychology, 22*, 5–55.

Locke, J. (1989). *Some thoughts concerning education* (J. W. Yolton & J. S. Yolton, Eds.). Oxford: Clarendon Press. (Original work published in 1693)

Lommel, A. (1966). *Prehistoric and primitive man.* New York: McGraw-Hill Book Company.

Loverance, R. (1988). *Byzantium.* Cambridge, MA: Harvard University Press.

Lowery-Palmer, A. (1980). *Yoruba world view and patient compliance.* Unpublished doctoral dissertation, Department of Anthropology, University of California, Riverside.

Maccoby, E. E., & Martin, J. (1983). Socialization in the context of the family: Parent-child interaction. In P. H. Mussen (Ed.), *Handbook of child psychology, v. 4, Socialization, personality, and social development* (pp. 1–102). New York: Wiley.

MacDonald, M. (1981). *Mystical Bedlam: Madness, anxiety, and healing in seventeenth century England.* Cambridge, England: Cambridge University Press.

Mahler, M. S., Pine, F., & Bergman, A. (1994). Stages in the infant's separation from the mother. In G. Handel & G. G. Whitchurch (Eds.), *The psychosocial interior of the family* (4th ed., pp. 419–448). New York: Aldine De Gruyter.

Mandler, J. M. (2004). *The foundations of mind: The origins of the conceptual system.* New York: Oxford University Press.

Marcel, A. J. (1983). Conscious and unconscious perception: Experiments on visual masking and word recognition. *Cognitive Psychology, 15*, 197–237.

Margolin, M. (1978). *The Ohlone way.* Berkeley, CA: Heydey.

Marshack, A. (1972). *The roots of civilization: The cognitive beginnings of man's first art, symbol, and notation.* New York: McGraw Hill.

Marshall, M., & Wendt, R. A. (1980). Wilhelm Wundt, Spiritism, and the assumptions of science. In W. G. Bringmann & R. D. Tweney (Eds.), *Wundt studies. A centennial collection* (pp. 158–175). Toronto: C. J. Hogrefe.

Maslow, A. H. (1954). *Motivation and personality.* New York: Harper & Row.

Masson, J. M. (1984). *The assault on truth. Freud's suppression of the seduction theory.* Toronto, Canada: Collins Publishers.

Mayo, E. (1933). *The human problems of an industrial civilization.* New York: Macmillan.

McClearn, G. E. (1991). A trans-time visit with Francis Galton. In G. A Kimble, M. Wertheimer, & C. White (Eds.), *Portraits of pioneers in psychology* (pp. 1–11). Hillsdale, NJ: Lawrence Erlbaum Associates.

McGraw, M. (1935). *Growth: A study of Johnny and Jimmy.* New York: Appleton-Century-Crofts.

McGue, M., & Lykken, D. T. (1991). Genetic influence on risk of divorce. *Psychological Science, 3,* 368–373.

McReynolds, P. (1987). Lightner Witmer: Little-known founder of clinical psychology. *American Psychologist, 42,* 849–858.

Megginson H. J. (1996). Rhesus incompatibility as a risk factor for schizophrenia in male adults. *Archives of General Psychiatry, 53,* 19–24.

Milar, K. (2000). The first generation of women psychologists and the psychology of women. *American Psychologist, 55,* 616–619.

Milar, K. S. (2000). The first generation of women psychologists and the psychology of women. *American Psychologist, 55,* 616–619.

Milgram, S. (1963). Behavioral study of obedience. *Journal of Abnormal and Social Psychology, 67,* 371–378.

Miller, D. T. (1999). The norm of self-interest. *American Psychologist, 54,* 1053–1060.

Miller, G. A. (1956). The magical number seven plus or minus two: Some limits on our capacity for processing information. *Psychological Review, 63,* 81–97.

Miller, G. A. (2003). The cognitive revolution: A historical perspective. *Trends in Cognitive Sciences, 7,* 141–144.

Miller, L. (1975). Israel and the Jews. In J. G. Howells (Ed.), *World history of psychiatry* (pp. 528–546). New York: Brunner/Mazel.

Minton, H. L. (1988). Charting life history: Lewis M. Terman's study of the gifted. In J. G. Morawski (Ed.), *The rise of experimentation in American psychology* (pp. 138–162). New Haven, CT: Yale University Press.

Mireaux, E. (1959). *Daily life in the time of Homer* (I. Sells, Trans.). New York: MacMillan. (Original work published in 1954)

Mitchell, S. A., & Black, M. J. (1995). *Freud and beyond. A history of modern psychoanalytic thought.* New York: Basic Books.

Montaigne, Michel. (1958). Man is no better than the animals. *Essays, Book II.* Stanford, CA: Stanford University Press. (Original work published in 1580)

Moore, R. L. (1977). *In search of white crows. Spiritualism, parapsychology, and American culture.* New York: Oxford University Press.

Morawski, J. G. (2000). Social psychology a century ago. *American Psychologist, 55,* 427–430.

Morawski, J. G., & Hornstein, G. A. (1991). Quandary of the quacks. The struggle for expert knowledge in American psychology, 1890–1940. In J. Brown & D. K. van Keuren (Eds.), *The estate of social knowledge* (pp. 106–133). Baltimore: Johns Hopkins University Press.

Morgan, C. D., & Murray, H. A. (1935). A method for investigating fantasies: The Thematic Apperception Test. *Archives of Neurology and Psychiatry, 34,* 289–306.

Morgan, C. L. (1904). *An introduction to comparative psychology.* New York: Scribner's.

Münsterberg, H. (1913). *Psychology and industrial efficiency.* Boston: Houghton Mifflin.

Murphy, G., & Murphy, L. B. (1968). *Asian psychology.* New York: Basic Books.

Napoli, D. S. (1981). *Architects of adjustment. The history of the psychological profession in the United States.* Port Washington, NY: Kennikat Press.

Neisser, U. (1967). *Cognitive psychology.* New York: Appleton-Century-Crofts.

Norcross, J. C., & Freedheim, D. K. (1992). Into the future: Retrospect and prospect in psychotherapy. In D. K. Freedheim (Ed.), *History of psychotherapy. A century of change* (pp. 881–900). Washington, DC: American Psychological Association.

O'Connell, A. N., & Russo, N. F. (1990). *Women in psychology. A bio-bibliographic sourcebook.* New York: Greenwood.

O'Donnell, J. M. (2002). The crisis of experimentalism in the 1920s: E. G. Boring and his uses of history. In W. E. Pickren & D. A. Dewsbury (Eds.), *Evolving perspectives on the history of psychology* (pp. 45–56). Washington, DC: American Psychological Association.

O'Hanlon, W. H., & Weiner-Davis, M. (1989). *In search of solutions: A new direction in psychotherapy.* New York: Norton.

Offenbach, J. (1959). *The tales of Hoffman* (R. Martin & T. Martin, Trans.). New York: G. Schirmer. (Original work produced in 1881)

Paludi, M. A., & Strayer, L. A. (1985). What's in an author's name? Differential evaluations of performance as a function of author's name. *Sex Roles, 10,* 353–361.

Papert, S. (1989). One AI or many? In S. R. Graubard (Ed.), *The artificial intelligence debate. False starts, real foundations* (pp. 1–14). Cambridge, MA: MIT Press.

Pechmann, C. (1996). Do consumers overgeneralize one-sided comparative price claims, and are more stringent regulations needed? *Journal of Marketing Research, 33,* 150–162.

Pepperberg, I. M. (1999). *The Alex studies: Cognitive and communicative abilities of Grey parrots.* Cambridge, MA: Harvard University Press.

Pepperberg, I. M. (2002). Cognitive and communicative abilities of Grey parrots. *Current Directions in Psychological Science, 11,* 83–87.

Perez, J. E. (1999). Clients deserve empirically supported treatments, not romanticism. *American Psychologist, 54,* 205–206.

Piaget, J. (1926). *The language and thought of the child.* London: Routledge.

Pickren, W. E. (2004). Between the cup of principle and the lip of practice: Ethnic minorities and American psychology. *History of Psychology, 7,* 45–64.

Pifer, A. (1973, August). The higher education of Blacks in the United States. *The Alfred and Winifred Hoernlé Memorial Lecture for 1973.* New York: Carnegie Corporation of New York.

Pignatti, T. (1969). *Pietro Longhi* (P. Waley, Trans.). London: Phaidon Press.

Pinel, P. (1962). A treatise on insanity. Academy of Medicine. *The History of Medicine Series.* New York: Hafner. (Original work published in 1801)

Plato. (1993). *Republic* (R. Waterfield, Trans.). New York: Oxford University Press. (Original work written ca. 380 BC)

Poe, E. A. (1992). The tell-tale heart. In J. Seelye (Ed.), *The complete stories.* New York: Alfred A. Knopf. (Original work published in 1842)

Popper, K. (1968). *The logic of scientific discovery.* New York: Harper & Row. (Original work published in 1935)

Popplestone, J. A., & McPherson, M. W. (1994). *An illustrated history of American psychology* (2nd ed.). Akron, OH: University of Akron Press.

Porter, K. (1972). *Through a glass darkly. Spiritualism in the Browning circle.* New York: Octagon Books.

Postman, L. (1973). Hermann Ebbinghaus. In M. Henle, J. Jaynes, & J. Sullivan (Eds.), *Historical conceptions of psychology* (pp. 220–229). New York: Springer.

Potts, T. C. (1980). *Conscience in medieval philosophy.* New York: Cambridge University Press.

Premack, D. (1976). *Intelligence in ape and man.* Hillsdale, NJ: Lawrence Erlbaum Associates.

Proctor, R. N. (1991). Eugenics among the social sciences. Hereditarian thought in Germany and the United States. In J. Brown & D. K. van Keuren (Eds.), *The estate of social knowledge* (pp. 175–208). Baltimore: Johns Hopkins University Press.

Purver, M. (1967). *The Royal Society: Concept and creation.* Cambridge, MA: MIT Press.

Rahman, F. (1952). *Avicenna's psychology. An English translation of Kitab al-Najat, Book II, Chapter VI with historico-philosophical notes and textual improvements on the Cairo edition.* London: Oxford University Press.

Raine, A., Meloy, J. R., Bihrle, S., LaCasse, L., & Buchsbaum, M. S. (1998). Reduced prefrontal and increased subcortical brain functioning assessed using positron emission tomography in predatory and affective murderers. *Behavioral Sciences and the Law, 16*, 319–332.

Ramos, S. de Paula (2003). Revisiting Anna O.: A case of chemical dependence. *History of Psychology, 6*, 239–250.

Reed, E. S. (1997). *From soul to mind. The emergence of psychology from Erasmus Darwin to William James.* New Haven, CT: Yale University Press.

Reid, T. (1969). *Essays on the intellectual powers of man.* Cambridge, MA: MIT Press. (Original work published in 1785)

Reisman, J. M. (1991). *A history of clinical psychology.* New York: Hemisphere.

Richards, R. J. (1982). Darwin and the biologizing of moral behavior. In W. R. Woodward & M. G. Ash (Eds.), *The problematic science. Psychology in nineteenth century thought* (pp. 43–64). New York: Praeger.

Robinson, D. N. (1989). *Aristotle's psychology.* New York: Cambridge University Press.

Rogers, C. R., & Dymond, R. F. (Eds.). (1954). *Psychotherapy and personality change: Coordinated studies in the client-centered approach.* Chicago: University of Chicago Press.

Romanes, G. J. (1882). *Animal intelligence.* London: Kegan Paul, Trench.

Romanes, G. J. (1884). *Mental evolution in animals.* New York: Appleton.

Romanes, G. J. (1888). *Mental evolution in man.* London: Kegan Paul, Trench.

Rovee-Collier, C. K., & Fagen, J. W. (1981). The retrieval of memory in early infancy. In L. P. Lipsitt (Ed.), *Advances in infancy research* (pp. 225–254). Norwood, NJ: Ablex.

Rumbaugh, D. M. (Ed.). (1977). *Language learning by a chimpanzee: The LANA Project.* New York: Academic Press.

Rush, B. (1811). Explanation of the plate of the tranquillizer. *The Philadelphia Medical Museum, 1*, 169–172.

Russell, B. (1945). *A history of Western philosophy.* New York: Simon and Schuster.

Russell, J. B. (1972). *Witchcraft in the Middle Ages.* Ithaca, NY: Cornell University Press.

Russell, J. B. (1980). *A history of witchcraft: Sorcerers, heretics, and pagans.* New York: Thames & Hudson.

Russo, M. (2003). *Herman Hollerith: The world's first statistical engineer.* Retrieved April 25, 2003, from Univeristy of Rochester Web site: http://www.history.rochester.edu/steam/hollerith/index.htm.

Rutter, M. (2002). Nature, nurture, and development: From evangelism through science toward policy and practice. *Child Development, 73*, 1–21.

Ryle, G. (1949). *The concept of mind.* London: Hutchinson & Company.

Sagan, C. (1996). *The demon-haunted world: Science as a candle in the dark.* New York: Ballantine.

Samelson, F. (1981). Struggle for scientific authority: The reception of Watson's behaviorism, 1913–1920. *Journal of the History of the Behavioral Sciences, 17*, 399–425.

Savage-Rumbaugh, E. S. (1988). A new look at ape language: Comprehension of vocal speech and syntax. In D. W. Leger (Ed.), *Comparative perspectives in modern psychology (Nebraska symposium on motivation 1987)* (pp. 201–255). Lincoln: University of Nebraska Press.

Sawyer, T. F. (2000). Francis Cecil Sumner: His views and influence on African American higher education. *History of Psychology, 3*, 122–141.

Scarborough, E., & Furumoto, L. (1987). *Untold lives: The first generation of American women psychologists.* New York: Columbia University Press.

Scarr, S. (1992). Developmental theories for the 1990s: Development and individual differences. *Child Development, 63*, 1–19.

Schacter, S. (1951). Deviation, rejection, and communication. *Journal of Abnormal and Social Psychology, 46*, 190–207.

Schachter, S., & Singer, J. E. (1962). Cognitive, social, and physiological determinants of emotional state. *Psychological Review, 69*, 379–399.

Schneider, K. J. (1999). Clients deserve relationships, not merely treatments. *American Psychologist, 54*, 206–207.

Schopenhauer, A. (1942). *Complete essays of Schopenhauer* (T. B. Saunders, Trans.). New York: Willey Book Company. (Original work published in 1844)

Schopenhauer, A. (1994). *Arthur Schopenhauer. Philosophical writings* (W. Schirmacher, Ed.). New York: Continuum Publishing. (Original works published in 1841–1852)

Schwartz, T. (1998, Summer). The bull and the bear and the woolly mammoth. *Oregon Quarterly*, pp. 23–25. Eugene: University of Oregon.

Scott, D. M. (1997). *Contempt and pity: Social policy and the image of the damaged Black psyche 1880-1996*. Chapel Hill: University of North Carolina Press.

Scott, W. D. (1913). *The psychology of advertising*. Boston: Small, Maynard.

Scull, A. (1993). *The most solitary of afflictions. Madness and society in Britain 1700–1900*. New Haven, CT: Yale University Press.

Scull, A., McKenzie, C., & Hervey, N. (1996). *Masters of Bedlam. The transformation of the mad-doctoring trade*. Princeton, NJ: Princeton University Press.

Searle, J. R. (1982, April 29). Myth of the computer [Review of the book *The mind's I: Fantasies and reflections on self and soul*]. *New York Review of Books*, pp. 3–6.

Sears, R., Pintler, M., & Sears, P. (1946). Effect of father separation on preschool children's doll play aggression. *Child Development, 17*, 219–243.

Sechenov, I. (1965). *Reflexes of the brain* (K. Koshtoyants, Ed. & S. Belsky, Trans.). Cambridge, MA: MIT Press. (Original work published in 1863)

Seligman, M. (1993, 1994). *What you can change . . . and what you can't*. New York: Fawcett Columbine.

Seligman, M. E. P., & Maier, S. (1967). Failure to escape traumatic shock. *Journal of Experimental Psychology, 74*, 1–9.

Shakespeare, W. (1623/1969). Macbeth. In A. Harbage (Ed.), *William Shakespeare the complete works* (pp. 1107–1135). Baltimore, Maryland: Penguin Books.

Shapiro, M. J. (1991). *Ellis Island. An illustrated history of the immigrant experience*. New York: Macmillan.

Sharp, S. E. (1899). Individual psychology: A study in psychological method. *American Journal of Psychology, 10*, 329–391.

Shelley, M. W. (1921). *Frankenstein*. New York: Dutton. (Original work published in 1818)

Sherif, M. (1935). A study in some social factors in perception. *Archives of Psychology* (No. 187).

Sherif, M. (1947). Group influences upon the formation of norms and attitudes. In T. M. Newcomb & E. L. Hartley (Eds.), *Readings in social psychology* (pp. 77–90). New York: Henry Holt.

Sherif, M., Harvey, O. J., White, B., Hood, W., & Sherif, C. (1961). *Intergroup conflict and cooperation: The robber's cave experiment*. Norman: Institute of Group Relations, University of Oklahoma.

Shermer, M. (1997). *Why people believe weird things*. New York: W. H. Freeman.

Shorter, E. (1997). *A history of psychiatry. From the era of the asylum to the age of Prozac*. New York: Wiley.

Siegler, R. S. (1994). The other Alfred Binet. In R. D. Parke, P. A. Ornstein, J. J. Rieser, & C. Zahn-Waxler (Eds.), *A century of developmental psychology* (pp. 175–202). Washington, DC: American Psychological Association.

Skinner, B. F. (1938). *The behavior of organisms*. New York: Appleton.

Skinner, B. F. (1948). *Walden two*. New York: Macmillan.

Skinner, B. F. (1971). *Beyond freedom and dignity*. New York: Alfred A. Knopf.

Sklar, K. K. (1971). Education of women: History. In L. C. Deighton (Ed.), *The encyclopedia of education* (Vol. 9, pp. 557–562). London: Macmillan.

Smith, M. (1944). *Handbook of industrial psychology*. New York: Philosophical Library.

Snelson, J. S. (1993). The ideological immune system. *Skeptic, 1*, 44–55.

Snyderman, M., & Herrnstein, R. J. (1983). Intelligence tests and the Immigration Act of 1924. *American Psychologist, 38*, 986–995.

Snyderman, M., & Rothman, S. (1988). *The IQ controversy, the media and public policy.* New Brunswick, NJ: Transaction Books.

Sokal, M. M. (1980). *Science* and James McKeen Cattell, 1894–1945. *Science, 209,* 43–52.

Spearman, C. (1904). General intelligence objectively determined and measured. *American Journal of Psychology, 15,* 201–292.

Spence, J. T., Deaux, K., & Helmreich, R. L. (1985). Sex roles in contemporary American society. In G. Lindzey & E. Aronson (Eds.), *Handbook of social psychology* (3rd ed., pp. 149–178). New York: Random House.

Spencer, H. (1880). *First principles.* London: Williams & Norgate.

Sperry, R. (1964). The great cerebral commissure. *Scientific American, 210,* 42–52.

Sperry, R. W. (1993). The impact and promise of the cognitive revolution. *American Psychologist, 48,* 878–885.

Spinoza, B. (1985). The emendation of the intellect. In E. Curley (Ed. and Trans.), *The collected works of Spinoza* (Vol. 1, pp. 7–45). Princeton, NJ: Princeton University Press. (Original work published in 1677)

Spock, B. (1946). *Baby and child care.* New York: Meredith Press.

Stevens, G., & Gardner, S. (1982). *The women of psychology. Vol. I: Pioneers and innovators.* Cambridge, MA: Schenkman.

Stone, M. H. (1997). *Healing the mind. A history of psychiatry from antiquity to the present.* New York: Norton.

Swift, J. (1966). A character, panegyric, and description of the Legion Club. In H. Williams (Ed.), *The poems of Jonathan Swift* (2nd ed., pp. 835–836). Oxford: Clarendon. (Original work published in 1736)

Szasz, T. S. (1960). The myth of mental illness. *American Psychologist, 15,* 113–118.

Szasz, T. S. (1970). *The manufacture of madness.* New York: Harper & Row.

Taylor, F. W. (1911). *The principles of scientific management.* New York: Harper & Brothers.

Terman, L. M. (1916). *The measurement of intelligence.* Boston: Houghton Mifflin.

Thomas, A., Chess, S., Birch, H. G., Hertzig, M. E., & Korn, S. (1963). *Behavioral individuality in early childhood.* New York: New York University Press.

Thomas, D. (1933). An attempt to develop precise measurement in the social behavior field. *Sociologus, 9,* 1–21.

Thomas, K. (1971). *Religion and the decline of magic.* New York: Scribner's.

Thompson, H. B. (1903). *The mental traits of sex.* Chicago: University of Chicago Press.

Thorndike, E. L. (1898). Animal intelligence: An experimental study of the associative processes in animals. *Psychological Review,* Monograph Supplement, 2 (8).

Thorndike, E. L. (1911). *Animal intelligence.* New York: Macmillan.

Thorne, B. M. (1997). Can apes learn a human language? In W. G. Bringmann, H. E. Lück, R. Miller, & C. E. Early (Eds.), *A pictorial history of psychology* (pp. 191–197). Chicago: Quintessence.

Titchener, E. B. (1898). The postulates of a structural psychology. *The Philosophical Review, 41,* 449–465.

Titchener, E. B. (1912). *A text-book of psychology.* New York: Macmillan.

Tolman, E. C. (1948). Cognitive maps in rats and men. *Psychological Review, 55,* 189–208.

Triplett, N. (1897). The dynamogenic factors in pacemaking and competition. *American Journal of Psychology, 9,* 507–533.

Tuchman, B. W. (1978). *A distant mirror: The calamitous 14th century.* New York: Alfred A. Knopf.

Turing, A. M. (1950). Computing machinery and intelligence. *Mind, 59,* 433–460.

Tversky, A., & Kahneman, D. (1973). Availability: A heuristic for judging frequency and probability. *Cognitive Psychology, 5,* 207–232.

Tweney, R. D. (1997). Edward Bradford Titchener (1867–1927). In W. G. Bringmann, H. E. Lück, R. Miller, & C. E. Early, (Eds.), *A pictorial history of psychology* (pp. 153–161). Chicago: Quintessence.

Tylor, E. B. (1924). *Primitive culture: Researches into the development of mythology, philosophy, religion, language, art and custom* (7th ed.). New York: Brentano's.

Unger, R. K. (1997). The three sided mirror. Feminists looking at psychologists looking at women. In R. Fuller, P. N. Walsh, & P. McGinley (Eds.), *A century of psychology: Progress paradigms and prospects for the new millenium* (pp. 16–35). London: Routledge.

University College London. *History*. Retrieved December 29, 2004, from http://www.psychol.ucl.ac.uk/info/history.htm.

van den Boom, D. C. (1989). Neonatal irritability and the development of attachment. In G. A. Kohnstamm, J. E. Bates, & M. K. Rothbart (Eds.), *Temperament in childhood* (pp. 299–318). New York: Wiley.

van Drunen, P. (1997). Psychotechnics. In W. G. Bringmann, H. E. Lück, R. Miller, & C. E. Early (Eds.), *A pictorial history of psychology* (pp. 480–484). Chicago: Quintessence.

Venables, P. H. (1996). Schizotypy and maternal exposure to influenza and to cold temperature: The Mauritius study. *Journal of Abnormal Psychology, 105*, 53–60.

Vesalius, A. (1952). *On the human brain* (C. Singer, Trans.). London: Oxford University Press. (Original work published as *De Humani Corporis Fabrica* in 1543)

Viney, W. (1996). Dorothea Dix: An intellectual conscience for psychology. In G. A. Kimble, C. A. Boneau, & M. Wertheimer (Eds.), *Portraits of pioneers in psychology* (Vol. 2, pp. 15–31). Washington, DC: American Psychological Association.

Viney, W. (2001). The radical empiricism of William James and philosophy of history. *History of Psychology, 4*, 211–227.

Vygotsky, L. S. (1978). *Mind in society* (M. Cole, V. John-Steiner, S. Scribner, & E. Souberman, Eds.). Cambridge, MA: Harvard University Press. (Original work published in 1930)

Vyse, S. A. (1997). *Believing in magic*. New York: Oxford University Press.

Wallach, M. A., & Wallach, L. (1983). *Psychology's sanction for selfishness*. San Francisco: W. H. Freeman.

Wallman, J. (1992). *Aping language*. Cambridge, England: Cambridge University Press.

Washburn, M. F. (1916). *Movement and mental imagery: Outline of a motor theory of consciousness*. Boston: Houghton Mifflin.

Washburn, M. F. (1936). *The animal mind. A textbook of comparative psychology* (4th ed.). New York: Macmillan. (Original work published in 1908)

Watson, J. B. (1913). Psychology as the behaviorist views it. *Psychological Review, 20*, 158–177.

Watson, J. B. (1928). *Psychological care of infant and child*. London: George Allen & Unwin.

Watson, J. B. (1930). *Behaviorism*. Chicago: University of Chicago Press.

Watson, J. B., & Rayner, R. (1920). Conditioned emotional reactions. *Journal of Experimental Psychology, 3*, 1–14.

Watson, R. I. (1979). *Basic writings in the history of psychology*. New York: Oxford University Press.

Wegner, D. M. (2003). The mind's best trick: How we experience conscious will. *Trends in Cognitive Sciences, 7*, 65–69.

Wegner, D. M. & Wheatley, T. (1999). Apparent mental causation. Sources of the experience of will. *American Psychologist, 54*, 480–492.

Weinberg, J. R. (1964). *A short history of medieval philosophy*. Princeton, NJ: Princeton University Press.

Weinstein, N. D. (1980). Unrealistic optimism about future life events. *Journal of Personality and Social Psychology, 39*, 806–820.

Wells, H. G. (1934). The invisible man. In *Seven science fiction novels of H. G. Wells* (pp. 183–306). New York: Dover. (Original work published in 1895)

Wertheimer, M. (1959). *Productive thinking*. New York: Harper. (Original work published in 1945)

Wertheimer, M. (1968). Experimental studies on the seeing of motion. In W. S. Sahakian (Ed.), *History of psychology: A source book in systematic psychology* (pp. 418–422). Itasca, IL: Peacock. (Original work published in 1912)

Wertsch, J. V., & Tulviste, P. (1994). Lev Semyonovich Vygotsky and contemporary developmental psychology. In R. D. Parke, P. A. Ornstein, J. J. Rieser, & C. Zahn-Waxler (Eds.), *A century of developmental psychology* (pp. 333–355). Washington, DC: American Psychological Association.

Wheeler, R. W. (1923). Introspection and behavior. *Psychological Review, 30*, 103–115.

Wiener, N. (1948). *Cybernetics*. New York: Wiley.

Wiggins, J. G., Jr. (1994). Would you want your child to be a psychologist? *American Psychologist, 49*, 485–492.

Wilde, O. (1992). The importance of being earnest. In J. Bristow (Ed.), *The importance of being earnest and related writings* (pp. 27–87). London: Routledge. (Original work published in 1899)

Wilford, J. N. (1996, October 29). Playing of flute may have graced Neanderthal fire. *New York Times*, p. C1.

Wilson, E. O. (1975). *Sociobiology: The new synthesis*. Cambridge, MA: Belknap.

Wilson, T. D. (2002). *Strangers to ourselves: Discovering the adaptive unconscious*. Boston: Harvard University Press.

Winter, A. (1997). The construction of orthodoxies and heterodoxies in the early Victorian life sciences. In B. Lightman (Ed.), *Victorian science in context* (pp. 24–50). Chicago: University of Chicago Press.

Winter, A. (1998). *Mesmerized. Powers of mind in Victorian Britain*. Chicago: University of Chicago Press.

Wogaman, P. J. (1977). *The great economic debate: An ethical analysis*. Philadelphia: Westminster.

Wollstonecraft, M. (1792). *A vindication of the rights of woman*. Boston: Thomas and Andrews.

Woody, T. (1966). *A history of women's education in the United States*. New York: Octagon Books. (Original work published in 1929)

Woolley, H. T. (1910). Psychological literature: A review of the recent literature on the psychology of sex. *Psychological Bulletin, 7*, 335–342.

Wundt, E. (1927). *Wilhelm Wundts Werk. Ein Verzeichnis seiner saemtlichen Schriften [Wilhelm Wundt's works. A list of his collected writings]*. Munich, Germany: Beck.

Wundt, W. (1916). *Elements of folk psychology* (E. L. Schaub, Trans.). London: George Allen & Unwin.

Wundt, W. M. (1969). *Outlines of psychology* (C. H. Judd, Trans.). St Clair Shores, MI: Scholarly Press. (Original work published in 1897)

Yaroschevskii, M. G. (1982). The logic of scientific development and the scientific school. The example of Ivan Mikhailovich Sechenov. In W. R. Woodward & M. G. Ash (Eds.), *The problematic science. Psychology in nineteenth-century thought* (pp. 231–254). New York: Praeger.

Zajonc, R. B. (1980). Cognition and social cognition: A historical perspective. In L. Festinger (Ed.), *Retrospections on social psychology* (pp. 180–204). New York: Oxford University Press.

Zax, M., & Klein, A. (1960). Measurement of personality and behavior changes following psychotherapy. *Psychological Bulletin, 57*, 435–448.

Zenderland, L. (1988). Education, evangelism, and the origins of clinical psychology: The child-study legacy. *Journal of the History of the Behavioral Sciences, 24*, 152–165.

Zinn, H. (1998). *The twentieth century. A people's history*. New York: HarperCollins.

ADDITIONAL READINGS

Abell, G. O., & Singer, B. (Eds.). (1981). *Science and the paranormal: Probing the existence of the supernatural*. New York: Scribner's.

Adams, G. (1931). *Psychology: Science or superstition?* New York: Covici Friede.

Adams, G. (1934). The rise and fall of psychology. *Atlantic Monthly, 153*, 82–90.

Altarriba, J. (Ed.). (1993). *Cognition and culture. A cross-cultural approach to cognitive psychology*. Amsterdam: North-Holland.

Amsel, A. (1987, 1989). *Behaviorism, neobehaviorism, and cognitivism in learning theory: Historical and contemporary perspectives*. Hillsdale, NJ: Lawrence Erlbaum Associates.

Anderson, J. R. (1990). *The adaptive character of thought*. Hillsdale, NJ: Lawrence Erlbaum Associates.

Augustine. (1931). *The city of God* (J. Healy, Trans.). New York: E. P. Dutton. (Original work written 413-426 CE)

Augustine. (1982). *The literal meaning of Genesis* (J. H. Taylor, Trans.). New York: Newman. (Original work written ca. 426 CE)

Bacon, F. (1915). *Of the advancement of learning* (G. W. Kitchin, Ed.). London: J. M. Dent & Sons. (Original work published in 1605)

Bakan, D. (1958). *Sigmund Freud and the Jewish mystical tradition*. Princeton, NJ: D. Van Nostrand.

Baumrind, D. (1993). The average expectable environment is not good enough: A response to Scarr. *Child Development, 64*, 1299–1317.

Beers, C. W. (1927). *A mind that found itself*. Garden City, NY: Doubleday, Page & Company. (Original work published in 1908)

Bretherton, I. (1994). The origins of attachment theory: John Bowlby and Mary Ainsworth. In R. D. Parke, P. A. Ornstein, J. J. Rieser, & C. Zahn-Waxler (Eds.), *A century of developmental psychology* (pp. 431–471). Washington, DC: American Psychological Association.

Brock, A. (1992). Was Wundt a Nazi? Völkerpsychologie, racism and anti-Semitism. *Theory and Psychology, 2*, 205–223.

Brown, J. (1991). Mental measurements and the rhetorical force of numbers. In J. Brown & D. K. van Keuren (Eds.), *The estate of social knowledge* (pp. 134–152). Baltimore: Johns Hopkins University Press.

Brush, S. G. (1988). *The history of modern science*. Ames: Iowa State University Press.

Burtt, E. A. (1932). *The metaphysical foundations of modern physical science* (Rev. ed.). New York: Humanities Press.

Carlyle, T. (1993). *On heroes, hero-worship, & the heroic in history*. Berkeley: University of California Press.

Carruthers, P. (1992). *Human knowledge and human nature*. New York: Oxford University Press.

Cohen, I. B. (1980). *Album of science. From Leonardo to Lavoisier 1450–1800*. New York: Scribner's.

Cowles, M. (2001). *Statistics in psychology. An historical perspective*. Mahwah, NJ: Lawrence Erlbaum Associates.

Danziger, K. (1979). The positivist repudiation of Wundt. *Journal of the History of the Behavioral Sciences, 15*, 205–230.

Danziger, K. (1980). The history of introspection reconsidered. *Journal of the History of the Behavioral Sciences, 16*, 241–262.

Danziger, K. (1990). *Constructing the subject. Historical origins of psychological research*. Cambridge, MA: Cambridge University Press.

de Waal, F. B. M. (1989). *Peacemaking among primates*. Boston: Harvard University Press.

DeCarvalho, R. J. (1990). A history of the "third force" in psychology. *Journal of Humanistic Psychology, 30*, 22–44.

Dewsbury, D. A. (1990). Early interactions between animal psychologists and animal activists and the founding of the APA Committee on Precautions in Animal Experimentation. *American Psychologist, 45*, 315–327.

Dolby, R. G. A. (1977). The transmission of two new scientific disciplines from Europe to North America in the late nineteenth century. *Annals of Science, 34*, 287–310.

Dunlap, K. (1920). *Mysticism, Freudianism and scientific psychology*. St. Louis, Mo: C. V. Mosby.

Ellenberger, H. (1970). *The discovery of the unconscious: The history and evolution of dynamic psychiatry*. New York: Basic Books.

Emde, R. N. (1994). Individual meaning and increasing complexity: Contributions of Sigmund Freud and René Spitz to developmental psychology. In R. D. Parke, P. A. Ornstein, J. J. Rieser, &

C. Zahn-Waxler (Eds.), *A century of developmental psychology* (pp. 203–231). Washington, DC: American Psychological Association.

Evans, R. B. (1984). The origins of American academic psychology. In J. Brozek (Ed.), *Explorations in the history of psychology in the United States* (pp. 17–60). Cranbury, NJ: Associated University Presses.

Farley, R. (1996). *The new American reality*. New York: Russell Sage Foundation.

Fay, J. W. (1966). *American psychology before William James*. New York: Octagon Books.

Festinger, L. (1950). Informal social communication. *Psychological Review, 57*, 271–282.

Flowers, C. (1998). *A science odyssey*. New York: William Morrow.

Foucault, M. (1980). *The history of sexuality*. New York: Pantheon.

Frame, D. M. (1958). *The complete works of Montaigne*. Stanford, CA: Stanford University Press.

Freedheim, D. K. (1992). *History of psychotherapy. A century of change*. Washington, DC: American Psychological Association.

Freud, S. (1947). *Leonardo da Vinci. A study in psychosexuality* (A. A. Brill, Trans.). New York: Random House.

Freud, S. (1949). *An outline of psychoanalysis* (J. Strachey, Trans.). New York: W. W. Norton. (Original work published in 1940)

Golden, M. (1990). *Children and childhood in Classical Athens*. Baltimore, MD: Johns Hopkins University Press.

Goodenough, F. L. (1926). *Measurement of intelligence by drawings*. Yonkers-on-Hudson, NY: World Book.

Green, C. D., Shore, M., & Teo, T. (Eds.). (2001). *The transformation of psychology. Influences of 19th century philosophy, technology, and natural science*. Washington, DC: American Psychological Association.

Greene, S. (1997). Child development. Old themes and new directions. In R. Fuller, P. N. Walsh, & P. McGinley (Eds.), *A century of psychology. Progress, paradigms and prospects for the new millenium* (pp. 36–53). London: Routledge.

Guilford, J. P. (1936). *Psychometric methods*. New York: McGraw-Hill.

Guthrie, R. V. (1998). *Even the rat was white* (2nd ed.) Needham Heights, MA: Allyn Bacon.

Hall, G. S. (1912). *Founders of modern psychology*. New York: D. Appleton and Company.

Hall, G. S. (1917a). Practical relations between psychology and the war. *Journal of Applied Psychology, 1*, 9–16.

Hall, G. S. (1917b). *Jesus, the Christ, in the light of psychology*. New York: Doubleday, Page & Company.

Hall, G. S. (1923). *Life and confessions of a psychologist*. New York: D. Appleton and Company.

Harris, B. (1979). Whatever happened to Little Albert? *American Psychologist, 34*, 151–160.

Harris, B. (1988). Key words: A history of debriefing in social psychology. In J. Morawski (Ed.), *The rise of experimentation in American psychology* (pp. 188–212). New Haven, CT: Yale University Press.

Hawkins, M. (1997). *Social Darwinism in European and American thought, 1860–1945. Nature as model and nature as threat*. Cambridge, England: Cambridge University Press.

Henle, M. (1971a). Did Titchener commit the stimulus error? The problem of meaning in structural psychology. *Journal of the History of the Behavioral Sciences, 7*, 279–282.

Henle, M. (1971b). *The selected papers of Wolfgang Köhler*. New York: Liveright Publishing.

Hilgard, E. R. (1987). *Psychology in America. A historical survey*. San Diego, CA: Harcourt Brace Jovanovich.

Humphrey, N. (1992). *A history of the mind*. New York: Harper Collins.

Hunter, R., & Macalpine, I. (1963). *Three hundred years of psychiatry 1535–1860*. London: Oxford University Press.

Huxley, T. H. (1959). *Evidence as to man's place in nature*. Ann Arbor: University of Michigan Press. (Original work published in 1863)

Huxley, T. H. (1989). *Evolution and ethics* (J. Paradis & G. C. Williams, Eds.). Princeton, NJ: Princeton University Press. (Original work published in 1893)

Jastrow, J. (1892). Psychology in American colleges and universities. *American Journal of Psychology, 3*, 275–286.

Keller, E. F., & Longino, H. E. (1996). *Feminism and science*. Oxford, England: Oxford University Press.

Kendler, H. H. (1985). Behaviorism and psychology. An uneasy alliance. In S. Koch & D. E. Leary (Eds.), *A century of psychology as science* (pp. 121–134). New York: McGraw-Hill.

King, D. B., & Wertheimer, M. (1994). The legacy of Max Wertheimer and Gestalt psychology. *Social Research, 61*, 907–936.

King, D. B., & Wertheimer, M. (2005). *Max Wertheimer and Gestalt theory*. New Brunswick, NJ: Transaction Publishers of Rutgers University.

Koch, S. (1951). Theoretical psychology, 1950: An overview. *Psychological Review, 58*, 295–301.

Koch, S. (1969). Psychology cannot be a coherent science. *Psychology Today, 3*, 64–68.

Koch, S. (1981). The nature and limits of psychological knowledge: Lessons of a century qua "science." *American Psychologist, 36*, 257–269.

Lazarus, R. S. (1991). *Emotion and adaptation*. New York: Oxford University Press.

Leahey, T. H. (2002). The mythical revolutions of American psychology. In W. E. Pickren & D. A. Dewsbury (Eds.), *Evolving perspectives on the history of psychology* (pp. 191–216). Washington, DC: American Psychological Association.

Lippmann, W. (1976). The Lippmann-Terman debate. The mental age of Americans. In N. J. Block & G. Dworkin (Eds.), *The IQ controversy* (pp. 4–44). New York: Pantheon Books.

Martin, L. H., Gutman, H., & Hutton, P. H. (Eds.). (1988). *Technologies of the self. A seminar with Michel Foucault*. Amherst: University of Massachusetts Press.

McNamara, J. A., Halborg, J. E., & Whatley, E. G. (1992). *Sainted women of the Dark Ages*. Durham, NC: Duke University Press.

Mead, M. (1943). *Coming of age in Samoa*. Middlesex, England: Harmondsworth, Penguin Books. (Original work published in 1928)

Medawar, P. B. (1985). *The limits of science*. Oxford, England: Oxford University Press.

Murphy, G. (1949). *Historical introduction to modern psychology*. New York: Harcourt Brace.

Murphy, G., Murphy, L. B., & Newcomb, T. M. (1937). *Experimental social psychology*. New York: Harper & Brothers Publishers.

O'Connell, A. N., & Russo, N. F. (1990). *Women in psychology*. New York: Greenwood Press.

Ogilvie, M. D. (2001). A biological reconstruction of mobility patterns at the foraging to farming transition in the American Southwest. *Dissertation Abstracts International, 61*, 4841.

Osborne, M. L. (1979). *Woman in Western thought*. New York: Random House.

Pagels, E. (1995). *The origin of Satan*. New York: Random House.

Parke, R. D., Ornstein, P. A., Rieser, J. J., & Zahn-Waxler, C. (1994). The past as prologue: An overview of a century of developmental psychology. In R. Parke, P. A. Ornstein, J. J. Rieser, & C. Zahn-Waxler (Eds.), *A century of developmental psychology* (pp. 1–75). Washington, DC: American Psychological Association.

Penrose, R. (1989). *The emperor's new mind*. Oxford: Oxford University Press.

Perez-Ramos, A. (1988). *Francis Bacon's idea of science and the Maker's knowledge tradition*. New York: Oxford University Press.

Piaget, J. (1966). *The psychology of intelligence*. Totowa, NJ: Littlefield, Adams & Co. (Original work published in 1947)

Plotkin, H. (1994). *Darwin machines and the nature of knowledge*. Cambridge, MA: Harvard University Press.

Pressman, J. D. (1998). *Last resort. Psychosurgery and the limits of medicine*. Cambridge, England: Cambridge University Press.

Ranke-Heinemann, U. (1990). *Eunuchs for the kingdom of heaven. Women, sexuality, and the Catholic Church.* New York: Penguin.

Richards, R. J. (1987). *Darwin and the emergence of evolutionary theories of mind and behavior.* Chicago: University of Chicago Press.

Robinson, D. N. (1995). *An intellectual history of psychology.* Madison: University of Wisconsin Press.

Rumbaugh, D. M. (1997). The psychology of Harry F. Harlow: A bridge from radical to rational behaviorism. *Philosophical Psychology, 10,* 197–210.

Ruse, M. (1985). *Sociobiology: Sense or nonsense?* Dordrecht, Netherlands: Reidel.

Samelson, F. (1980). J. B. Watson's Little Albert, Cyril Burt's twins, and the need for a critical science. *American Psychologist, 35,* 619–625.

Sarton, G. (1952). *A history of science: Ancient science through the golden age of Greece.* Cambridge, MA: Harvard University Press.

Schachter, S. (1964). The interaction of cognitive and physiological determinants of emotional state. In L. Berkowitz (Ed.), *Advances in experimental social psychology* (pp. 49–80). New York: Academic Press.

Shakow, D., & Rapaport, D. (1964). The influence of Freud on American psychology. *Psychological Issues, IV, 1, Monograph 13.* New York: International Universities Press.

Sherif, C. W. (1983). Carolyn Wood Sherif. In A. N. O'Connell & N. F. Russo (Eds.), *Models of achievement. Reflections of eminent women in psychology* (pp. 279–293). New York: Columbia University Press.

Shields, S. (1991). Leta Stetter Hollingworth: "Literature of Opinion" and the study of individual differences. In G. A. Kimble, M. Wertheimer, & C. White (Eds.), *Portraits of pioneers in psychology* (pp. 242–255). Hillsdale, NJ: Lawrence Erlbaum Associates.

Shore, M. (2001). Psychology and memory in the midst of change: The social concerns of late 19th century North American psychologists. In C. D. Green, M. Shore, & T. Teo (Eds.), *The transformation of psychology. Influences of 19th century philosophy, technology, and natural science* (pp. 63–86). Washington, DC: American Psychological Association.

Shweder, R. A., & LeVine, R. A. (Eds.). (1987). *Culture theory. Essays on mind, self, and emotion.* Cambridge, MA: Cambridge University Press.

Siegel, R. (1981). Life after death. In G. O. Abell & B. Singer (Eds.), *Science and the paranormal* (pp. 159–184). New York: Scribner's.

Simon, B. (1978). *Mind and madness in ancient Greece. The classical roots of modern psychiatry.* Ithaca, NY: Cornell University Press.

Smith, L. D. (1986). *Behaviorism and logical positivism. A reassessment of the alliance.* Stanford, CA: Stanford University Press.

Stagner, R. (1988). *A history of psychological theories.* New York: Macmillan.

Strong, D. E. (1965). *The Classical world.* New York: McGraw-Hill.

Suplee, C. (2000). *Milestones of science.* Washington, DC: National Geographic Society.

Thelen, E., & Adolph, K. E. (1994). Arnold L. Gesell: The paradox of nature and nurture. In R. D. Parke, P. A. Ornstein, J. J. Rieser, & C. Zahn-Waxler (Eds.), *A century of developmental psychology* (pp. 357–387). Washington, DC: American Psychological Association.

Thomas A., & Chess, S. (1989). Temperament and cognition: Relations between temperament and mental test scores. In G. A. Kohnstamm, J. E. Bates, & M. K. Rothbart (Eds.), *Temperament in childhood* (pp. 263–282). New York: Wiley.

Thurstone, L. L. (1927). The method of paired comparisons for social values. *Journal of Abnormal and Social Psychology, 21,* 384–400.

Thurstone, L. L. (1929). Theory of attitude measurement. *Psychological Review, 36,* 222–241.

Turner, F. M. (1974). *Between science and religion. The reaction to scientific naturalism in late Victorian England.* New Haven, CT: Yale University Press.

van Gelder, T. (1996). Dynamics and cognition. In J. Haugeland (Ed.), *Mind design II. Philosophy, psychology, artificial intelligence* (pp. 421–454). Cambridge, MA: MIT Press.

Voltaire, M. F. A. (1932). *Dictionnaire philosophique.* New York: Coventry House. (Original work published ca. 1760)

Vygotsky, L. S. (1978). *Mind in society.* Cambridge, MA: Harvard University Press.

Wade, N. J., & Brozek, J. (2001). *Purkinje's Vision. The dawning of neuroscience.* Mahwah, NJ: Lawrence Erlbaum Associates.

Wagar, W. W. (1992). *A short history of the future.* Chicago: University of Chicago Press.

Webster, R. (1982). *Why Freud was wrong. Sin, science, and psychoanalysis.* New York: Basic Books.

White, M. (1972). *Science and sentiment in America. Philosophical thought from Jonathan Edwards to John Dewey.* New York: Oxford University Press.

White, M. (1997). *Isaac Newton. The last sorcerer.* Reading, MA: Addison-Wesley.

Whitehead, A. N. (1929). *The function of reason.* Boston: Beacon Hill Press.

Witmer, L. (1907). Clinical psychology. *The Psychological Clinic, 1,* 1–9.

Woodward, W. R., & Ash, M. G. (1982). *The problematic science: Psychology in nineteenth-century thought.* New York: Praeger.

Wright, D. B., & Loftus, E. F. (1998). How misinformation alters memories. *Journal of Experimental Child Psychology, 71,* 155–164.

Zupan, M. L. (1976). The conceptual development of quantification in experimental psychology. *Journal of the History of the Behavioral Sciences, 12,* 145–158.

Name Index

Subject Index